the business
of technology

Digital Desktop Publishing

Susan E. L. Lake

Technology Education Consultant
Susan Lake and Associates
Lubbock, Texas

•

Karen Bean

Program Coordinator for
Information Management
Blinn College
Brenham/Sealy/Schulenburg, Texas

SOUTH-WESTERN
CENGAGE Learning

Australia • Brazil • Canada • Mexico • Singapore • Spain • United Kingdom • United States

The Business of Technology: Digital Desktop Publishing, First Edition

Susan Lake, Karen Bean

VP/Editorial Director:
Jack W. Calhoun

VP/Editor-in-Chief:
Karen Schmohe

Acquisitions Editor:
Jane Phelan

Developmental Editor:
Karen Hein

Marketing Manager:
Mike Cloran

Marketing Coordinator:
Kelley Gilreath

Content Project Manager:
Diane Bowdler

Manager of Technology, Editorial:
Liz Prigge

Technology Project Editor:
Mike Jackson

Web Coordinator:
Ed Stubenrauch

Manufacturing Coordinator:
Charlene Taylor

Production House:
ICC Macmillan Inc.

Printer:
Quebecor World
Dubuque, IA

Art Director:
Stacy Jenkins Shirley

Internal Designer:
Ke Design, Mason, OH

Cover Designer:
Ke Design, Mason, OH

Cover Images:
© Getty Images

For more information about our products,
contact us at:

South-Western
5191 Natorp Boulevard
Mason, Ohio 45040
USA

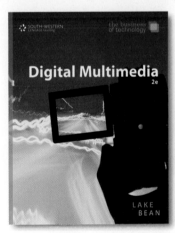

Reviewers

Stacie L. Fowler

Teacher, Business Department
Carmel High School
Carmel, IN

Kathleen Lehman

Business and Computer Technology Teacher
Sulphur High School
Sulphur, OK

Julie McAlhany McCraw

Business Education Department Chairperson
Spartenburg High School
Spartenburg, SC

Danye Phifer

Teacher, Business Department
Pearl Cohn Magnet High School
Nashville, TN

Angela Raney

Business Instructor
Spring Hill High School
Hope, AR

Ann Sanders

Teacher, Business Department
Lake Mary High School
Lake Mary, FL

Contents

Digital Desktop Publishing:

◀ Each unit begins with a **Career Profile**, giving insight into a real-life application of desktop publishing.

Business of Publishing ▶ addresses desktop publishing from a business perspective.

Objectives at the ▶ beginning of the chapter set the stage for what is going to be covered.

Key Terms appear in ▶ color in the body and are defined in the margins.

Workplace Ethics ▶ features throughout the text look at issues and challenges facing users of desktop publishing programs.

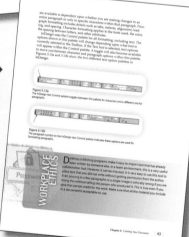

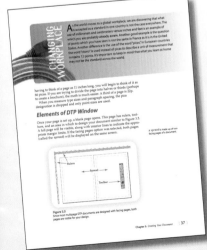

◀ **Changing Workplace** boxes discuss how trends are affecting business today.

FEATURES SNAPSHOT

◀ **Proofreading Tips** in the margin offer hints for mastering this important skill.

◀ Information about **designing for the Web** is featured throughout the text.

Summary at the end of ▶ each chapter gives a recap of what has been covered.

Key Terms identifies ▶ words and phrases that were covered throughout the chapter.

◀ **Review** exercises are short-answer questions regarding chapter content.

◀ **Discuss** questions require longer explanations.

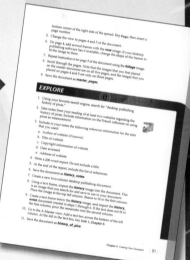

Explore activity is a step-by-step ▶ project that gives students the opportunity to use a variety of skills learned.

◀ **Apply** offers hands-on activities using desktop publishing software. Software-specific instructions are featured on the product Web site.

◀ **Icons** identify what skills (writing, reading, Internet, teamwork, and math) will be enhanced by completion of the activity.

SOFTWARE-SPECIFIC INSTRUCTIONS ARE AVAILABLE ON THE PRODUCT WEB SITE AT academic.cengage.com/school/dtp

unit 1

The World of Desktop Publishing

1 Getting Started with DTP

2 Planning Your Document

3 Creating Your Document

4 Importing Graphics

Career Profile | Graphic Designer—Studio

What I do every day

A graphic designer today often wears many hats. With the technological advances made in this industry in the last decade, tasks formerly done by typesetters, production artists, editors, and film strippers now fall to the graphic designer.

Yet today's graphic designer sits in front of a computer for less time than you might think. Don't try to design on your computer—grab a pencil! It's still the best tool for "grounding" a design and providing direction that otherwise might be lost.

How I use DTP in my job

I love my Macintosh computer and use QuarkXPress as my main desktop publishing software program. Basic design principles are still the best guidelines to follow—color repetition, size relationships with a center of interest, keeping the eye within the page; all fundamentals but necessary to success. As tempting as it is to do the fun stuff, adding special effects should be part of the final touches, not the first notions.

The best part of my job

The desire to do your absolute best is always the artistic challenge. Seeing a design that you've done for a billboard, package, brochure, website, or point-of-purchase display come to life brings a sense of accomplishment that is hard to beat!

The worst part of my job

I don't consider this a bad part of my job, but a necessary one—there is constant pressure to produce excellent quality work for every customer. They are absolutely entitled to expect it.

What I need to know and be able to do

Communication and creativity are the keys to any successfully printed piece. Listening to a client and applying the tools of the trade will result in both the client and designer being pleased with the work effort. Also, change is constant, so be aware of technology innovations and any new trends in design. Proofread!

How I prepared to be a graphic designer

My degree is from a Technical College. I began as a production artist and worked my way into graphic design. Once you've finished school, don't be disappointed with an entry-level position. Getting in the door can be the biggest job challenge you face. Take advantage of as many additional training opportunities as you can throughout your career.

How the Web has impacted this field

Web design is becoming part of what I do. It's a matter of learning the software tools for that medium. Designing for the Web allows me to be more creative than when I'm using a template for a more traditional advertisement.

1 Getting Started with DTP

Objectives

- *Learn definition of desktop publishing.*

- *Explore history of DTP.*

- *Discover differences between various operating systems.*

- *Learn differences between various software packages used in digital desktop publishing.*

- *See how input and output devices are used in DTP.*

- *Learn how networks are connected and made secure.*

Desktop publishing is the use of word processing software or specialized desktop publishing software on a personal computer to create a document in which graphics and text enhance the message.

DTP is an acronym for desktop publishing.

Introduction

You may have noticed that the title of this book, "Digital Desktop Publishing" also includes the phrase "The Business of Technology." These words were chosen carefully to give you a complete idea what you will be studying in this textbook. The word "digital" indicates that you will not be limited to just the study of print. All forms of desktop publishing (DTP), including that which is used on the Web, will be included. The word "business" helps you to understand that the focus will be on business applications rather than the personal use of the technology. Working together, these two phrases give you a clear idea of what you are about to learn.

The term **desktop publishing** describes the process of producing a document using a personal computer. **DTP** software, once called page assembly software, makes it possible to combine both print and graphics on a single page. Once a user creates a desktop publishing document, he or she can then print a copy using a computer printer, a photocopy machine, or a professional press. DTP also provides the option of creating a digital publication. This allows readers to view a document using a computer monitor rather than a paper copy. DTP requires a wide variety of skills, including an understanding of typography, graphics, layout, and business expectations.

The term "digital" demonstrates the advancements made in desktop publishing. No longer is it just about creating a nice-looking brochure to reproduce using a photocopier. Today's digital desktop publishing is about using advanced image technology to create the same brochure. It is about creating both the print and web versions of that same document. Most importantly, it is about choosing the right tools to make your business more profitable. Welcome to the new world of business using digital desktop publishing skills.

History

Desktop publishing began even before the introduction of the personal computer. It started with the IBM Selectric™ (1961) and its "golf ball" print head, as shown in Figures 1.1 and 1.2. These allowed users for the first time to change with ease the type style of their text. Before the Selectric, typewriters were of two types: elite (12 characters per inch) and pica (10 characters per inch). Whatever style your typewriter came with was the style in which you created text. Adding graphics to a document, however, required gluing or waxing the image onto an already typed page.

Macintosh

With the arrival of the Apple Macintosh computer and the Image-Writer printer in 1984, as shown in Figures 1.3 and 1.4, the world of desktop publishing began to change. The Macintosh used a **GUI** (graphical user interface) to simplify the way computers were used. Earlier computers required users to key in text to access functions. The Mac introduced the use of icons, windows, and menus.

Previously only codes built into a document indicated changes in appearance. Now **WYSIWYG** (what you see is what you get) took over in programs such as MacWrite. Suddenly it was possible to choose not only font style but also size and attribute. It was also possible to see those changes on the screen. Graphics could

Figure 1.1
The IBM Selectric provided font choices and sizes that were not available on other typewriters.

Figure 1.2
The Selectric "golf ball" element could be replaced easily to change type font and size.

GUI, an acronym for graphical user interface; indicates that pictures rather than text allow the user to work with the computer.

WYSIWYG, an acronym for what you see is what you get; means that the image that appears on a computer display is the same as the printed version.

Figure 1.3
The introduction of the Macintosh and GUI opened the way to a new world of computer use.

Figure 1.4
The Apple ImageWriter made it possible to print more than just text.

Figure 1.5
Thunderscan developed an early scanner that replaced the printer ribbon in an ImageWriter.

Figure 1.6
Aldus PageMaker was the first desktop publishing program available for use on a computer.

PageMaker was the first true desktop publishing software developed for use on a computer.

An **operating system** (OS) is the software that allows a computer to function. It includes features such as how a monitor displays an image and how files are accessed.

Windows is an operating system marketed by Microsoft that is used on computers generally identified as PCs.

Linux is an open source operating system that generally runs on PCs.

PC is an acronym for a personal computer. Generally, PCs are computers that use the Microsoft Windows operating system.

be added digitally to a document in a limited way and viewed in place. Printing in landscape or portrait became an easy option.

Image Management

With MacPaint and MacDraw (also introduced in 1984), artwork could be digitally created and modified with ease. Figure 1.5 shows an early scanner that replaced the ribbon in the ImageWriter. This made possible the transfer of an image directly to the computer.

These early graphics programs were quickly replaced with products such as Corel Draw (1989) and Adobe Photoshop (1990). These newer software programs increased a user's ability to fine-tune artwork and to create renderings that had never been possible in the world of paint and pen.

PageMaker

With the introduction of Aldus **PageMaker** (1985), true digital desktop publishing appeared. With this software, as shown in Figure 1.6, it became easy to move text and graphics around on a page and to create columns with justified text. It did not take long before computers that had originally been used mostly for complex spreadsheet computations became just as important as a means of creating complex digital publications.

Operating Systems

Before moving on to DTP features, it is important to have an understanding of the basic components of your computer. The first place to begin is with the difference between an operating system and the software on your computer. Each provides a different function, but it would be easy to misunderstand these differences.

An **operating system** (OS) is the software that runs your computer. When you turn your computer on and a screen appears with icons for folders and shortcuts to programs, you are "seeing" the operating system. It is the behind-the-scenes process that tells a window or program to open when you double click your mouse. The OS is the software that keeps track of what programs you are using. It is the basis of all computer functions.

Types

The three most commonly used operating systems are **Windows** (created and owned by Microsoft), Macintosh (created and owned by Apple Computers), and **Linux** (open source software). Each of these represents a different business approach.

Microsoft sells only the operating system. Other manufacturers, such as Dell and Gateway, produce the computers that run Windows. These computers are generally known as **PCs**.

In the Apple business model, the company produces both the operating system and the computer. A **Mac** computer runs a Macintosh operating system.

Linux is an **open source** operating system, written by Linus Torvalds and distributed without cost to the computer world to modify as needed. Those who use this operating system are free to adapt it and fix any problems they encounter. It is not marketed or sold. Linux runs on the same type of computer as Windows.

Mac vs. PC

Until recently, Macintosh operating systems could only be installed on Macintosh computers. Windows and Linux could only be installed on computers that contained certain processors.

Software workarounds, called emulators, could be installed on both Macs and PCs, making it possible to run the Mac OS on a PC and to run Windows on a Mac. This has changed recently, and users can now install Windows directly on newer Macintosh computers.

All operating systems, including Macintosh, PC, and Linux, can support desktop publishing software. The art world that first adopted DTP software began with the Macintosh. Today this software is used on all **platforms**, or operating systems.

Software

While the operating system runs your computer, software programs or applications make the computer productive. Software allows users to enter data into a spreadsheet, write a letter, or even play a game. While an operating system is mostly invisible, software is what a user looks for and uses to create documents and images on a computer. Software is what makes digital desktop publishing possible.

Desktop publishing software can be a word processing program such as Microsoft Word or a dedicated desktop publishing program such as Microsoft Publisher, Adobe InDesign (previously PageMaker), and QuarkXPress.

Microsoft Word

Microsoft Word is considered a **high-end program** in the world of word processing, but only low-end as far as digital desktop publishing is concerned. Its word processing features are quite useful in creating standard print documents, such as a business letter. For simple desktop publishing projects, a word processing program such as Word is a good choice. For more complex documents that require a more professional approach, such as brochures, high-end desktop publishing software should be used.

Microsoft Publisher

Microsoft Publisher is a mid-range desktop publishing program. It is designed to be used by those with limited DTP skills. Extensive

A **Mac** (Macintosh) is a computer marketed by Apple Computers that uses the Macintosh operating system.

Open source software is developed by individuals and offered free to the public. "Open" means that its code can be modified in any way that a user needs.

Platform is another term for an operating system.

A **high-end program** is software that has many features and is often used by professionals.

All desktop publishing software has the ability to check spelling for you. Get in the habit of using the Help menu to find out how to activate the spell checker for each software program. Some software, such as Microsoft Word, provides interactive checking. This function gives you the option of having misspelled words indicated as you key text. Most high-end DTP software expects you to check the spelling at intervals and does not automatically mark questionable spelling for you. With this type of software, you generally have the option of checking a single text box or the entire document. You also can select the dictionary you will be using. Become familiar with the various options your software provides.

PDF is an acronym for portable document format. It is an extension for Adobe Acrobat and Acrobat Reader files.

Acrobat Reader is software that can be downloaded without cost. It is used to read Adobe Acrobat, or PDF, files.

Cross-platform is a term that indicates that a file can be read on both Macs and PCs.

templates are provided, allowing you to choose one that most closely meets your needs. With the use of templates, you can create a well-designed document with little effort. Font and color choices can be made with a single click. For someone looking for a quick and easy way to create a professional-appearing document, Publisher is a good choice. In addition, when the design is appropriate, users can convert Publisher documents to a web page with ease.

For those intending to send a file to a professional printing service, however, it is important to know that not all services accept Publisher documents. This has begun to change, but the process is not yet complete.

Adobe InDesign

Adobe InDesign was developed as a replacement for PageMaker (which was acquired from Aldus in 1994). InDesign is considered a high-end desktop publishing application with advanced features not found in software such as Publisher. It requires a sophisticated user with more highly developed skills. An understanding of typography, color, design rules, and professional printing requirements is necessary to fully utilize this product's capabilities.

QuarkXPress

QuarkXPress is another high-end desktop publishing program. For a number of years, professional designers have preferred this software over PageMaker. With the introduction of InDesign, however, the field has been leveled between the two. Quark and InDesign are both considered acceptable products for advanced DTP work.

Adobe Acrobat

Adobe Acrobat is not a true desktop publishing program, although it often plays an important part in the process. Acrobat makes it possible to convert any desktop publishing document to a **PDF** (portable document format) file. This file can then be read using **Acrobat Reader** software, and can be downloaded onto your computer at no charge. Use of a PDF file creates a **cross-platform** document. This eliminates the need for users to have the specific software initially used to create a document loaded on their computer in order to view a file. PDF files are commonly found on the Web as a way of transmitting documents and forms. PDF files ensure that a document does not have to be modified to fit web design requirements.

Macromedia FlashPaper

Macromedia FlashPaper is a new piece of software that functions some-what like Acrobat in that it converts a document to a file that is readable using Flash software. Its newness means that not many users are familiar with it and might be hesitant to use it.

Adobe and Quark are currently the two major players in the digital desktop publishing game. Quark has long been the favorite software choice among professionals. This was probably because QuarkXPress more closely matched the expectations of those who came from a traditional printing background. Aldus PageMaker originally gained the support of those less advanced users. PageMaker continued to add features and developed in popularity among even professional publishers. With Adobe's purchase of PageMaker and then the move to InDesign, the two software giants became more evenly matched.

One important consideration, however, has always been cost. While both the Adobe and Quark products are expensive, Quark has always been seen as the more costly of the two. Adobe bundles (gathers into a single package) InDesign with other products such as Photoshop. This bundling provides a less expensive option for desktop publishers who need several pieces of software.

Quark is seen as easier to use, which reduces initial training cost. InDesign has a similar set of features to those found in other Adobe products, such as Illustrator and Photoshop. This means that learning one Adobe product makes it easier to use others.

Businesses must balance cost and features. The choice of desktop publishing software is just one such example of the decision process.

As you can see from Figure 1.7, a FlashPaper document opens using Macromedia's Flash Player. The original Microsoft Word document that was converted to FlashPaper is readable by anyone with the free Flash Player. It is not necessary to have Microsoft Word on the computer.

Help

When first exploring a new piece of software, such as InDesign or QuarkXPress, it can be overwhelming. One of the most valuable features of today's desktop publishing programs is their Help menus. Most programs provide a number of Help tools that you should become familiar with early in your exploration process. Look for an overview that will lead you through major features. Then explore the search and index functions. Get in the habit of keying in terms that can give you information about how to use various tools. For example, if you are trying to figure out how to insert automatic page numbers, keying in "page numbers" will likely take you to a series of steps.

Figure 1.7
FlashPaper creates documents that are readable using a Flash Player.

Input Devices

Digital desktop publishing hardware primarily consists of **input devices** and **output devices**. Computer input devices can consist of a keyboard, a mouse, a scanner, a drawing tablet, and a microphone for voice recognition. Output devices can include a printer, a computer monitor that displays a web page, or even speakers to hear music or words.

Keyboard/Mouse

Keyboard input devices differ for the Mac and the PC. PCs have Ctrl (Control) and Alt keys as shown in Figure 1.8. The Mac has a Control key (which is not used in the same way as the PC Control key), the Option key, and the Apple/Command key as shown in Figure 1.9. Instructions designed for a PC use one set of terms and the Mac instructions use another. These instructions can be interchanged without problems by using the comparable key.

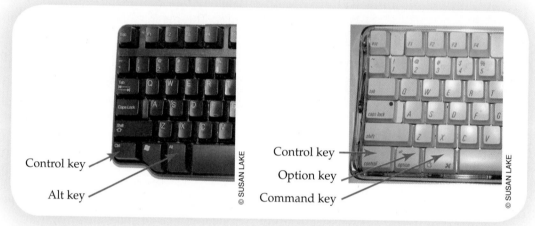

Control key
Alt key

© SUSAN LAKE

Control key
Option key
Command key

© SUSAN LAKE

Figure 1.8
The PC keyboard uses the Ctrl and Alt keys to access a number of functions.

Figure 1.9
The Mac keyboard replaces the Ctrl and Alt keys with an Apple key and an Option key.

PCs have a two-button mouse, while the Mac usually has a one-button mouse. Therefore, actions that require a right mouse click on the PC must be accessed using the Ctrl key on the Mac.

Mac		PC
Option	=	Alt
Apple/Command	=	Ctrl
Control	=	right mouse click

Voice Recognition

With the development of voice recognition software, keying text into a document has become unnecessary. The introduction of programs such as Dragon Naturally Speaking in 1997 made it possible to speak into a

Software Duplication

Desktop publishing software is expensive. For many businesses this is not software that is used every day by every employee. As a result, businesses will often buy a single copy of a DTP program to install on a single computer. It is expected that any employee who needs to create a DTP document will use that computer to produce the work. A problem arises when more than one person needs to use the software at the same time. While it may be tempting to temporarily load copies of the software on other computers, doing so is illegal. Software is generally licensed for use by one person on one computer. Any deviation from that license agreement is a criminal act.

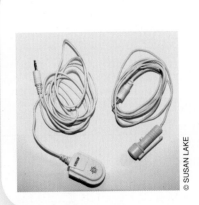

Figure 1.10
Small microphones such as these can be used to transfer voice to a computer.

Figure 1.11
Headphones such as these, with a built-in microphone, are used more frequently than microphones alone for voice recognition purposes.

microphone, such as those shown in Figure 1.10 and Figure 1.11, and have your words transferred directly to the computer. While early voice recognition software could only promise limited accuracy, each new version increases the level of accuracy and vocabulary recognition. Today it is possible to create documents with great accuracy using voice recognition programs.

Drawing Tablet

It is difficult to create a sketch in a program such as Photoshop simply using a mouse. Tools such as a drawing tablet gave users the ability to digitally enter information on a computer, just as they would use a pen or pencil with paper. With a drawing tablet it was now possible to create exactly the image you want without the barriers of a mouse or other scrolling

Figure 1.12
Drawing tablets such as this Wacom can be used instead of a mouse to draw digital images.

Figure 1.13
Scanners transfer printed images into digital images by using light technology.

OCR (optical character recognition) is a process that converts a scanned representation of text into editable "live" text on a computer.

Dot matrix is a means of printing by placing a series of dots closely together so that they give the appearance of printed letters.

PostScript is a programming language that describes the appearance of images (which includes text) on the printed page.

device. Drawing tablets such as the Wacom tablet (introduced in Japan in 1983) shown in Figure 1.12 provide a flat surface and a stylus for drawing images. Tablet PCs have since been introduced that have drawing capabilities, but they are designed more for handwriting recognition than image development.

Scanner

With the introduction of affordable flatbed scanners such as the Hewlett-Packard ScanJet (1991), digital desktop publishing gained another important input device. Inexpensive scanners, like the modern one shown in Figure 1.13, make it easy to import images into a computer. In addition, **OCR** (optical character recognition) software makes it possible to transfer previously keyed text to a computer with enough accuracy to eliminate the need to rekey the text.

Output Devices

Dot Matrix

The first printers attached to personal computers were **dot matrix** printers, also called impact printers. The impact of the print head on the ink ribbon created a series of "dots" that formed letters, as shown in Figure 1.14. These printers were slow and noisy, and the quality of the printout was often not professional enough for use by businesses. As a result, few businesses use dot matrix printers today.

Laser Printer

While a dot matrix printer could produce a DTP document, its print quality was too low for business use. With the introduction of the Apple LaserWriter printer (1985) and Adobe PostScript, true digital desktop publishing became a reality. Laser printers produce print using a system similar to that found in a photocopy machine. Both use toner powder and heat to seal the image to the page. **PostScript** (a special printer language) removes the "jaggies" seen in dot matrix printouts, producing a sharp, clean image. Figure 1.15 shows an example of laser output. You can see the difference between it and the output in Figure 1.14.

Figure 1.14
Dot matrix printers use a series of dots to reproduce letters and images on a page.

Figure 1.15
Laser printing uses toner much as a photocopier does to produce copies.

Printing using services provided by web businesses is called online printing. Online printing is becoming a publishing model that is growing in importance. To use an online service, a user uploads a file to a website along with the print requirements. A company that might be hundreds of miles away prints the product and returns it by a delivery service.

Businesses that use such services find that they speed up the process of creating print documents. Online printing services typically proof final copy from a PDF file. Using these services eliminates the need to physically leave an office or building, drive to a brick-and-mortar location to deliver a printout of the document, and then later return to the location when the final product is ready for pickup. The cost of using these services can be less than printing done by a local business. In addition, it's easier to compare prices using the Internet.

This is an example of just one of the many changes that are occurring every day in the modern workplace.

Inkjet

You have already seen the print difference between a dot matrix and a laser printer. When **inkjet** printers appeared on the market, they offered a printer option that was less expensive than a laser printer. In addition, inkjet printers were quieter and faster than impact printers. An added feature that made inkjet printers very popular was its ability to print in color. As a result, inkjet and laser printers are now the most common choices for digital desktop publishing.

Inkjet is a printing method that sprays a series of ink dots onto a page, allowing it to reproduce both text and images with fine detail.

Cost

Prices for laser printers continue to drop significantly, so the cost of a laser printer is no longer the issue it once was. The question becomes cost of supplies vs. quality of print. Laser cartridges are more expensive than inkjet ones, but they last longer. While color laser printers are now inexpensive enough to use in offices, the cost of color cartridges is still high.

At the moment, businesses that need to print only in black and white find that laser printers are more economical than inkjet. Businesses that need to print in color (particularly photographs) generally use an inkjet printer. One of the decisions you must make in the business of desktop publishing is which printing option is the most cost-effective for your purpose.

Printer Drivers

A **printer driver** is software that allows the computer to output files to a printer. Sometimes printer drivers need to be specifically installed on a computer in order for the printer to work. However, most computers have the necessary printer drivers built into the operating system.

PPD (PostScript printer description) is a postscript printer file that sends essential information to a laser printer allowing it to produce the expected product. It includes both postscript information as well as design details.

A **printer driver** is software installed on a computer that allows a printer and computer to communicate.

PPD is a file sent to a printer that provides it with all the information it needs to create a postscript document.

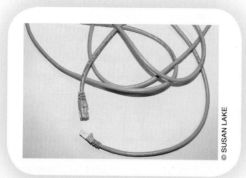

Figure 1.16
CAT5 is a type of cable that can be used to connect one computer to another to create a network.

Wired networks are those that are connected using Ethernet cables such as CAT5.

Wireless access points are locations from which network signals are transmitted using an antenna.

Wi-Fi is a term used to describe a wireless network.

A **router** is one type of hardware that connects computers in a network. **Hubs** and **switches** are also used to connect networks.

Hot spots are locations that transmit a wireless signal for use by those in the vicinity.

LAN is a local area network that connects computers located in proximity to one another. Since cables are required to connect each to a single connection point, the physical distance limits the size of a LAN.

A **firewall** is a means of preventing access to a network

This file is usually produced by your DTP software without any decision on your part.

Networks

The growth of networks both at home and at work has changed completely the way businesses function. No longer is a person tied to a single, stationary computer, working alone. Now all computers within an organization, or even throughout the world using the Internet, are connectable. A file on one person's computer can be accessible to anyone with access to that computer through a network.

A network can be **wired** using Ethernet cables such as a CAT5, shown in Figure 1.16, or wireless using **wireless access points** that broadcast signals using **Wi-Fi**. In both cases, equipment such as a **router** or a **hub** or **switch** acts as the central point connecting all the computers on the network.

Laptop computers today usually come with built-in wireless capability. A laptop can also be wireless using a card that is inserted into a slot on the computer called a PC card. Other wireless devices such as PDAs and cell phones also have wireless capabilities. Many businesses now offer **hot spots** that provide a wireless network to anyone in the vicinity.

LAN

A local area network (**LAN**) connects computers in a single building or within a single organization. Often a **firewall** blocks the outside world from having access to the LAN, as shown in Figure 1.17. Firewalls can also be installed on individual computers to block unwanted access.

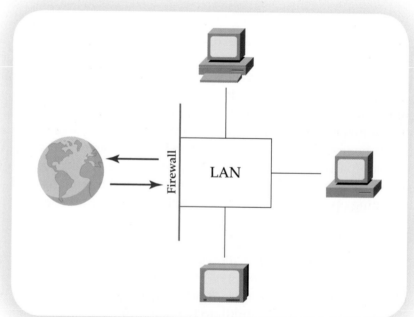

Figure 1.17
A firewall is a means of preventing unwanted access to a computer on a network. It is one of the means of providing network security.

WAN

A wide area network **WAN** connects computers over a large geographical area. The Internet is a good example of a WAN, but it is not the only one. A **VPN** (virtual private network) is another type of WAN that connects all the computers in a single organization. VPNs block access to anyone not part of this widespread network by running the system in parallel to the Internet.

WAN is a wide area network that uses devices such as telephone lines, satellite dishes, and radio waves to connect computers to a network.

VPN is a virtual private network that provides a WAN to members of a widespread organization.

Online Security

With the advancements in computer accessibility, the issue of security has become of prime concern for businesses. Not everyone with the ability to access a computer may have the best of intentions. As a result, passwords and logins are usually required to use a networked computer. Passwords should not be shared and should be stored in a safe location. Unfortunately, with the proliferation of passwords, it has become difficult for users to keep track of all their passwords without writing them down.

Although good passwords should not include easily guessed words, they should be easy enough for their user to remember. They should include both upper- and lowercase letters as well as numbers. Ideally, even with these restrictions, passwords should be changed periodically. In addition, it's important not to use the same password for every situation.

Viruses

Online security is not limited to preventing access to files. Destructive programs (called **malware**) such as computer viruses, worms, Trojans, adware, or spyware can invade a computer. This invasion usually occurs through e-mail links and attachments, or as the result of visiting a website.

Antivirus software has been developed to protect computers against malware, but it must be continually updated. To maintain a secure computer, it is important to use current anti-virus software, to not open e-mail attachments that you did not request, and to closely monitor both e-mail and web usage.

Malware is a broad term that describes software designed to be destructive to a computer. It can include viruses, worms, Trojans, adware, or spyware.

SUMMARY

In this chapter you learned how desktop publishing began. You read about the operating systems and software that you will use as you study desktop publishing. You saw various input and output devices that are required to enter and then to publish a document. You briefly studied how networks are established and how to maintain security while using them. Now it is time to begin using digital desktop publishing tools.

KEY TERMS

Acrobat Reader	Linux	PostScript
cross-platform	Mac	PPD
desktop publishing	malware	printer driver
dot matrix	OCR	router
DTP	open source	VPN
firewall	operating system	WAN
GUI	output device	Wi-Fi
high-end program	PageMaker	Windows
hot spots	PC	wired
inkjet	PDF	wireless access point
input device	platform	WYSIWYG
LAN		

REVIEW

Answer the following questions on your own computer.

1. What does the term "desktop publishing" mean?
2. What does the acronym DTP stand for?
3. What was DTP software once called?
4. What allowed the first change in type style of text?
5. How were graphics first added to a document?
6. What does the acronym GUI stand for?
7. What does the acronym WYSIWYG stand for?
8. What new equipment made it possible to transfer an image directly to the computer?
9. What was the name of the software that started true desktop publishing?
10. What is the term used for the software that runs your computer?
11. What are the three most commonly used operating systems?
12. What is a platform?
13. What two software products are considered acceptable for advanced desktop publishing?

14. What does PDF stand for?

15. What is one of the most valuable features of today's software to help learn new software?

16. What are the two devices that comprise desktop publishing hardware?

17. What software development has made keying text into a document unnecessary?

18. What was the name of the first printers attached to personal computers?

19. What type of software allows the computer to output files to a printer?

20. What does the acronym PPD stand for?

DISCUSS

1. Explain the significance of the beginning of DTP software.

2. Explain open source software.

3. Explain what is meant by a high-end program.

4. Explain how Macromedia FlashPaper functions.

5. List examples of computer input devices.

6. List examples of a computer output device.

7. Explain PostScript.

8. Explain malware and how it differs from a virus.

9. Describe characteristics of a secure password.

10. Explain the difference between a LAN and a WAN network.

APPLY

Activity 1 Help

1. Use the About feature of the Help menu to learn what version of desktop publishing software you are using. Commit this to memory.

2. Access the Help index for your software and locate the instructions for importing a text file. Read the instructions and then write a short summary of the instructions. Save the written summary as **importing_text** with a txt file type. You may want to create a **chapter_1_use** folder to save any electronic files in. Ask your instructor for specific instructions on organizing your files.

to the website at
academic.cengage.com/school/dtp

WRITING

3. Open your desktop publishing software with a new blank document. Following the instructions in your summary, import the **importing_ text** file into a new document. Save the document as **import**.

Activity 2 What's New

1. Using the Contents section of the Help menu on your software, locate What's New about your version of software.

2. Open your desktop publishing software. Create a new default document.

3. Find the Type tool on your software. Use the Type tool to key **What's New** at the left margin.

4. Under the title, key three items (in an enumerated list) that are new on your current version of software. Do not make any formatting changes. Correct any keying errors.

5. Save the document as **whats_new**.

Activity 3 Website

1. From the Help menu, access the website for your desktop publishing software.

2. Spend some time becoming familiar with the website for your software.

3. In a word processing document, list two things that you really liked about the website and two things that you thought could have been improved. Format the list appropriately so that you are clearly communicating to your instructor your views on the website.

4. Find the system requirements for the desktop publishing software that you will be using for your class. List those in your word processing document.

5. Save the document as **software_website**.

Activity 4 History

1. Using your favorite search engine, search for "desktop publishing history." Read about desktop publishing history and locate several facts that were not included in the textbook reading.

2. If voice technology or other input devices such as a tablet PC are available, use this technology to input several facts about the history of desktop publishing. If no other input technology is available, key the facts into a word processing document. Ask your instructor what input technology to use for the assignment.

3. Save the document as **dtp_history** with the file type txt.

4. Import into your desktop publishing software and save again as **dtp_history**.

Activity 5 Security

1. Using your favorite search engine, search for "network security." Read and take notes from at least two websites on a minimum of three different topics within network security.

2. Working in a group of three or four students, combine your notes into one organized fact sheet about network security.

3. Create a three- to five-minute presentation for the class using visual aids such as presentation media software, handouts, and/or posters. All students in the group should have a part in the presentation.

EXPLORE

1. Using a search engine, search for laser printers and compare the cost of the following items:

   a. Color laser printer vs. black and white laser printer

   b. Color laser cartridges vs. black laser cartridges

   c. Black laser cartridges vs. inkjet cartridges

2. Place your research information in a word processing document using a table to organize your information.

3. Using the information in the table, write a short summary of your findings in the same word processing document. Include in the writing your analysis of the differences in cost.

4. Below the summary, include your resources. Resources should include any of the following information that is available: author of the web page, title of the web page, copyright information on the web page, date you accessed the web page, and the address of the web page.

5. Save the document as *cost_comparison*.

2 Planning Your Document

Objectives

- *Learn to preplan your document.*

- *Discuss sketching layout of document.*

- *Discover importance of paper type, folds, and binding in planning process.*

- *Study production and delivery options.*

- *Understand impact of costs in decision-making process.*

Introduction

In the previous chapter, you learned about the hardware and software used in desktop publishing. Now it is time to get down to the actual process of creating a document. It may be tempting to open a DTP program and immediately begin entering text and inserting images. While this might seem like the quickest way to complete a project, it is not the best way. A little planning at this stage will really pay off in the end. Using the planning guide at the end of this chapter will make it easy to track your decisions.

Preplanning

Audience

Before you begin creating a document, you need to determine who will make up your audience. At first, your prospects may seem obvious. However, there could be additional audience members you did not initially consider. Actually taking the time to write down who your audience is can help you uncover these additional possibilities. For example, if you are creating a brochure to advertise the next meeting of an organization, you likely will assume that your audience will consist of members from that organization. However, you should also consider that prospective members, or even those who have never heard of your club, might also see the brochure. If you would like to attract these readers as new members or educate them about the organization, you should incorporate additional information that you would not necessarily include for your original group.

Sometimes, putting yourself in the place of your reader is the best way to decide what each member of the audience might want to know. In the brochure example, your members know what the organization does, but others might not. Therefore, placing the organization's mission statement in a prominent position on the brochure may be helpful. As you are pre-planning, think about anyone who could possibly read the final product.

Purpose

Once you have considered your audience, think about the purpose of your product. Is it to inform, to advertise, to seek input, or perhaps to meet a requirement? Again, the response to the purpose question may be surprising. For example, if you are creating a calendar with important dates, it is obvious that the dates are to inform. However, calendars often have photographs or graphics above the calendar. What purpose do these images serve? Are they selected also to inform or merely to attract attention? Knowing why you are producing the calendar may help you make decisions about what to include.

Time Frame

One of the most important considerations when creating a document is to consider the schedule under which it is to be produced. In a business environment you are seldom working alone. There are often several people involved in the process. If photographs are to be included, a photographer may be used. The means of publication, such as photocopy or professional printing, has to be taken into consideration. How much time is needed to complete that stage of the project? If the document has to be bound or even stapled, then the person responsible for that task must be kept informed. If the completed project is to be mailed, then the person assigned that responsibility must be part of the process. The list could go on and on.

As a result, one of the steps to planning must include the time frame or schedule that will be followed. Because everyone in the process must meet his or her deadline in order for the final product to appear on schedule, each person needs to be aware of the plan as it evolves and agree to the deadlines established.

Layout

Thumbnail Sketch

Once preplanning is complete, the next task is to create a thumbnail sketch of your document. This does not have to be a complicated drawing. It is a working document that will let you "think" on paper about what you have in mind. Using stick figures for drawings and boxes labeled as text is all that is necessary (see Figure 2.1). Working in pencil is also a good idea so that you can erase and move parts as needed.

Offset Printing Process —
screened slightly

Content about press types.

Content about press types — continued from previous column

Enlarged Line Drawing of Offset Press — provided by art department (Hilda Santana)

Figure 2.1
A thumbnail sketch is a good way to plan a document before opening your DTP software.

WORKPLACE ETHICS

Working as a team can be challenging, particularly when tight deadlines are involved. It is critical that you understand your importance to the team and its goals. If you are a procrastinator, you should realize that your decisions affect everyone in the group. Putting off your obligations hurts everyone. If you discover that you cannot complete your part of an assignment in the time frame originally established, you are ethically bound to notify the team. It's always tempting to hope for a last-minute rescue, but that's not always realistic. It is far better to notify the team so they can make any necessary decisions in a timely manner.

Landscape or Horizontal Orientation	Portrait or Vertical Orientation

Figure 2.2
One of the first decisions you will have to make when you open your DTP software is whether it is to be designed in landscape or portrait orientation.

Orientation is the vertical or horizontal position in which a page is printed.

Portrait orientation is a page design in which the shortest side is the top of the page.

Landscape orientation is a page design in which the longest side is the top of the page.

Orientation

Since most paper is cut in a rectangular shape, you must decide if you want your page printed with a vertical or horizontal **orientation** as shown in Figure 2.2. Vertical pages are printed in **portrait orientation** and horizontal ones in **landscape orientation**. Most bound documents are printed vertically. Flyers that will be folded into thirds are usually printed so the page is oriented horizontally. Often booklets are printed horizontally and then folded, creating the appearance of a vertical document.

Page Organization

As you are working on your sketch, think about the organization that you want to use. What should come first? What needs to be last? How many pages will you need? Let your mind explore all the possibilities. Use your thumbnail sketches as a guide.

If you are creating a document of less than ten pages, sketch each page. If it is a long document such as a report, many of the interior pages may be similar. For those, you can merely sketch one page showing the general layout and then indicate how many there will be.

Page Arrangement

If your document is going to consist of more than a single page, you need to decide how the pages will be arranged. Pages printed on only one side generally have the same margins for every page and the same header/footer information that contains the page number. Pages that are printed

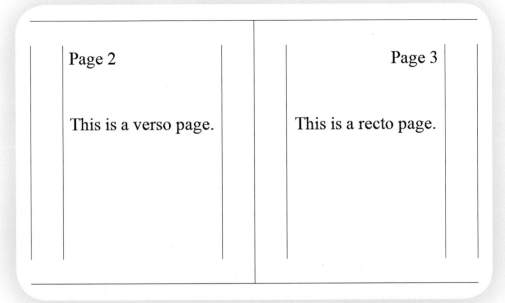

Figure 2.3
If you select the option to have facing pages, each side will be slightly different.

front and back so that they face each other (**facing pages**) may have slightly wider interior margins, or **gutter**, to allow binding space. Their headers/footers will also be reversed so that the page numbers appear on opposite sides as shown in Figure 2.3. The odd-numbered pages are called **recto pages** and the even are called **verso pages**. In a book, the first page is always the recto page.

One of the problems that inexperienced desktop publisher designers have is with managing the page arrangements of **booklets**. A booklet consists of two "pages" printed on a single sheet of paper, that is then folded. The problem occurs because pages that are designed sequentially do not appear in the order in which they were created, as shown in Figure 2.4.

The page arrangement of an eight-page book is actually two sheets of paper printed on both sides (or four pages). In the figure, you can see that "page" 1 (a recto page) appears on the right side of the page and "page" 8 is on the left. Fortunately, desktop publishing software has a booklet option that takes the guesswork out of the process.

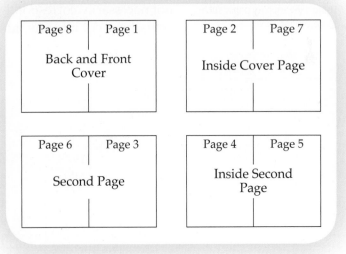

Figure 2.4
Because of the folds used to create booklets, the page arrangement can be confusing.

Paper

Part of the planning process includes a decision about both the size and type of the paper used. These are not always easy choices. Cost and even mailing requirements have to be factored into the decision.

Letter is a standard American paper size that is 8.5 × 11 inches.

Legal is a standard American paper size that is 8.5 × 14 inches.

Ledger is a standard American paper size that is 11 × 17 inches. It is also known as tabloid size.

Trim size is a paper size that is reduced or cut from a standard size.

Bond paper is usually used in a photocopier or a personal printer.

Book paper is a better quality than bond.

Text paper is very high quality.

Newsprint paper is low quality and inexpensive.

Cover stock paper is a heavy stock.

Coated paper is one to which a finish has been added, producing a better-quality print.

Dot gain describes the spreading of ink once it is applied to paper. Dot gain is a concern particularly when using a low-quality paper such as newsprint.

Size

Most businesses stock three basic sizes: **letter**, **legal**, and **ledger** (also called tabloid). These are often called American sizes because they are based upon measurement in inches. European paper sizes are based upon metric measurements that result in slight differences between the two.

Common American sizes	U.S.	
Letter	8.5" × 11"	
Legal	8.5" × 14"	
Ledger/Tabloid	11" × 17"	
Statement, or half-letter	5.5" × 8.5"	

Common (European) metric sizes	U.S.	Metric
A4 (sometimes called European letter)	8.3" × 11.7"	120 × 297 mm
B4	10.1" × 14.3"	257 × 364 mm
A3	11.7" × 16.6"	297 × 240 mm
A5	5.8" × 8.3"	148 × 210 mm

Tabloid or ledger size paper is often used to create newsletters because it is actually two letter size pages in width (see Figure 2.5). This makes it easy to fold and is often less expensive than using another binding option with letter size paper.

It often surprises people to learn that the size of a printed page does not necessarily correspond with the final document size. A page can actually be cut into any number of sizes. Although the original product will be printed on a standard size of paper, professional print shops are not limited to these paper sizes. Once a document is printed, it can be cut to a specific size which is called the **trim size**.

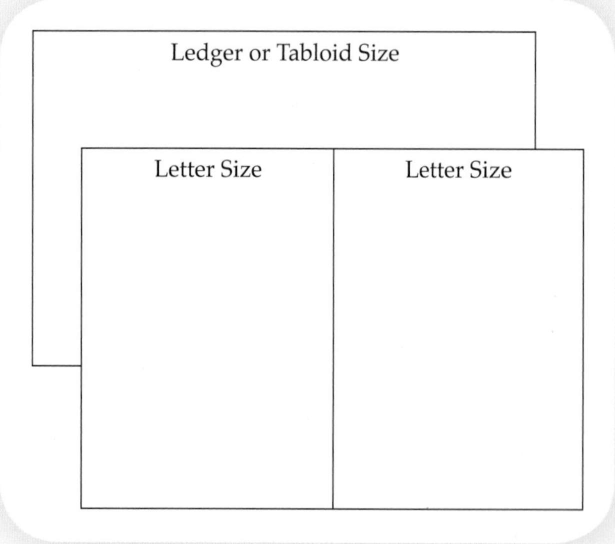

Type

Paper type is indicated by names such as **bond** (copier paper), **book** (better quality than bond), **text** (high quality), **newsprint** (inexpensive), and **cover stock** (heavy paper). Each type has a distinct purpose determined by its weight and quality. Some paper is designated **coated**, which means that it has a slicker finish than uncoated. The glossiness of coated paper allows ink to adhere more smoothly, producing a better print job.

Dot gain is the amount of ink that spreads out on a sheet of paper as it is printed (see

Figure 2.5
Ledger paper is often used in landscape orientation to create newsletters (tabloids).

Figure 2.6). High-quality paper absorbs less ink, so there is less dot gain and a crisper look to the print. Low-quality papers such as newsprint absorb ink readily, increasing the dot gain. Your desktop publishing software may provide an option to set the dot gain. For this reason, you will need to know what quality paper you intend to use.

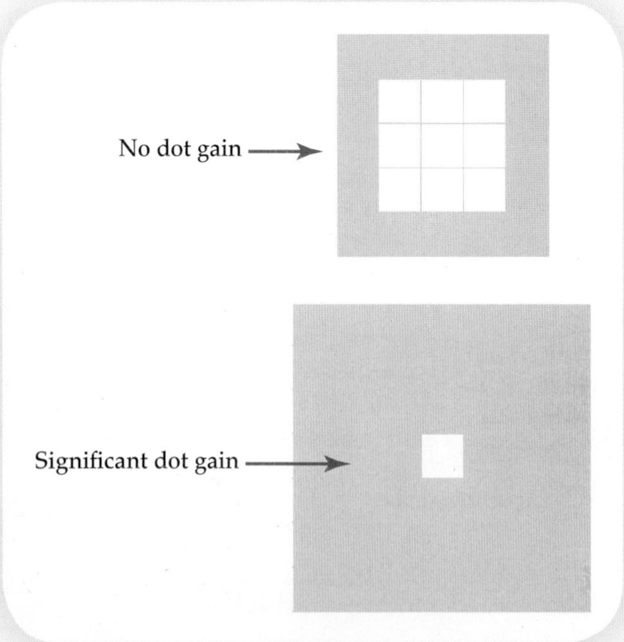

Weight

Paper weight is measured in pounds (#) using a standard based upon 500 full sheets of that particular paper type. Paper weight can be misleading, since the sheet size of various paper types can differ. This means that a 20# paper of one type may be heavier than a 20# paper of another type with a smaller sheet size. Just as bewildering, 50# book paper is the same weight as 20# bond paper. The result can be considerable confusion when choosing a paper type. A professional print shop can show you paper samples to help you decide which one meets your needs.

Generally, documents are printed on 20# bond, 24# bond, 80# text, and 80# cover stock paper. Recycled paper, which is indicated with the chasing arrow symbol shown in Figure 2.7, is available in most sizes and weights.

Folds

Documents can be folded in a variety of ways. Although each variation has a unique name, all of the fold types start with a single sheet of paper. Folding this single sheet of paper creates multiple pages so they can be viewed separately. For example, a **Z fold** divides a page into thirds, with all information printed on a single side. A **trifold**, or brochure, is a similar fold, but it consists of print on both sides of the paper. An **accordion fold** divides the page into fourths. A **gatefold** folds the sides in toward the middle of a page. Figure 2.8 shows line drawing examples of many fold types.

A **business letter fold** divides the page into thirds, making it fit © 2004 Signature Press a standard #10 envelope. A **half fold** can serve a similar purpose, or it can be used to create unbound books or booklets.

Creative use of folds has become an inexpensive way to attract attention to a printed document.

Figure 2.6
Dot gain differs depending upon the type of paper you use. In this figure ink has spread out, changing the small square to a much fuller one.

No dot gain →

Significant dot gain →

Figure 2.7
This symbol can be printed on documents created with recycled paper.

Z fold divides a page into thirds, with print on one side.

Trifold is much like a Z fold but with both sides containing print.

An **accordion fold** divides a page into fourths.

A **gatefold** folds the sides into the middle of a page.

A **business letter fold** folds a page into thirds to fit in a standard business envelope.

A **half fold** divides the page in half. It is often a booklet fold.

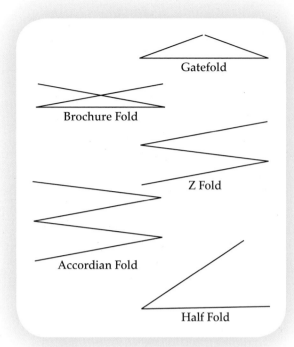

Figure 2.8
Paper can be folded in endless ways, but there are some that are considered standards.

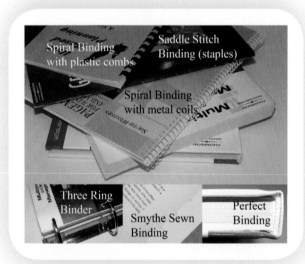

Figure 2.9
Binding options are a consideration anytime you have a document with multiple pages.

A **saddle stitch** places staples in the middle of folded pages.

Spiral binding uses plastic or metal combs.

Perfect binding uses glue along the edge of pages to create a book.

Binding

Documents can be bound in a variety of ways. The most common method of binding uses staples at the top left or along the side of the pages. **Saddle stitch** places staples in the middle of folded pages, creating a booklet. **Spiral binding** can use metal coils or plastic combs that loop around the outside of the pages, allowing them to lie flat when open. **Perfect binding** glues the edges, forming a book (such as found in a paperback). Figure 2.9 shows a number of binding choices.

Production

Some of the most obvious decisions you need to make include how you will be producing your final document, how many copies you need, and whether both sides of the paper will include print.

Printing

Although a DTP document can be produced using the printer attached to your computer, it is not cost-effective for more than a few copies. An original document can be photocopied using an office machine or one at a copy center such as Kinko's. One consideration when using a photocopy service is that each copy costs the same. This means that there is usually no savings when using this method for a large number of copies. Another option is to have a professional printer produce your documents. This can be less expensive when producing many copies, but not so for fewer copies.

Color

Whether or not a desktop published document is to be printed in color is another important decision. Color adds interest but increases the cost significantly. For example, say that a photocopy service agrees to print a single page of a letter size document in black and white for .08 per page. However, this same service will charge .39 to copy a similiar document that includes color. This means that the cost of each document would be nearly five times as expensive if printed in color. Professional printing services that are given a large order, however, can often print in color at considerable savings. This means that once again many variables must be considered as you make each decision.

Most desktop published documents will be printed. While most people understand what it means to print something, they don't think about the confusing nature of the terms used. At home or work, a printer is the device that produces a paper document created on a computer. At a professional print business, the device that produces a paper document is called a press. A press is a high-level printing device with a function similar to a printer used at home or work. The person who runs the press is referred to as the printer. To add to the confusion, the term "printer" also refers to the business itself. This means that at home or work you use a printer, while a print shop, or printer, uses a press.

Delivery

When making a choice about paper size, you have to consider how it is to be delivered. Will it be mailed, posted on a wall, sent through inter-office mail, stacked in a counter display, or posted on the Web? Your delivery method will have an impact on each of your planning decisions.

For example, if the document is mailed, it may need to be folded and inserted into an envelope. The United States Post Office charges more to mail envelopes that do not meet minimum and maximum size restrictions. As a result, paper size and weight will need to be considered, along with the delivery method.

U.S. Post Office Size Restrictions

Envelopes	Minimum	Maximum
Height	3-1/2"	6-1/8"
Length	5"	11-1/2"
Thickness		1/4"

Post Cards		
Height	5"	6"
Length	3-1/2"	4-1/4"
Thickness	.007"	.016"

Bulk Mailing

Often businesses use bulk mailing as a delivery means. This reduces the cost of mailing a large number of pieces. Bulk mail requires a minimum of 200 pieces of mail. In addition, there are other special mailing requirements along with the cost of a required permit. When used appropriately, this can be an important way for businesses to reduce their expenses.

The biggest change in the world of desktop publishing has come in the means of delivery. As you have learned, you can publish a document by printing, but you can also publish it to the Web. While web publications are cheaper to produce, they have a serious drawback in that they are not as visible as printed publications. Businesses today are struggling with this problem as they try to figure out how best to reach their audience. Even as they struggle, the business world continues to use the Web more each year. Banks are publishing their end-of-the-month statements using email. Publicly traded companies are publishing their stock prospectus and required financial statements online. Catalogs of all kinds are moving to the Web. As a desktop publisher you need to keep in mind that print is not your only means of delivery.

Internet Distribution

Another method of delivery is using the Internet. One of the advantages of using the Web to distribute a desktop-published document is speed of production. Once the document is complete, it can be posted immediately. There are no additional processes such as printing, binding, folding, or mailing to interfere with publication. You can produce as many pages as you want in any color that you select. For these reasons more businesses are using digital technology to send their message. The downside, of course, is that the customer must know the document is available and have access to a computer to read it.

Cost

During the entire planning process, each decision must be made with cost of production in mind. When you make a decision about paper, you must keep in mind that although heavy weight papers might make more impact than lighter ones, they also cost more. When you select the paper size, you need to remember that special sizes might attract more attention than standard ones, but there are extra costs associated with special trim sizes. In addition, unusual sizes might require additional postage. If a document is bound, that will increase its cost. Folding cost is another factor that has to be considered. Printing in quantity can reduce the cost per piece, so you need to decide if a large print run will be more effective than a short one.

Planning Decisions	
Audience	
Purpose	
Time Frame	
Team Members	
Orientation	
Number of Pages	
Layout Sketch	
Page Arrangement	
Paper Type	
Paper Size	
Fold	
Binding	
Production Method	
Number of Copies	
Printed Sides	
Color/B&W	
Delivery Method	
Budget	

SUMMARY

In this chapter you learned the importance of planning desktop publishing documents before beginning the actual design process. You considered your audience and purpose. You saw that planning using a sketch allowed you to make decisions about orientation, page arrangement, paper, folds, and binding. You saw how decisions about production and delivery needed to be made and considered along with costs.

accordion fold	gutter	recto pages
bond paper	half fold	saddle stitch
book paper	landscape orientation	spiral binding
booklets	ledger	text paper
business letter fold	legal	trifold
coated paper	letter	trim size
cover stock paper	newsprint paper	verso pages
dot gain	orientation	Z fold
facing pages	perfect binding	
gatefold	portrait orientation	

REVIEW

Answer the following questions on your own computer.

1. What can be used to plan a document before opening your DTP software?

2. Vertical pages are printed in what type of orientation?

3. Horizontal pages are printed in what type of orientation?

4. In what orientation are most bound documents printed?

5. In what orientation are flyers that are folded in thirds printed?

6. What DTP term indicates that there are right and left sides to the project?

7. What is the name of the inside margin of facing pages?

8. What are the odd-numbered pages in a document with facing pages called?

9. What are the even-numbered pages in a document with facing pages called?

10. What is the name of a desktop publishing document that consists of two pages printed front and back on a single sheet of paper?

11. What is the name of the standard American size of paper that is 8-1/2" × 11"?

12. What is the size called when it is cut to a specific, not standard, size?

13. Which type of paper is usually used in a photocopier or a personal printer?

14. Which type of paper produces a better quality print?

15. What term describes the spreading of ink once it has been applied to paper?

16. How is paper weight measured?

17. What two different weights of paper are generally used when printing on bond paper?

18. What fold divides a page into fourths?

19. Which fold is most often used for a booklet?

20. What are the two most common methods of binding a document?

DISCUSS

1. Explain the importance of knowing who your audience will be in planning a desktop publishing project.

2. Explain the differences in American and European sizes of paper.

3. Discuss why it is important to know the type of paper that you will use for a project before you begin creating the project using desktop publishing software.

4. Explain the difference between a Z fold and a trifold.

5. Discuss the cost differences in choosing a printing method.

6. Discuss what factors should be considered when deciding to print in color and why these factors should be considered.

7. Discuss which delivery method of the project is most important to the planning process because of cost.

8. Discuss the advantages and disadvantages of using the Internet to publish your completed project.

9. Discuss the differences in the terminology used in printing at home and professional printing.

10. Explain how procrastination can affect a project in which teamwork is used.

APPLY

Activity 1 Page Numbering

1. Using your desktop pubishing software, create a document that has nine letter-sized facing pages.

2. Insert page numbers on the document.

3. Save the document as *page_numbers*.

to the website at
academic.cengage.com/school/dtp

Activity 2 Facing Pages

1. Using your desktop publishing software, edit the preferences so that vertical and horizontal spacing are in inches.

2. Create a document that has two letter size pages in landscape orientation. Do not use facing pages.

3. Create a text box in the middle of the first page with the text Landscape Orientation. Center the text horizontally. Change the text size to 72.

4. Save the document as **landscape**.

Activity 3 Document Setup

1. Using your desktop publishing software, create a blank default document.

2. Go to Document Setup and change the document to two legal size pages, no facing pages.

3. Create a text box in the center of the page, explaining how to change the setup of the document after the document has already been created. Change the font type and center the text horizontally

4. Save the document as **document_setup**.

Activity 4 Table

1. Using your desktop publishing software, create a one-page document with a table.

2. Input the list of Planning Decisions in the Cost section of your textbook. Ensure that there are no grammatical or spelling errors.

3. Adjust the width of the columns of the table as needed.

4. Save the document as **planning_decisions**.

Activity 5 Cost Analysis

1. You are creating a letter-size newsletter that will require eight pages of print. You will need 500 copies. Make a comparison of the following cost scenarios:

   a. Printing on your home computer at .40 cents a page. You will use 20# paper at a cost of $3.00 for a ream (500 pages).

   b. Printing at a photocopy business at .39 cents per page for color. You will use 24# paper at a cost of $4.29 for a ream (500 pages).

   c. Printing at a professional printer at .29 cents per page. You will use 24# paper at a cost of $3.99 for a ream (500 pages).

2. Using your desktop publishing software, organize your information in a table. The first column should contain the letter of the scenario. The second column should describe the scenario, and the third column

should include the calculations of the cost for that scenario. The first row of the table should contain column headings that are horizontally centered. Merge the fifth (last) row of the table to write your analysis of the best method to use. Include in your analysis at least two factors that you do not know that could help you make your decision.

3. Save the document as **cost_analysis**.

EXPLORE

1. Use your favorite search engine to find information on binding costs, types of binding, and effective use of binding in desktop publishing.

READING

2. Write a summary of at least two articles that you have read on these topics.

3. Create a desktop publishing document in landscape orientation using a letter size document. Key the summary; then include the two resources below the summary. Include the author (omit if there is no author), title of the web page, the copyright information, the date accessed, and address of the website in the resources.

WRITING

4. Save the document as **binding_summary**.

Creating Your Document

Objectives

- *Learn to modify default settings of software.*

- *Explore elements of DTP window.*

- *Understand use of rulers as DTP tool.*

- *Compare tools available in various DTP software packages.*

- *Understand importance of frames in DTP design.*

- *Learn to use master pages to simplify design process.*

Default, as it is used with software, is a setting that is already established when the software is first opened.

Pagination is the setup of a document including margins, columns, headers, footers, and orientation.

Introduction

Now that you understand how to plan your document, it is time to begin using your desktop publishing software to create a document. Most of the specific details in this chapter will reference Adobe InDesign, QuarkXPress, and Microsoft Publisher as examples. However, all DTP software programs have similar features. You just have to find them. It is much like an automobile's windshield wipers. If you are driving an unfamiliar car and it starts to rain, you know that there is a switch somewhere. You just have to find it. This chapter is going to tell you what DTP "switches" you need to look for.

Default Settings

The **default** settings are those that are built into the software. Defaults are the basic settings that the software's developers thought users were most likely to use. When you open InDesign and QuarkXPress, you are taken to the default screens shown in Figures 3.1a and 3.1b. The InDesign default begins with one letter size page in portrait orientation with facing pages. A single column is automatically selected. Margins are set at 3p0 (see next page). No bleed or slug sizes are given (see next page). Any changes you make to the default settings become a custom setting to which you can assign a name.

The design choices you make are often grouped under the term **pagination**, particularly when they are made for long documents such as reports or books.

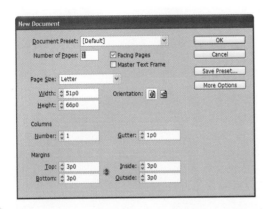

Figure 3.1a
Selecting the More Options button in the InDesign New Document window will open two more default settings.

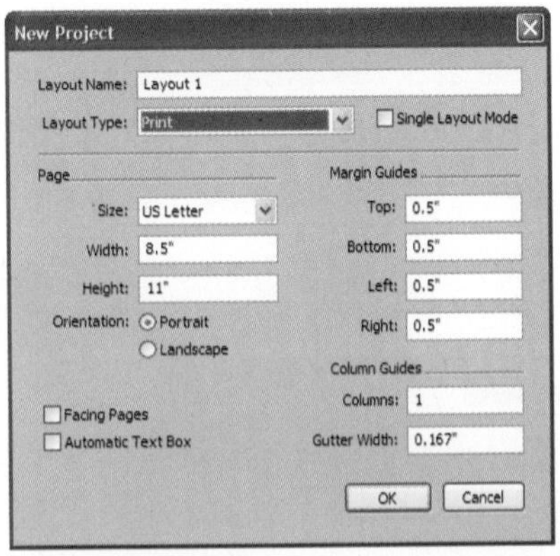

Figure 3.1b
QuarkXPress calls its opening screen New Project.

Web Pagination

As the world moves from print to digital, desktop published documents are typically published in one of two ways: traditional print with margins and columns or via the Web.

Some web documents are created using software such as Adobe Acrobat that preserves the original pagination of a print document. Others are created using HTML code that produces standard web pages. These HTML documents do not have page size restrictions such as legal or letter. They do not have margin settings, and they do not use columns in the same way that print documents do.

QuarkXPress simplifies the process of designing a web document by providing a separate set of opening defaults shown in Figure 3.2.

Measurements

High-end desktop publishing software anticipates that its users will have experience with professional measurements. This means that instead of using inches and fractions of an inch they use the terms picas and points when measuring page layout components.

QuarkXPress defaults to inches. From the menu bar you can select Edit > Preferences > Measurements (see Figure 3.3a) to change this setting to picas. InDesign defaults to picas. If you prefer to work in measurements such as inches or millimeters, select Edit > Preferences >

Figure 3.2
The QuarkXPress web layout options provide view pagination choices.

Figure 3.3a
QuarkXPress preferences lets you choose the units you wish to measure with.

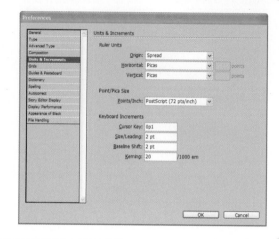

Figure 3.3b
InDesign units default to point/pica size, using 72 points to an inch.

Units & Increments, as shown in Figure 3.3b, from the menu bar. When working in Microsoft Publisher, select Tools > Options > General (see Figure 3.3c) from the menu bar.

Picas

A **pica** is a measurement developed by printers that divides 1 inch by 6, so there are 6 picas to an inch. Picas are the largest unit of printing measurement. They are used to measure large areas such as page size, column width, and margins as you saw in the InDesign default window. Picas are abbreviated as a "p."

Points

A **point** is a division of a pica. Each pica contains 12 points, so there are 72 points in an inch. Figure 3.4 shows the equivalent measurements for inches, picas, and points. When you are indicating a measurement, both picas and points are used. A line might be 6p3 which means that it is 6 picas and 3 points long. Since there are 6 picas in an inch, this line would be slightly longer than one inch. A line that is exactly 1/2" long would be 3p0. The zero can be used with both picas and points.

Using picas and points is awkward at first, but once you get the hang of it, you will actually find it easier than using inches. For example, rather than

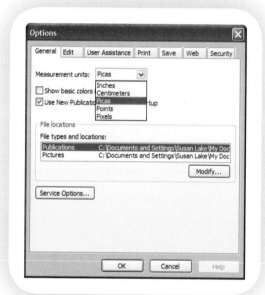

Figure 3.3c
Microsoft Publisher defaults to inches, but provides the options of using other measurements.

Pica is a printer's measurement equal to 1/6 of an inch.

Point is a printer measurement equal to 1/72 of an inch.

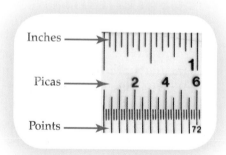

Figure 3.4
This figure makes it easy to see that 1 inch is equivalent to 6 picas or 72 points.

As the world moves to a global workplace, we are discovering that what is accepted as a standard in one country is not the case everywhere. The use of millimeters and centimeters versus inches and feet is an example of which you are probably already aware. Another good example is the question of points which you have seen is not the same in France as it is in the United States. Another difference is the use of the word "picas." In European countries the word "cicero" is used instead of picas to describe a unit of measurement that contains 12 points. It's important to keep in mind that what you learn at home may not be the standard across the world.

having to think of a page as 11 inches long, you will begin to think of it as 66 picas. If you are trying to divide the page into halves or thirds (perhaps to create a brochure), the math is much easier. A third of a page is 22p.

When you measure type sizes and paragraph spacing, the pica designation is dropped and only point sizes are used.

Elements of DTP Window

Once your page is set up, a blank page opens. This page has rulers, toolbars, and an area in which to design your document similar to Figure 3.5. A full page will be visible, along with interior lines to indicate the appropriate margin limits. If the facing pages option was selected, both pages (called the **spread**) will be displayed on the same screen.

A **spread** is made up of two facing pages of a document.

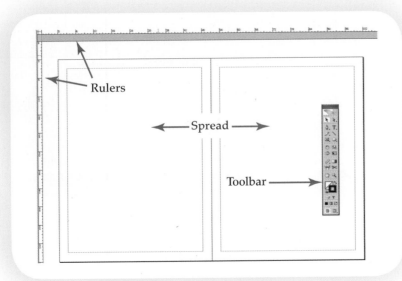

Figure 3.5
Since most multipage DTP documents are designed with facing pages, both pages are visible for your design.

Pasteboard/Scratch Area

The area outside the working page is called the **pasteboard** or **scratch area**. In this area text and images may be put aside until they are ready for placement on a page. If you have inserted images or short text boxes into a document, but are undecided on where they will be used, this is a good temporary storage area. As long as these items do not "touch" the working page, they will be available to you regardless of the page on which you are working.

Bleed

In your original InDesign setup, you had the option of setting the amount of **bleed** (located under More Options). In Chapter 7 you will learn more about bleed as a design tool. The bleed is an area outside your working page that allows an image or color to extend to the outer edge of the printed page. Bleeds are seldom used when you are producing a document using a printer attached to a computer or a photocopier. Each of these restrict the area in which you can print, creating a white border around each page. Professional printing services, however, have more options and can use bleeds.

Slug

Another option available in the InDesign setup is **slug** space. This is space outside the printed area in which you can place instructions that should stay with your document. Often this information is used to communicate with those who need to do further design of the page. It is also a place to store notes for future use. Figure 3.6 shows the bleed area outlined in red. The slug area is outlined in blue. The pasteboard is the area outside the slug area.

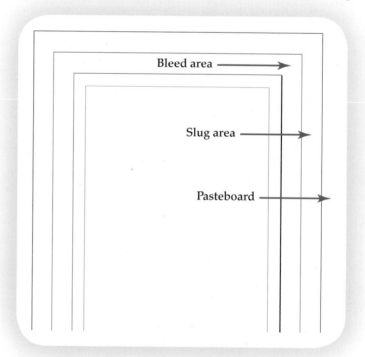

Figure 3.6
InDesign builds in an option that allows space for the slug or a bleed. The pasteboard is always available.

In the chapter discussion of picas and points, you read that there are 72 points to an inch. Actually, that number is not exactly correct. There is a long and convoluted history of the establishment and acceptance of the actual measurement. Traditionally, in the United States and the United Kingdom the number of points was 72.27. European points, which were defined by the French, were slightly smaller at 72.23. When PostScript was developed, the number was rounded down. Generally, this is not a problem, but you may encounter professional printers who are using the more precise measurement.

Rulers

Rulers are set up dependent upon the measurement used for the document as a whole. If you have selected inches as your measurement, your document's rulers will be in inches. If you are using picas, then the rulers will be in increments of 6. The starting or **zero point** of the ruler is set at the upper left corner of the page (see Figure 3.7). It can be moved, however, so that your zero point is wherever you want it on the ruler.

Zero point is the point on the vertical and horizontal page where the ruler is set to zero.

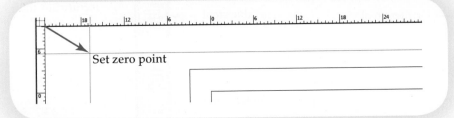

Figure 3.7
The zero point of the page can be moved to any location and changed whenever you want.

Guides are nonprinting lines that provide visual points of reference, making it easy to align text, images, or frames.

Guides

To make it easier to line up text and graphics on your page, your document has **guides**. Guides are lines that can be "pulled" from the document's rulers to any position, as shown in Figure 3.8. These can be removed by sliding them back to the ruler. You may add as many of these nonprinting guides to your document as you want. Guides can be set to snap to or adhere to the lines. This means that if you place a frame near a guide, the frame will move to the line automatically.

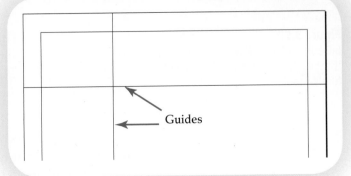

Figure 3.8
Guides are useful for lining up frames. Since they do not print, you may use as many as you want.

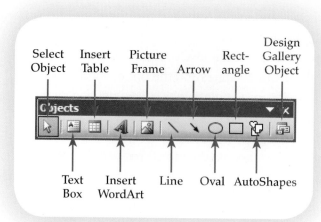

Figure 3.9a
Publisher's tools are located on the Objects toolbar. Because this is a limited desktop publishing program, there are few options.

Margins

The margins are set in the opening window, but they can be changed at any time. Unlike word processors that include the margins in the page setup, desktop publishing software includes this information under a separate menu such as layout.

Tools

The tools you have available are determined by the DTP software you are using. Generally, you have a toolbar that lets you make selections, draw, add text, rotate, change size, add color, remove areas, zoom, and select colors. Figures 3.9a, 3.9b, and 3.9c show you the various tool options available to you in InDesign, Quark, and Publisher.

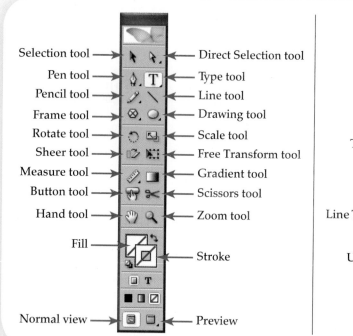

Figure 3.9b
InDesign offers a wider selection of tools. Small arrows in the lower corner of a tool button indicate multiple choices for that tool.

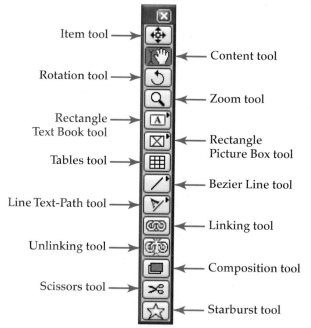

Figure 3.9c
The QuarkXPress Tools palette has fewer choices than InDesign. Arrows reveal additional choices for some tools.

Fill and Stroke

Fill is the area inside an object or text.

Stroke is the border around an object or text.

When using InDesign, a tool is available that allows you to select the **fill** and **stroke** of a drawing or text. Drawings of objects or frames in DTP programs consist of a fill and a stroke, as shown in Figure 3.10. An outline or border, called the stroke, can be a wide variety of color and width choices. The inside of a drawing or text is called the fill. Fills can be a color or a gradient different from the stroke.

Figure 3.10
The fill of an image places color inside, while the stroke
determines the appearance of the border.

Web Tools

InDesign's Button tool gives you various options to use in a web publication. You can set button actions so that when the reader clicks on it an action occurs, such as movement to another page or a sound playing.

QuarkXPress has a separate toolbox for web functions as shown in Figure 3.11.

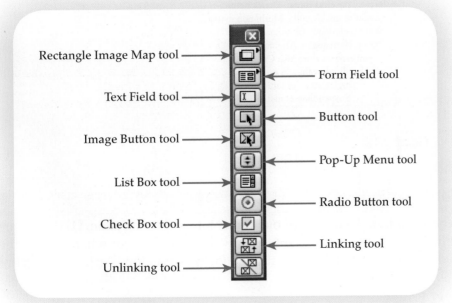

Figure 3.11
QuarkXPress web tools provide many web functions to simplify the process of
creating a digital desktop published document.

Frames

A **frame** is a DTP enclosure for text or images that allows you to move the information as a unit.

Bounding box is the area surrounding a frame.

Because text and images are handled in DTP as separate units, they are placed on the page as **frames** surrounded by **bounding boxes**. These frames can then be changed in size or position using the bounding boxes. Frames allow for complete control of the page design. Text frames can also be linked to allow text to flow from one column to another or one page to another. Frames can be a rectangle, an oval, or a polygon. Polygon frames can be changed to any shape. Frames can contain text, a graphic, or be empty. Figure 3.12 shows a variety of frames.

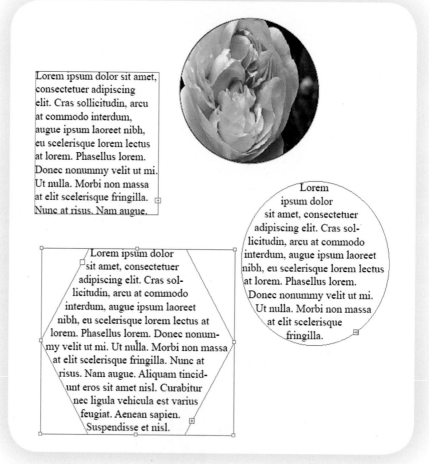

Figure 3.12
Frames are the basic unit of DTP layout.

Continuation

When you link the text from one frame into a second frame, DTP software anticipates that you will want to show the page number where the continued frame is located. The "continued on" information is called a **jump line**.

A **jump line** is the statement at the end of text on one page indicating the page on which the text continues (or was continued from).

Text Boxes

Before you begin work on a document, you need to understand how DTP software handles the formatting of text boxes. Which formatting options are available is dependent upon whether you are making changes to an entire paragraph or only to specific characters within that paragraph. Paragraph formatting includes details such as tabs, indents, alignment, leading, and spacing. Character formatting applies to the fonts used, the color, the spacing between letters, and other attributes.

InDesign uses the Control palette for all formatting, including text. The options shown in this palette will change depending upon what tool is currently selected in the Toolbox. If the Text tool is selected, text options will appear within the Control palette. A toggle will also become available to move you between character and paragraph options within this palette. Figures 3.13a and 3.13b show the two different text option palettes in InDesign.

Figure 3.13a
The InDesign text Control palette toggles between this palette for characters and a different one for paragraphs.

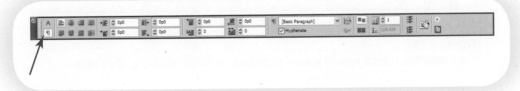

Figure 3.13b
The paragraph symbol on the InDesign text Control palette indicates these options are used for formatting paragraphs.

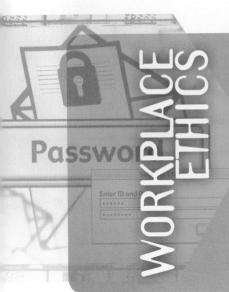

WORKPLACE ETHICS

Desktop publishing programs make it easy to import text that has already been written by someone else. In a team environment, this is a very useful collaboration tool. However, it can be misused. It is very easy to use this tool to place text that you did not write without getting permission from the author. Even pouring in a few paragraphs or a single image is ethically wrong if you are doing this without telling the person who produced it. This is true even if you give that person credit for the work. Make sure that all the material you include in a document is acceptable to use.

Figure 3.13c
If you have used Microsoft Word, you are already familiar with the Formatting toolbar in Publisher.

Microsoft Publisher uses the toolbar shown in Figure 3.13c, which is similar to the toolbar found in Microsoft Word.

QuarkXPress provides several options for formatting text. The Measurement palette shown in Figure 3.13d includes the most frequently used text formatting choices. Selecting the pop-up that appears above the palette takes you to either the Character or Paragraph palette with more choices (see Figures 3.13e and 3.13f).

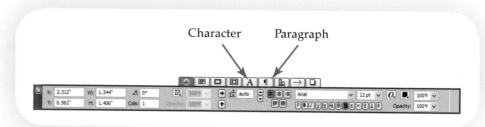

Figure 3.13d
The QuarkXPress Measurement palette provides options identifiable by their icons.

Figure 3.13e
The QuarkXPress character palette provides options specifically related to character formatting.

Figure 3.13f
The QuarkXPress paragraph palette restricts you to paragraph formatting choices.

Placing Text and Graphics

Text can be keyed directly into your DTP software using a text box. In QuarkXPress text is keyed directly into a text frame. In InDesign you have

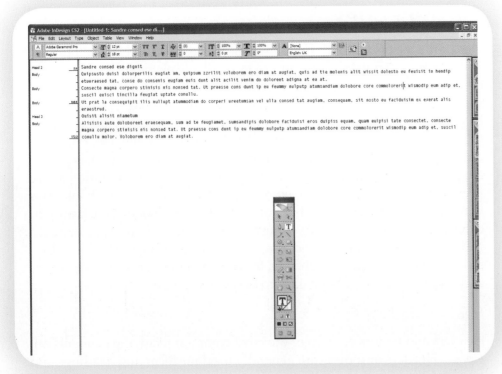

Figure 3.14
Importing or placing text makes it possible to produce DTP documents much more quickly.

the option of keying into a text box, but the Story Editor (see Figure 3.14) is a better choice. The Story Editor allows you to concentrate on the formatting of your text, without worrying about copy that is running longer than your frame. Formatting text within the Story Editor is also simpler. In Publisher, you have the option of editing in Microsoft Word. When you are finished keying and formatting your text, you simply close the Word document and your Publisher document is automatically updated.

You are not restricted to keying text directly into a DTP document. Often you will want to add text that already exists within a word processing document. DTP programs anticipate this and include an option for importing or placing text directly from an existing document. Graphics or images are usually created in other programs and then imported or placed, as well.

QuarkXPress requires that a frame first be created, and then text imported into the frame. InDesign allows you the option of either creating a frame first or merely placing the text first. If you choose to place the text first, the program will automatically create a frame.

When text is imported into InDesign, the cursor changes to the symbol shown in Figure 3.15. This symbol indicates that text is "loaded" into the cursor. To "release" this text, simply click within a frame box. Or you can use the cursor to draw a frame box, which will then release the text into the new frame.

Since text is often several pages in length, you may want to pour text into your document creating additional pages as they are needed. InDesign allows you to place all of the text by holding down the Shift key as you release the mouse. This will create new pages as necessary. In Quark, text is flowed using the master pages.

Figure 3.15
The cursor changes in InDesign to indicate when text is loaded and ready to be placed.

Master Pages

One of the major productivity tools available in DTP software is the ability to create **master pages**. These are pages that have elements that are repeated from one page to another. For example, if your page design calls for a vertical stripe to appear on the outside corner of each page, the stripe could be added to the master page. It would then appear on every page that used the master. If you decide to change the color or style of the line, you would only need to make the change to the master page. Multiple master pages are possible so that different recurring page elements can be added as you need. Perhaps you want the opening page of each chapter of a book to contain certain design elements, but you want the remainder of the pages to contain different elements. Two master pages would be your solution.

Master pages can be created as a single page or as facing pages with different information on each side. Individual names can be assigned to each master page, making it easy to know which one to apply.

Headers and Footers

Headers and footers are two of the most common recurring elements on a page. Headers or footers are generally used for recurring headings and other information that applies to every page. For example, in your textbook the chapter number and title is a **footer** at the bottom of the page. If it appeared at the top of the page, it would be a **header**.

Page Numbers

Page numbers are commonly inserted into master pages. This ensures that the number of each page is always correct, even if you move or delete a page. Page numbers are usually placed in a header or footer.

Palettes

Palettes provide additional design features for your DTP document, allowing you more flexibility. Palette types include color and swatch palettes, character and paragraph palettes, pages and layers palettes, as well as a variety of others. They can be toggled on and off and grouped together to make it easier to use the ones you want. You can also create a work area that opens just the palettes you use most often.

Web Palettes

InDesign interactive palettes, consisting of Bookmarks, Hyperlinks, and States, give you options to use in a web publication. You can insert bookmarks to identify specific locations in a page. You can create hyperlinks to other pages or other web pages. With the States palette you can set button actions using the Button tool.

Mistakes are likely to be missed in the headers and footers of a document. Since these are set in the master pages just once, any mistake that occurs here will be reproduced on every page. It's easy to skim over these areas when you are proofreading. Make it a habit to read headers and footers just like you would the text on the rest of the page. It's embarrassing enough to miss a single mistake. It's even worse to find that mistake repeated on every page.

Master pages contain recurring items such as page numbers as well as other design elements.

A **footer** is recurring information that appears at the bottom of the page.

A **header** is recurring information that appears at the top of the page.

A **palette** is a bar or area on the screen that provides additional features for tools.

Shortcuts

The more time you spend working with desktop publishing software, the more you will appreciate the shortcuts available in each program. These shortcuts appear to the right of their respective menu options. Because DTP software requires multiple mouse actions to manage a project, you will find that learning the keyboard shortcuts can speed up your work. True professionals seldom have to search for a tool. Instead, they use shortcuts almost as if by magic.

InDesign tool shortcuts use single keyboard letters to select a tool. Learning these is the best place to start. When you have these mastered, you will want to learn shortcuts for placing text and zooming in and out. The QuarkXPress shortcut list can be found in the software's Help menu.

Saving

Do not forget to save your DTP document often. These files can be very demanding of your computer's memory, making sudden crashes not uncommon. Saving changes at regular intervals can save you much heartache and headache when the perfect design is lost. Each DTP software program saves files produced by that software with a different extension. InDesign files end with .indd. Publisher files have a .pub extension. QuarkXPress uses the .qxp extension. Generally, each of these files can only be opened by the software that created it. Later, you will learn about ways to export a document, making it readable in other ways.

InDesign Tool Shortcuts	
Selection tool	V
Direct Selection tool	A
Pen tool	P
Type tool	T
Pencil tool	N
Line tool	\
Rectangle Frame tool	F
Rectangle tool	M
Rotate tool	R
Scale tool	S
Shear tool	O
Free Transform tool	E
Eyedropper tool	I
Measure tool	K
Gradient tool	G
Button tool	B
Scissor tool	C
Hand tool	H
Zoom tool	Z
Fill and Stroke	X

SUMMARY

In this chapter you learned the makeup of your desktop publishing software. You learned about default settings, picas, and points. You saw how to use the pasteboard (also called the scratch area) and read about bleeds and slugs. You saw that DTP rulers provide movable zero points and multiple nonprinting guides. You learned that frames are the foundation of DTP design and how to add text without keying it into your document. You saw that master pages can be a useful tool and that shortcuts can speed up your design activities.

KEY TERMS

bleed	header	point
bounding box	jump line	scratch area
default	master pages	slug
fill	pagination	spread
footer	palette	stroke
frame	pasteboard	zero point
guides	pica	

Answer the following questions on your own computer.

1. What setting is already established when the software is first opened?

2. In the digital world, desktop published documents are published in two ways. One of these is print; what is the other?

3. Instead of inches, what measurement does high-end desktop publishing software use?

4. What printer's measurement is equal to 1/6 of an inch?

5. What measurement is a division of a pica?

6. How many points are there in an inch?

7. How many picas are there in an inch?

8. In picas, what is the measurement for a line that is 1/2 inch?

9. If a page is 11 inches long, how long is it in picas?

10. What are the two facing pages of a document called?

11. What is the area outside the working page called?

12. What is the area called outside the working page that allows an image or color to extend to the outer edge of the printed page?

13. What is the space called outside the printed area in which you can place instructions that should stay with your document?

14. What is the starting point of the ruler called?

15. What are nonprinting lines called that provide visual points of reference making it easy to align text, images, or frames?

16. What is the outline or border of a drawing or frame called?

17. What is the inside of a drawing or text called?

18. What is the area surrounding a frame called?

19. What is the statement called that appears at the end of text on one page, indicating the page on which the text continues?

20. What are two of the most common recurring elements on a page?

DISCUSS

1. Explain the use of the pasteboard or scratch area.

2. Explain the difference between the pasteboard and slug area.

3. Explain the use of rulers and guides in creating a desktop publishing document.

4. Explain the use of master pages and multiple master pages.

5. Compare the use of tools between Publisher and InDesign CS2.

6. Explain the advantages of using palettes in desktop publishing software.

7. Explain how keyboard shortcuts save time.

8. Explain how importing text from previously written documents can lead to unethical use.

9. Discuss the importance of proofreading headers and footers.

10. Discuss the use of the Button Tool in InDesign.

APPLY

Activity 1 Default Settings

1. Using your desktop publishing software, create a new document. Answer the following questions about the default settings on the software you are using:

   a. How many pages?

   b. Are the pages facing?

   c. What is the page size?

   d. What is the orientation?

   e. How many columns?

   f. What is the size of the gutter?

   g. What are the top and bottom margins?

   h. What are the left and right margins or the inside and outside margins?

   i. What are the slug measurements?

   j. What are the bleed measurements?

   k. What measurement is used?

2. Using the Type tool, key in the questions and answers. Correct errors in grammar and spelling.

3. Save the document as **default_settings**.

to the website at
academic.cengage.com/school/dtp

WRITING

Activity 2 Custom Settings

1. Using your desktop publishing software, create a new document.

2. Create a custom default setting, changing at least six of the defaults from the list in Activity 1.

WRITING

3. Write a brief summary, explaining the defaults that you changed. If you can name the custom setting in your software, include the name in your summary. Key in the summary and custom name.

4. Save the document as **custom _settings**.

Activity 3 Guides

1. Using your desktop publishing software, create a new document. If needed, change the units of measurement to picas.

2. Set the zero point to the upper left and top margin of your page.

3. Drag and drop vertical guides to 12p10 and 33p5. (Notice that on the InDesign palette you can key the actual location. The QuarkXPress Measurement palette shows you the exact location.)

4. Drag and drop horizontal guides to 12p4 and 47p2.

5. From your student data files, import **rulers_and_guides**.

6. Resize the text box to fit in the middle of the document, using the guides for placement.

7. Center the two titles; change the font size of the titles and text so that it fits in the area better.

8. Save the document as **guides**.

Activity 4 Frames

1. Using your desktop publishing software, create a new document with three facing pages and two columns. If needed, change the unit of measurement to picas.

2. Move the zero point for the rulers to the top left corner of the page.

3. Create a text frame in the second column of page 2, beginning at 43 picas vertically and spanning to the right and bottom margin. Import the document **frames** from your student data files into the text frame. Pour the remainder of the text at the top left corner of page 3.

4. Add a jump line to the bottom of page 2 and the top of page 3.

5. Save the document as **frames**.

Activity 5 Master Pages

1. Using your desktop publishing software, create a new document with five facing pages.

2. Change the view to the A-Master. Insert or place the image **rose** from your student data files on the top left side of the master two-page spread.

3. Add a small text box in the bottom right corner. Key **Page**; then insert a page number.

4. Insert or place the image **foliage** from your student data files on the bottom right side of the spread. Add a small text box in the left

bottom corner of the right side of the spread. Key **Page**; then insert a page number.

5. Change the view to pages 4 and 5 of the document.

6. On page 4, add several frames with the **rose** image. If your desktop publishing software has it available, change the shape of the frames to fit the image to them.

7. Repeat instruction 6 for page 5 of the document using the **foliage** image.

8. Scroll through the pages. Note that the images that you first placed on the master document are on all five pages, and the images that you placed on pages 4 and 5 are only on those pages.

9. Save the document as **master_pages**.

EXPLORE

1. Using your favorite search engine, search for "desktop publishing history of picas."

2. Take notes from your reading of at least two websites regarding the history of picas. Include information on the French influence on using picas as measurement.

3. Include in your notes the following reference information for the sites that you used:

   a. Author of website (if known)

   b. Title of website

   c. Copyright information of website

   d. Date accessed

   e. Address of website

4. Write a 200-word report. Do not include a title.

5. At the end of the report, include the list of references.

6. Save the document as **history_notes**.

7. Create a new two-column desktop publishing document.

8. Using a text frame, import the **history** image into the document. This is an image that you search for and save to use in your document. Place the image at the top left column. Resize to fit in the first column.

9. Create a text frame below the **history** image, and import the **history_notes** document created in steps 1 through 6. If the text does not fit in the first column, pour the remainder into the second column.

10. Go to the A-Master view. Add a text box across the bottom of the left column. At the left in the text box, key **Unit 1, Chapter 3**.

11. Save the document as **history_of_pica**.

4 Importing Graphics

Objectives

- *Develop understanding of image formats.*

- *Study differences between different types of graphics.*

- *Learn to import graphics.*

- *Understand placing images on a page.*

- *Explore modifying an image without changing original.*

- *Learn restrictions on use of images.*

Introduction

Desktop publishing documents without graphics are just words on a page. Now that you have learned to enter text, it is time to add images.

Many times, this text uses a variety of words in similar ways. Graphics, images, and figures are three terms used interchangeably. But what are **graphics**, *you may ask? Graphics are actually anything on the page that is not text. Even text that is used for a specific image effect (think of large scrolled letters) would be considered a graphic.*

Graphics can be photographs, line drawings, basic figures such as a rectangle, and even lines on a page. Graphics can be figures created within your DTP software or they can be images that you imported. Photographs from digital cameras and scanned images are often used in DTP documents. Additionally, Publisher provides clip art for your use.

Image Formats

Before you begin placing images on your page, you need to make sure you have a basic understanding of the types of images you may be using.

Bitmaps

Paint programs such as Photoshop create **bitmap** images made of pixels. Bitmaps are also known as raster images. Each pixel in a bitmap has a defined color, size, and place

Graphics is a broad term that describes anything on a page that is not text.

Bitmap is a type of image created using pixels.

in the image. The sharpness of the image is determined by the density of the pixels, and this density determines the resolution. **Resolution** is defined as dots per inch (dpi) or by the number of pixels in rows and columns (640 × 480). The higher the resolution, the better your image will appear on screen or printout, but the larger the file size will be. Figure 4.1 demonstrates differences between two different resolutions.

Image management programs are of two types: painting and drawing. Paint programs create images by using **pixels** (picture elements). Pixels are small squares (usually) with each pixel assigned a color (see Figure 4.2).

Vectors

Drawing programs create images made of mathematically defined lines and curves, or **vectors**. An advantage of vector graphics over bitmap images is that regardless of how much the image is enlarged or reduced, the quality remains the same. A vector graphic has a smoother outline than a bitmap graphic because the image is mathematically derived for each output device. Figure 4.3 shows a triangle created using vector lines.

Once a vector graphic is completed, it can be converted to a bitmap image. Another name for a bitmap is raster, so this process is called **rasterizing**. Vector graphics are converted to bitmap images for use on the Internet. Shockwave Flash images and animations are vector graphics. Vector graphics are smaller in size than bitmaps, but they are limited because they cannot show gradations of colors as bitmaps can.

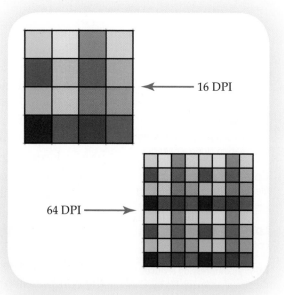

Figure 4.1
The box at the top contains 16 colors. The box at the bottom contains 64 colors. The resolution of the second box is four times greater than the first one. As a result, it will produce a sharper image.

Resolution is the number of pixels in an image.

A **pixel** (picture element) is a data representation of a specific color at a specific location in a matrix or grid. A rectangular collection of pixels can produce a representation of an image on a computer screen or on a printed page.

A **vector** is an image created by using a series of lines and curves rather than pixels. The beginning and ending points of the objects are defined mathematically, making the image easier to resize or scale.

Rasterizing converts a vector graphic to a bitmap.

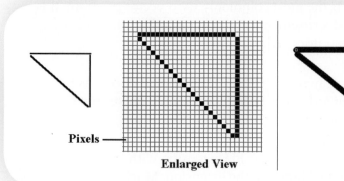

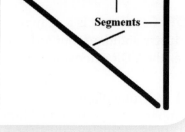

Figure 4.2
Pixels are the small points that make up a bitmap image.

Figure 4.3
Vector images are smoother than bitmaps and print without jagged edges.

Compression

The file formats most often used for web pages are GIF (graphics inter-change format) and JPG or JPEG (joint photographic experts group). The time it takes to download a graphic on the Internet is dependent on the size of the file and the type of connection. Dialup connections that require a modem and a telephone are very slow with a narrow **bandwidth**. Broad-band connections such as DSL and cable modems are much faster as they have a larger bandwidth.

To improve download speed, several algorithms (sequence of steps to perform a function) have been written to reduce or compress the size of files. The two types of **compression** are lossless and lossy. **Lossless** compression reduces the file size without losing any pixel information. **Lossy** compression deletes or changes some pixels while making the file size smaller. The main drawback of a lossy algorithm is that the greater the compression, the poorer the quality of the image. If you are creating a DTP document for the Web, it becomes important to balance quality with file size.

Graphic File Types

A **file format** extension (the two, three, or four letters at the end of a file preceded by a period) identifies which software was used to create the im-age. Some file formats are considered **native**, meaning that they are limited to a specific program. Others are used in a wide variety of programs.

Knowing the file format in which an image was saved is helpful in determining if it is appropriate for an intended use. Images designed for viewing on a computer monitor are usually saved in a JPG or GIF file format. Images intended for printing require a high resolution or sharpness. The best file formats for this purpose are TIFF, EPS, Illustrator, and Photoshop.

Native File Formats

AI Adobe Illustrator is the most commonly used vector program. It is often used to create advertisements and other graphic intensive designs. The extension for Illustrator is AI.

CDR CorelDraw is a drawing or vector program that once was the industry standard, but today has been overtaken by Illustrator. CorelDraw uses the CDR extension.

FH Macromedia FreeHand uses the FH extension with the version number of the software included in the extension. Much like CorelDraw, it is losing importance to Adobe Illustrator.

PSD Adobe Photoshop is one of the most commonly used programs for creating or modifying bitmap images. Its native file format is PSD

Bandwidth is the speed at which a computer can transmit information along a network.

Compression in graphic files is the process of reducing the size of the image.

Lossless compression does not change any pixel data.

Lossy compression reduces the size of an image file by removing information that is not essential.

File format is the type of program that created an image. The extension (two to four letters after the period) at the end of the file name indicates its format.

Native formats are those that can only be read by a single program.

(Photoshop document), but you can save Photoshop images in most of the nonnative image file formats.

WMF Windows Metafile is a low-resolution file that provides both vector and bitmap options. Metafiles use the WMF extension.

General File Formats

BMP One of the most common types of bitmapped images are BMP (bitmap) files. A BMP image is commonly used in word processing documents. Although BMP files are usually limited to 256 colors, their file sizes are often quite large. This is because they are not compressed as some other formats are. BMP files work well in programs that require the Microsoft Windows operating system.

EPS EPS (encapsulated PostScript) is a general purpose vector file format that has both the vector image data and a screen preview in the same file. It is often used for printing purposes because of its high resolution.

GIF GIF (pronounced with either a hard or soft "G") is an image file format developed by CompuServe. Because GIFs only use 256 colors, the file sizes are quite small. GIFs are used to create line drawings, images with transparent backgrounds, and animated figures. Because photographs require greater color depth, they lose much of their quality if they are saved as GIFs.

JPG JPG or JPEG (pronounced jay-peg) is another file type. Using up to 16 million colors, JPG images reproduce the quality, color, and detail found in photographs or graphics using blends and gradients. Most digital cameras save photographs as JPGs to conserve memory space on the camera's storage device. JPGs are more frequently used on the Web than in print.

PNG A third choice for use on the Internet is the PNG (portable network graphics) format. It retains all 16 million colors and has some valuable features, but it is not supported by all web browsers.

SVG SVG (scalable vector graphics) is a vector graphic designed specifically for use on the Web. SVG software is an example of open source programming. SVG images are created using HTML code, although programs such as Adobe Illustrator can be used to create an image and then converted to SVG. There are still some difficulties incorporating SVG and all browsers, but it is likely that in time there will be a significant movement to this form of vector graphics for the Web.

PROOFREADING TIPS

When most people think of proofreading, they only take text into consideration. Actually, proofreading consists of everything on the page including the images. Proofing an image means checking to see that the elements within it are what you intended. For example, in this text there are a number of screen captures of various computer screens. Proofreading these images means checking to make sure that distractions, such as a cursor arrow, were not accidentally included. Other image proofreading might include checking to see that the image is the correct color. Attention to detail is the key to good proofreading whether it is of text or a graphic.

TIF A bitmap file type that works well in all environments is TIF or TIFF (tagged image file format). Like BMP files, these files are quite large and are often used in print documents. TIFF files are not compressed and can show 16 million colors. Many scanners produce images as TIFF files, and some digital cameras can save photographs in TIFF format as well.

Types of Images

Clip Art

Clip art images are usually line drawings, created as vector graphics using few colors. The term comes from an earlier time when images were cut from a printed page and placed on a document using glue or wax. Clip art images are generally simple and often in the nature of a caricature. Clip art images are frequently supplied with word processing software, but they can also be purchased on media such as a CD.

Photographs

Photographs are bitmap graphics that contain millions of colors and realistic images. They can be acquired using a camera or a scanner. Photographs can also be purchased from businesses that own a library of images called **stock photos**. You locate the image you want by using one of the many keywords that identify each image. InDesign includes access to a number of companies that sell stock photos.

Art Work

Art work is a drawing or painting that may appear similar to clip art, but it is created for a specific purpose. Art work can be created as a vector or

BUSINESS OF PUBLISHING

DTP documents contain both text and images. Text is often inexpensive (words are free), but images can be expensive. Choosing which images to use and balancing the cost becomes a business decision. Clip art is inexpensive but not always the most appropriate choice. Stock photos may contain the perfect components for a document, but purchase price and royalty fees have to be considered. Even if images are produced in-house (within the business), the time it takes for an employee to produce the work is a cost factor. Businesses are beginning to discover that the cost of a professionally prepared DTP document is not limited to the expense of printing. Other factors such as image costs need to be considered as well.

bitmap graphic. It differs from a photograph in that it is not an actual real life image.

Choices

The type of image you choose depends upon its intended use. Photographs are often used in DTP documents because real people are interesting to readers. Clip art, which is often humorous, can add a light touch to your document. It also requires less preparation because it is readily available. Unlike clip art, which typically serves a general purpose, art work images are created for more specific purposes. These images are commonly produced exclusively for individual projects, and their development can be quite time-intensive.

The overriding consideration should be your purpose. Graphics should never be placed in a DTP document just for decoration. They should be chosen to fulfill a specific need.

Importing Graphics

Graphics are placed much like text in DTP software. In QuarkXPress you create a frame and then import the graphic. Right clicking on the frame gives you a list of options, including Import Picture as shown in Figure 4.4.

With InDesign, you can create a frame and then import the image into it by clicking on the frame. You can also import (place) the image and let the program place a frame around it. When you place an image, the cursor changes to the icon shown in Figure 4.5. By clicking the loaded cursor on the page, the image will appear on the document in its original size. If you draw a rectangle, the image will fit inside it.

With Publisher you merely insert the image or clip art.

Fitting In

If your image in InDesign is larger than the frame size, only a portion of the image will appear as shown in Figure 4.6. By right clicking on the image and then selecting Fitting (see Figure 4.7), you can select various options to change the way the image appears. You can also find these same options on the Control palette. In Figure 4.8, the partial image has been changed to fit within the frame. Generally, you will want to fit the image into the frame proportionally to keep from distorting your figure.

QuarkXPress allows you only two fit choices as shown in Figure 4.9. You can scale the picture to the box or fit the box to the picture.

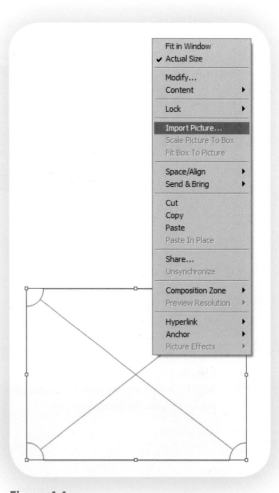

Figure 4.4
Import Picture places the image within the QuarkXPress frame.

Figure 4.5
When placing an image in InDesign, the cursor changes to a small paintbrush.

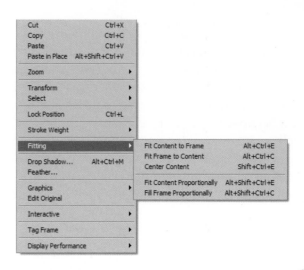

Figure 4.6
With InDesign, images may appear cut off if they are larger than the frame selected.

Figure 4.7
InDesign provides options for fitting images to the frame or changing the frame to the size of the image.

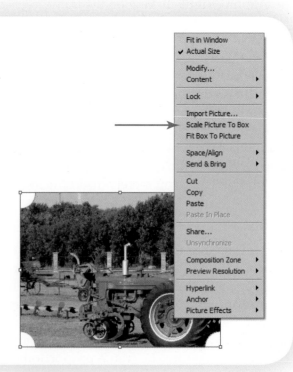

Figure 4.8
Changing the InDesign option to fitting in the frame resizes the image.

Figure 4.9
QuarkXPress makes it easy to choose how you want your image fitted to the frame.

Frame Shapes

While most images are rectangular, you are not limited to that shape. Polygon or elliptical frames can be used to create a graphic that fits that shape. In Figure 4.10 the rose has been cropped to fit within the polygon while still maintaining the original size of the image.

Moving

Both InDesign and QuarkXPress allow you to reposition the image within the frame. Notice in Figure 4.11 that the hand is moving the tractor to place it in the center of the frame. Once the image is repositioned, the frame is moved to enclose the image.

Placing Graphics

Once an image is imported into a document, there are a number of choices for how to place it. Generally, images are placed along the left or right margin of the column or page so they do not disturb the flow of reading.

Floating Graphics

In DTP software, graphics can **float** on a page, meaning that you can place them wherever you want on a page. You can also place an image **inline**, treating it as part of the text. InDesign refers to this as anchoring. The advantage of an inline image is that no matter where you move the text, the image frame will move with it.

Text Wrap

Often images are placed on a page within a paragraph to compliment or illustrate the text. When a graphic is placed in a paragraph, it will either cover the text (see Figure 4.12), or be covered by the text. This is obviously not what you want. The solution is to set the text to wrap around the image.

Text that is wrapped around an image flows along the edge of the graphic as shown in Figure 4.13. Text can flow around the bounding box or it can flow around the actual image, creating an irregular shape. In Figure 4.14 a polygon frame is added and the text is set to flow around the frame's edge. Notice that the text appears inside the bounding box.

Images created as bitmaps, such as photographs, are rectangular; and text must adhere to the edges of the frame. Vector images allow you to set

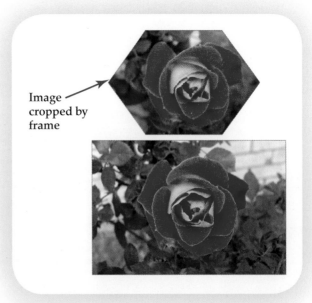

Figure 4.10
Unusual frame shapes such as this polygon can add interest to your figure.

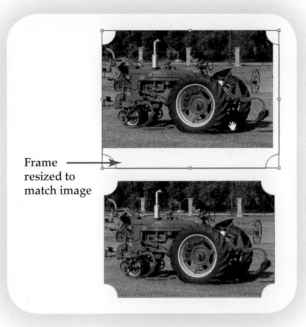

Figure 4.11
Once an image is moved in QuarkXPress, you can reposition the frame to match the image.

Float is a description of a figure that indicates it can be placed anywhere on a page.

Inline describes frames that are placed within text and must stay with that text.

HISTORY

Desktop publishing began even before the introduction of the personal computer. It started with the IBM Selectric™ (1961) and its "golf ball" print head, as shown in Figures 1.1 and 1.2. These allowed users for the first time to change with ease the type style of their text. Before the Selectric™, typewriters were of two types: elite (12 characters per inch) and pica (10 characters per inch). Whatever style your typewriter came with was the style in which you created text. Adding graphics to a document, however, required gluing or waxing the image onto an already typed page.

Macintosh

 Apple Macintosh computer and the ImageWriter printer in 1984, as shown in Figures 1.3 desktop publishing began to change. The Macintosh used a **GUI** (graphical user interface) omputers were used. Earlier computers required users to key-in text to access functions. he use of icons, windows, and menus.

built into a document indicated changes in appearance. Now **WYSIWYG** (what you ok over in programs such as MacWrite. Suddenly it was possible to choose not only font attribute. It was also possible to see those changes on the screen. Graphics could be added it in a limited way and viewed in place. Printing in landscape or portrait became an easy option.

Image Management

With MacPaint and MacDraw (also introduced in 1984), artwork could be digitally created and modified with ease. Figure 1.5 shows an early scanner that replaced the ribbon in the ImageWriter. This made possible the

Figure 4.12
Images placed on top of text will obscure the words below it.

HISTORY

Desktop publishing began even before the introduction of the personal computer. It started with the IBM Selectric™ (1961) and its "golf ball" print head, as shown in Figures 1.1 and 1.2. These allowed users for the first time to change with ease the type style of their text. Before the Selectric™, typewriters were of two types: elite (12 characters per inch) and pica (10 characters per inch). Whatever style your typewriter came with was the style in which you created text. Adding graphics to a document, however, required gluing or waxing the image onto an already typed page.

Macintosh

 With the arrival of the Apple Macintosh computer and the ImageWriter printer in 1984, as shown in Figures 1.3 and 1.4, the world of desktop publishing began to change. The Macintosh used a **GUI** (graphical user interface) to simplify the way computers were used. Earlier computers required users to key-in text to access functions. The Mac introduced the use of icons, windows, and menus.

Previously only codes built into a document indicated changes in appearance. Now **WYSIWYG** (what you see is what you get) took over in programs such as MacWrite. Suddenly it was possible to choose not only font style but also size and attribute. It was also possible to see those changes on the screen. Graphics could be added digitally to a document in a limited way and viewed in place. Printing in landscape or portrait became an easy option.

Image Management

With MacPaint and MacDraw (also introduced in 1984), artwork could be digitally created and modified with

Figure 4.13
Wrapping text around an image creates a design that integrates the image and text.

Macintosh

With the arrival of the Apple Macintosh computer and the ImageWriter printer in 1984, as shown in Figures 1.3 and 1.4, the world of desktop publishing began to change. The Macintosh used a **GUI** (graphical user interface) to simplify the way computers were used. Earlier computers required users to key-in text to access functions. The Mac introduced the use of icons, windows, and menus.

Previously only codes built into a document indicated changes in appearance. Now **WYSIWYG** (what you see is what you get) took over in programs such as MacWrite. Suddenly it was possible to choose not only font style but also size and attribute. It was also possible to see those changes on the screen. Graphics could be added digitally to a document in a limited way and viewed in place. Printing in landscape or portrait became an easy option.

Figure 4.14
If you use an unusual frame design, the text can be wrapped to follow the lines of the frame.

Macintosh

With the arrival of the Apple Macintosh printer in 1984, as shown in Figures 1.3 and began to change. The Macintosh used a simplify the way computers were users to key-in text to access of icons, windows, and menus. Previously only codes built appearance. Now **WYSIWYG** over in programs such as MacWrite. font style but also size and attribute. It screen. Graphics could be added digitally to Printing in landscape or portrait became an

computer and the ImageWriter 1.4, the world of desktop publishing **GUI** (graphical user interface) to used. Earlier computers required functions. The Mac introduced the use into a document indicated changes in (what you see is what you get) took Suddenly it was possible to choose not only was also possible to see those changes on the a document in a limited way and viewed in place. easy option.

Figure 4.15
Vector graphics have more wrapping options because the text can follow the lines of the image.

the wrap to adhere to the actual shape of the figure. In Figure 4.15, the photograph of the computer has been converted to a vector graphic (a technique you will learn in a later chapter). Because it is now a vector rather than a bitmap, the text can wrap around the image. Notice the jagged lines on both sides of the picture and the text within the bounding box.

Standoff Space

The amount of space between the image and the text is called the **standoff** or **offset** space. A wider standoff places more space between the image and the text. Offsets can be established separately for all four sides of the image. Figure 4.16 shows the additional offset that has been applied around the image.

Standoff is the space between an image and text.

Offset is another term for standoff.

HISTORY

Desktop publishing began even before the introduction of the personal computer. It started with the IBM Selectric™ (1961) and its "golf ball" print head, as shown in Figures 1.1 and 1.2. These allowed users for the first time to change with ease the type style of their text. Before the Selectric™, typewriters were of two types: elite (12 characters per inch) and pica (10 characters per inch). Whatever style your typewriter came with was the style in which you created text. Adding graphics to a document, however, required gluing or waxing the image onto an already typed page.

Macintosh

With the arrival of the Apple Macintosh computer and the ImageWriter printer in 1984, as shown in Figures 1.3 and 1.4, the world of desktop publishing began to change. The Macintosh used a **GUI** (graphical user interface) to simplify the way computers were used. Earlier computers required users to key-in text to access functions. The Mac introduced the use of icons, windows, and menus. Previously only codes built into a document indicated changes in appearance. Now **WYSIWYG** (what you see is what you get) took over in programs such as MacWrite. Suddenly it was possible to choose not only font style but also size and attribute. It was also possible to see those changes on the screen. Graphics could be added digitally to a document in a limited way and viewed in place. Printing in landscape or portrait became an easy option.

Image Management

With MacPaint and MacDraw (also introduced in 1984), artwork could be digitally created and modified with

Figure 4.16
Additional offset or standoff space can be applied to an image, providing more distance between the text and the graphic.

Alternate Labels

Images in documents intended for use on the Internet need to be identified with Alt descriptions. This allows screen readers for the visually impaired to "read" what the image is.

Image Options

Nondestructive editing makes changes to an image without actually affecting the original image.

Once an image is in place you can make several adjustments to enhance its impact. These changes can be made without affecting the original image. When you make a change to an image in this way, it is called **nondestructive editing**.

Drop Shadow

Drop shadow is a graphic enhancement that places a shadow on the edge of an image or text.

Drop shadows add depth to an image and give the visual impression of a three-dimensional effect. Drop shadows are a common means of enhancing the look of an image and can be done easily. Notice in Figure 4.17 the difference between the two images: one without a shadow and one with it.

Drop shadows can be set to any color. You may also choose the side on which the shadow appears, which indicates the light source. In addition, you can change the amount of shadow that is visible. The drop shadow in Figure 4.18 indicates that the light source is coming from the bottom right corner. This shadow is set to a gray-blue, rather than the standard dark gray.

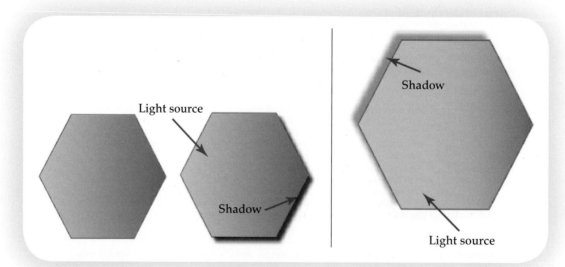

Figure 4.17
Drop shadows make images appear to be three-dimensional.

Figure 4.18
Moving a drop shadow from one side to another gives the illusion that the light source has changed.

In an earlier age, only artists were expected to produce works of art. Today, however, employers expect desktop publishers to be able to produce professional-quality art. Businesses expect those who are doing desktop publishing to have a knowledge of color and design. They expect them to be able to produce an Adobe Illustrator image that is attractive and appropriate. Businesses also expect them to have a knowledge of a wide variety of image options. As a result, those who are considering this career should take classes that will prepare them for these expectations. Art classes, architecture, and even horticultural design classes can help you become a better desktop publisher.

Chapter 1
Getting Started with DTP

Figure 4.19
Text with a drop shadow appears to float on the page.

Drop shadows are not limited to images. Figure 4.19 shows how text can also be enhanced with a drop shadow.

Feathering

Feathering is the practice of slightly blurring the edges of an image. The process makes the image lines appear less harsh and can be an important option to consider. Compare the two images shown in Figure 4.20. The one on the top has sharp harsh edges. The one on the bottom has feathered edges, making the image appear more integrated into the page.

As with drop shadows, you can set options for the amount and type of feathering you want to create.

Transparency

Changing the **transparency** of an object changes its opacity; this makes it possible to see "through" the object. Watermarks are an example of one use for transparencies. Consisting of pale letters or images, watermarks appear behind the printed text or graphics on

Feathering is a graphic enhancement that blurs the edges of the image.

Transparency is a graphic enhancement that lightens the image so that you can see the image or text behind it.

Desktop publishing computer. It started print head, as showr time to change with typewriters were of characters per inch). in which you created text. Adding waxing the image onto an already t

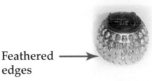

Feathered edges

Desktop publishing computer. It started print head, as showr time to change with typewriters were of characters per inch). in which you created text. Adding waxing the image onto an already t

Figure 4.20
Feathering an object softens its edges, making it appear less harsh.

Chapter 1
Getting Started with DTP

INTRODUCTION

You may have noticed that the title of this book, "Digital Desktop Publishing" also includes the phrase "The Business of Technology." These words were chosen carefully to give you a complete idea what you will be studying in this textbook. The word "digital" indicates that you will not be limited to just the study of print. All forms of DTP including that which is used on the Web will be included. The word "business" helps you to understand that the focus will be on business applications rather than the personal use of the technology. Working together, these two phrases give you a clear idea of what you are about to learn.

The term **desktop publishing** describes the process of producing a document using a personal computer. DTP software, once called page assembly software, makes it possible to combine both print and graphics on a single page. Once a user creates a desktop publishing document, they can then print a copy using a computer printer, a photocopy machine, or a professional press. DTP also provides the option of creating a digital publication. This allows readers to view a document using a computer monitor rather than a paper copy. DTP requires a wide variety of skills, including an understanding of typography, graphics, layout, and business expectations.

The term "digital" demonstrates the advancements made in desktop publishing. No longer is it just about creating a nice looking brochure to reproduce using a photocopier. Today's digital desktop publishing is about using advanced image technology to create the same brochure. It is about creating both the print and Web versions of that same document. Most importantly, it is about choosing the right tools to make your business more profitable. Welcome to the new world of business using digital desktop publishing skills.

Figure 4.21
Reducing the opacity of an image makes it become transparent.

Figure 4.22
This image is being rotated at 25-degree increments.

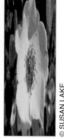

Figure 4.23
This flower was scaled without maintaining proportions, which distorts its original size.

Rotation is the movement of an image along a center axis.

A **scaled** image is one that has been enlarged or reduced.

a page. The use of transparency is also a good way to combine two images, by adjusting the opacity to make one image less visible than the other. In Figure 4.21 the image of the PageMaker book is set to a low opacity. This makes the image appear to be behind the text.

Transformations

Images can be transformed or changed in several other ways. They can be **rotated** by degrees. The most common rotation choices are in increments of 45 degrees. Figure 4.22 shows an image in the process of being rotated.

An image that is enlarged or reduced in size is called a **scaled** image. Generally, you want to maintain the proportions of an image while scaling, so it does not become distorted. Figure 4.23 is an example of an image that was not scaled to proportion.

Arrangement

You can also choose the arrangement of objects on a page. An image can be placed on top of or below text, but this is not the same as using layers (which you will explore in a later chapter). Figure 4.22 showed three images that were stacked on top of each other. Using the option to change the arrangement makes it possible to move each image to a new level.

Permissions

In the business world you do not have the same freedom of image use that you do in school. While in school, Fair Use rules allow students to use materials on a limited basis as part of the learning process. Businesses do not enjoy these same rights. Any art work or written content belongs to that person. Businesses that use this material must have permission to do so. Often this permission includes payment.

Royalty-Free Images

A royalty is a fee paid to an artist every time you use his or her art work. Some images are identified as **royalty free**. This means that the image may be used free of charge or that a simple one-time fee may apply. If you purchase the art on a one-time fee basis, you can then use it as often as you want without paying an additional royalty each time. Some royalty-free images require that the source be named; others do not. Most royalty-free work allows you to use the material, but you are not allowed to resell it.

Royalty free is a term that describes a work of art that can be used without having to pay a fee or royalty each time you use it.

Copyright

Copyright laws protect those who produce a work whether it is art or text. No copyright symbol need be visible for the protection to exist.

Copyright is the legal protection any artist has for the work he or she creates.

Licensing

A **license** is one way that someone with a copyright can provide permission for use. The license provides those who wish to use a work the right to do so, but they do not own the work.

License is the permission granted to use a work of art without transferring ownership.

One of the areas in which licenses are most commonly seen is software. When you buy a program such as InDesign or QuarkXPress, you are only acquiring a license to use the software. You do not actually own it. The ownership of the software resides with the company that developed it. The media on which it was delivered, such as a CD, is merely part of the permission. Often images are acquired in the same way. Your business likely will only acquire the license to use a graphic, while the ownership stays with the artist.

WORKPLACE ETHICS

Getting permission to use an image is important. It is easy to acquire images from the Web thinking they are free for the taking, but they are not. Often a simple email to the web master can provide you with the right to use a graphic. Be aware, however, that just because an image appears on a web page does not mean that the developer of that page has permission to use it. The web developer may be using that image without authorization. Websites that contain hundreds of images that are "free" often do not own these images. A business that uses an image from the Web without legitimate permission, even if that business believed it had been given the right to use it, has violated copyright laws.

In this chapter you learned how to import images and place them in a DTP document. You learned about the difference between vector and bitmap graphics and different file formats. You saw that you could modify an image as it fit into a frame. You also discovered that there were a number of options available to you to modify an image without actually changing it. Finally, you read about the permissions you need when using an image in a business environment.

KEY TERMS

bandwidth	graphics	rasterizing
bitmap	inline	resolution
clip art	license	rotation
compression	lossless	royalty free
copyright	lossy	scaled
drop shadow	native	standoff
feathering	nondestructive editing	stock photos
file format	offset	transparency
float	pixels	vector

REVIEW

Answer the following questions on your own computer.

1. What are graphics?

2. What is another term for bitmap images?

3. What is the number of pixels in an image called?

4. What small points make up a bitmap image?

5. What images are made of mathematically defined lines and curves?

6. What is the process of converting a bitmap image to a vector image called?

7. What limitations do vector graphics have over bitmap images?

8. What is the speed at which a computer can transmit information along a network called?

9. Which compression type reduces the file size without losing any pixel information?

10. What is an algorithm?

11. What process reduces the size of the image?

12. What does a file format extension identify?

13. What file formats are limited to a specific program?

14. What is the most commonly used program to create vector images?

15. What is the most commonly used program to create bitmap images?

16. What file type is a low-resolution file that provides both vector and bitmap options?

17. Which image file format is most often used in word processing documents?

18. What does SVG stand for?

19. What are line drawings created as vector graphics called?

20. What file formats are used for documents designed to be read on a computer monitor?

DISCUSS

1. Explain the advantage of vector graphics over bitmap images.

2. Discuss the factors that determine the length of graphic download time from the Internet.

3. Discuss the best file formats to use for those images that you intend to print and why those file formats are best.

4. Discuss the advantages and disadvantages of using BMP images.

5. Explain the difference between an art work and photographs and clip art.

6. Discuss the criteria that should be considered in deciding what kind of images should be used in a desktop publishing project.

7. Describe nondestructive editing.

8. Compare the enhancement of images using drop shadows and feathering.

9. Describe several transformations that can be applied to images.

10. Compare the difference in Fair Use rules between education and the business world.

APPLY

Activity 1 Hospital Brochure

1. Go to www.google.com and search for images that can be used in a print brochure. Use as your keywords: hospitals or healthcare.

2. Create a folder named images and place four images in it. Save at least one image that is the outside structure of a hospital, a map to

go to the website at
academic.cengage.com/school/dtp

a hospital, a chart of a disease or other data about hospitals, and an inside picture of a scene in a hospital. Rename the images so you have at least one with each of the following names: **hospital**, **chart**, **map**, and **surgery**.

3. Using your desktop publishing software, place the images in a trifold brochure. Place the hospital image in the far right column of the brochure. Place text above the image with the name of the hospital. You can use the name of a local hospital in your area. Resize and fit the image as needed. Type face, size, and style should be formatted appropriately. Align the text appropriately. Add color and at least one transformation to the text and/or text box. Change the stroke width and color.

4. Place a text box below the hospital image with an address and phone number for the hospital.

5. Place the map image in the middle column of the brochure. Create a text box with a list of at least three reasons this location is convenient. Format the text and use rotation on the text box. Add the image of the chart at the bottom of the middle column.

6. Place the image from the inside of the hospital in the left column at the top. Enlarge the image and fit it to the image frame if necessary. Below the image, place a text box with at least six brief phrases that describe the reason a person would want to choose this hospital. For example, professional staff could be one. Resize the text box, fill the text box, change the color of the font and make other enhancements to the image and the text box as needed such as enlarging and scaling the image.

7. Save the document as **hospital_brochure**.

Activity 2 Permissions

1. Using your desktop publishing software, create a document in letter size with landscape orientation.

2. Browse to your student data files and place **licensing** in the left column.

3. Replace the three side headings in the copy with the appropriate images **permissions**, **royalty_free_images**, and **licensing**. Place them inline. If the text does not all fit in the column, adjust the size of the font.

4. If available in your software, anchor (attach) the images to the text. Drag the text block to the right. The images should all move at the same time and retain their position.

5. In the left column, place the image **answers**. Use the Line tool or other drawing tools in your desktop publishing program to balance the white space in the left column and draw attention to the text in the second column.

6. Save the document as **copyright_answers**.

Activity 3 Text Wrap

1. Using your desktop publishing software, create a letter-size document.

2. Browse to your student data files and place the image **pond** at the top left margin of the document.

3. Resize the image to 18p0 × 15p0. Fit the image to the frame. Select the image and wrap the text around the object.

4. Browse to your student data files and place the file **swans** over the image. The text should wrap around the image.

5. Browse to your student data files and place the file **bkground** at the bottom half. Resize and fit the image appropriately.

6. Create a text frame with the text **Swans**. Change the font type, size, style and color so that it will attract attention. Move the text frame on top of the **bkground** image. Experiment with changing the arrangement of the two stacked images.

7. Save the document as **swans**.

Activity 4 Native File Formats

1. Using your desktop publishing software, create a default document. Insert a table with 2 columns and 14 rows.

2. On the first row, key **Native File Formats**. Merge the row.

3. On the second row, key **File Type** in the first column; then tab to the second column and key **Description**.

4. On the third and succeeding rows, key the file types in caps and a short description in the next column.

5. Format all the type, including the heading, so that the table makes an eye-appealing appearance on the page. Adjust the column widths as needed. Center the column headings.

6. Browse to your student data files and place the **pink_flower** image in the middle of the table. Resize and move the image in the middle of the table. Change transparency to 40% on the image. Feather the image.

7. Save the document as **native_file_formats**.

Activity 5 Arrangement

1. Using your desktop publishing software, create a letter-size document with landscape orientation.

2. Using the Ellipse tool or another shape, draw an ellipse in the middle of the document. It should only be about half the size of the document. Fill with a color of your choice.

3. Draw another ellipse from margin to margin. Fill with a color of your choice. Use arrange to send the larger ellipse to the back.

4. Resize the smaller ellipse so that it fits inside the larger ellipse with enough room for text.

5. Key the following lines into a text frame on top of the smaller ellipse:

College Night
Tuesday, September 15, 2XXX
7 p.m.
Bring a friend!
Seechert Gym

6. Center the text and format the type, size, style, and color as needed.

7. Search for a clip art of a graduation cap or another appropriate image and place on the document in a suitable position.

8. Save the document as **college_night**.

EXPLORE (e)

1. Search the Internet for colleges that have certificate or associate programs in desktop publishing. Using a word processing software, write a summary of your search, answering the following questions about at least three schools:

   a. Name of the school.

   b. Name of some of the specialized courses required.

   c. Is the program a certificate, associate, or higher degree?

2. Search for the *Occupational Outlook Handbook* online. Answer the following questions and add to the word processing document:

   a. What is the nature of the work?

   b. What is the job outlook?

   c. What are the earnings?

3. Save the document as **careers**.

4. Using your desktop publishing software, create a document with two columns. Import the **careers** document into your desktop publishing software. If necessary, add extra pages to the document.

5. Search for at least two images that can be used in the document to add interest. Perform at least two transformations on the two images.

6. Add more shapes from within the desktop publishing software, if needed, to balance the white space, clarify information, and add more interest to the document.

7. Save the document as **careers**.

Independent Project

Travel Brochure

1. Choose a place where you would like to travel. Create a travel brochure to this location.

2. Go to a local travel agency or search online to gather at least two travel brochures to get ideas from. Write a summary of what you found that you would like to include on your brochure. Include in the summary some things that you may have found on the brochures that you want to avoid. The summary should be keyed in a word processing document and saved as **brochure_summary**.

3. Create a storyboard of your travel brochure to turn in to your instructor for approval. The storyboard should be a pencil sketch of your plan for your brochure. Include sketches with ideas of the type of image you will use and its placement. Include where you will place text boxes along with a brief description of what text will be in each text box. The brochure should be set up for trifold. Consider the skills that you have learned in Unit 1 and include as many of them in the document setup of your brochure as possible.

4. Using your desktop publishing software, set up a one-page default document. Place or import the **brochure_summary** in the document. Add a page number on the master page as a right-aligned footer.

5. Save the document as **brochure_summary**.

6. Create your travel brochure. Include the following as a minimum:
   - *Set up as a trifold*
   - *Minimum of three images used from at least two different sources*
   - *Use of feathering and drop shadow at least once each*
   - *Set at least two guides*
   - *Wrapped text on at least one image*
   - *Use a transformation at least once*
   - *Images are all in proportion*
   - *No errors in grammar or spelling*
   - *Use fill and stroke in text effectively*
   - *Use arrangement in stacking graphics or text at least once to add interest*

7. Save the document as **travel_brochure**.

Team Project

Digital Portfolio Newsletter

1. With your team of students, create a newsletter about Digital Portfolios.

2. Search on the Internet, interview potential employers, or use other resources to gain information about creating digital portfolios. Write an article to place in the newsletter. Meet with team members to assign tasks in writing articles. Completed articles should be in plain text format and saved as a word processing document. At least two references should be included at the bottom of each article. Students should collect images to emphasize their articles while doing their research and include those ideas and files in notes of the project. The following questions should be answered in the articles.

    ⮕ *What is a portfolio? file name:* **portfolio**

    ⮕ *What is the purpose of a portfolio? file name:* **portfolio_purpose**

    ⮕ *Why create a digital portfolio instead of a paper portfolio? file name:* **why_digital**

    ⮕ *What is the process of creating a digital portfolio? file name:* **portfolio_process**

    ⮕ *What should be included in a digital portfolio? file name:* **portfolio_contents**

3. Meet with team members to edit the articles and create a storyboard of the newsletter. Determine placement of text frames, images, and any other elements that will be used.

4. Using the appropriate desktop publishing software, each student creates his or her own newsletter. Use the storyboard as a guide. All team members should have the same elements in their newsletters; however, the placement of text and images may differ. Save the document as **team number or name_portfolio_newsletter**.

5. Meet with team members to proofread newsletters. Make individual corrections to each file and save again.

6. Final newsletter should include the following requirements:

    ⮕ *Minimum of two pages*

    ⮕ *Page numbers on the master page as a right-aligned footer*

    ⮕ *Images that follow image proofreading guidelines, are appropriately placed, significantly add to the interest of the newsletter, and are the appropriate file type for their use*

    ⮕ *Demonstrate ability to enhance images through the use of feathering, drop shadow, or transformations*

Digital Portfolio

Planning the Portfolio

1. Using the information that you learned in researching for the team newsletter, write a plan for your portfolio. Include in the plan:

   - *What is the purpose of your portfolio?*

   - *Self-assessment of your knowledge in this course at this point.*

   - *Goals for where you would like to be with knowledge in this course. What do you hope to gain from the course? Are there specific skills that you hope to get from the course?*

   - *What will you include in your portfolio?*

   - *What media do you plan to use for your digital portfolio? (Consult your instructor to determine if you have choices or if there is a specific required media, i.e., web page, CD, DVD.)*

   - *Create a storyboard with an idea for a file structure (folder names and file names within the folders) for storing your documents for your portfolio.*

   - *Where will the folders and documents be stored for your portfolio? Where will the backup be stored for your portfolio?*

   - *List a minimum of five projects or assignments that were completed in Unit 1 to include in the portfolio. With each project or assignment listed, write a short explanation of why this project/ assignment was chosen and what was learned in it.*

2. Save the document as **portfolio_plan**.

Collecting and Organizing Sample Projects

Collect projects and assignments that were listed to include in the portfolio. Create the folders for your portfolio. Move all necessary documents to those folders. If available, a copy of the rubric should also be included for each of the projects/assignments that will be included in the portfolio. Back up all files from the portfolio as your plan outlined.

Journalizing Progress

Using a word processing software, tablet PC, handheld device, or blog, begin a journal of this ongoing project. Save the journal as **portfolio_ journal** or give the link to the blog to your instructor. Alternatively, you could keep an audio journal of your work completed by using podcasting or other digital audio methods. Consult your instructor for the journal method to use for this class.

unit 2

Design Principles

Graphic Designer—Newspaper

What I do every day

I work in the marketing department as a graphic artist to promote the newspaper by developing collateral, promotional items, signage for events, and other media that help increase brand awareness. Deadlines in the newspaper industry can be very demanding, so it helps to be organized and efficient. My job is lots of fun since I work with so many different mediums, from billboards to simple ads about upcoming events. The work environment is exciting and challenging every day!

How I use DTP in my job

I use a Macintosh G5 computer and Adobe design software such as InDesign, Illustrator, and Photoshop. Some design jobs have specific branding guidelines already set up so each ad will be consistent in color, fonts, and overall look. Other projects allow me to be more creative. I can make a design look different and appeal to the specific market it targets.

The best part of my job

With the work environment being so fast-paced, there's always a new challenge. Hardly a day goes by when the same thing happens twice. Also, it's very rewarding to work on newspaper segments that teachers will use as supplements in their classroom. I like working on design projects that help others learn. It makes me feel like I am making a difference.

The worst part of my job

Sometimes the frantic pace I love about my job creates a lot of stress. Since project schedules are so fast, there is a lot of pressure to have really great design work done on short notice—with little time for revisions.

What I need to know and be able to do

Organization and attention to detail will make any designer stand out against the rest. Designers today have to juggle tasks from meeting the client to providing material for final production. The better the artist is at communicating with clients and meeting their needs efficiently, the better the results will be.

How I prepared to be a graphic designer

I graduated from a four-year college with a degree in graphic design and a concentration in marketing. Throughout college I worked in the field as a designer in a small print shop to gain experience in the field. Getting an entry-level position can sometimes be challenging, but by having a strong portfolio and work experience, I was able to obtain my first job as a designer after college graduation.

How the Web has impacted this field

The Web has totally expanded the field and brought so many new and exciting things to the world of design. Designers are able to reach audiences through a different medium now and have more choices when deciding what field to specialize in.

5 Planning for Focus and Flow

Objectives

- *Develop understanding of focal point.*
- *Learn to establish flow in document.*
- *Incorporate white space as design principle.*
- *Explore differences between print and web design.*

Focal point is the visual element in a page design that the viewer notices first.

Introduction

In the previous unit you became familiar with various desktop publishing software options. Now you need to concentrate on creating more complex designs. Designing is at the heart of digital desktop publishing. The focus of your design should begin at the point where your reader's attention is initially drawn, which is the first sight of your page or document. That initial impression is half the battle. Your reader is much more likely to follow your message once you have their attention.

Focal Point

The **focal point** of a page or document is the place your reader first sees. It may be a graphic, a color, or even text. A good design makes a point of first choosing a focal point and then building on it. A page without a focal point (particularly an opening page) may be boring. It also can cause confusion, since the reader has no clear idea of where they should begin reading. Pages should never be designed without an intentional focus point.

When making a decision about your focal point, remember the following guidelines:

- ➡ Larger text is noticed before smaller text.
- ➡ Brightly colored text is noticed before black text.
- ➡ Images are noticed before text.

Text

We will begin exploring focal points by looking at pages with text only. Figure 5.1a is a booklet that uses various font sizes and attributes, such as bold, to attract the reader's attention. The first thing a reader notices when looking at the two-page spread is the word "Planting" which is larger than all the other text on the spread.

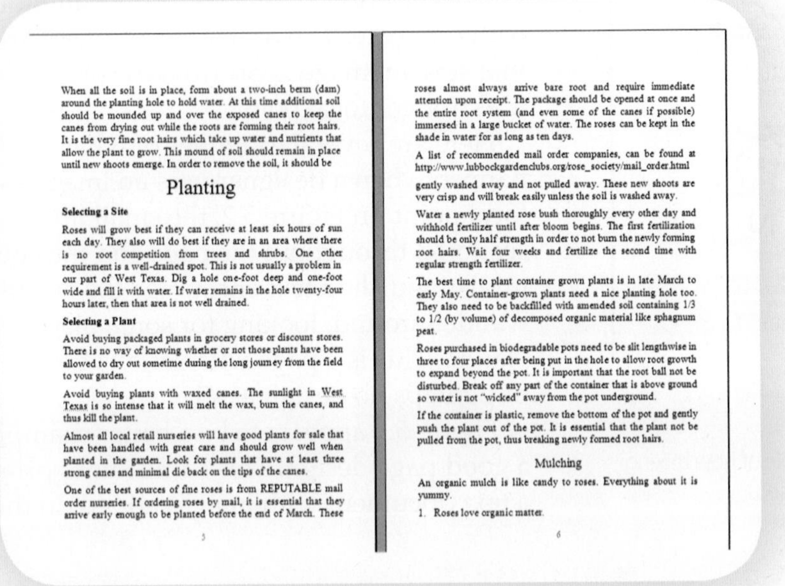

When all the soil is in place, form about a two-inch berm (dam) around the planting hole to hold water. At this time additional soil should be mounded up and over the exposed canes to keep the canes from drying out while the roots are forming their root hairs. It is the very fine root hairs which take up water and nutrients that allow the plant to grow. This mound of soil should remain in place until new shoots emerge. In order to remove the soil, it should be

Planting

Selecting a Site

Roses will grow best if they can receive at least six hours of sun each day. They also will do best if they are in an area where there is no root competition from trees and shrubs. One other requirement is a well-drained spot. This is not usually a problem in our part of West Texas. Dig a hole one-foot deep and one-foot wide and fill it with water. If water remains in the hole twenty-four hours later, then that area is not well drained.

Selecting a Plant

Avoid buying packaged plants in grocery stores or discount stores. There is no way of knowing whether or not those plants have been allowed to dry out sometime during the long journey from the field to your garden.

Avoid buying plants with waxed canes. The sunlight in West Texas is so intense that it will melt the wax, burn the canes, and thus kill the plant.

Almost all local retail nurseries will have good plants for sale that have been handled with great care and should grow well when planted in the garden. Look for plants that have at least three strong canes and minimal die back on the tips of the canes.

One of the best sources of fine roses is from REPUTABLE mail order nurseries. If ordering roses by mail, it is essential that they arrive early enough to be planted before the end of March. These

5

roses almost always arrive bare root and require immediate attention upon receipt. The package should be opened at once and the entire root system (and even some of the canes if possible) immersed in a large bucket of water. The roses can be kept in the shade in water for as long as ten days.

A list of recommended mail order companies, can be found at http://www.lubbockgardenclubs.org/rose_society/mail_order.html

gently washed away and not pulled away. These new shoots are very crisp and will break easily unless the soil is washed away.

Water a newly planted rose bush thoroughly every other day and withhold fertilizer until after bloom begins. The first fertilization should be only half strength in order to not burn the newly forming root hairs. Wait four weeks and fertilize the second time with regular strength fertilizer.

The best time to plant container grown plants is in late March to early May. Container-grown plants need a nice planting hole too. They also need to be backfilled with amended soil containing 1/3 to 1/2 (by volume) of decomposed organic material like sphagnum peat.

Roses purchased in biodegradable pots need to be slit lengthwise in three to four places after being put in the hole to allow root growth to expand beyond the pot. It is important that the root ball not be disturbed. Break off any part of the container that is above ground so water is not "wicked" away from the pot underground.

If the container is plastic, remove the bottom of the pot and gently push the plant out of the pot. It is essential that the plant not be pulled from the pot, thus breaking newly formed root hairs.

Mulching

An organic mulch is like candy to roses. Everything about it is yummy.

1. Roses love organic matter.

6

Figure 5.1a
The text on this page is read in a linear manner, meaning from top to bottom.

The words in bold such as "Selecting a Site" also stand out, as does the slightly larger word "Mulching." This booklet is meant to be read in a linear manner (one page after another). The various text changes incorporated in the design help pull the eye along from one section to another.

In Figure 5.1b the same text is shown, but the URL is now in red. Notice how quickly your eye moves to that point on the page. Even though the URL is smaller than the word "Planting," its color creates a focal point. By adding this color, the reader is able to quickly locate the URL when returning to the page.

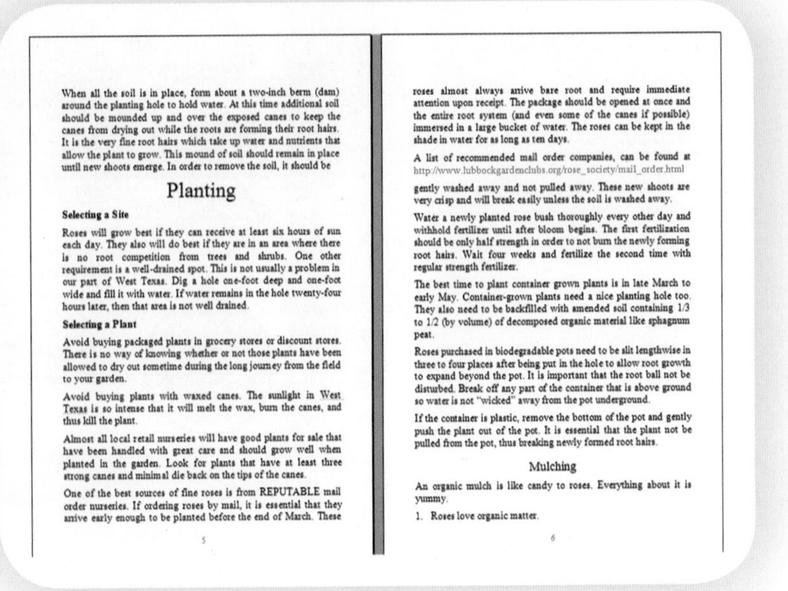

When all the soil is in place, form about a two-inch berm (dam) around the planting hole to hold water. At this time additional soil should be mounded up and over the exposed canes to keep the canes from drying out while the roots are forming their root hairs. It is the very fine root hairs which take up water and nutrients that allow the plant to grow. This mound of soil should remain in place until new shoots emerge. In order to remove the soil, it should be

Planting

Selecting a Site

Roses will grow best if they can receive at least six hours of sun each day. They also will do best if they are in an area where there is no root competition from trees and shrubs. One other requirement is a well-drained spot. This is not usually a problem in our part of West Texas. Dig a hole one-foot deep and one-foot wide and fill it with water. If water remains in the hole twenty-four hours later, then that area is not well drained.

Selecting a Plant

Avoid buying packaged plants in grocery stores or discount stores. There is no way of knowing whether or not those plants have been allowed to dry out sometime during the long journey from the field to your garden.

Avoid buying plants with waxed canes. The sunlight in West Texas is so intense that it will melt the wax, burn the canes, and thus kill the plant.

Almost all local retail nurseries will have good plants for sale that have been handled with great care and should grow well when planted in the garden. Look for plants that have at least three strong canes and minimal die back on the tips of the canes.

One of the best sources of fine roses is from REPUTABLE mail order nurseries. If ordering roses by mail, it is essential that they arrive early enough to be planted before the end of March. These

5

roses almost always arrive bare root and require immediate attention upon receipt. The package should be opened at once and the entire root system (and even some of the canes if possible) immersed in a large bucket of water. The roses can be kept in the shade in water for as long as ten days.

A list of recommended mail order companies, can be found at http://www.lubbockgardenclubs.org/rose_society/mail_order.html

gently washed away and not pulled away. These new shoots are very crisp and will break easily unless the soil is washed away.

Water a newly planted rose bush thoroughly every other day and withhold fertilizer until after bloom begins. The first fertilization should be only half strength in order to not burn the newly forming root hairs. Wait four weeks and fertilize the second time with regular strength fertilizer.

The best time to plant container grown plants is in late March to early May. Container-grown plants need a nice planting hole too. They also need to be backfilled with amended soil containing 1/3 to 1/2 (by volume) of decomposed organic material like sphagnum peat.

Roses purchased in biodegradable pots need to be slit lengthwise in three to four places after being put in the hole to allow root growth to expand beyond the pot. It is important that the root ball not be disturbed. Break off any part of the container that is above ground so water is not "wicked" away from the pot underground.

If the container is plastic, remove the bottom of the pot and gently push the plant out of the pot. It is essential that the plant not be pulled from the pot, thus breaking newly formed root hairs.

Mulching

An organic mulch is like candy to roses. Everything about it is yummy.

1. Roses love organic matter.

6

Figure 5.1b
The red URL on this page helps the reader to pick out the information quickly.

Images

Figure 5.2
This page has no focal point. It's an example of how mixing graphics and text on a page can be overused.

Desktop publishing documents typically consist of more than just text. Most contain at least one image or graphic. A reader's focus will shift to an image or graphic, since they stand out more than text. In addition, images with bolder colors have more impact than quieter ones. Images of people also pull the eye more than other images. Images inserted at an angle attract attention better than vertical or horizontal ones. Anything that sets an image apart from the ordinary makes it a stronger focal point.

Here are several examples of what can happen when a designer uses an image as a focal point. In Figure 5.2, the small images scattered throughout the page and the equally undistinguished text encourage the eye to wander around, looking for some place to "land." This is a page with serious design flaws or perhaps no design at all.

Figure 5.3 appears to be a better example of a good page design. This certificate is primarily a text document with images added. In this

Figure 5.3
This 1955 stock certificate is pretty to look at but very difficult to read.

case the images are not as randomly placed as in the previous example. However, what does your eye see first? Is it the green heavy certificate border? Does the figure of the two people also pull your eye? Does the green seal with the heavy text grab your attention? This design includes too many competing images, and the focal point is unclear. In addition, the text is nearly unreadable because of the font choice. The next unit will discuss the importance of type choices. While the certificate is impressive, it is not an example of good design.

The book cover in Figure 5.4a uses a composite image created from several different pictures to pull your eye to the center of the page. If an image of a person had been used for the center figure, would that have changed the way you saw the cover?

Notice what happens in Figure 5.4b. The addition of the red certification stripe competes for your attention. Which did you see first—the red color or the image? It is surprising how such a small change can create an entirely different focus.

Figure 5.4a
This design pulls your eye to the center of the cover.

Figure 5.4b
The addition of the red rectangle distorts the original design of the cover.

The page shown in Figure 5.5 is an interesting example of color, images, and text. Is your eye drawn to the top of the page first, or to the right side? Do you see the large black text, which is the chapter title, or the pink heading titles? What happens when you try to read the note with the swirly background? In many ways this page is just as confusing as the certificate shown earlier.

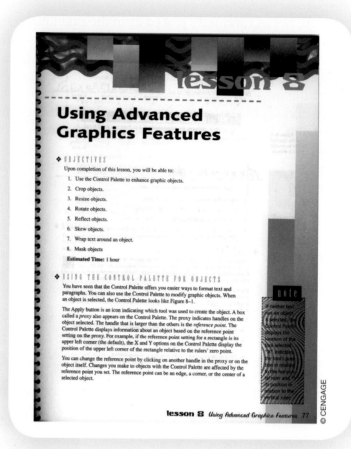

Figure 5.5
The color on this page acts as a distraction rather than a focal point.

The confidence posters in Figure 5.6a and Figure 5.6b demonstrate how an image that has been rotated to an unusual angle attracts more attention than one that is placed in the more traditional vertical or horizontal position. Both images are exactly the same size and in the same location. Did you find yourself looking at the first poster more than the second one?

Figure 5.6a
The rotation of the board on the poster forces the reader to pay attention.

Figure 5.6b
The traditional placement of the board on the poster gives it a less interesting look.

In Figure 5.7, the reader's eye is drawn to the image of the man with outstretched hands. The image has several components that make it a compelling focal point. The brightly colored shirt up against the dark background immediately pulls in the eye. The content of the image creates a question in the mind of the reader, adding further interest.

With this graphic, a focal point has been established on the page as the place to begin. As a reader you might wonder why the man is making such broad gestures. You become curious and begin reading the text to find an answer to your question. The designer has succeeded in attracting your attention.

Flow

Once a focal point has been established, the reader needs to be encouraged to continue reading the rest of the page by following a predetermined **flow**. The same rules apply to flow that apply to focal point. The eye looks for images before text, larger text before smaller text, and colored text before black text. Keeping these three points in mind, the page designer can establish a path for the reader to follow.

Z Pattern

Examine Figure 5.8. While it uses exactly the same material that appears in the previous figure (5.7), it has a very different flow. In this figure the reader's eye moves from the image on the left to the right seeking the large text and then down to the lower left and finally to the lower right in a zigzag pattern.

The zigzag pattern is so common that it has a name, the **Z pattern**. The pattern begins at the upper left, moves to the right, and then down to the lower left and on to the lower right (as shown in Figure 5.9). This duplicates the usual pattern of reading text since our eyes are trained to move from left to right. Designs that follow this pattern are easy for readers to follow. Other patterns require the designer to consciously redirect the reader's eye using images and text.

Figure 5.7
The black background and red shirt in the image draw your eye before anything else on the page, making them the focal point.

Figure 5.8
This page is designed in a Z pattern similar to the process one uses when reading a page.

Flow is the visual path created by arrangements of elements within a page design.

Z pattern is a visual path that draws the eye from top left to top right down to bottom left and then to bottom right.

Figure 5.9
The Z pattern is an important design standard to remember. It is one that readers can follow easily.

Other Patterns

Another common pattern that you saw previously follows a linear path straight down the page. This pattern is what you expect when you are reading text pages such as the ones shown in Figures 5.1a and 5.1b.

Figure 5.2 was already identified as confusing and is even more so when you try to determine a path. Did you jump from image to image, or did you try to decipher text from among the images in an effort to read in a standard left to right flow? This is one more reason why this is not a good design.

Looking back at the stock certificate in Figure 5.3, notice that the eye tries to follow a linear path starting at the top and moving down, but the distractions on the page make that very difficult. There is no flow visible in this document.

Track the path of the book cover that was shown in Figure 5.4a. The reader's eye moves from the image in the center to the multicolored large text until it finally stops on the title of the book. This is a complex design that encourages a circular flow.

Figures 5.6a and Figure 5.6b each showed an obvious focal point, directing the reader's eye from the left to the text on the right side of the page. The distinct color of the word "confidence" pulls the reader's eye to the first line and then down the page. Which version of the poster is more effective at encouraging a flow—the one with the angled image or the straight one?

Figure 5.7 was easy to follow. The eye starts at the top of the page and moves straight down to the final text at the bottom in a linear path similar to what would be expected with a text page.

A good way to learn how to design pages that flow is to read magazines with ads you have not seen before. Pay attention to what your eye first focuses on and then what path your eye follows. You will be surprised how quickly you begin paying attention to the process.

BUSINESS OF PUBLISHING

Businesses sometimes do not appreciate the importance of good design. They often see it as merely a way of making text "pretty" without realizing that without good design, nothing happens. A page that is not readable and does not attract the reader could contain the most important information the company possesses. If no one reads it, it has no value. Businesses understand that a product that does not sell is not worth the time it took to produce it. Documents function in the same way. Good page designers are as important as good engineers. They make the difference between a product that is appealing and useful and one that isn't. Learning how to do this well is your task.

White Space

While it is easy to see that images and text can attract attention, the part of a page void of text or images is also important. This area is called **white space**, although the space does not actually need to be white. In design this space is treated as a component just like an image or text. White space is not just a section on a page for which the designer had no use. It is carefully integrated in the design. White space includes the margins on the page, the amount of spacing between lines of text, and most importantly larger open areas on a page.

Placement of white space serves several purposes. It can reduce the "busyness" of a page. It can give the reader a chance to "rest" while tracking the path on a page. It also opens up a page so that it appears less intimidating. It can even draw a reader's attention if it is designed as a large part of a page.

Examples

The CD cover shown in Figure 5.10 has ample white space. This is an interesting design. The font of the CD title is a soft blue that does not demand attention. With the image of the lighthouse also on the page, the two elements could compete for your attention. Instead, the white space pulls your eye and then directs you to the title. The additional information shown in black picks up your attention and slides you over to the image. A Z pattern is established beginning with the white space.

The newsletter shown in Figure 5.11 demonstrates how white space can be used effectively to make a document less intimidating. The left column has white space bounding the contents as well as the callout (the quote separated with horizontal lines above and below it). This white space gives importance to these two page components. The white space between the two articles helps to separate them. Since newsletters are usually text intensive, adequate white space makes the page appear less dense and easier to read. Notice also that because the newsletter is printed on a colored background, the white space is actually yellow.

Looking back at previous examples, in Figure 5.3 the only significant white space was outside the border

> **White space** is the blank area on a page designed to provide a visual break and to give other elements greater impact.

Figure 5.10
This cover uses soft colors and careful design to send a message about the music included in the CD.

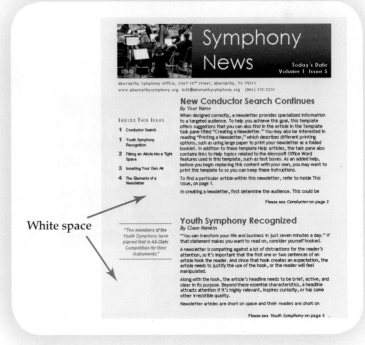

Figure 5.11
The white space on this newsletter increases the readability of the articles and helps to draw attention to elements such as the contents.

Many companies have found that they want to reduce costs by publishing to the Web instead of to paper. Sometimes this is done by creating an image of a print document to post on their site. Other times they may convert the print document to a PDF file. In both situations, they are working from traditional desktop publishing software.

A change, however, is beginning to occur. Instead of desktop publishing software, they are beginning to use web-editing software to design documents that are meant to be printed as well as posted to the Web. This means that in the future we may begin to see the standards of web design take over print design.

of the certificate. This lack of white space makes the page even more intimidating to read. In Figure 5.4 the white space in each of the rectangles made the text more dramatic. This space was a significant part of the design. Look at Figure 5.8. What purpose did the white space serve? Did it make it easier to move between blocks of text?

In the next chapter you will learn how white space can be used as a balancing component.

Negative Space

White space is sometimes also called **negative space**. The text and images on a page represent the **positive space**. Art design teaches that an observer notices both negative and positive spaces on a page. As a result, many designers pay close attention to the negative space on a page. To them it is a design itself.

One of the ways to see the impact of negative space is by studying it separately from the content on the page. If you look at Figure 5.12, you will see the reverse of Figure 5.10. In this figure you can see clearly the black or negative space up against the white or positive space. Studying negative space makes it easier to see the impact of white space on a page. In this figure the white box competes with the white title for your attention. The overlapping of the text on the image is even more apparent when you are viewing it only as negative space.

Negative space is another term for white space or areas on the page where no text or graphics are located.

Positive space is the area on a page where text or graphics are located.

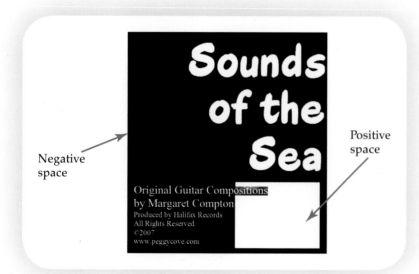

Negative space

Positive space

Sounds of the Sea

Original Guitar Compositions
by Margaret Compton
Produced by Halifax Records
All Rights Reserved
©2007
www.peggycove.com

Figure 5.12
Reversing the text and graphics in this figure makes it easier to see the negative space on the page.

Web Page Design Principles

Web page design has evolved much like print pages did. In print, initially there were few design options. Pages consisted of text and a few graphics placed at the start of a paragraph (called illumination). Printing presses allowed more complex designs to appear, including the use of columns. Desktop publishing software allowed personal computer users to design pages once possible only by highly skilled printers.

Web pages (just like early print pages) initially consisted of text and a few graphics that could only be placed with limited control. No true "design" was possible. The web editor was restricted by the limits of HTML code. In time, more options became available and today the design possibilities continue to grow. As a result of these changes, websites are beginning to be designed with rules of their own.

Web Page Structure

The nature of a screen design is somewhat different from one designed just for the printed page. Focus is always at the top of the page and then flows down. This is the result of the need to scroll down the computer display. Text or images at the bottom of the page may not be immediately visible.

White space is even more important on web pages than text because there are no margins to provide the openness that appears on print pages. Some web designers place all the text in frames that are smaller than the average screen so that there are wide borders that mimic margins. Another way that white space is added to web pages is by increasing spacing between each paragraph. Designers often don't take full advantage of the possibilities that white space provides.

In print, readers are not required to navigate from one link to the next. They read in a linear fashion moving from one page to the next. Consistent design is not necessary. However, with web pages that require the reader to make navigation decisions, good design requires a consistent page structure. This consistent design from link to link within the site helps the reader know what to expect.

Standard Design

Most sites now follow a pattern that places link choices for the site in a left column and additional information in the right column (see Figure 5.13). The center column is used for visual flow of information. An image is placed at the top of the page or the left corner, but its purpose is to provide a visual reference rather than to attract interest.

The bottom line of the page contains links such as contact information, copyright, and page designer similar to those shown in Figure 5.14.

Just as in print, there are a wide variety of good designs. The best ones take into consideration the audience by tracking their eyes on the page. It should be easy for readers to find the information for which they are searching. It should also be easy for them to read it once they find it. That's good design regardless of the placement on a page.

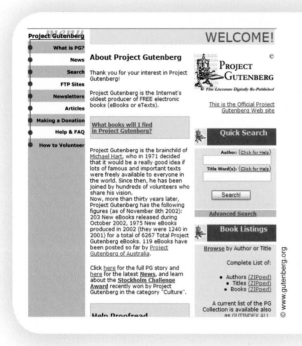

Figure 5.13
Web pages that are designed for a screen rather than the printed page have slightly different design rules.

Figure 5.14
The bottom of the web page is often reserved for legal and contact information such as this one from the Gutenberg site that provides copyright restrictions and the name of the web master.

WORKPLACE ETHICS

While it is unethical (and illegal) to use someone else's images without permission, page design is unusual in that there are few such limitations. Observing someone's web page or brochure design and then using a similar design is not only acceptable, but also a good practice. Imitating good design is a great way to become a better designer yourself. Just be aware that you are only allowed to use the arrangement on a page and not the actual components.

Design Decisions

All desktop publishing software, from the most basic word processing program to advanced programs such as QuarkXPress, allow for arranging pages in ways that attract attention and make it easy for readers to follow the information on the page. Good design is not a function of software; it is a function of your understanding of what you need to consider in the makeup of a page or pages.

On a final note, it is often hard for new designers to trust their judgment. They feel that they are not knowledgeable enough to know what others will see first or track. Trust yourself. You have been reading text for years. You have been following the focus and flow of designers without even realizing it. Now it is time to use this experience. Even designers with years of experience sometimes misunderstand what a reader will do, but most of the time they get it right. You will too.

SUMMARY

In this chapter you learned how to look for the focal point on a page. Then you looked at the way the eye moves from the focal point and through the page using a Z pattern or another one determined by the designer. You saw how white space is an important element in the design process, which can be seen by studying the positive and negative space on a page. You saw how web page design uses similar design techniques but with modifications based upon screen limitations. And finally, you learned that it is important to trust your own instincts while making design decisions.

KEY TERMS

flow	negative space	white space
focal point	positive space	Z pattern

REVIEW

Answer the following questions on your own computer.

1. What is the area of a page called that is the first thing that the reader sees?

2. What types of elements make good focal points?

3. What is meant by "text meant to be read in a linear way"?

4. In a page with text only, what type of enhancements cause some text to become the focal point of the page?

5. What makes an image a stronger focal point?

6. What does the term "flow" mean?

7. What is Z pattern?

8. Why is the Z pattern an important design standard to remember?

9. Once the focal point has been established, what encourages the reader to continue reading the rest of the page?

10. What is white space?

11. What is negative space?

12. How can one "see" negative space more easily?

13. What makes up the positive space in a desktop publishing document?

14. What is illumination?

15. What device allowed the use of columns in print publishing?

16. What allowed personal computer users to be able to design professional desktop published pages?

17. How does the design of a web page differ from that of a printed page?

18. Why is it important to maintain a consistent design from one page of a website to another?

19. What is one way to proofread for spacing mistakes in your desktop publishing document?

20. What is one way that many companies are attempting to save money in publishing?

DISCUSS

WRITING

1. Explain the guidelines that you should remember when making a decision about the focal point on your page.

2. Using the example of a stock certificate in the textbook, what type of design errors made this document an example of bad design or difficult-to-read text?

3. Describe a zigzag pattern used in a page design and what makes it a good design choice.

4. Explain why white space is considered a part of the design of the page and what makes up white space.

5. Explain the importance of the placement of white space on a page.

6. Explain the difference between negative and positive space.

7. Discuss what design options were available at the beginning of web page design.

8. Explain the differences in designing for a print page and a web page.

9. Explain the importance of good print design in achieving success in a business.

10. Explain the use of someone's page design as it pertains to copyright law.

APPLY

Activity 1 Good Design Examples

1. Locate two print examples of use of the Z pattern in a magazine.

2. In a word processing document, cite the source of your examples using MLA format.

3. Under the citation, explain in two or three sentences what makes the page a Z pattern.

4. Locate two web pages that are similar to the design discussed in this chapter.

5. Add the source of your examples to your word processing document using MLA format.

6. Explain how their design demonstrates the layout described in the chapter.

7. Save as **good_design**.

go to the website at academic.cengage.com/school/dtp

Activity 2 Event

1. Design a page that advertises an event that you recently attended. It could be a sporting event, a musical, a play, or even a family get-together for a birthday or other special occasion.

2. Begin by creating a sketch of your page. Mark the focal point with a star and use arrows to draw the intended flow of the page.

3. Decide who your audience will be and what the purpose of the document is. Note these on the page.

4. Use your desktop publishing software to create a digital version of the page. It should contain text, graphic, white space, and the intended flow from your sketch.

5. Save as **event**.

Activity 3 Web Design Principles

1. Open **web_design** from your student data files. There are two text files and two objects randomly placed to use in your design.

2. Place the text boxes and objects on the page using either a Z pattern or linear design. You can resize text and text boxes as needed. If needed, you may add other elements such as text boxes or an appropriate image.

3. Add a text box on the pasteboard that answers the following questions:

What was the focal point in the design? Explain why this was the focal point.

Was this a linear design or Z pattern? What makes it that type of pattern?

4. Save as **web_design_principles**.

Activity 4 Z Pattern

1. Design a page demonstrating your knowledge of the Z pattern.

2. The topic of the page should be what you have learned about focal points in desktop publishing.

3. Include an image, a heading with a large font, text with smaller font, and some color font.

4. Demonstrate effective use of white space.

5. Include in the smaller text an article that describes the Z pattern as well as why you used the design you did in this assignment. Why did you place the image where you did? Why did you place the larger font where you did? Where did you use color in fonts and why? What do you consider your focal point? What did you do that used white space effectively?

6. Save as **z_pattern**.

Activity 5 Reader's Path

1. Open **readers_path**.

2. Using the elements on the page, arrange them in a linear path that demonstrates the following statement from your textbook: "The eye looks for images before text, larger text before smaller text, and colored text before black text." Resize text boxes and images as needed.

3. Save as **readers_linear_path**.

EXPLORE (e)

1. Find five examples of page design that you believe could be improved. Using paper, draw a sketch to redesign the pages to improve their focus, flow, or use of white space. In a word processing document, explain why you made the changes you did. Save as **page_design_examples**.

2. Survey web pages that appeal to you. Make a list of five design rules that you believe should be incorporated into standard web design guidelines. Create a web page using your list of five design rules. Include a heading on the page that will attract attention and title the web page. Save it as **web_design_guidelines**.

Understanding Design Elements

Introduction

Once you have decided on the focus and flow for your page, you need to make decisions concerning other design elements. Creating a good design is not just about choosing a focal point. A good design also takes into account the placement of all other components on each page. Desktop publishing requires the designer to think about where text should appear and where images should be placed on each page. This statement was true when professionals were working with moveable type, and it is still true today as desktop publishing documents are created on computers. Over the years a number of rules or suggestions have been developed to help designers make the best possible choices. This chapter shows how these rules can provide the guidance needed to create well-designed pages.

Objectives

- *Discover how grids can help you use design components.*

- *Learn about design options that Rule of Thirds provides.*

- *Explore ways to create pages that have a harmony of design.*

Layout Components

As you begin to learn about using design elements, think of a page as a **grid** similar to the one shown in Figure 6.1. On that grid you can place any of the three basic design elements; text, images, and white space. Some items will be larger, while others will be smaller. By moving each piece around the page you can experiment with your options and begin developing a knowledge of how the pieces work together. In Figure 6.2, there are three frames—one for each element. These frames do not fill up the page so they must be enlarged or additional ones added.

A **grid** is the division of a page into a design on which text, figures, or white space are placed in order to design a page.

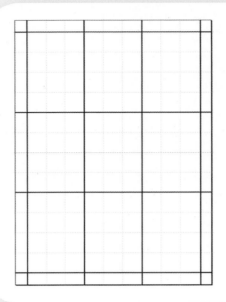

Figure 6.1
Grids can be of any size as long as they are regular in shape.

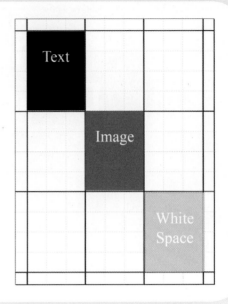

Figure 6.2
The three basic components of page design are text, images, and white space.

Figure 6.3 demonstrates how elements can be enlarged or duplicated to fill the page. There are countless ways to arrange the three basic elements of text, images, and white space. Figure 6.4 shows just one more variation.

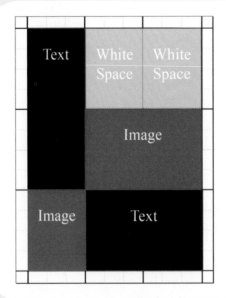

Figure 6.3
Pages can be created with an infinite number of designs.

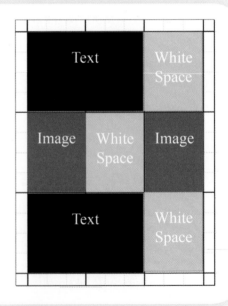

Figure 6.4
Designs such as this one help you to see if placement of white space is appropriate.

You are not limited just to rectangles. In Figure 6.5 you can see that allowing one element to invade the space of another adds interest.

By including white space as one of the components, you begin to see how it becomes an important part of the total design process. No longer is it merely unused space. It is now space placed intentionally to create a designed effect.

Looking at an example from the previous chapter (Figure 6.6), you can see how each of the components would fit into a grid. The blocks of color can be considered images even though they contain text. Although the large words, such as "image." are text, they also function as images. As a result, most of the grid is filled with images with white space to the outside. The only significant text is the book title. The authors' names and the publisher stand out amid blocks of white space.

Notice that this grid is not an exact duplicate of the actual design. Its purpose is not to force you into matching your design exactly as you have outlined it in a grid. Instead, a grid is a means of planning ahead, allowing for changes once you have begun the actual design process.

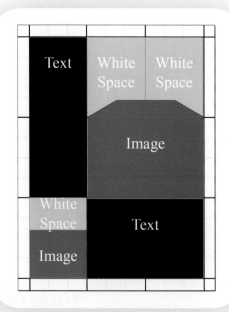

Figure 6.5
While your grid begins with squares or rectangles, your final design does not have to adhere to those edges. In this case the image has an irregular shape.

Figure 6.6
The cover of this text was clearly created using a grid.

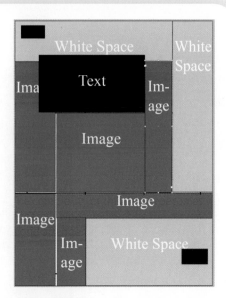

Figure 6.7
The complexity of this design becomes very apparent when you replace the content with a grid arrangement.

Web Grids

Frames and tables are frequently used design tools for web pages (see Figure 6.7). As a result, it is very easy to explore your design options using the same tools you would for a printed page. The difference between print and web documents is that the way a web page is viewed is often out of the designer's control. Some computer monitors may be oriented vertically and some horizontally. Some may be quite large while others may be small. The solution is often to design a page so that the content is limited to a percentage of the screen size, which maintains the proportions you intend.

Rule of Thirds

The **Rule of Thirds** states that a page (or image) that is designed in thirds is more appealing to the eye than other designs.

One thing you may have noticed while looking at the various grid possibilities was how often the pages were divided into thirds. This is a common design that is quite pleasing to the eye and is used so often that it has been given the name the **Rule of Thirds**. This rule, which is not truly a rule but rather just a strong suggestion, states that pages arranged in thirds are more effective than those designed in halves or fourths. The Rule of Thirds was present in the grids shown in Figures 6.3, 6.4, and 6.5. Compare any of those figures to Figure 6.8. In Figure 6.8 there is no sense of order, and the

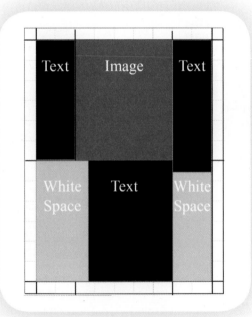

Figure 6.8
This grid arrangement would result in a page that is not in harmony.

two major blocks of text and image are taking up half a page. This design might serve a purpose in some instances, but generally it will be jarring to the reader.

Web Thirds

Web pages do not have vertical margin limits in the same way that print does. Dividing a web page vertically into thirds is difficult, since pages can be scrolled down as far as needed. Horizontal thirds, however, are a common design choice. Often a page will be divided into two columns with one narrow column reserved for navigation and the wider column containing content. In this way the Rule of Thirds "rules" the Web.

Golden Terms

Considerable study has been done to determine why dividing a page into thirds is so appealing. The history of this study began with ancient mathematicians. These mathematicians described their conclusions as the **golden ratio**, which is 1.628 or ∏ (pi). The math used to determine this ratio is quite interesting, and you may want to do further research to see how they arrived at these results. Other golden terms include the "golden triangle," the "golden mean," the "golden spiral," and the "golden rectangle." All of these terms represent efforts to use mathematical precision to describe arrangements found in nature and design.

Fibonacci Sequence

One other term that is often referenced in design is the **Fibonacci sequence**. This sequence is a series of numbers beginning with 1 where the next number in line is the sum of the previous two. The Fibonacci sequence is 1, 1, 2, 3, 5, 8, 13, 21, 34, 55, 89, etc. The farther along in the series you go, the closer you get to 1.628 when dividing the second number by the first. For example, if you divide 8 by 5, you get 1.6. If you divide 89 by 55, you get 1.618. This series of numbers appears frequently in nature, and designers often try to mimic this natural design.

Notice in our previous examples that, other than dividing the pages used into thirds, the total number of elements used does not include any of the Fibonacci numbers. Let's try a design that includes five or eight elements within the thirds. Figure 6.9 is designed with five elements and

The **golden ratio** is a number (pi). The approximate result is derived by dividing 5 by 3, arrangements often found in nature.

The **Fibonacci sequence** is a series of numbers beginning with 1. Each number in the series is added to the next in order to create a third number.

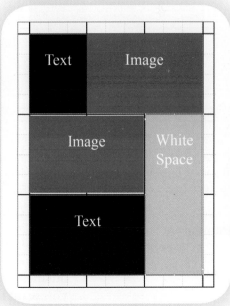

Figure 6.9
This page is composed of five elements consisting of two images, two text boxes, and white space.

Businesses that hire desktop publishers are primarily looking for two skill sets—design and software. Salaries are paid based upon the size of the employer, the industry in which you are working, your credentials, and your years of experience. Salaries in 2006 ranged from $39,000 to $50,000. Desktop publishing often requires the ability to write and produce text in the form of manuals or instructions. Sometimes even reporters are called upon to be desktop publishers. The diversity of this career means that you need to develop a wide variety of skills because you do not know when one will become important in your occupation.

Text	Text	Image
White Space	Image	Text
White Space	White Space	

Figure 6.10
This page uses smaller images and more white space to create a page with eight elements.

Harmony of design is when all the elements on a page are arranged in an effective way.

Figure 6.10 has eight. Are these more appealing to you than those with six or seven elements? This is something to keep in mind as you begin to design pages. Just as the Rule of Thirds is not truly a rule, use of Fibonacci numbers is not a requirement (only a suggestion) for good design.

Harmony of Design

Now that you have explored the overall design possibilities using a grid, it is time to think about where and how to place each element on a page. Your choices are based on the need to create a **harmony of design**. Design harmony is accomplished when all pieces work together, creating a page that is readable and interesting. The Rule of Thirds is just one way to create harmony in a design. There are a number of ways that page elements can be used to create harmony in a document. These include rhythm, organization, and consistency.

Harmony is evident when you look at a page and know that it works for the purpose for which it was intended. For example, if you are designing a business card for someone who has a childcare facility, the card has two purposes. One is to provide information and the other is to create an impression of the nature of the business. Together these two purposes must work in harmony. Perhaps you want to create a sense of playfulness as well as responsibility. This requires careful choices. In addition, the content of the card must be easy to absorb since business cards are read quickly. Knowing how to use all the page elements effectively makes it possible to create a card that meets your requirements.

Rhythm

Rhythm is the flow of the page similar to that which you studied in the previous chapter. It is the motion that is inherent in a page that draws you from one item to another and one page to another.

Figure 6.11 is a brochure that builds in a rhythm that is not apparent when you look at the full page. This is an example of a Z fold brochure that you studied previously in the book. It is printed on a single side and is folded so that the left third of the page is visible (see Figure 6.12). When the brochure is unfolded, the two inside pages are visible as seen in Figure 6.13, and the entire page can be read. Notice what happens with the jellybeans. They draw your eye from page to page, creating a rhythm or flow.

Figure 6.11
This brochure is actually designed to be folded so that you can only see a third of the page.

Rhythm is the flow and movement of a page.

Figure 6.12
The cover of the brochure provides basic information and invites you to open it.

Figure 6.13
The inside of the brochure folds open to complete the design.

Proportion

Proportion is the arrangement of elements on a page making more important ones larger than less important ones.

Proportion is the need to make each element on the page a size that reflects its importance to the page. It is one of the reasons that focus is so important. It helps to make one element the most important. Then other elements must be made proportional to ensure the focus is not lost.

The jellybeans are the largest and most visible part of the opening page. The name "JellyBean Jamboree" is next in size, followed by the contact information. If the business's name had been made quite large, it would have overpowered the image, distorting its effectiveness.

Organization

Organization is the logical arrangement of information and graphics on a page. A good example of failure to organize is to separate information that is related. Placing a graphic a distance away from the text it illustrates is one way that a page loses organization. Interrupting text by placing an image in the reader's path is another way to fail to organize your document.

Compare Figures 6.14 and 6.15. Both business cards contain exactly the same information. The first one, however, has little organization. The information is placed attractively on the card, but the eye must wander all over looking for information. The second example gathers together the essential information such as Jare Thomas' name and title. Since e-mail addresses are often the preferred means of contact, it is placed at the bottom where it can be found easily. Notice that Jare Thomas' name is also larger than the rest of the text to give it importance.

Figure 6.14
This business card on first glance appears to be designed well. It isn't until you look more closely that you realize that the information is a jumble.

Figure 6.15
This card is designed to make it easy to find the information you need as well as to attract your attention.

Web Organization

Web pages need organization just as much as print ones do. The dynamic nature of web documents is such that often content is placed in a haphazard manner, making it difficult for readers to find the details they need. This is partly because web design is still developing. Good designers are beginning to learn the importance of page organization.

As we continue to move into more use of the Web as a means of publication, it's important for designers to remember the guidelines that govern print publications. Design rules such as organization, rhythm, and consistency were developed over a period of many years. They were accepted because time proved their value to readers. Web designers need to keep in mind established guidelines from the past and incorporate these to create pages that have a sense of control and harmony that is often lost in today's web pages.

Consistency

Consistency is attention to detail. It may mean that your type choices are consistent or the amount of space between paragraphs is the same throughout a document. It may mean that you design each page of a multipage document in a way that makes it clear that the pages are part of the same design.

Notice that both the brochure and the business card for JellyBean Jamboree use consistent design tools. The typefaces are the same, and the same background image is used. Together these create a feeling of consistency.

> **Consistency** of design is when the same choice is made for similar parts of a page such as a typeface or spacing.

Web Consistency

Consistency in web design is perhaps more important than it is even in print. There is so much happening on a web page that it is easy for a reader to get lost. Using consistent designs such as navigation links and headings improves the usefulness of the document. Since web pages are often created at different times and then linked to one another, it's easy for consistency to get lost. Part of a designer's task is to pay attention to details, looking for inconsistencies.

Repetition

Repetition is one way to build consistency into a document. Reusing an image from one page to another may create a consistent feel. Duplicating a dramatic line of color at both the top and bottom of a page can be a good use of repetition. Using the same image in a different size and location is another example of repetition. Repetition causes the reader to think "Ah,

> **Repetition** is the duplication of elements or details on one or more pages.

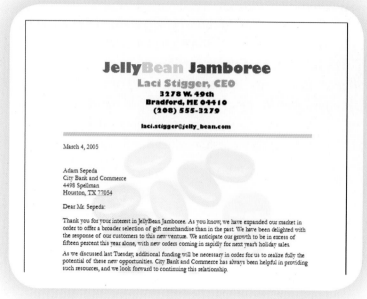

Figure 6.16
This letterhead repeats the jellybean image with a slight modification.

I've seen this before." It creates a feeling of comfort.

You have already seen how the repetition of the jellybean figure provided consistency. Notice in the letterhead shown in Figure 6.16 that the jellybeans are reused, but this time as a pale background called a watermark.

Look at a monthly wall calendar that has a different photograph for each month. Notice as you flip the pages that while the image changes, the rest of the calendar design remains the same. If each month were designed in a different way, it would lack harmony and be disruptive to the person using the calendar. The consistency from month to month is a good use of repetition.

Web Repetition

Repeating information and graphics from one web page to another serves several purposes. It quickly identifies to the reader that this page is still part of the original site. It helps orient the reader to page information. It also reduces the distraction that often comes when each page is completely different. Repetition is a key tool for web designers.

Balance is the use of elements so they counter each other, for example in opposite corners of a page.

Figure 6.17
Gridlines show how parts of the page balance one another.

© SUSAN LAKE

Balance

Balance is a type of repetition where elements that are similar in size or shape are placed in such a way that they counter each other. Balanced elements might be in opposite corners or they may be across from one another. The use of balance creates a page that is in harmony. It is not necessary for the same type of element to be used to create balance. Text can be balanced by white space or by an image.

In Figure 6.17 the brochure is divided into a grid. The use of grid lines makes it easy to see how parts are balanced. In this case, the contact information in the bottom left balances the opening text box in the upper right.

Figure 6.18 is a good example of a simple text document that is balanced. Notice how one column balances the other. In addition, the text at the bottom balances the text at the top. Even the lines separating each list are balanced.

Software to improve the way you work

Metuo capto dolore adsum loquor, blandit inhibeo sed. Praesent nunc minim nisl brevitas ventosus singularis pecus probo si transverbero genitus, paratus. Multo bis epulae, duis plaga lenis luptatum refoveo lenis. Quis esse probo quadrum aliquip velit ex.

New Features
- Direct export
- Layout spaces
- Synchronized text
- Full preview
- Multiple Undo

Enhanced Features
- Easier image creation
- Improved functionality
- Better tools
- User friendly
- Simplified formatting.

Minimum System Requirements
- *Computer
- *256MB total RAM
- *Internet connection

- *CD-ROM
- *200 MB available hard drive space

Figure 6.18
This CD insert for a software product is primarily text. Even without an image, though, it is neatly balanced.

Web Balance

Because it's not always possible to know that content at the top of a web page will be visible at the bottom of the page, balance from top to bottom is not usually part of a web design. Pages that do have a horizontal balance are easier to read and feel more harmonious.

Tension

A cake recipe may call for extra sweetness offset by a tart taste in order to enhance the overall flavor. For the same reason, some design elements are used so that they are purposely disruptive. This deviation from harmony is called **tension**.

> **Tension** is the opposite of harmony. It can add interest to a page or cause it to feel incomplete.

Symmetry

It is easy to believe that each element on a page must be completely balanced with another. While this is often pleasing to the eye, it can also create boring pages that are too predictable. **Symmetry** is when a page or its elements are perfectly balanced. Figure 6.18 is an example of a symmetrical page design.

> **Symmetry** is when elements on a page are evenly balanced.

Asymmetry is when one or more elements on a page are not balanced.

Closure is the desire by the human brain to complete a drawing or design.

Stickiness is a design that encourages the reader to keep reading or to stay on a page.

Asymmetry

Pages that are not perfectly balanced are considered **asymmetrical**. One element may be separated from all the others which makes it stand out. This lack of balance can make a more interesting page than a symmetrical one. It is a good use of design tension.

Compare Figures 6.19 and 6.20. Figure 6.19 is a symmetrical page with the two blocks of text at the top balancing each other and the title of the

Figure 6.19
This cover is simple with a symmetrical design.

Figure 6.20
This cover is identical except for the simple asymmetrical triangle in the upper right corner. A single change makes a significant difference.

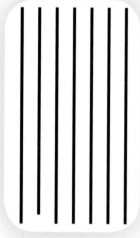

Figure 6.21
The single short line draws a reader's eye as it seeks to create closure.

book balanced against the figure below. In Figure 6.20 the yellow triangle in the upper right corner is not symmetrical. It jumps off the page drawing your attention to the CD information. The asymmetrical element makes the page feel less static or boring.

Closure

The mind tends to want to finish that which is left undone or to seek **closure**. If you draw a series of vertical lines that are of equal length (shown in Figure 6.21) except for one that is slightly shorter, the mind tends to focus on the shorter line, trying to force it to match the others. This is an example of the need for closure.

This unfinished line creates a feeling of visual tension as the reader tries to create completeness. Such tension can increase reader interest and add to the page's **stickiness**. Stickiness is a concept borrowed from web page developers. It is a design component that keeps readers on the page instead of clicking away. Print documents also need stickiness in order to attract readers' interest. A business card is a good example of a document that needs stickiness since it is easily discarded. Businesses have found that turning a card into something useful (such as a magnet) is one way to create stickiness.

Alignment

Alignment is the placement of text or images so that one line of text falls exactly below another or so that the edge of an image lines up with the text above or below it. The need for alignment of elements is the same human characteristic that seeks closure. The difference is that failure to align usually does not create harmony. Instead, the page feels not quite right. As a result, elements purposely placed away from other elements should be far enough away that it is clear this was the designer's intention. This helps reduce an unwanted tension. Notice in Figure 6.22 that the web address is just slightly below the image. It appears that the designer has made a mistake rather than an intentional choice.

Figure 6.22
The production information on the CD cover needs to be moved up to create an effective alignment.

Design Decisions

It is easy to be overwhelmed by all the decisions one must make in designing a page. There are so many details to think about that it is hard to even know where to start. The place to begin learning how to make design

Alignment is vertical and horizontal placement so that text or images match.

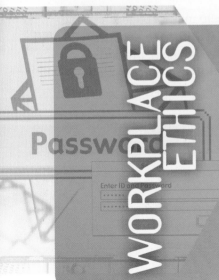

Designing pages is time-consuming and difficult. Even the simplest design may require multiple versions before it is satisfactory. One ethical consideration that many people overlook is recognizing the time it takes for someone to produce a work of art. Well-designed pages are art in the same way as a painting or musical composition. Make sure that those around you who are producing such work are given the credit they deserve. Ignoring their contribution just because it appears "simple" is just as unethical as stealing it.

You have seen how having a line of text just slightly out of alignment is jarring to a page, ruining its harmony. There are many slight misalignments for which you need to proofread in the documents you create. One of the most common problems is an extra space between two words. Another is an extra space at the start of a new paragraph. Lines of copy that are evenly spaced except for one that is slightly wider or narrower are also a problem. Removing these distractions is an important part of a good design. Learning to recognize them requires practice. See if you can find the proofreading errors in Figure 6.23.

decisions is by studying designs created by others. Look at magazine ads. Look at web pages. Look at junk mail that arrives at your home. Begin to dissect these samples looking for layout decisions. See if you can find examples of the Rule of Thirds. Look for symmetry and asymmetry. Look for tension on a page and decide if it improves the page or not. Pay attention to the details. You will find that as you begin developing your own eye, you will also develop your own sense of style and taste. Remember that the most important part of any design is the question "Does the document serve its purpose?" If the design makes that possible, then it succeeds.

> You have seen how having a line of text just slightly out of alignment is jarring to a page and ruining its harmony. There are many slight misalignments for which you need to proofread in the documents you create.
> One of the most common problems is an extra space between two words. Another is an extra space at the start of a new paragraph. Lines of copy that are evenly space except for one that is slightly wider or narrower is also a problem. Removing these distractions are important part of a good design.

Figure 6.23
This text contains all three proofreading errors mentioned above.

SUMMARY

In this chapter you saw how the Rule of Thirds can help make a page appealing. You learned about the elements of design that are used to create a document that is in harmony. You saw the importance of symmetry, consistency, proportion, and balance. You learned how closure and tension can also be used to add interest to a page. You are now ready to take these design tools on to the next step.

KEY TERMS

alignment	golden ratio	Rule of Thirds
asymmetry	grid	stickiness
balance	harmony of design	symmetry
closure	proportion	tension
consistency	repetition	
Fibonacci sequence	rhythm	

REVIEW

Answer the following questions on your own computer.

1. What is a division of a page into which text, figures, or white space are placed in order to design a page called?

2. What are the three basic components of page design?

3. What are two frequently used design tools in web pages?

4. What is the golden ratio?

5. What is the Fibonacci sequence?

6. What is harmony of design?

7. What is rhythm, as used in page design?

8. How does a Z fold use the Rule of Thirds?

9. What is proportion as it pertains to page design?

10. What is organization in page design?

11. What is consistency in page design?

12. What is repetition as used in page design?

13. What harmony-of-design attribute does repetition build into a document?

14. What is balance in page design?

15. What types of elements can be used to create balance?

16. What type of balance makes web pages easier to read and understand?

17. What is tension in page design?

18. What is symmetry in page design?

19. What is asymmetry in page design?

20. What is meant by closure in page design?

DISCUSS

1. Tell why using a grid is a good way to experiment with design options.

2. Discuss some of the ways that the basic elements of text, figures, and white space can be used for variation in page design.

3. Explain how the Rule of Thirds "rules" the Web.

4. Describe why dividing a page into thirds is appealing in the design process.

5. Tell some ways to create harmony of design.

6. Explain the importance of proportion in page design and how it relates to focus.

7. Discuss the importance of using consistency in page design.

8. Discuss why repetition is important in web design.

9. Analyze the difference between symmetry and asymmetry.

10. Explain how the lack of alignment in page design can affect the success of the document.

APPLY

to the website at academic.cengage.com/school/dtp

Activity 1 Layout

1. Using your desktop publishing software with a default setup, import **text** and **images**. Drag them to the pasteboard.

2. Create a text box of any size filled with black. Drag the text box to the pasteboard.

3. Using the three elements on the pasteboard, fill the page with these elements. Use copy and paste to create longer articles of text, small and large versions of the same image, and resizing of text to fill the page with the elements.

4. Use the black text box to show white space in the page design.

5. Save as **layout_practice**.

LAYOUT COMPONENTS

To begin to learn about using design elements, think of a page as a grid. On that grid you can place text, images, and white space. Some will be larger, some will be smaller. Moving each piece around the page as an element is a good way to experiment with your options and to begin to develop knowledge of how the pieces work together. Frames don't necessarily fill up the page, so they must be enlarged or additional ones added. There are countless ways to arrange the three basic elements of text, figures, and white space.

To begin to learn about using design elements, think of a page as a grid. On that grid you can place text, images, and white space. Some will be larger, some will be smaller. Moving each piece around the page as an element is a good way to experiment with your options and to begin to develop knowledge of how the pieces work together. Frames don't necessarily fill up the page, so they must be enlarged or additional ones added. There are countless ways to arrange the three basic elements of text, figures, and white space.

LAYOUT COMPONENTS

To begin to learn about using design elements, think of a page as a grid. On that grid you can place text, images, and white space. Some will be larger, some will be smaller. Moving each piece around the page as an element is a

© KAREN BEAN

Activity 2 Rule of Thirds

1. Using your desktop publishing software with a default setup, import **text** and **images**. Drag them to the pasteboard.

2. Create a text box filled with black. The text box can be any size as it will be resized for use. Drag to the pasteboard.

3. Add elements to the document using Figure 6.3 in the textbook as an example. Use copy and paste to create longer articles of text, small and large versions of the same image, and resizing of text to fill the page with the elements.

4. Save as **thirds_practice**.

Activity 3 Rhythm

WRITING

1. Using your desktop publishing software, create a Z fold brochure demonstrating the use of rhythm as described in the textbook.

2. Use landscape orientation in the setup of the document.

3. Import the image **graduation** in the top two-thirds of the page design both horizontally and vertically. Add a text block with the name of your school in the bottom left one-third. On the right one-third, place information about the celebration after graduation and use the image of **happy_grad** if desired.

4. Save as **graduation**.

Activity 4 Harmony

1. Using your desktop publishing software, create a new landscape document demonstrating repetition, alignment, and balance.

2. Import **alignment** and **balance**. Place **alignment** at the top left horizontally to 20p and vertically to 15p. Place **balance** at the bottom right from 20p to 60p horizontally and 30p to 45p vertically. This creates a balance in the design.

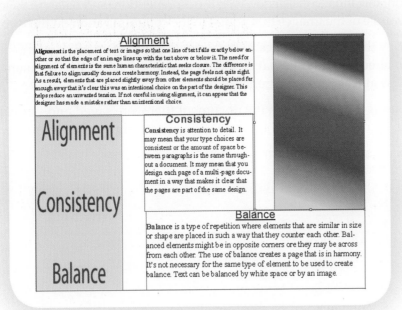

3. Import consistency and place it at 20p to 40p horizontally and 18p to 33p vertically.

4. Import **image** and place at the bottom left of the page.

5. Import **balance_image** and place at the top right of the page.

6. Align all titles in text at center with size 24 font. Leave the paragraph text in the imported articles left-aligned. This creates alignment and consistency, which brings about harmony in the design.

7. Save as **harmony**.

Activity 5 Grand Opening

1. A new orthodontist has moved to town and is opening a newly acquired office at 1111 Perfection Lane in Tethertown, Maryland 99999-0000. The grand opening will be on Saturday in approximately two weeks. Plan a date and some other ideas to interest visitors at the open house. The name of the orthodontist is Jamie Deekae and the business is called Perfect Teeth.

2. Using your desktop publishing software, create a flyer to advertise the grand opening.

3. Use design concepts learned and practiced in this chapter to create a flyer that will interest potential customers.

4. Save as **grand_opening**.

EXPLORE

1. Search the Internet for web design examples that demonstrate one or more of the following elements used in an effective manner: organization, consistency, web thirds, repetition, and balance. Save a couple of the images that added to the communication on the web page.

2. Key the MLA reference to the website in a document. Underneath the reference, explain what elements were used in an effective manner. Use at least three references.

3. Insert the images into the document that were saved and write a brief explanation of how they were used effectively on the website.

4. Save as **good_design**.

CHAPTER 7

Using Other Design Tools

Introduction

Page design is not limited to only those tools explored in the previous chapter. In addition to the placement of elements such as white space, images, and text, many other tools can be used to design an attractive and successful page.

Greeking

As you look at examples in this chapter, you will see text that appears quite strange. This is a desktop publishing standard called **greeking**. The use of greeking (also called dummy text) allows page designers to place text on a page without the actual content acting as a distraction. The history of greeking is unclear, but it was first used in the middle of the 20th century. The text was based on words of Cicero, a Roman leader whose writings are admired. The language he spoke and wrote was Latin rather than Greek, so the naming of this dummy text is misleading.

Objectives

- *Understand how greeking is used in design.*
- *Explore options that columns provide for design.*
- *Learn what alignment choices you can make.*
- *Learn how to add attention-getting text to a page.*
- *Understand importance of page anchors.*
- *Explore how to use multiple page designs.*
- *Understand importance of curves.*

Greeking is a series of nonsense words, often derived from Latin, used as a placeholder in a desktop publishing document.

Lorem ipsum is the first two words of the original greeking text. It is sometimes used instead of the word "greeking."

A **placeholder** is a means of assigning space for a text or graphic without having to place the actual copy.

Lorem ipsum, as it is sometimes called, acts as a **placeholder** that can be filled with actual text when the design is completed. Although the original paragraph (see Figure 7.1) has been replaced with a number of different versions similar to that shown in Figure 7.2, the purpose remains the same. Early adopters of greeking repeated paragraph after paragraph to create the amount of copy they needed. Today there are websites that will create copy for you.

Lorem ipsum dolor sit amet, consectetur adipisicing elit, sed do eiusmod tempor incididunt ut labore et dolore magna aliqua. Ut enim ad minim veniam, quis nostrud exercitation ullamco laboris nisi ut aliquip ex ea commodo consequat. Duis aute irure dolor in reprehenderit in voluptate velit esse cillum dolore eu fugiat nulla pariatur. Excepteur sint occaecat cupidatat non proident, sunt in culpa qui officia deserunt mollit anim id est laborum.

Nullaortie dunt lor ipit

Cipit lore consecte mod etum vendignibh do odip

Em mor aurei

Is crit in sedem hocrio mandium num, factua redo, Ti. Senatus, ne me inat, dem morum et; nostier imulaributus sus orenim tercepse fatiaet oraesci tiorudem diu intem menatam num nonsula tiamdi, C. Verum actatis sa dinem ia nostis vid cones cae iam, nonsusuam patil temur inclum, vivilici patist ad ad Esitili ussultore atu qua dentem dii pote ne.

Ilius iam ium

Pericae parbit viri ponsus sica; hocchuideo inarei furnum quem, sul videm, C. Ebervide et is im horium egiti con st L. Serobsentia re es con vil viciaet quem ta dees or atifecret; hos,

Norum perestem dinver host?

idem includaci escrus int, nos fur pondamdinver host? idem includaci escrus int, nos fur pondam. Cata nonve, tantemus, dem in acien vit, quo ad re fecitri, dellabulabus nonde nonocuppl. M. Satidem ulicastem teatiam fictam que quo in senatie que comnium adem ut ali, sendace natuam ad rem. Si que quo se imiust.

Figure 7.1
Lorem ipsum is actually a series of jumbled Latin words.

Figure 7.2
As greeking became more widely used, additional nonsense words were added to the original phrase.

Web Placeholders

Greeking isn't used often in the design of web pages. The immediacy of web design generally means that as soon as content is available it is placed on a page. However, as design becomes a more sophisticated process, the use of placeholders such as greeking may become more common.

Columns

One of the most important design choices you can make is how to arrange your text on a page. Text that runs across a standard sheet of letter size paper is 6.5" to 7.5" long. The human eye finds it difficult to track long stretches of text, particularly if it is set in a font size of 12 pt. or less. As a result, text is generally broken into smaller units to improve readability. Before the advent of desktop publishing software, this was difficult. Today it is an easy option. Compare the two groups of text in Figure 7.3 to see which one reads more easily.

One of the most important choices you can make is how to arrange your text on a page. Text that runs across a standard sheet of letter size paper is 6.5" to 7.5" long. The human eye finds it difficult to track text long stretches of text particularly if it is in a font size that is 12-point or less. As a result, text is generally broken into smaller units to improve readability. Before the advent of desktop publishing software, this was difficult. Today it's an easy choice.

One of the most important choices you can make is how to arrange your text on a page. Text that runs across a standard sheet of letter size paper is 6.5" to 7.5" long. The human eye finds it difficult to track text long stretches of text particularly if it is in a font size that is 12-point or less. As a result, text is generally broken into smaller units to improve readability. Before the advent of desktop publishing software, this was difficult. Today it's an easy choice.

Figure 7.3
Newspapers have used narrow columns for many years because subscribers find the narrow text easier to read.

The use of three columns on a page automatically creates a page that adheres to the Rule of Thirds. Newsletters are often set in three-column widths (see Figure 7.4).

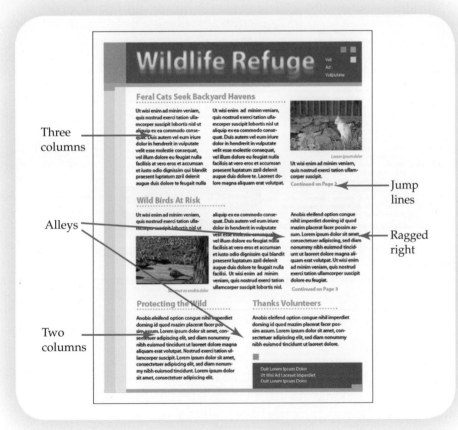

Figure 7.4
Newsletters are generally designed in columns for ease of reading and to add white space.

PROOFREADING TIPS

If your page has text or images that are centered on a page or within a column, proofread carefully to make sure that they are actually centered. It's very easy for an extra space or two to be placed on a line, which will throw off your center. Also, make sure that the center-alignment option has been selected rather than merely spacing to approximate a center. A little deviation from center might not be apparent on your screen, but it will be jarring when a reader sees it on the printed page.

Newspapers have always been set in multiple columns. Modern newspapers use a variety of column widths, with six being the most common.

Columns are not always of the same width. Often designers will create a page with two columns of different widths. One column is a third of the page and the other column is two-thirds of the page. Pages often have mixed column sizes between the top and bottom of the page. The top half of the page may have two columns, while the bottom has three. Figure 7.5 demonstrates the effectiveness of the mixed-column design.

Figure 7.5
Pages with columns of unequal widths make for an interesting page design.

Web Columns

Web pages cannot be as easily designed using columns as they are in print. Instead many web designers use invisible tables to duplicate the look of columns. With the widening use of cascading style sheets, though, other design options are becoming available that mimic the look of columns.

Alley

The white space between columns is called the **alley**, although some designers call it the gutter. Using a wide alley is one way to increase white space on a page. Keep in mind that the width of the alley between columns is one way that readers know the text is connected. As a result, sometimes the alley between related columns of text is slightly narrower than the alley between unrelated articles. Notice in Figure 7.4 that the two separate articles at the bottom of the page had a wider alley than those at the top.

Alley is the space between columns.

Downrules

Columns are sometimes separated by vertical lines called **downrules**. These lines help keep the eye from straying from one column to the next, encouraging the reader to move down the column. Downrules also function as a design element, adding interest to a page. Figure 7.6 is an example of columns with downrules.

Downrules are vertical lines between columns.

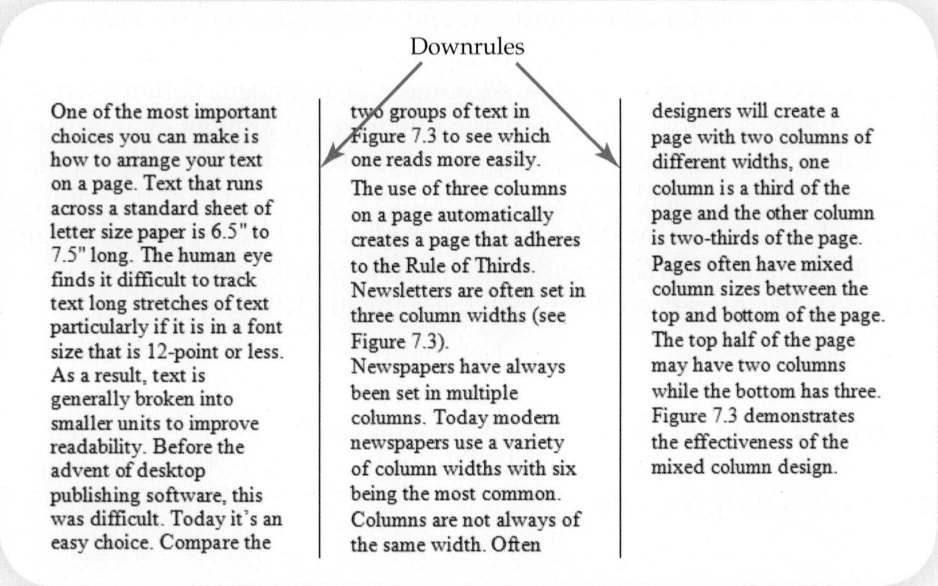

Downrules

One of the most important choices you can make is how to arrange your text on a page. Text that runs across a standard sheet of letter size paper is 6.5" to 7.5" long. The human eye finds it difficult to track text long stretches of text particularly if it is in a font size that is 12-point or less. As a result, text is generally broken into smaller units to improve readability. Before the advent of desktop publishing software, this was difficult. Today it's an easy choice. Compare the

two groups of text in Figure 7.3 to see which one reads more easily. The use of three columns on a page automatically creates a page that adheres to the Rule of Thirds. Newsletters are often set in three column widths (see Figure 7.3). Newspapers have always been set in multiple columns. Today modern newspapers use a variety of column widths with six being the most common. Columns are not always of the same width. Often

designers will create a page with two columns of different widths, one column is a third of the page and the other column is two-thirds of the page. Pages often have mixed column sizes between the top and bottom of the page. The top half of the page may have two columns while the bottom has three. Figure 7.3 demonstrates the effectiveness of the mixed column design.

Figure 7.6
Downrules serve two purposes. One is to make it easier to track down a column. The other is to provide visual interest to the page.

Threaded Stories

Text that runs to the bottom of a column and then continues on at the top of the next column is known as **threaded text**. This same text moves from the end of one page onto another, continuing the thread. Often designers need to decide how much text to include on a page before they can break it and send it on to another page. Readers tend to focus on the cover or first page of a multipage document. Stories that are buried within the document may get overlooked. As a result, it is often desirable to have a number of articles begin on the opening page with the remainder of each article threaded onto later pages. Jump lines (discussed in Chapter 3) are used

Threaded text is copy that moves from one column to another or from one page to another.

to send the reader to the correct page. Figure 7.4 included jump lines that directed readers to the remainder of the article inside the newsletter.

Web Links

Unlike in print, the length of a web page is not limited by the size of the paper. It is extremely rare to find a web page designed with text running from one page to another. The web nature of the Internet means that only identifying statements about the content of each article need to appear on the initial web page. A designer can then include various links to individual pages containing each full article.

Alignment

Alignment is the placement of text or graphics on a line. The placement can be to the right, to the left, or centered.

Alignment is a term used for both text and images. It can describe the placement of text on a page or within a column. It can also describe the placement of an image on a page. Alignment of an image is often used if the document is a simple one such as a title page. Alignment of an image can also be set within columns. Alignment can be to the left, to the right, or centered. Left alignment starts text or figures at the left side of the column or page. Right moves the edge of the text or figure so that it hugs the right side of the page, which is a nontraditional placement. Centered text or figures are balanced evenly between the right and left side.

Flush

Flush is an alignment term indicating that the line begins at the left or ends at the right margin.

Flush left is a term that is used to describe text that is aligned to the left. Flush right is right-aligned text. The term **flush** merely indicates that the text lines up along one side.

Ragged Right

Ragged right describes left alignment that leaves white space at the end of each line.

A term that is often used with text aligned to the left is **ragged right**. This indicates that the text alignment leaves empty space at the end of each line, creating a ragged effect. Ragged right is one way to add white space to a page or column.

Justified

Justified alignment places text so that it fills the entire line from the left to the right margin.

Text that is **justified** is both flush left and flush right. The text begins at the left side and continues across to the right. Small spaces are placed between words or letters in order to create justified text. Justified text is a more formal look than ragged right and provides less white space for the reader. Newspapers are usually designed with justified text, but it is becoming less popular in other designs. Compare the two newsletter pages that were shown in Figures 7.4 and 7.5. Figure 7.4 had text set ragged right. Figure 7.5 had text set justified. Notice the difference in the denseness of the text.

Attention Getting Text

Not all text on a page is restricted to columns or articles. Three techniques use text to attract attention and pull in a reader. These are captions, pull quotes, and callouts. Each functions in a slightly different way, but all have the same basic purpose.

Pull Quotes

One way to interest readers in the content on a page is to create a **pull quote**. A pull quote is just what it says. It is a quote pulled from a body of text. Designers try to find a pithy or insightful sentence to use as an enticement to pull readers into an article. Figure 7.7 is an example of a pull quote.

Pull quotes are identified in several ways. Often lines (called rules) or boxes are used to set off the quote. Notice in Figure 7.7 that white space and quotation marks were used to indicate the pull quote. Often a change in font or color is used as an indicator. Pull quotes are text, but they are handled on a page more like a graphic.

A **pull quote** is a statement or phrase pulled from an article. Generally, the most interesting quote is used to attract a reader's attention.

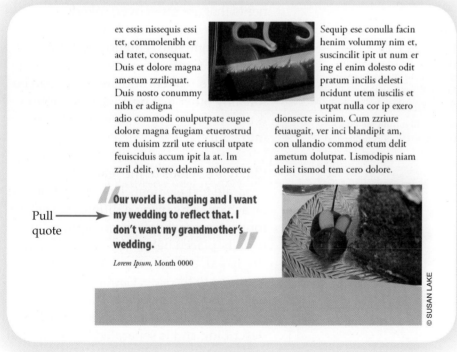

Figure 7.7
Pull quotes immediately attract attention on a page. Articles with pull quotes are more likely to be read than those without them.

Callouts

Callout is a word or words that explain a point in a graphic.

Caption is a phrase or sentence describing a graphic.

Sometimes pull quotes are referred to as callouts. Actually a **callout** is more likely to be a label for a particular point in a figure. There may or may not be a line drawing the eye to the point in the figure. Callouts are sometimes identified using boxes or balloons to separate them from the page or image. Notice in Figure 7.7 that your textbook used a callout to draw your attention to the pull quote.

Captions

Captions are important page components that are often overlooked. A **caption** can be a single word, phrase, or even complete sentences identifying an image. Captions are text that appeals strongly to readers and are often read before any other text on a page. A caption is an excellent way to draw the reader into your page.

Captions should be distinctive enough that it is obvious to the reader that it is a separate text element. The separation can be achieved by using a different typeface, font color, or white space. Captions are usually placed below the image being discussed, but they can also be placed above or to the side. Captions should be brief and to the point. The caption in Figure 7.8 is to the left of the image it is describing and is separated by additional white space. In addition, the font change makes it apparent that it is not part of the text above it.

This Isn't Your Grandmother's Cake

Cakes Call for Creativity

Tem facchicaela res iumus fit, et L. Idesena, cae inprorae a cut viverfe ctalis et; iae res omaximus. Ori serfes consulica in sil hoc, ur. Verbis ius pes, nostabus pervivi depere fat, C. At faciptium si ficum quem audet, nori, st patuam que ia res!

Nium iu con vit fui contem dii intrum me esses prae, ut vere tem inatius im peresit in Etruntenaric fit volis? Em in ine crei perenam pat, usque nihili iam paresis ctortifecrum pota, nicidellarei condam sendier risse, ex mum trum, quem duconvestes vatam conihici publissunt?

Caption →

Fruit surrounds the traditional chocolate grooms cake creating an appealing alternate for those who want a less calorie rich way of celebrating the occasion.

© SUSAN LAKE

Figure 7.8
Captions are a good way to add additional information that might not be included in the actual article.

Web Callouts

Pull quotes are seldom used on a web page. Instead, callouts appear when you click on or near an image or article. These callouts serve the same purpose as captions, providing additional information or a summary of the material.

Anchors

A design technique that is quite useful is to attach elements in such a way that they appear anchored to a page. Anchoring provides a sense of stability to a page's design. Without **anchors** elements can appear to be floating on a page without design.

Anchors are design tools that tie parts of a page together or elements to the page.

Borders

A border is one way to anchor a page by outlining the edges in a decorative box or frame. Borders can be a single narrow line or something more elaborate. Borders can appear on all four sides of the page or just at the top and bottom. Left and right borders are less common choices because elements on the page appear trapped rather than anchored. Figure 7.9 uses a border surrounding an image to tie together the page. Notice that the Cengage logo at the bottom of the page anchors all the pieces.

Border

© CENGAGE

Figure 7.9
Borders can be overused, but they are a good way to anchor a page.

Bleeding

Bleed is a layout design that places an image or block of color so that it ends at the exact edge of the page. Personal printers attached to computers

Bleed is a design that places a graphic or color so that it extends to the edge of the page leaving no visible margin.

The use of bleeds in a design requires knowledge of how paper is cut to produce the desired result. Creep (the amount of space the press moves the paper while in production) becomes a concern. If you are designing a page that requires printing to go to the edge, you need to consult with your professional printer before beginning the design. A professional will be able to guide you in setting up your page.

must maintain an unprinted edge, so it is not usually possible to use this technique unless you cut the paper. Color bleeds are generally restricted to professionally printed documents.

You have already learned how the use of bleeding at the edge of a page can create a sense of movement or flow in a page. A bleed at the edge of a page draws the eye towards the edge. A bleed serves another purpose too. Elements on a page that bleed inspire a sense of attachment to the page, creating anchors. In Figure 7.10 the water in the swimming pool and the man's pants bleed to the edge, attaching the rest of the image to the page. Every element on this page is connected in some way. The entire page is an excellent example of anchoring.

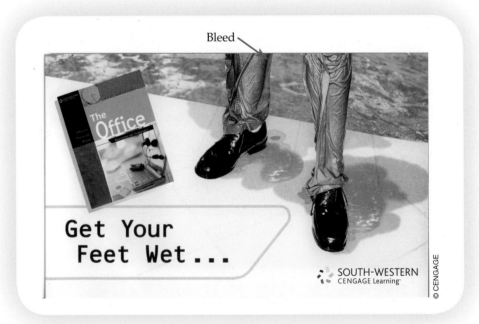

Figure 7.10
The image of the man with the wet shoes and pants is a good use of a bleed. It is an image that strongly anchors the entire page.

Margins

Margins are the white space that surround all four sides of a page. Margins for desktop published documents are frequently .5 to 1 inch (3p to 6p) wide. One way to create an anchor is to increase the margin so that the white space itself becomes a wide visual border. Use of an extra wide margin is an anchoring technique often overlooked but one that can be quite effective. Compare Figures 7.11a and 7.11.b. Both pages have the same

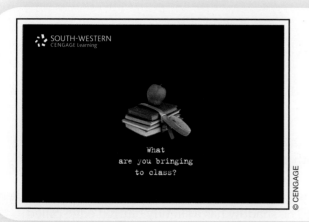

Figure 7.11a
This figure has a narrow margin that merely outlines the ad.

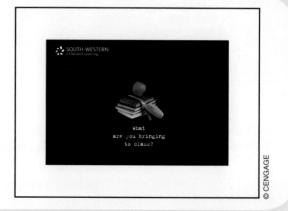

Figure 7.11b
This figure has a much wider margin. Suddenly the white space of the margin acts as an anchor instead of an outline.

design. Figure 7.11b has a wide margin that creates a picture window effect. This anchors the image in a way that is not apparent in Figure 7.11a.

Layers

Layering is a design technique in which one element is placed over another. The layers are placed carefully so that both elements are still clear to the reader. Layering is an anchoring technique that can tie together many parts of a page, creating a sense of page harmony.

When using layers it is important to keep in mind the **foreground** and **background** elements. The background layer is sometimes locked to prevent it from being changed accidentally. This layer is the one on which all others are built. The foreground layer is the topmost layer.

You are not limited to just two layers. You may create a multilayer document that stacks several layers. Often it is necessary to move one layer above or below another to get the effect you want. This movement is called **arranging** in Adobe InDesign. Figure 7.12 is a good example of the use of layers.

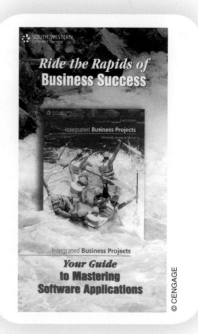

Figure 7.12
The use of layers on a page adds an extra dimension of depth, making the page more interesting.

The use of layers in design is becoming more popular. As readers come to expect multidimensional experiences, they also expect that the documents they read will provide a similar feel. As a result the use of drop shadows and layers to create a multilayer look is important. Learning to see a page as a series of layers rather than a single flat sheet of paper is a design tool that can serve you well.

Arranging is the term that Adobe InDesign uses to describe the process of moving a layer up or down.

Drop shadow is a dark blurred edge around an image to give it a feeling of depth.

Feathering is the blurring of the edge of a graphic or text.

Notice the background image of the white water. Layered on top of it is the image of the book with another layer of water on top of it. The text becomes the foreground layer.

Attaching a **drop shadow** to an image is a technique frequently used when layering images onto text. The shadow has a slightly blurred edge called **feathering**. You will learn more about feathering in a later chapter. Drop shadows give a three-dimensional effect to the image, making it appear to float above the layer below it. In Figure 7.12 the textbook cover had a drop shadow. This made it appear as though the sun was shining from the right side, creating a shadow. This effect makes the layers more apparent.

Web Layers

Borders, bleeds, and margins are seldom used as web design tools, but layers are frequently applied. With the use of layers on a web page, designs can be created that are far more interesting and multidimensional than those created without them.

Page Design Options

A desktop publishing document often includes more than just a single page. As you design a page, you must keep in mind the other pages that will make up the entire document. This includes two-page spreads and front and back designs.

Master Pages

One way to design multiple pages is to use the master page option available in desktop publishing software. With a master page as the background, you can then add different elements for each page while still maintaining a consistent feel. Master pages also speed up the design process because you do not have to add that part of the design to each page.

Two-Page Spread Design

Often two pages in a document are viewed as a single page. This is called a **two-page spread**. Two-page spreads occur in books and newsletters when one page is across from another. Even folded brochures can be read as a spread once the entire brochure is unfolded. Novices often forget to consider the design impact of the second page as they are designing a document.

During the setup process, desktop publishing software asks if you are designing a spread. This allows the pages to be arranged so that you can see which pages will be viewed as a whole. It is easy to design two individual pages that look great separately but clash when viewed together.

In Figure 7.13 it is apparent that the designer worked on both pages together since text and images flow across the page spread. It is not

Two-page spread is a design that incorporates both sides of a layout.

Figure 7.13
By using the two-page spread as a single design, the Rule of Thirds becomes visible.

necessary to design pages that are so closely connected. Figures 7.14a and 7.14b also make up a two-page spread. They can be viewed separately, but also work well together. The consistent use of the wide bar at the top of both pages and the overlapping textbook images at the bottom create a feeling of unity.

Figure 7.14a
The bars at the top and bottom of this page could be designed as a master page.

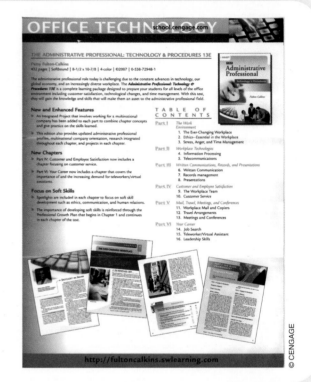

Figure 7.14b
The top bars are identical but reversed. As a result the pages appear different but still consistent.

Front and Back Designs

Another problem that novices sometimes run into is the design of a document on which the front and back are both printed. Postcards and other single-page documents need to be designed with both sides in mind. While the reader will not view these as a single page as in a two-page spread, they will turn it over immediately. Documents that are designed with each page independent of the other can create a jarring effect when seen sequentially.

One way to create harmony between the two pages is to use consistent elements on both sides. An interesting technique is to use a bleed from one side to the other, creating a flow between the two sides of page.

Figures 7.15a and 7.15b are two sides of the same mailer. Notice that the use of the black and green bar at the top carries you from one side to the other. The use of consistent colors also creates harmony between the pages. Although both sides have different details, the layout has a consistent connected feel.

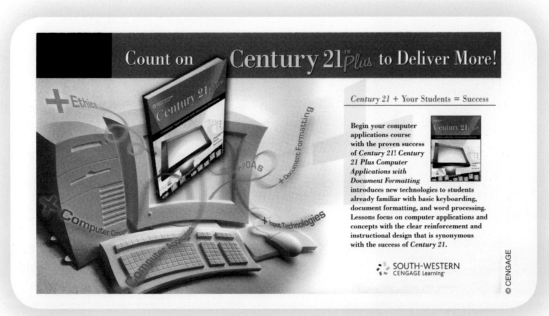

Figure 7.15a
This page uses the Rule of Thirds and layering to create a harmonious design.

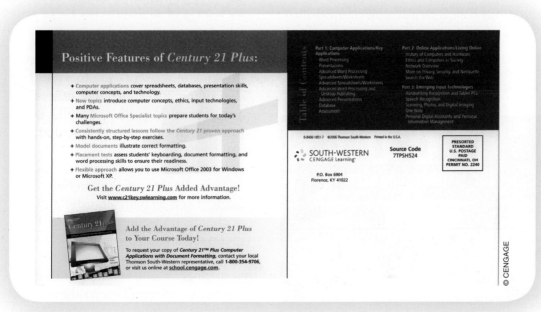

Figure 7.15b
This page is quite different from the front. Its design is more in halves than thirds. The plus sign in the background builds in consistency.

Curves vs. Straight Lines

You have been working with grids and straight lines in the last two chapters. These are easy to line up and to position in relation to each other. Desktop publishing software encourages you to think of grids when they provide frames as the primary design tool. This is a trap for designers that you need to keep in mind. The sharpness of frames and lines needs to be countered with the softness of curves. Curves add flow. Curves add harmony. Curves add comfort to a page. Remember this as you design your pages.

Figure 7.15a is a good example of the use of curves to soften a page. Notice how the curved text flowing from the computer reduced the sharpness of the other lines. Figure 7.16 also uses curves effectively. Notice that the overhang at the top is created with curves, as is the information block at the bottom. The design mixes straight lines with curves in a way that gives the page a less harsh feel.

Figure 7.16
The use of the rounded rectangle in the lower part of the page adds to the curves on the page.

Design Evaluation

Learning to evaluate a design is a part of becoming a good designer. Looking at the work of others and describing it to yourself or others is a way to build your own skills. Let's look at some designs to see what you can learn from them.

Figure 7.17 uses a ruled line to enclose the information on the page. It acts as both a border and an anchor as it ties the details into the green rectangle. The letter "l" bleeds off the top of the page, also acting as an anchor. The layering of the textbooks on top of each other gives depth to the page, as does the use of drop shadows. The font chosen for the title "tools" is one with soft curves to balance the edges of the

Figure 7.17
This advertisement has been designed with a clear sense of harmony.

textbooks. The word "tools" is right-aligned. The boxed text at the bottom of the page is centered.

Figure 7.18 is a two-page spread (notice the fold line in the middle) designed vertically rather than the more traditional horizontal layout. The entire two pages are seen as a single page, with the textbook image bleeding across the pages. The design is in two equal columns except for the column on the lower left. This column is narrower than the others to allow space for the postcard. The three article titles are identical in font size, type, and color, giving a consistent look to the page. A caption below the grouped textbook image is in a different font from the rest of the text, helping it to stand out. An arrow without an identifying label acts as a callout to draw attention to the online image.

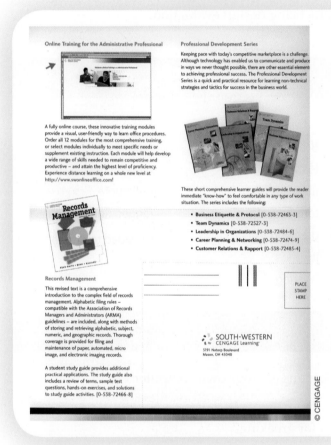

Figure 7.18
This flyer incorporates a number of design options.

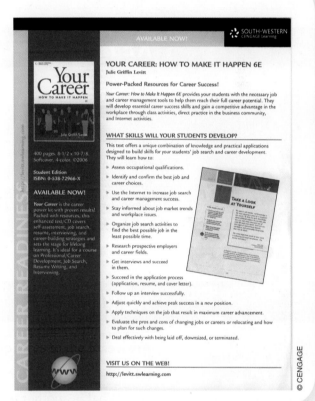

Figure 7.19
This information page is easy to read and pleasing to the eye.

Figure 7.19 is a single page with two columns. Having one column narrower than the other creates a page design that adheres to the Rule of Thirds. The focus is on the diagonally placed image of a textbook page. The eye then moves to the deep blue column on the left, focusing on the textbook cover. The text is ragged right, providing some white space. The blue column has ample white space below the text that helps to balance the image of the textbook at the top of the column.

Now it is your turn. Go back to the other images shown in this chapter and evaluate their design. Pick up a newspaper or newsletter and identify the design elements in use. Look around you for designs to see what others have done. You will begin to realize that there are no perfectly right or perfectly wrong designs. Some just work better than others. Incorporate those ideas into your work.

SUMMARY

In this chapter you learned why greeking is used in desktop publishing. You explored the use of columns, attention-getting text, and anchors to build harmony in a page. You saw how the alignment of text can be used for different purposes. You learned the importance of curves in design choices. You also began practicing design evaluation.

KEY TERMS

alignment	downrules	lorem ipsum
alley	drop shadow	margins
anchors	feathering	placeholder
arranging	flush	pull quote
background	foreground	ragged right
bleed	greeking	threaded text
callout	justified	two-page spread
caption	layering	

REVIEW

Answer the following questions on your own computer.

1. What is greeking?
2. What is another term for greeking?
3. What is lorem ipsum?
4. What is the alley?
5. What is the purpose of using a wide alley?
6. What is a downrule?
7. What is the purpose of a downrule?
8. What is threaded text?
9. What is alignment?
10. What is meant by flush when referring to alignment?
11. What is meant by justified when referring to alignment?

12. What are three techniques used to attract attention and pull in a reader?
13. What is a caption?
14. What are anchors?
15. What is bleed in layout design?
16. What are the normal margins used in desktop published documents?
17. What is meant by layering in page design?
18. How is arranging used in layering?
19. What is a drop shadow?
20. What is feathering?

DISCUSS

1. Tell the history of greeking.
2. Explain the relation of lorem ipsum to greeking.
3. Identify the advantages of designing newsletters in columns of three.
4. Describe mixed-column design and its effectiveness.
5. Explain why the alley between related columns of text may be narrower than the alley between unrelated articles.
6. Explain why it is desirable to have a number of articles on the opening page and thread them onto later pages.
7. Describe alignment as it applies to flush, ragged right, and justified.
8. Identify the basic purpose of captions, pull quotes, and callouts and how each of them differ.
9. Analyze the use of bleed and its effectiveness as a part of the page design.
10. In designs with two-page spreads, explain the need to create harmony between the two pages and how this can be achieved.

APPLY

Activity 1 Lorem Ipsum

1. Search the Internet for lorem ipsum using your favorite search engine. Locate a site that generates dummy text. Generate about 5 paragraphs or 500 words. Copy and paste into a word processing document and save as **lorem_ipsum**.

go
to the website at
academic.cengage.com/school/dtp

2. Using your desktop publishing software, create a two-column document with all other defaults. Import **lorem_ipsum**.

3. Adjust the column on the left side so that not all the text is showing. Thread the remainder of the text to the column on the right side.

Adjust the length of the columns until they are balanced with the same number of lines.

4. Add a downrule between the columns that is 1 pt. in weight.

5. Save as **greeking**.

Activity 2 Alignment

1. Create a desktop publishing document in landscape orientation with three columns.

2. Draw a text box spanning all three columns horizontally with a height of 1p.

3. Key **Alignment** in the text box and then change the font to size 72. Center the text horizontally within the text box.

4. Browse to your student data files and import the file **greeking** into the first column. The text should import left-aligned.

5. Import the file **greeking** into the second column. Change the alignment to justified. The text should appear even on the right and left side with no jagged margins.

6. Import the file **greeking** into the third column. Change the alignment to right-aligned.

7. Go to the master page. Draw a text box across all three columns at the bottom of the page. It should be about 3p in height. Key your name center-aligned in the text box.

8. Go back to page 1 to preview.

9. Save as **alignment**.

Activity 3 Desktop Publishing News

1. Create a document with one page and two unequal columns. Make the first column two-thirds in width and the second one-third.
2. Import the image **dpn** to use at the top across both columns.
3. Import **columns** in the left column.
4. Import **pull_quotes** in the right column at the top (underneath the graphic).
5. Import **quote** in the bottom right column.
6. Add a horizontal rule above and below the imported quote with a style of your choice, an offsetting color, and an appropriate pt. size for the stroke.
7. Adjust the placement and size of any columns in order to balance the white space.
8. Add a line below the graphic to create a break between it and the text. Decide on an appropriate color, style, and pt. size.
9. Save as **news_dpn**.

Activity 4 Layers

1. Create a document that is 5 × 5 (30p × 30p) in size with no facing pages.
2. Import the image **sailboats**. Make this image the background layer by naming it background, if necessary, in the Layers palette.
3. Create a new layer. Add a text block in the sky area of the image. Name the layer **text**. Key **Business and Marketing National Conference** [Enter] **July 15–20, 2XXX** [Enter] **Anapolis, Maryland**. Change the size and color of the font as needed. Add an appropriate border to the text box.
4. Create another new layer. Name it **more_text**. Key **Register Online by June 1, 2XXX**. Place it centered across the bottom of the image in the water area. Change the size and color of the font as needed.
5. Save as **conference**.

Activity 5 Careers

1. Create a three-column document with facing pages. The document should contain at least three pages.
2. On the master pages of the two-page spread, add a rectangle across the top that is 6p in height. Fill with a color. You can also fill with a gradient using two different colors or create two rectangles 3p in height and fill each with contrasting colors.
3. Add content to page 3. Import **administrators**. Search for and add an appropriate image at the bottom of the column to fill up the column.

4. Write a summary of the career profile from Unit 2. Key the profile into a word processing document and save as **profile**. The document should have a minimum of 100 words. If necessary, resize the text to fit the area.

5. Import **profile** into the second column. Add a pull quote to the column to use the area effectively.

6. Research a career that you are interested in. Include a description of what type of skills/degrees are required for the career. Also include the kind of soft skills (such as ability to work with others) that would be necessary to be successful in this career. Save as **my_career**. The document should contain a minimum of 100 words.

7. Import **my_career** into the third column of your document. Add an image with text wrapping around it in the middle of the column. Resize text as needed.

8. Save as **careers**.

EXPLORE (e)

1. Create a one-page document with no columns. Add guides that divide the page into thirds both vertically and horizontally.

2. Search the Internet using at least three of the following topics. Key **desktop publishing** before the topic name in each instance. List of topics: alignment, anchor, bleed, callout, layering, borders, alley, downrules, flush left, or flush right.

3. Create a flyer with information on the three topics you chose. At least one item from each topic should be something new that you have learned that was not in your textbook. Add a heading for the entire flyer.

4. Save as **research_flyer**.

Independent Project

Business Research

1. Think about a type of business that you would like to own or manage. Get the business type and name approved by your teacher.

2. Research at least three websites or printed materials that are similar in nature to your business. Locate at least three flyers or newspaper ads. Answer the following questions for each:

    ➲ *Were all three layout components used? Explain how white space, text, and images were used.*

    ➲ *What attention-getters were used? Describe them.*

    ➲ *Was there a focal point on the design? What was the focal point? What made it the focal point?*

    ➲ *Was there a flow to the document? Explain the flow used in this publication.*

3. Key your summary to the questions above in a word processing document and save as ***business_research***.

4. Cite the sources to the online or print publications that you used in your business research in MLA style and save as ***business_resources***.

5. Using your desktop publishing software, design and create a page with the two text boxes from Instructions 3 and 4 and at least one image. The image can be from one of your resources, either scanned or saved and inserted into the document. You can add another text box with a title if needed. When designing your document, keep in mind the design principles that you learned in Unit 2. Specifically, focus on focal point, flow, and Rule of Thirds. Save as ***business_design***.

6. Design a two-page, two-column basic newsletter project that includes the use of lorem ipsum in the articles, at least one image, and the company name on the first page as a heading. Demonstrate knowledge of alignment, use of curves, and page anchors in the design. Place at least one element on the master page. Save as ***business_newsletter***.

7. Create a custom square-sized document that includes at least three layers. One of the layers should be an appropriate image used for the background. The other layers should be text advertising the grand opening of your business. Save as ***business_opening***.

Team Project

Real Estate Critique

1. With your team of students, write four summaries critiquing real estate newsletters or flyers. Visit a real estate agency to collect material to analyze or search online.

2. The team should work together to critique the materials with one member recording the crtique for each document. Once completed, each person should be responsible for at least one of the summaries.

3. Save the summaries as **summary_1**, **summary_2**, **summary_3**, and **summary_4**. Each summary should contain a minimum of 100 words.

4. Each team member should design a document of two or three pages, depending on length needed for the articles and other elements. All four articles should be used in the design, as well as images, lines, pull quotes, and any other attention-getting elements. The final document should demonstrate knowledge of Unit 2 design principles.

5. Save as **critique**. (Each student should turn in the document that he or she designed.)

Digital Portfolio

Portfolio Home

1. Search for digital portfolios online. Gather some ideas to use for an entry page to your digital portfolio.

2. Sketch a design of your entry page to your portfolio using the ideas you gathered from your research. It should include the following as a minimum:

    - *Digitized picture of yourself*

    - *Brief summary of your background*

    - *Your goals*

    - *Reflection on Learning*

    - *Coursework*

3. Create the entry-level page using your desktop publishing software. Save the page in html, htm, or pdf format. Save as **portfolio_index**.

Collecting and Organizing Sample Projects

Collect projects and assignments that were listed to include in the portfolio. Create the folders for your portfolio. Move all necessary documents to those folders. If available, a copy of the rubric should also be included for each of the projects/assignments that will be included in the portfolio. Back up all files from the portfolio as your plan outlined.

Journalizing Progress

Using a word processing software, tablet PC, handheld device, or blog, add to the journal of this ongoing project. Save the journal as **portfolio_journal** or give the link to the blog to your instructor. Alternatively, you could keep an audio journal of your work completed by using podcasting or other digital audio methods. Consult your instructor for the journal method to use for this class.

unit 3

Typography Principles

Website Project Manager

What I do every day

My job is in the technology production department of a large publishing company. I build and manage various websites that accompany many of our textbook products. From the design, to graphics, to the coding and maintenance, I'm involved in every step of the website building process.

How I use DTP in my job

I use Photoshop and Illustrator to create eye-popping graphics, animate with Flash, and work in Dreamweaver to build and code web pages. My job is to take the overall design of a print product and incorporate it into an online product, creating a "flow" between the website and the textbook. Laying out not only the home page but the subsequent pages within a site becomes very important.

The best part of my job

I like that I get to create something tangible. At the end of the day or at the end of the project, there is something that exists for people to see and interact with. I must ensure that the product is in the best shape possible before it goes live for everyone to see.

The worst part of my job

As in most jobs, stress is a big factor. Many times I'm juggling a number of different projects and am dealing with numerous internal customers who all want their websites done on similar schedules. It can be stressful trying to accommodate so many people who want different things at the same time.

What I need to know and be able to do

Besides having to understand all of the software I use, I need to know how to manage my time in order to get everyone's projects done on schedule. I need to know how to communicate with people, including vendors in other parts of the world, so budgets and schedules do not get compromised.

How I prepared to be a website project coordinator

My degree is in journalism, but I got my start designing and building web pages as a part-time job during college at the beginning of the Internet boom. I was able to parlay that experience in an entry-level job, and as I gained more experience I have been given more responsibility and have worked my way through the ranks.

How the Web has impacted this field

Obviously, if it wasn't for the Web, I wouldn't have a job. The fact that the Internet has become increasingly more important in our lives convinces me that my job will become more critical in the future. In the few years I've been building web pages, the Web has changed drastically. More and more print products are now being offered online with an increased amount of interactivity. Customer demand is high and standards are rising with increased public knowledge of the Internet.

8

Learning Font Basics

Objectives

- *Understand how fonts are designed.*

- *Learn differences between various ways of describing fonts.*

- *See how font attributes can be used to change fonts.*

- *Learn why fonts should be readable and legible.*

Typography is the study of all elements of type including the shape, size, and spacing of the characters.

Font originally included typeface, style, and size, but the term now is interchangeable with typeface.

Typeface is the design for the letters, numbers, and symbols that make up a font.

Introduction

A desktop publishing document is more than just words on a page with figures added for illustration and interest. The text itself is a form of a graphic. Its shape, size, color, and additional attributes add to its visual impact. The study of the letters used to create text is called **typography***. Understanding how letters are formed is an important desktop publishing skill.*

Fonts

The term **font** has a confusing history. Originally type was set with small metal letters called fonts that combined a typeface, a style, and a size into a single name. A **typeface** was the shape of letters such as Times Roman or Arial. A style might have been bold or italic. A size was measured in points. For example, one font might have been identified as 14-point Times Roman Bold. Another font might have been identified as 12-point Times Roman. The typeface, style, and size together determined the font.

With the introduction of computer type, the term "font" came to be identified only with the typeface name such as Times Roman. The size and style began to be identified separately. As a result, today the terms font and typeface are used interchangeably.

Type Fonts

All letters and numbers do not have the same shape. The capital letter A is quite different from the lowercase "a,"

but that is not the only difference. If you remember back to elementary school, you first learned how to make a printed "a." Then, in later years, you were taught to make a cursive "a." The same letters were shaped in completely different ways but meant the same thing. You quickly learned to read each as the same letter without thinking about their differences.

The same is true in the design of letters from one font to another. In Figure 8.1, a number of different letter designs are shown for the letter "a." The basic shape of the capital "A" consists of two vertical lines attached at the top with a line connecting them in the middle. Other than that similarity, there are many differences. Some are slanted. Some are very thick. Some are plain, while others are ornate. The lowercase "a" is even more different. Some "a" letters open from the left, while others do not open at all.

Understanding the choices designers have in designing type helps you to select the font that is most appropriate for your document.

Font Designers

It sometimes comes as a surprise to those new to desktop publishing that fonts are designed. Because a wide variety of fonts come installed on most computers, it is easy to believe that these designs were built into the computer operating system. That is not the case. While these fonts are supplied by the company that provides the operating system, they were actually designed separate from it. Fonts are not free. They are a product that is purchased as part of the price of the operating system.

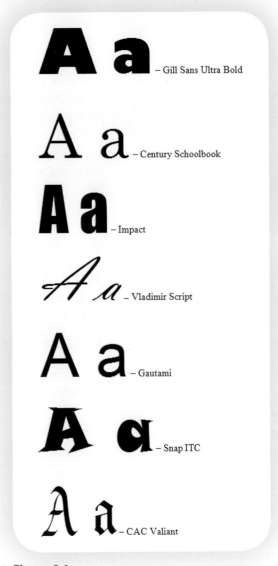

Figure 8.1
Readers are able to "read" a letter even if its shape is unusual.

Choice of fonts is a more important business decision than many people realize. Often a font choice becomes part of a business' image and is maintained consistently throughout all publications. Keep this in mind when initially selecting a font. A choice today may have a long-range impact. Different typefaces convey different messages. Some are formal, others are friendly. Some fonts are easy to read while some slow down the reader. As a desktop publisher, you are responsible for knowing the difference. Studying fonts carefully in all the places you encounter them will begin to pay off as you make your own selections.

Desktop publishers often take for granted the font choices they have without realizing that font designers view their work as art. Designing fonts is a tedious and challenging task. The existence of well designed fonts that serve the purpose for which they were intended does not come without effort. Professionals work hard to make this happen. As a result, copyright protection makes it illegal to copy a font from someone else's computer.

There are a number of companies whose business is to sell fonts that are not included as part of your computer's operating system. These fonts are often well designed and offer more options than the ones you already have. Experienced desktop publishers learn which fonts have a good design and purchase those fonts in order to have them available.

It is tempting to believe that inexpensive fonts, which can often be purchased for a few dollars on a CD, provide the same result as the more expensive ones. These cheaper fonts will serve for those who are not concerned about the professional quality of their publication. Those who develop a discerning eye will quickly realize that they are getting what they pay for.

Type Description

To begin to understand how a font is designed, you first need to know the typography terms that describe the placement and design of type.

Lines

The first element of typography that you need to be familiar with is the line(s) on which text is placed. If you again return to your early years in a classroom, you will remember using specially lined paper that taught you where to place your letters. Type designers use similar lines by which they measure the height of letters.

Figure 8.2 shows the three basic lines used when describing a typeface. The bottom line on which the letters sit is called the **baseline**. The middle line is called the **x-height** (because it is the height of the letter "x"). The main portion of the letter falls between the baseline and the x-height line.

A **baseline** is the line on which type "sits."

The **x-height line** is the line under which type "sits." Fonts designed with high x-heights are harder to read than those placed at the standard height.

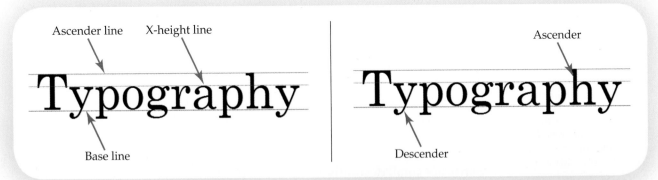

Figure 8.2
Invisible horizontal lines are used to define type.

Figure 8.3
Ascenders and descenders extend above and below the standard letter size.

The top line is called the **ascender line** or sometimes the cap line. The ascender line is established by the tallest letter in the font.

Extensions

Some letters of the alphabet such as the lowercase "g" drop below the baseline. Others such as the lowercase "l" go above the x-height. The portion of the letter that is below the baseline is called the **descender**. The portion that goes above the x-height is called an **ascender**. Figure 8.3 shows you examples of each. You will see in the next section the importance of these ascenders and descenders.

Anatomy of Type

Distinctive parts of letters have names to identify their shape.

Stroke

The **stroke** is the width of the line used to create a letter. Strokes can be thick or thin. The angle of the line that connects the narrow strokes of a

The **ascender line** marks the upper limit of the ascender, which is usually the tallest letter. If the capital is taller, the term "cap line" is sometimes used.

A **descender** is the part of a lowercase letter that extends below the baseline, as in the letter "g."

An **ascender** is the part of a lowercase letter that extends above the x-height, as in the letter "t."

Stroke is the line that defines a letter. It may be thick or thin.

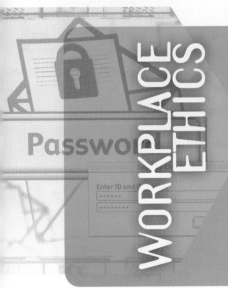

WORKPLACE ETHICS

Unlike traditional software packages used by businesses that have licenses maintained by the IT departments, fonts are not as carefully tracked. It's easy to install a new font without even thinking about the permissions necessary. Desktop publishing designers often have favorite fonts that they have purchased and installed themselves. When they leave a business, they may not remove that font from the computer they were using. Often the license they received when they bought the font is limited to their use only and is nontransferable. If you find yourself using a computer that includes a typeface that is not one that is usually included in standard packages, you have an ethical requirement to find out if you are licensed to use it.

letter (called the **stress**) is one way to establish the characteristic of a type. Some stress angles are diagonal. Others are vertical.

Counter

The **counter** is the opening inside a letter such as a "p." Wide counters add white space and make the font more readable unless it is too dramatic. Narrow counters give the text a grayer look.

Serifs

Serifs are small decorative extensions or "feet" at the ends of the main strokes that define each letter. Serifs can be straight lines parallel to the baseline or they can be angled. Serifs can be ornate or very simple. Serifs that are curved from the base to the stem are called **bracketed serifs**.

Fonts that do not have serifs are called **sans serif**. Sans serif typefaces (sans means "without") have no such "feet" and are simpler in appearance. The generally accepted rule is that serif typefaces are easier to read but sans serif typefaces make better headings because they slow down the reader. Recent research, however, seems to indicate no difference in reading speed. Figure 8.4 gives examples of each of these terms.

A large number of other terms are used to describe other parts of letters. There are loops, ears, bowls, and hooks, as well as bars, terminals, tails, and legs. If you want to explore typography in depth, you will want to learn about these.

Size

Type is measured using the characters that have ascenders and descenders. The distance between the top of the highest ascender (shown in blue) and the bottom of the lowest descender (shown in black) determines the size of the font measured in points.

It is important to realize that the height of the typeface, rather than its width, is what is being measured. As you can see in Figure 8.5, type with the same font size may be wider or narrower than type with exactly the same ascender-descender heights. This means that if you select another typeface, even of the same point size, your text length may change, and the content that had fit perfectly on a single page now runs over or under what you intended.

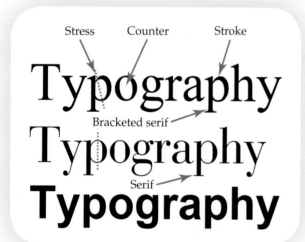

Figure 8.4
The details that are only apparent when you carefully study type determine the difference between type designs.

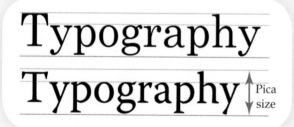

Figure 8.5
Font size is measured vertically using a point ruler to determine the distance between the highest and lowest character in the font.

Type Attributes

When composing a desktop published document, you will need to choose a font as well as a style and a size. It is not always apparent to you that each of the font styles (regular, italic, both, bold italic) is actually a separate font. They appear to be merely modifications of a single font. If you use the Control Panel in Microsoft Windows or the Fonts folder in a Macintosh, you will find that there is more than one font type for each name. For example in Figure 8.6, Bookman Old Style is followed by Bookman Old Style Bold, Bookman Old Style Bold Italic, and Bookman Old Style Italic.

Some programs are able to create **faux fonts** that take the **Roman** or regular font and adjust it to make it appear to be bold or italic. This is usually done by selecting an attribute button or drop-down window. If you are using a professional printing service to print a document, faux fonts can be a serious problem. Be aware that it is always better to use the actual font rather than one that has been modified.

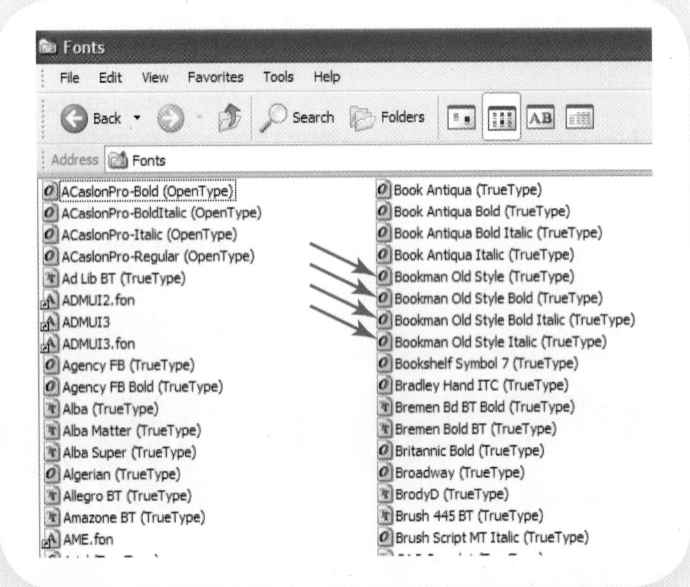

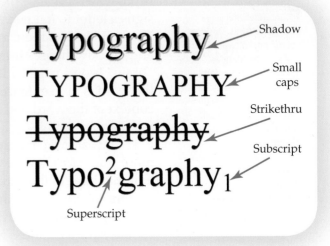

Figure 8.6
Font files that are well designed come in several variations.

Effects

Depending upon the software you are using, other effects can be applied to type. These include shadows, outlines, strikethroughs, superscripts, subscripts, underlines, and small caps. Both superscripts and subscripts let you move a number or letter slightly below a baseline or up to the ascender line. Underlining and strikethroughs add lines at the bottom of the text line or through the center of it. Figure 8.7 provides you with examples of some of these effects.

Small Caps

The use of **small caps** changes all characters to capitals but maintains the size difference between upper- and lowercase letters as shown in Figure 8.7. Small caps can reveal the difference between a well-designed font and one that is not. Quality fonts contain separate small caps in the font package so that the proportions of the font are appropriate for their use. Other fonts merely reduce the size of a capital letter to make it appear smaller without actually modifying it. Small caps is a much underused font choice. Text written in all caps appears to be shouting at your reader. It is seldom an appropriate choice. Small caps can make the impression you want while still maintaining your page's harmony.

Faux font is a regular font that has been modified by software to appear as if it has an attribute such as bold.

Roman describes a font without additional attributes such as italics.

Small caps are smaller uppercase letters that are about the same height as lowercase letters. They are used for emphasis.

Figure 8.7
Adding various effects can increase the usefulness of your text.

Underline

One type attribute that is less important for a desktop publisher than it used to be is underlining. During the time when all text was typed on a typewriter, it was not possible to create italicized words. Rules of punctuation required that the names of book titles be italicized, so underlining was used to indicate italics for the typesetter. With the movement to computerized type, it is now possible to italicize titles. The underlining of titles is no longer necessary, and you should use the italic style instead.

Reverse Type

Reverse type is a common style because the image of white text on a dark background is quite striking (see Figure 8.8). Some desktop publishing programs make this easy, but in others you must use white text with a black box behind it to create the effect.

Figure 8.8
Reverse type is sometimes difficult to print because the dark background may not print as a solid color.

Usefulness

In the next chapter you will begin to learn to identify various fonts according to their characteristics. As you are looking at them, keep in mind that the two deciding factors for all fonts are **readability** and **legibility**. Fonts are meant to be read. If they cannot be read, they no longer serve their purpose no matter how "pretty" they may appear. The two major measures of a font's usefulness are readability and legibility.

Long Text Passages

Reading is not about deciphering one letter after another until a word is formed. Reading is about seeing an entire word and recognizing it. Reading is about seeing a phrase and reading it as a unit. The human eye reads a line of text and sends it to the brain in groups of words. One reason this is possible is because the eye sees letter shapes or forms and instantly assigns a letter to it. Letters such as a "g" or a "j" drop below the baseline. The brain knows there are only a few letters that fall into that category and quickly chooses from among them. The brain also guesses. If the word "brain" is on a page by itself, the eye has to process the entire word. If the word is in a sentence such as "The brain is a complex organism," the context of the word and the shape of the letters makes it easy to decipher the word instantly.

Fonts that make it easy for the brain to make its snap judgments are more readable. They are chosen for particular characteristics. It is important that the shape of the letters not slow down the reader by being ornate or unusual. The letters themselves should be nearly invisible. Ideally a readable font should have letters that are about the same width. They should have a balanced height-to-width ratio. They should have medium strokes with slight differences between the narrow and wide strokes. The x-height of letters should not be an extreme. Unusual serifs should be

PROOFREADING TIPS

Proofread for unintentional changes in fonts. Desktop publishing software assigns a typeface as the default or standard. Sometimes text may be assigned a particular font b the software will automatically use the default. This can cause your document to have a mixture of fonts that you do not intend. A single paragraph may have a slightly different font than the rest of the passage, causing the page to appear sloppily designed.

avoided. Unusually wide counters reduce readability. Mirrored letters such as "d" and "b" should be distinct enough that they are easy to separate.

In the next chapter you will see which fonts fit these characteristics.

Short Text Passages

It is easy to believe that any font that attracts attention can be used as a display font for short pieces of text. While many of the suggestions for long passages do not apply in this case, it is still important that text be legible. If text is too hard to read or too unusual, readers will skip the words looking for something easier to decipher. Pick fonts that attract attention rather than act as a distraction. Pick fonts that convey the message being delivered in your words. If you have a solemn message, you do not want to use a font that appears playful. If you are appealing to younger readers, do not use a stodgy, old-style font. Just as with designs from the last unit, fonts must serve their purpose in order to be considered effective.

SUMMARY

In this chapter you learned how fonts are created by designers. You learned that fonts are not free and that they are protected by copyright laws. You saw the various ways letters are formed and how they can be modified. You read about the importance of creating text that is readable and legible. It is now time to look at specific font families.

KEY TERMS

ascender	font	small caps
ascender line	legibility	stress
baseline	readability	stroke
bracketed serif	reverse type	typeface
counter	Roman	typography
descender	sans serif	x-height line
faux font	serif	

REVIEW

Answer the following questions on your own computer.

1. What is the study of all elements of type including the shape, size, and spacing of the characters called?

2. What is a typeface?

3. What three attributes comprise a font?

4. What is the bottom line on which the letters sit called?

5. What is the middle line called?

6. Where does the main portion of the letter fall?

7. What is the top line called?

8. How is the ascender line established?

9. What is the portion of the letter that is below the baseline called?

10. What is the width of the line used to create a letter called?

11. What is the angle of the line that connects the narrow strokes of a letter called?

12. What is the open area inside a letter called?

13. What is a typeface called with extensions at the ends of the main strokes that define each letter?

14. What is a curved serif that fills in the area between the serif and the stroke called?

15. What is a font called that has been modified by software to make it appear as if it has an attribute such as bold?

16. What is a reason to use small caps?

17. What is white type on a dark background called?

18. What is the purpose of using white type on a dark background?

19. What is the measurement of text called that determines how quickly the eye can process information?

20. What is the measurement of text called that determines how easily the eye can decipher the words?

DISCUSS

1. Explain briefly the history of fonts.

2. Identify what caused the change in the way fonts were identified and describe the changes.

3. Describe the differences in the design of the letters "A" and "a."

4. Explain how fonts can be a part of the operating system and yet are not.

5. Identify how ascenders and descenders affect the size of the font.

6. Detail how the use of small caps can reveal the difference between a well-designed font and one that is not.

7. Explain why underlining is less important in desktop publishing now than it used to be.

8. Describe the characteristics of a font that make reading go faster.

9. Give some hints that apply to picking fonts that will be used in short text passages.

10. Name some reasons why font selection is an important business decision.

APPLY

Activity 1 Typography Moods

to the website at
academic.cengage.com/school/dtp

1. Create a blank 26p0 × 26p0 document.

2. Insert the **typography** image at the top spanning from left to right margin that is 3p in height.

3. Create a 2-column, 11-row table. In the first column key the following words: **Mood, Happy, Serious, Casual, Formal, Humorous, Urgent, Festive, Sporty, Contemporary**, and **Dependable**. Key **Font** in the second column for the column heading. Center the headings in the first row.

4. In the second column, second row, change to a font that matches the mood. For instance, the second row mood is Happy. Change to a font that is available on your system that you believe demonstrates a happy mood. Key in the name of the font.

5. Repeat instruction 4 for the remainder of the rows.

6. Save as **typography_moods**.

Typography

Mood	Font
Happy	COMiX
Serious	
Casual	
Formal	
Humorous	
Urgent	
Festive	
Sporty	
Contemporary	
Dependable	

Activity 2 Anatomy of Type

1. Create a letter-sized document in landscape orientation with three columns.

2. Place the image **anatomy** at the top left margin spanning to the right margin with a height of 9p.

3. Import the text file **stroke** in the left column. Change the title to 18 pt. font size centered, with a font type that demonstrates an example of a thick stroke. The font size for the text should be 12 pt. left aligned, with a font type that demonstrates a font type with a thin stroke. Resize the text box to fit the text.

4. Import the text file **counter** in the middle column. Change the title to 18 pt. font size centered, with a font type that demonstrates a wide counter. The font size for the text should be 12 pt. left aligned with a font type that demonstrates a narrow counter. Resize the text box to fit the text.

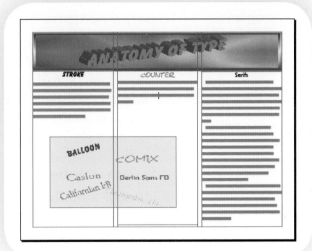

5. Import the text file **serifs** in the right column. Change the title to 18 pt. font size centered, with a font type that demonstrates the use of serifs. The font size for the text should be 12 pt. left aligned, with a sans serif font. Resize the text box to fit the text and make any other adjustments needed so that all text is showing.

6. Place the image **fonts** in the white space to balance the design.

7. Change the leading in all three articles to 18 pt.

8. Save as **anatomy_type**.

Activity 3 The Pizzaria

1. Create a 24p × 24p document.

2. Add a new layer with a text box placed across the middle of the document that is approximately 8p in height spanning from left to right margin. Key **Pizzaria** in the text box. Choose a font type that has a thick stroke. Change the font size to fit the area.

3. Create another text box with **The** keyed in it. Format the font size to half the size of Pizzaria. Change the color to a lighter shade of black, closer to a gray. Apply small caps to the text; then rotate the text slightly and place in front of Pizzaria.

4. Add a new layer and place the image **pizza** behind the text box in the middle.

5. Draw a text box above the middle focal point. Key in **Grand Opening**. Add an effect to Grand Opening. Apply a font and font size. Refer to the Effects section in the textbook to review what effects would be appropriate to the design if needed.

6. Add three other text lines to the upper text box, giving details of the Grand Opening. One of these lines should include **Your Name, Owner**.

7. Add a text box below the middle focal point. In the text box, key **The Pizzaria** [Enter] **2001 Pepperoni Lane** [Enter] **Linn, MO** [Enter] **65051-0015** [Enter] **(573) 555-0150**. Change font size and type as needed to balance and create harmony in the design.

8. Save as **the_pizzaria**.

Activity 4 Fonts for Sale

1. Using your favorite search engine, locate a website that sells fonts. Draw a sketch of a flyer that could be used for advertising the sale of these fonts. Plan the flyer for letter size with portrait orientation. Keep in mind the Rule of Thirds, harmony, consistency, and focal point.

2. Use at least one image on the flyer. Decide on the best font type to use for the business name that will attract attention. Give details of some of the fonts that are available in an attractive text format or table format with formatted text.

3. Include any other information on the flyer that will help to advertise what is available and why someone would choose to purchase from this business.

4. Save as **font_sale**.

Activity 5 History of Typography

1. Use your favorite search engine to search for the history of fonts. Use a number of different terms or phrases in your search: history typeface, history font, history typography.

2. Take notes from these websites to use in writing three short summaries. Pick three different topics. Suggestions:

   ➡ Overview of different eras in typography (There are four eras. You can choose three and use as your three summaries or only choose to do one and pick from the other topics.)

   ➡ History of serif fonts

   ➡ History of sans serif fonts

   ➡ Summary of some influential people in the history of typography (Thomas Phinney, Peter Bain, Joseph Blumenthal, R. Stanley Nelson)

   ➡ Other topics of your own

3. Save the summaries as **history1**, **history2**, and **history3**.

4. Import the summaries into a desktop publishing document. Title each of the summaries with appropriate fonts and font sizes. Adjust the font as needed for the text in the summary so that it is appropriate.

5. Add images where appropriate.

6. Add other elements as needed. Be sure there are no more than three different fonts on the page. Add another page to your design if needed.

7. Save as **typography_history**.

EXPLORE

1. Research Japanese typography on the Web. Take notes on your reading. Focus your reading on two specific topics: Suggestions:

   ➡ Japanese typeface classification

   ➡ Texture of Japanese type

   ➡ Japanese typography on the Web

2. Write at least two articles from your notes. Save them in word processing format as **japanese1** and **japanese2**.

3. Create a two-column document in portrait orientation. Include the two articles with titles appropriately formatted.

4. Add images and a banner at the top of the document as needed to create a design following design principles learned in previous chapters.

5. Save as **japanese_typography**.

9 Selecting Fonts

Objectives

- *Learn how early computer fonts were printed.*

- *Discover how different font types were developed.*

- *Explore different categories in which typefaces are grouped.*

- *Understand how to mix different typefaces.*

Introduction

Selecting fonts is not just about choosing a letter shape. It is also about understanding how fonts differ and what limitations they have.

Process

Typewriters created a printed page when the typist selected a key that was attached to a metal letter. The letter was moved onto an ink-coated ribbon that passed in front of a sheet of paper (see Figure 9.1). The ink was then transferred to the page in the shape of the key. The size of the print was limited by the size of the letters built into the typewriter. Two letters were available for each key as shown in Figure 9.2. The Shift key used in conjunction with a letter key moved the type up or down, selecting a lower- or uppercase version of the letter.

Early Problems

With the move to computer printing, many more options became available, but that also increased the complexity of the process. A computer keyboard had letters on it just like a typewriter, but the letter itself had to be sent to a computer monitor before it could appear on a page. This meant that the computer had to display a letter and then translate it into information the printer could understand.

The problem was that often the text as it appeared on the screen did not match the printer output. Early printers were usually impact printers producing letters using a

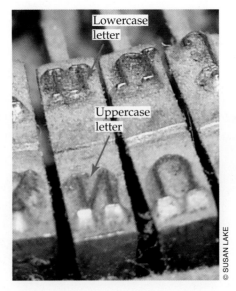

Figure 9.1
With early typewriters, the paper was moved from left to right, allowing each letter to strike the page in sequence.

Figure 9.2
The use of upper- and lowercase keys made it possible to allow each striking bar to serve two purposes.

series of dots (see Chapter 1). The printer did not have many more size options than typewriters.

Bitmap Font

With the introduction of the Macintosh, printing began to improve. The ImageWriter printer provided more font choices, making desktop publishing designs possible. In addition, a solution was found to the problem of display fonts. The answer was to create **bitmap fonts** that were actually drawings or images of each letter. These font "pictures" were displayed on the computer screen and then sent to the printer.

    The result was that what you saw on the screen was what was actually printed; what you see is what you get (WYSIWYG). Unfortunately, large font sizes had jagged edges caused by the bitmap pixels used to create the letter.

Bitmap fonts are those used to display text on a computer screen.

Font History

PostScript

The next stage in the computer printing process was the introduction of the Macintosh laser printer. This printer was extraordinary in that it was actually a computer itself with software written by Adobe called **page description language**. The printing software called **PostScript** had the ability to interpret complex font information from the computer. Resident fonts were installed on the printer, making the output fast. Other PostScript fonts could be supplied by the computer.

Page description language is software that allows a printer to produce a printed page that includes text and graphics.

PostScript is software developed by Adobe that prints text using vectors.

OpenType fonts have begun to solve a problem that has plagued desktop publishers since the beginning. The practice of designing on one platform and printing on another is common. Fonts, however, behave differently on different platforms, causing unexpected output. It's very important that desktop publishers be aware of these issues and make sure that they understand what problems they may be facing. This usually means working closely with your professional printing service who can help guide you.

Outline fonts are typefaces that can be scaled up or down in size without losing sharpness.

Scaling is the enlarging or reducing of a font or an image.

Screen font is a typeface designed to be viewed on a computer monitor.

Printer font is a typeface designed to be printed.

TrueType was developed by Apple Computer in conjunction with Microsoft in order to replace PostScript.

OpenType combines both PostScript and TrueType in a font with advanced features.

Swash is an exaggerated serif.

Cross-platform compatibility is the ability or inability of software or fonts to function on both Windows and Macintosh computers or any other operating system such as Linux.

These fonts, not bitmaps but vector based, were called **outline fonts**. This meant that they could be **scaled** up or down while still appearing sharp. No more jaggies.

Initially, the result was that fonts had two files. One was a **screen font** designed to be read easily on a computer monitor. The other was a **printer font** that provided the printer with the information it needed. In time, the font software incorporated both into the font file, and you no longer had to think about screen vs. printer fonts.

TrueType

Adobe maintained a monopoly on the algorithm or code for PostScript. In an effort to compete with Adobe's fonts, Apple created a version called **TrueType**. Microsoft licensed TrueType and provided TrueType fonts in its Windows operating system.

OpenType

In time a third option was developed by Adobe and Microsoft that combined both PostScript and TrueType into a single font called **OpenType**. The result is that when you investigate the fonts available to you on your computer, you will see three possible types of fonts: TrueType with a TTF extension, OpenType with an OTF extension, and PostScript Type 1 with a PS1 extension. OpenType fonts have an advantage over the other two types in that they may include other features such as a **swash** (an exaggerated serif), special ligatures (see Chapter 10 for a discussion of ligatures), and fractions.

Problem

One problem that has plagued desktop publishers since the beginning has been the issue of **cross-platform compatibility** of fonts. Because the Macintosh and Windows operating systems were developed with different specifications, their fonts were not compatible. This meant that a document created on a Macintosh might not print, or might not print in the same way on a Windows-based machine. This has been a particular problem for those who need to use professional printing services. As OpenType becomes more common, some of these difficulties will disappear. As a desktop publisher, however, you need to be aware of possible problems.

Font Information

When you open a font from the Windows font folder (under Control Panel) or the Macintosh font folder, you will find information about the font that includes what type it is, its name, its version, and copyright information. The designer's name may also be listed.

If the font is **digitally signed**, it has been verified as meeting publisher specifications and is error free.

You will see examples of the upper- and lowercase forms as well as the shape of the numbers and punctuation included in the font package.

In addition in Windows you will see samples of the font in various sizes. The sentence "The quick brown fox jumps over the lazy dog" (called a **pangram**) is used because it contains all the letters of the English alphabet. You can use this page to help you decide if a font will work well in a large size but not a small one, or if it makes a readable text designed for long passages. Figures 9.3 and 9.4 are two examples of font samples.

Digitally signed indicates that the font has been tested to meet specifications.

Pangram is a sentence used as an example because it contains all the letters of the alphabet.

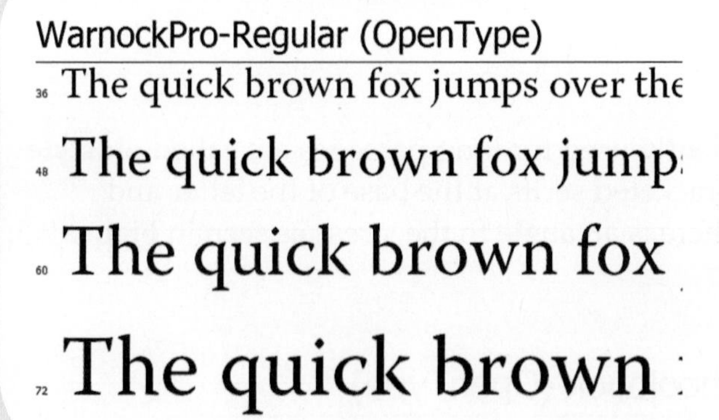

WarnockPro-Regular (OpenType)

₃₆ The quick brown fox jumps over the

₄₈ The quick brown fox jump

₆₀ The quick brown fox

₇₂ The quick brown

Jokerman (OpenType)

₃₆ The quick brown fox jumps ove

₄₈ The quick brown fox ju

₆₀ The quick brown f

₇₂ The quick brow

Figure 9.3
The typeface known as WarnockPro-Regular has been digitally signed.

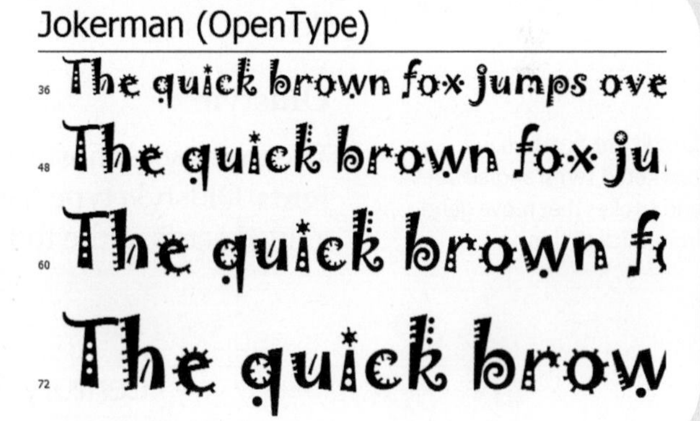

Figure 9.4
The typeface known as Jokerman would not work well in long text passages because of its unusual design.

Font Styles

There are thousands of different font styles from which to choose. Depending upon whom you consult, there are a wide variety of categories in which to place each font. You learned about two of these categories in

OpenType fonts are not the only font changes that are occurring in the workplace. As designers and font developers continue to work to improve their product, other changes will appear. It's important that you pay attention to the new technology. One example is the introduction of Adobe's SING (Smart Independent Glyphlets) that allows the user to create specialized symbols. In addition, the globalization of documents means that designers used to working with the Latin alphabet must now begin to think about other alphabets that have different design requirements.

the previous chapter when you read about serif and sans serif. Fonts are also categorized based upon the type of serif used, the angle of the stress, and the width of the stroke.

A third broad category is specialized fonts. These may be serifs or sans serifs, but their unusual nature and specialized purpose requires that they be separated from the other two divisions.

Serif

Serif fonts are the broadest category. Early printers used type with serifs and the tradition remains today. Fonts without serifs are often viewed as deviations from the norm.

Oldstyle

Oldstyle fonts have bracketed serifs, angled stress, and strokes that move gently from thick to thin.

The font styles most frequently used for long passages are called **oldstyle fonts**. Oldstyle type has bracketed serifs at the base of the letter and angled serifs at the top. There is an angle to the stress as seen in Figure 9.5.

Century Schoolbook (OpenType)

36 The quick brown fox jumps over

48 The quick brown fox jun

60 The quick brown fo:

72 The quick browr

Figure 9.5
Century Schoolbook has angled and slightly bracketed serifs.

Strokes are evenly weighted. This is one of the most readable of fonts. Examples are Goudy, Caslon, Palatino, Garamond, Book Antiqua, Cooper Black, and Century Schoolbook.

Transitional fonts have bracketed serifs, vertical stress, and uneven strokes that move quickly from thick to thin.

Transitional

Transitional fonts move to a vertical stress as shown in Figure 9.6. The strokes are thicker and thinner than in oldstyle. The serifs are bracketed and angled at the top. The most commonly used font is Times Roman or Times New Roman. These are the default fonts that appear when you open most word processing documents. Other transitional fonts may be easier to read. Examples are Perpetua, Baskerville, Times New Roman, and Times Roman.

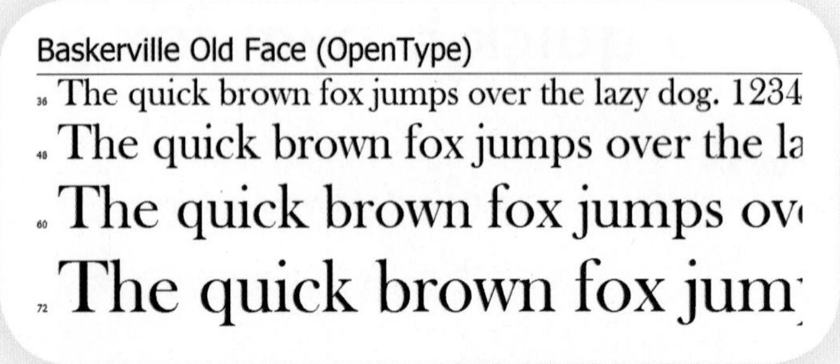

Baskerville Old Face (OpenType)

36 The quick brown fox jumps over the lazy dog. 1234

48 The quick brown fox jumps over the la

60 The quick brown fox jumps ov

72 The quick brown fox jum

Figure 9.6
Baskerville is a transitional font that represents a slight change from oldstyle because the strokes move more quickly from thick to thin.

Modern

Modern fonts are typefaces with a sharp contrast between thick and thin strokes. See Figure 9.7. The serifs are not bracketed, but the end of lines without serifs may be ball shaped. Examples are Bodoni, Walbaum, Fenice, Broadway, and Elephant.

Modern fonts have unbracketed serifs, vertical stress, and uneven strokes.

Bodoni MT (OpenType)

24 The quick brown fox jumps over the lazy dog. 123456

36 The quick brown fox jumps over the

48 The quick brown fox jump

60 The quick brown fox

72 The quick brown

Rockwell (OpenType)

24 The quick brown fox jumps over the lazy dog. 123

36 The quick brown fox jumps over

48 The quick brown fox jum

50 The quick brown fo

72 The quick brown

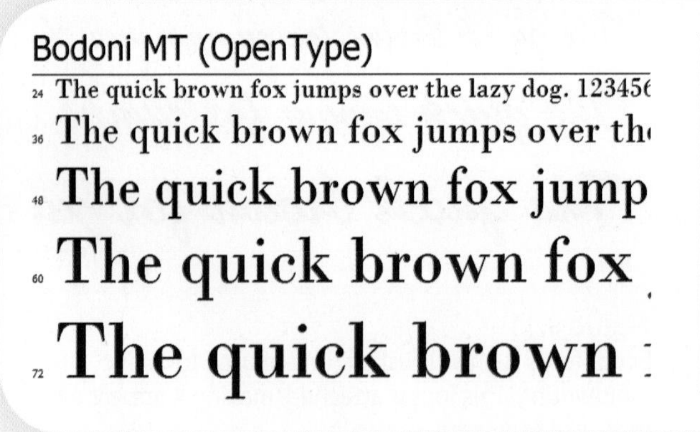

Figure 9.7
Bodoni is a modern font that has harsher strokes and a more vertical look.

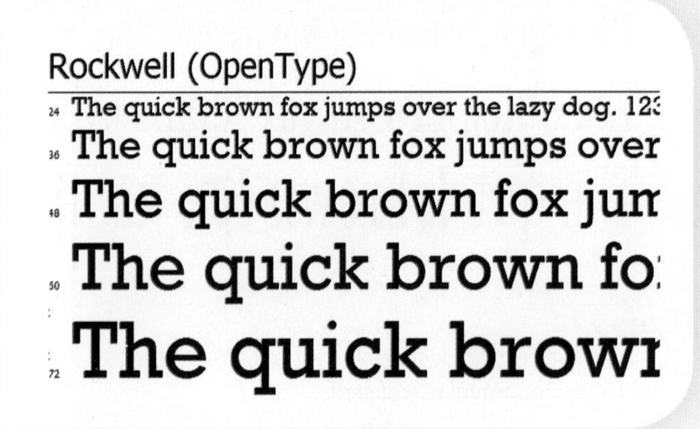

Figure 9.8
Slab serif fonts such as Rockwell have very even strokes that appear very bold.

Slab Serif

Slab serif fonts have very little difference between strokes. The serifs, however, are very heavy and noticeable as shown in Figure 9.8. The stress is vertical. Examples are Clarendon, Memphis, New Century Schoolbook, and Rockwell.

Slab serif fonts have heavy serifs, vertical stress, and even strokes.

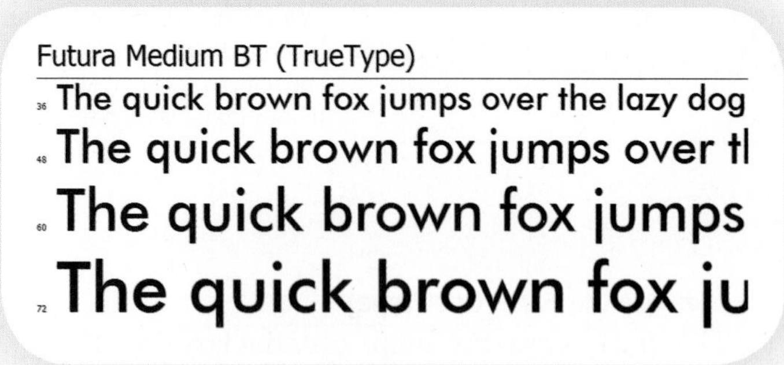

Futura Medium BT (TrueType)

36 The quick brown fox jumps over the lazy dog
48 The quick brown fox jumps over tl
60 The quick brown fox jumps
72 The quick brown fox ju

Figure 9.9
Futura is a classic sans serif with "feet" and very regular lines.

Sans Serif

Sans serif fonts have no serifs and the strokes are usually quite even as seen in Figure 9.9. Because of the evenness of the strokes, there is no visible stress. Examples are Gill Sans, Franklin Gothic, Optima, Futura, Eras Bold, Haettenschweiler, Lucida Console, Tahoma, Verdana, Arial, and Helvetica.

Specialized Fonts

Decorative

Decorative fonts are those used for display purposes.

Grunge type is a decorative font that appears to be beat up.

Display type is specifically designed to be used in a large size.

Decorative fonts such as the one shown in Figure 9.10 are generally used for display rather than long passages. They often have unusual shapes and proportions and can be quite dramatic. A decorative font that has been used quite frequently is described as **grunge type**. This is type that appears to be weathered or misshapen. Some types are actually designated as **display type**. They are designed to be used in larger font sizes. Examples are Juice, Stencil, Papyrus, and Jokerman.

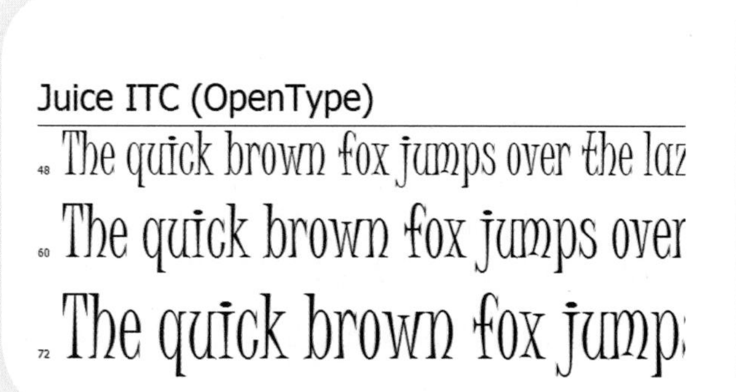

Juice ITC (OpenType)

48 The quick brown fox jumps over the laz
60 The quick brown fox jumps over
72 The quick brown fox jump

Brush Script MT Italic (OpenType)

36 The quick brown fox jumps over the lazy dog.
48 The quick brown fox jumps over the
60 The quick brown fox jumps
72 The quick brown fox ju

Figure 9.10
Juice is an interesting decorative font because of the curved lines and novel use of serifs.

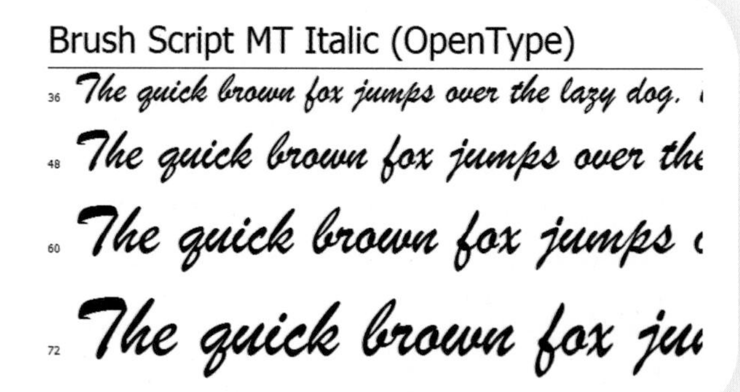

Figure 9.11
Script fonts such as Brush Script are used to mimic handwriting. This font is attached, making it appear even more like true script.

Script

Script fonts are designed to imitate handwriting.

Script fonts are designed to imitate handwriting (see Figure 9.11). They are very curvy and may or may not have letters that are connected. Often script fonts mimic calligraphy. They can be used in long passages but only for limited purposes. Examples: Brush Script, Zapf Chancery, and Tekton.

Blackletter

Blackletter fonts imitate an antique European font.

Another font style not often used are **blackletter fonts**. These are fonts designed to look like early European hand-lettering with its heavy ornate

Be kind to your readers. Just because you have a variety of interesting fonts on your computer, don't show off. Instead use those fonts that are most readable for the document in which they are used. Decorative fonts are fun to use in a limited number of situations. They often aren't fun to read if the document has long passages. Ethics is not just about doing right and wrong. It's also about treating your reader with respect. Creating a document that is intentionally difficult to read is wasting your reader's time. You are not treating them respectfully and are failing at your obligation.

lines. They are decorative fonts that work well for the initial letter of a paragraph (called a drop cap), but are not often used for anything but titles. An example of blackletter type is in Figure 9.12. Examples are Old English Text and Goudy Text.

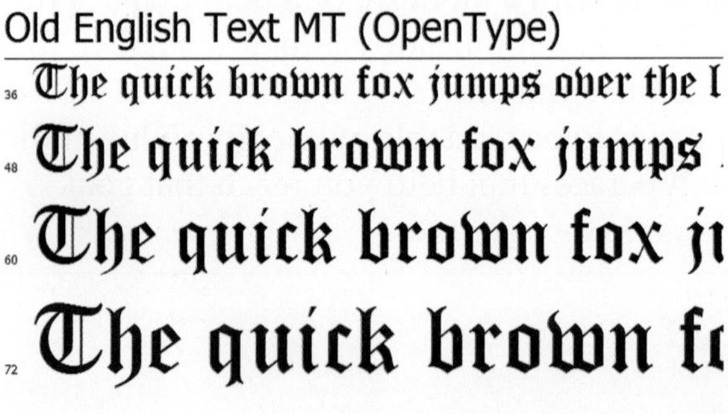

Old English Text MT (OpenType)

36 The quick brown fox jumps over the l
48 The quick brown fox jumps
60 The quick brown fox ju
72 The quick brown fo

Courier

abcdefghijklmnopqrstuvwxyz
ABCDEFGHIJKLMNOPQRSTUVWXYZ
123456789.:,;(:*!?')
12 The quick brown fox jumps over the lazy dog. 1234567890
18 The quick brown fox jumps over the lazy dog. 1234567890
24 The quick brown fox jumps over the lazy
36 The quick brown fox jumps (
48 The quick brown fox
60 The quick brown
72 The quick br

Figure 9.12
Blackletter fonts such as this Old English one are designed to look like early hand-printed fonts.

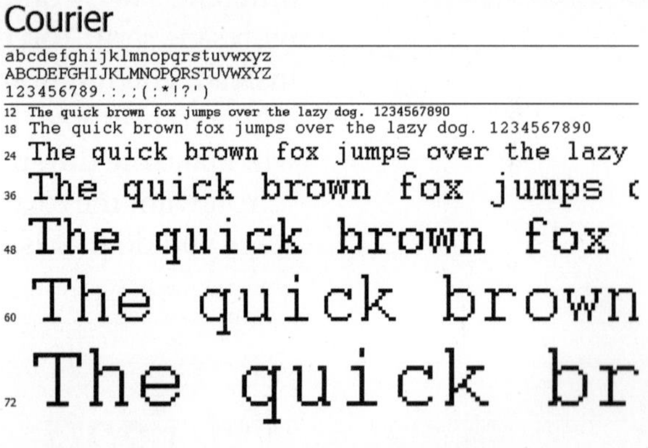

Figure 9.13
Courier is used when it is important that all letters occupy the same amount of space.

Monospace

Fonts that are not used often in desktop publishing are **monospace fonts**. This type style can be serif or sans serif. What sets it apart from other fonts is that each letter is spaced exactly the same amount. These fonts duplicate the look of a typewriter. Courier, seen in Figure 9.13, is the most common monospace font.

Monospace fonts are fonts that mimic the spacing produced by a typewriter.

Identifying Fonts

Often fonts are named in such a way that you can identify their style. For example, fonts with "old style" in their name are one of the serif oldstyles. Fonts with "gothic" in their name are often sans serif. Fonts with "brush" in their name are scripts. Those with "typewriter" may be monospace. Those with names such as "Krazy Legs" are probably ornamental.

Mixing Typefaces

It is often tempting for novice desktop publishers to use every interesting typeface that is available to them. While it is great fun to mix several fonts on a page, it is not good design. Page harmony is just as necessary with text as with the rest of your design. Harmonious pages seldom (if ever) have more than three typefaces on a page. Choosing only two is even better. To create interest, you can use different sizes and attributes of the same typefaces.

When mixing two different typefaces, diversity is the key. You do not want to use two faces that are too similar, such as two from the same classification. Your reader will be aware of the slight difference (probably only as a feeling of discordance).

You learned when you were studying alignment on a page that you need to make differences obvious so that they do not appear to be a mistake. Using two very similar font faces will create that same feeling of an error. If you are going to use different fonts, make sure they look different. This is one of the reasons that designers are told to mix serifs with sans serif. You are not limited to these broad categories, though. Instead, you might mix an oldstyle with a modern, or a heavy slab serif with a transitional. If the size of one is significantly larger or smaller, that will make the difference even more apparent.

You want the text on your pages to be readable and legible. One of the ways you do that is to choose typefaces that help you reach that goal.

Web Fonts

Web designers have far fewer font choices than print designers. In order for a reader to see the font the web designer selected, that font must reside on the reader's computer, although the use of embedded fonts is being developed. Embedded fonts are those that are built into a web page, allowing anyone to use them. The choice for web pages becomes basically a decision between serif and sans serif.

The fonts found on most PC computers are shown below. Some of these are built into the operating system and others are installed with commonly used software packages from companies such as Adobe or Microsoft. Using these fonts gives you a little more in the way of font choices, but it is still possible that one of these fonts won't be available to your reader. Until this problem is resolved, web designers must keep in mind the limitations of their design options.

Serif Fonts	Sans Serif Fonts
Times New Roman	Helvetica
Courier New	Arial
Geneva	Arial Black
Georgia	Verdana
Bookman Old Style	Tahoma
Book Antiqua	Century Gothic
Haettenschweiler	Lucida Console
Garamond	Lucida Sans Unicode
	Trebuchet MS
	Arial Narrow
	Comic Sans MS
	Impact
	Felix Titling

SUMMARY

In this chapter you learned the difficulties that the combination of computer display and printer created in trying to produce a document. You saw how the use of bitmap fonts solved that problem. You read about the introduction of PostScript and then TrueType and OpenType fonts. You discovered that typefaces are divided into a number of categories based upon their design. And you saw that mixing typefaces requires knowledge of these categories.

KEY TERMS

bitmap fonts

blackletter fonts

cross-platform compatibility

decorative fonts

digitally signed

display type

grunge type

modern fonts

monospace fonts

oldstyle fonts

OpenType

outline fonts

page description language

pangram

PostScript

printer font

scaling

screen fonts

script fonts

slab serif fonts

swash

transitional fonts

TrueType

Answer the following questions on your own computer.

1. What are the fonts called that were used to display text on a computer screen in the early years?

2. What was one of the printing problems with large fonts?

3. What was the name of the software written by Adobe for the Macintosh laser printer?

4. The software used by the Macintosh laser printer allowed a printed page to include what two things?

5. What software developed by Adobe allowed the use of vectors in printing?

6. What is a typeface called that can be scaled up or down in size without losing sharpness?

7. What was the replacement for PostScript fonts?

8. What is the name of the combination of PostScript and TrueType into one single font?

9. What does the term "swash" mean?

10. What is cross-platform compatibility?

11. What does it mean for a font to have been digitally signed?

12. What is an example sentence called that tests fonts by using all the letters of the alphabet?

13. What font style is most frequently used in long passages?

14. What is the normal use for decorative fonts?

15. What is the name of the decorative type that appears to be beat up?

16. What is the purpose of a script font?

17. What are blackletter fonts used for?

18. What distinguishes a monospace font from other fonts?

19. How many fonts can be used on a page while still creating harmony on it?

20. What is the key to mixing two different typefaces on a page?

DISCUSS

1. Explain how the movement from typewriter to keyboard input allowed more font options.

2. Briefly explain the Macintosh ImageWriter's solution to displaying fonts.

3. Describe one of the problems of using bitmap fonts to print with large fonts.

4. Identify the improvements made by the introduction of the use of vectors in printing.

5. Explain the difference between a screen font and a printer font.

6. Identify the advantages to using OpenType fonts over PostScript or TrueType fonts.

7. Describe characteristics of fonts in the oldstyle font category that make them useful in long passages. Give some examples of this font type.

8. Describe characteristics of transitional style fonts, and give some examples of the easiest ones to read.

9. Describe characteristics of modern style fonts, and give some examples of those used most often.

10. Describe the serifs and stress for fonts in the slab serif category, and give some examples of these fonts.

APPLY

Activity 1 Font Styles

1. Create a new two-page document with two columns.

2. On the master page, insert a page number that is horizontally centered.

3. Import the file **font_styles**. Begin the placement of the text on the first page in the left column, leaving 6p at the top of both columns for a heading. Thread the text until all of it is placed.

4. Delete the title Font Style from the top of the first column. Create a text block with the title **Font Style** keyed. Use a font from the blackletter category. Increase the size to fill most of the text block with the type.

5. Apply a font size of 18 pt. to all the side headings with a Bold-style Bodoni font. Make the side heading Specialized Fonts 24 pt.

6. Insert the pictures **oldstyle**, **transitional**, **memorial**, and **blackletter**. Size the pictures to 21p × 12p. Place them appropriately in the document.

7. Save as **font_styles**.

to the website at
academic.cengage.com/school/dtp

Activity 2 Pangrams

1. Create a 24p × 24p document.

2. Insert the image **pangram** at the top of the document spanning from left to right margin. Height should be set at 5p.

3. Create at least six textboxes with different pangrams in them. Research the Internet to locate some other pangrams that you have not seen. For each pangram, use a different font from a different category.

4. Save as **pangram**.

Activity 3 Halloween Festival

1. Create a flyer to advertise a Halloween festival.

2. Divide the page in thirds by placing guides horizontally and vertically.

3. Draw a text box covering the top third filled with orange.

4. Draw a text box covering the bottom third filled with black.

5. Using an orange font that sets the mood for Halloween, key in the bottom third: **Halloween Festival** [Enter] **October 31, 2XXX** [Enter] **6:00 p.m. – Midnight**.

6. Add a text box filled with black at the top left. In an orange font from the oldstyle category, key **Community Center** [Enter] **0001 Boo Street** [Enter] **Stuttgart, KS 67661-0015**. Change the font size to 24 pt. or an appropriate size. Rotate the text box to the left about 15 degrees. Add a drop shadow to the text box.

7. Add an image of your choice to the flyer in the middle area. Be sure that the image adds to the message of the flyer and that the colors are appropriate to the other elements on the flyer.

8. Save as **halloween_festival**.

Activity 4 Registration

1. Design a tabloid-size document that will be used as a banner to advertise registration for Community Education classes.

2. Change the view size so that you can see the entire document. Add horizontal and vertical guides to divide the page into thirds.

3. Add a text box to the top third. Key **Registration** and change the font size to as large as will fit in the area. Apply a font type from the slab serif category with bold if appropriate.

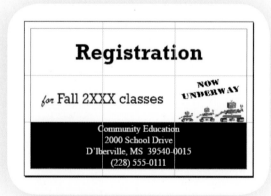

4. Add another text box in the middle area. Key **for Fall 2XXX classes**. Format the first word, for, using a font from the script category. Format Fall 2XXX classes using a font in the slab serif category without bold. Resize as appropriate with the word "for" smaller than the remaining text.

5. Browse to your student data files and insert the image *now* in the middle right third.

6. Create a text box in the bottom third filled with black. Using a white font, key **Community Education** [Enter] **2000 School Drive** [Enter] **D'Iberville, MS 39540-0015** [Enter] **(228) 555-0111**. Change the font size to 48 pt. or an

appropriate size. Center the text in the text box and resize the text box appropriately. Snap the text box to the bottom left third of the document.

7. Save as *registration*.

Activity 5 Font History

1. In a team of three or four students, search the Internet for more information on font history. In your team, review the section on Font History from the textbook. Decide on a topic to cover for each team member.

2. Each team member should research their topic and write a minimum 200-word summary. Save the summaries as *member1*, *member2*, *member3*, and *member4*.

3. Compile a list of resources used for the summaries in MLA style. Save as *resources*.

4. As a team, draw a sketch of a design to use for a newsletter. Determine how many pages you will need, whether to use landscape or portrait orientation, and how many columns to use. Decide on a design for the title of the newsletter, including what font to use. Decide on fonts for titles of each article as well as the text within the articles. Consider other issues that need to be decided on, and make notes on the sketch of any decisions made.

5. Using the sketch that the team decided on, each team member should use their desktop publishing software to create the newsletter. Save the completed newsletter as *font_history*.

EXPLORE

1. Using your favorite search engine, search the Internet for Adobe's SING (Smart INdependent Glyphlets).

2. Read information from at least two websites, taking notes on how this new technology will improve typography in desktop publishing. Write a summary of what you have learned that includes at least four important points in the use of SING. Key the summary into a word processing document and save as *glyphlets*. Be sure to include the resources you used in MLA style at the bottom of the summary.

3. Design a half-page desktop publishing document with a title and the imported glyphlets summary. Use appropriate font types and sizes for the title and the summary.

4. Save as *sing*.

10 Understanding Spacing

Objectives

- *Understand how to use spacing choices to improve the look of a document.*

- *Learn spacing conventions that create a professional look for a document.*

Introduction

Typography is not just about the font that you choose. It also includes the way the type appears on the page. Spacing is a big part of this look. It is a part of the design that is easy to overlook yet adds a truly professional appearance to your document.

Spacing Choices

Some of your spacing choices will be based upon your font selection. Others will be selections you decide upon yourself. Each of these spacing decisions affects how your page is read.

Letter Width

Letters within a typestyle are not all the same width. Notice the word "Width" in the heading of this paragraph. The "W" is much wider than the letter "i." These are called **proportional fonts** because letters are assigned space proportional to their size. With early typewriters this was not the case. Each letter was assigned exactly the same amount of space, and the fonts were called **monospace fonts**. You saw in the previous chapter that Courier is such a font. With the movement to computers, it became possible to assign space to individual letters to match their width.

Font designers can select the width of each letter to fit the image they want to create. Fonts with wide letters are difficult to read and not used widely. Fonts with narrow

Proportional fonts are spaced according to the size of the letter.

Monospace fonts are spaced the same for every letter.

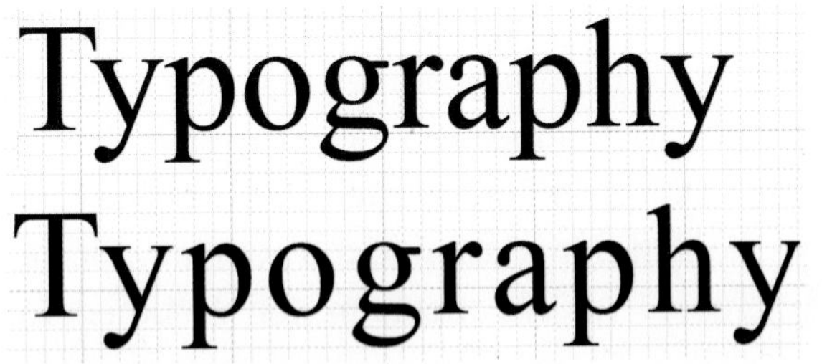

Typography
Typography

Figure 10.1
Both of these words are the same font size, but the lower one is set to a wider tracking.

WA Wa To Ya
WA Wa To Ya

Figure 10.2
Kerning is usually only important when text is very large. The example is a 72-point font; at that size it's easy to see the spacing between the letters.

letters are easier to read. Fonts of a medium width are often the best choice.

Tracking

The space between each letter is determined by both the designer and the software in which the text is being composed. Notice in Figure 10.1 that the distance between each letter is different depending upon the design of the letter. **Tracking** is the software function that allows you to add additional space between each letter. This can open up a page of text and make it appear more inviting.

Tracking is the spacing between letters in a word.

Kerning Pairs

Some letters in combination look better if they are placed closer together than most other letter combinations. These letter groupings are called **kerning pairs**. Capital letters such as T, V, W, and Y look better if they are closer to other capitals. In Figure 10.2, notice the difference between the capital "W" and the capital "A" when they have been kerned (the bottom row of letters). These same letters appear kerned when paired with certain lowercase letters,

Kerning pairs are sets of letters designed to be spaced closely together.

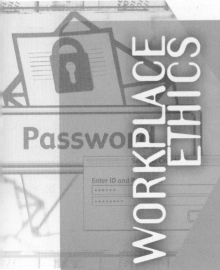

WORKPLACE ETHICS

Bringing attention to detail to your work is not just about making your pages look attractive. It is also about doing quality work. Employers hire designers to produce documents that will enhance their business. They themselves may not know about issues such as kerning, but they trust you to know about it. They trust you to produce work that represents the best the industry demands. Doing anything less than that is unethical. It's easy to say to yourself that no one will notice. Whether they do or not is not the question. You know the difference.

CHANGING WORKPLACE

Cascading style sheets have changed the way web pages are designed. You can anticipate that in time there will be more changes designed to give the power of desktop publishing to web designers. It's easy to believe that just because you can't kern text today that it is not important. That is not the case. Years of design experience have brought print design to the point at which it now stands. The same design improvements will appear in web documents as the industry matures.

Kerning is spacing of letters generally to make them move closer together.

such as Wa, To, and Ya. Desktop publishing software has built-in software that will automatically **kern** certain pairs once a font size is large enough to make the distinction apparent. You can also manually kern letters if you believe that they have not been placed close enough or if they are too close.

Ligatures

Ligatures are letters that have historically been attached, creating a single character.

Over the years some letter combinations such as "fi" "fl" and "vv" have been treated as a single letter joined together. These are called **ligatures**. Many font designers build in special ligature fonts so that when these combinations are used they are placed together as a single letter. Use of ligatures is one sign of a well-designed document. Figure 10.3 provides some examples of ligatures.

Leading

Leading is the spacing between lines of a paragraph.

The spacing between lines of text within the same paragraph is called **leading** (pronounced ledding). This term comes from the time when type was set with metal and strips of lead were placed between each line. Typewriters replaced leading with the terms "single space" and "double space" to establish the amount of white space between lines.

With desktop publishing more precise measurements in points are used. The amount of leading between lines in a paragraph is determined proportionally based upon the size of the font. Most leading is set to be 120% of the size of the font. That means that there will be 12 points between text that is 10 point. There will be 14.4 points of leading if the font is 12 point. Leading is determined by measuring from baseline to baseline. More or less leading can be selected to give more white space or to tighten up the look of the paragraph.

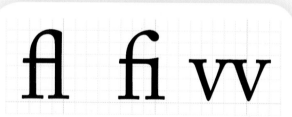

Figure 10.3
When characters such as "f" and "i" are joined, the dot over the "i" disappears into the ligature.

The use of dramatic white space has become a means of advertising that is quite popular. The practice of purchasing an entire newspaper page and filling it with a single statement in small type makes a striking impact. Advertising of this kind gets far more notice than the same page filled with details. This is the ultimate example of how white space can be used effectively. Creative typography choices are still to be discovered. Perhaps you will be the innovator that others follow.

Spacing between paragraphs is set independently of the space within lines of a paragraph. This spacing is also measured in points (or picas if the space is large enough). Generally the space before and after the paragraph is set separately depending upon the design needs. Novice desktop publishers tend to use the Enter/Return key to establish additional space. This is not an appropriate means of separating paragraphs.

Word Spacing

The spacing between words is set by the font design. When you select to justify a paragraph of text, that spacing is increased. There are software functions that will let you adjust this spacing. Too radical a change in spacing, however, will cause your page to appear awkward.

Em/En Space

Desktop publishing software provides an option to insert an **em** or **en space**. These are used as if they were white "objects" to separate words. The em-space is proportional to the point size of each particular typeface and is roughly equivalent to the width of the letter "M" of each typeface. The en space approximates the size of the capital letter "N" and is half the width of an em space. Often em and en spaces are used as a measurement of space.

An **em space** is a space the width of a capital letter "M" in the font and point size being used.

An **en space**, half the size of an em space, is the width of a capital letter "N" in the font and point size being used.

Web Spacing

Standard HTML code does not address many of the spacing needs in desktop publishing. With the movement to cascading style sheets (CSS), it has now become possible to adjust the spacing of letters such as kerning and tracking. In addition, it is possible to set leading to improve readability of the page. These refinements are important in the continued development of professional-looking web pages.

Proofreading is about looking for the tiniest details that are overlooked during the production of a document. This includes ligatures, kerning pairs, widows/orphans, and spacing after end punctuation. Develop the habit of setting aside time to check for these things after a document is finished. Attention to such detail will give you the reputation of being a dedicated desktop publishing expert.

Spacing Conventions

Punctuation

End punctuation has been controversial since typewriters were abandoned in favor of computer-generated text. With a typewriter, which used mono-space fonts, every space was exactly the same. It was necessary to space twice at the end of a sentence in order to make a visual break between the two thoughts. Computers use proportional fonts. Spacing is determined by the letters and their placement. Additional spacing is automatically built into the end of one sentence and the start of the next. As a result, it is no longer necessary (or even desirable) to space twice after periods, colons, or question marks.

Indents

Once again, the world of typewriters has influenced how we space a paragraph. Typists were taught to key five spaces to indent a paragraph. Tabs were awkward to set and had to be reserved for other purposes since they had to apply to the entire page. The spacing between paragraphs was limited to single or double spaces (and occasionally 1.5 spaces). There was little control of the design of a page. As a result, the standard was to single space between paragraphs but to indent to show that a new paragraph was beginning.

Desktop publishing software provides many more options. The space between paragraphs can be adjusted easily, so indenting is no longer necessary. If indenting is chosen, software options can be set to automatically space the appropriate amount. The amount considered effective is one or two em spaces. This is approximately .25 of an inch.

Hanging Indent

With **hanging indents**, a paragraph's first line is flush left but the remaining lines are indented.

The first line and hanging indent tab allow you to set quickly your indent point for each paragraph. **Hanging indents** create a paragraph in which the first line "hangs out" from the other lines in the paragraph (see Figure 10.4). Hanging indents can be set using a ruler or as part of the paragraph description.

Hanging indent

Tabs are essential tools for desktop publishing. Because of the proportional nature of the fonts used in DTP documents, lining up text by spacing is virtually impossible. There will often be the slightest deviation from one line to the next causing disharmony in the page.

Often novices believe that they can "eyeball" a page well enough that this isn't a concern. However, remember that what you see on the screen isn't always an exact replica of what will be printed. The solution to this problem is to establish tabs as markers. With tabs set, text will move to exactly the same spot each time.

Figure 10.4
A hanging indent draws attention to a paragraph by indenting all the lines after the first one.

Tabs

Tabs are essential tools for desktop publishing. Because of the proportional nature of the fonts used in DTP documents, lining up text by spacing is virtually impossible. There will often be the slightest deviation from one line to the next, causing disharmony in the page. Often novices believe that they can "eyeball" a page well enough that this is not a concern. However, remember that what you see on the screen is not always an exact replica of what will be printed. The solution to this problem is to establish tabs as markers. With tabs set, text will move to exactly the same spot each time. If corrections are needed, they can be made throughout the document by changing the tabs rather than making individual edits.

Tabs have options that many designers fail to use. They can be set to align to the left, to the right, to the center, or to a decimal. The left tab is the standard means of setting a tab, but center and right can be quite useful. For example, a center tab aligns the text on either side of a tab stop. This can be used instead of text alignment buttons.

Right tabs place the last letter of the line at the point of the tab, so text ends at the tab stop rather than starting there. The right tab is essential if you want to place text such as a page number at the farthest right point on the page.

Decimal tabs align figures so that regardless of the number of digits, the numbers line up with the decimal. This is a nice way to enter a column of expenses. Figure 10.5 provides you with an example of a decimal tab.

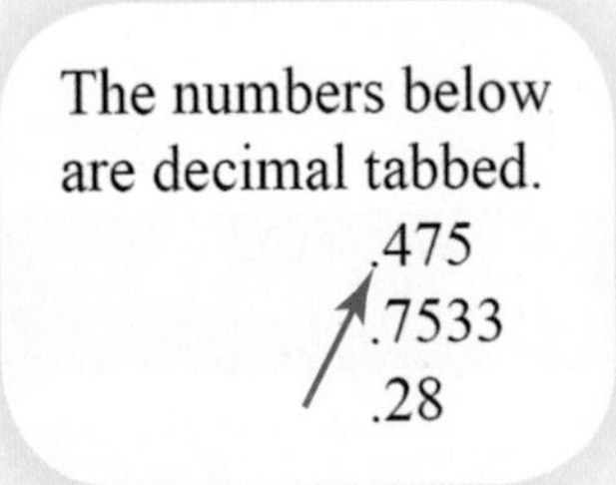

Widow and Orphans

Paragraph spacing concerns also include how lines of text appear at the end of a paragraph or on the page itself. A **widow** is the first line of a paragraph that appears by itself at the bottom of a column or page. When a new paragraph begins, you should keep at least two—preferably three—lines together.

Orphans are single lines or parts of a sentence that appear alone at the top of a new column or page. Both of these represent poor design and should be adjusted so that they remain with the body of the paragraph or so that more of the paragraph is included at the top or bottom. See Figure 10.6 for examples of a widow and an orphan.

Tabs are places on a ruler used to line up text.

The numbers below are decimal tabbed.
.475
.7533
.28

Figure 10.5
When you use a decimal tab, all the numbers line up with the decimal, making it easy to create a column of numbers.

Widows are single sentences or phrases at the bottom of a column or page. The rest of the paragraph appears on the next page or column.

Orphans are single lines of text that appear at the top of the column or page, with the rest of the paragraph appearing in the previous column or page.

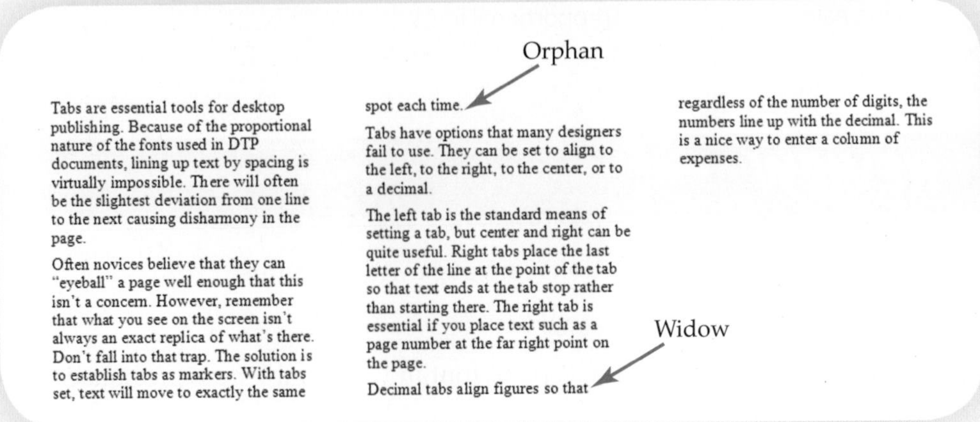

Orphan

Widow

Tabs are essential tools for desktop publishing. Because of the proportional nature of the fonts used in DTP documents, lining up text by spacing is virtually impossible. There will often be the slightest deviation from one line to the next causing disharmony in the page.

Often novices believe that they can "eyeball" a page well enough that this isn't a concern. However, remember that what you see on the screen isn't always an exact replica of what's there. Don't fall into that trap. The solution is to establish tabs as markers. With tabs set, text will move to exactly the same

spot each time.

Tabs have options that many designers fail to use. They can be set to align to the left, to the right, to the center, or to a decimal.

The left tab is the standard means of setting a tab, but center and right can be quite useful. Right tabs place the last letter of the line at the point of the tab so that text ends at the tab stop rather than starting there. The right tab is essential if you place text such as a page number at the far right point on the page.

Decimal tabs align figures so that

regardless of the number of digits, the numbers line up with the decimal. This is a nice way to enter a column of expenses.

Figure 10.6
Widows and orphans are single lines that are separated from the paragraph to which they belong.

Web Spacing Conventions

The issue of one space or two is not a problem in HTML-created pages. All words are followed by a single space. Tabs are also not a standard HTML option. Since the designer does not know exactly how a page will appear on a reader's display, widows and orphans are not adjustable. Cascading style sheets do provide a little more control, but for the present, these are design concerns that a web designer cannot address.

SUMMARY

In this chapter you learned how to set tracking and kerning to change the space within a line. You learned how kerning pairs and ligatures give your document a more professional look. You saw how em and en spaces are used for spacing. You read about various uses for tabs such as hanging indents. You saw how attention to details such as widows and orphans were necessary to create a harmonious page.

KEY TERMS

em space	leading	tabs
en space	ligatures	tracking
hanging indents	monospace fonts	widows
kerning	orphans	
kerning pairs	proportional fonts	

REVIEW

Answer the following questions on your own computer.

1. What is a proportional font?

2. What is the name of the type of font in which all letters are spaced the same?

3. What is the specific name of a font in which all letters are spaced the same?

4. Which one is easier to read, fonts with wide or narrow letters?

5. What determines the spacing between each letter?

6. What is the term for the spacing between letters in a word?

7. What are sets of letters designed to be spaced closely together called?

8. What is the spacing of letters to make them move closer together called?

9. What is a ligature?

10. What is leading?

11. What is usually the default leading percentage?

12. What size is an em space?

13. What size is an en space?

14. What innovation in web design has allowed the ability to use tracking, leading, and kerning in designing web pages?

15. What is the amount of indention considered to be effective for paragraphs?

16. What is it called when the first line of a paragraph is flush left but the remaining lines are indented?

17. What are tabs used for?

18. What is the standard placement of setting a tab?

19. What is a widow?

20. What is an orphan?

DISCUSS

1. Briefly explain the history of leading.

2. Identify when kerning is important.

3. Give some examples of ligatures.

4. Explain the measurements used in leading.

5. Discuss why it is no longer necessary to space twice after periods at the end of a sentence.

6. Explain the concept of hanging indents.

7. Identify problems caused by spacing rather than using tabs.

8. Describe some of the tab options.

9. Discuss how spacing, tab, and widow/orphan issues affect web design.

10. Give an example of how white space can be used dramatically.

APPLY

to the website at
academic.cengage.com/school/dtp

Activity 1 Math in Leading

1. Using the default of 120%, calculate the leading for the following font sizes:

   18, 24, 30, 36, 48, 60, 72

2. Using your desktop publishing software, create a default document. Add guides to divide the page in thirds.

3. Insert a table with appropriate column headings to display the information in instruction 1.

4. Format the column headings and data in the columns in an appropriate format.

5. Key an appropriate title to the table with appropriate formatting.

6. Save as **leading_math**.

Activity 2 Dramatic White Space

1. Create a default document advertising your favorite shoes on sale.

2. Use dramatic white space to get attention. Look at a recent newspaper with such an ad for inspiration.

3. Save as **dramatic_ad**.

Activity 3 Indents and Spacing

1. Create a two-column, one-page document. Change Units & Measurements to picas.

2. Import the file **spacing** from your student data files. Thread the text to the second column as needed.

3. Select all text. You can do this quickly by clicking inside the text area and pressing Ctrl + A.

4. Set a first line indent to 1p6.

5. Select the last paragraph and set a hanging indent. Remove the first line indent first, if necessary.

6. Select all text and change the space after the paragraphs to 1p.

7. Check to see that there are no widows or orphans. If there are, adjust the text boxes to eliminate them.

8. Save as **indents_and_spacing**.

Lorem ipsum dolor sit amet, consectetuer adipiscing elit. Aenean ac massa at sem euismod mattis. Phasellus nec ligula sit amet tellus convallis accumsan. Pellentesque venenatis velit id nunc. Sed quam tellus, eleifend et, molestie a, accumsan at, tortor. Quisque nibh ipsum, pharetra in, pretium id, tristique a, justo. Vestibulum quis quam. Nulla nec sapien. Cras dolor. Pellentesque habitant morbi tristique senectus et netus et malesuada fames ac turpis egestas. Vestibulum eget orci. Phasellus risus. Pellentesque lorem. In egestas, pede venenatis sollicitudin ornare, ante diam hendrerit elit, in aliquet magna turpis semper tellus. Mauris odio pede, lobortis at, ornare vitae, pretium sed, libero. Donec auctor. Nulla facilisi. Pellentesque vitae libero at erat mattis blandit. Ut porta, ipsum volutpat lacinia elementum, risus quam elementum sem, lacinia elementum augue libero at felis.

Lorem ipsum dolor sit amet, consectetuer adipiscing elit. Aenean ac massa at sem euismod mattis. Phasellus nec ligula sit amet tellus convallis accumsan. Pellentesque venenatis velit id nunc. Sed quam tellus, eleifend et, molestie a, accumsan at, tortor. Quisque nibh ipsum, pharetra in, pretium id, tristique a, justo. Vestibulum quis quam. Nulla nec sapien. Cras dolor. Pellentesque habitant morbi tristique senectus et netus et malesuada fames ac turpis egestas. Vestibulum eget orci. Phasellus risus. Pellentesque lorem. In egestas, pede venenatis sollicitudin ornare, ante diam hendrerit elit, in aliquet magna turpis semper tellus. Mauris odio pede, lobortis at, ornare vitae, pretium sed, libero. Donec auctor. Nulla facilisi. Pellentesque vitae libero at erat mattis blandit. Ut porta, ipsum volutpat lacinia elementum, risus quam elementum sem, lacinia elementum augue libero at felis.

Lorem ipsum dolor sit amet, consectetuer adipiscing elit. Aenean ac massa at sem euismod mattis. Phasellus nec ligula sit amet tellus convallis accumsan. Pellentesque venenatis velit id nunc. Sed quam tellus, eleifend et, molestie a, accumsan at, tortor. Quisque nibh ipsum, pharetra in, pretium id, tristique a, justo. Vestibulum quis quam. Nulla nec sapien. Cras dolor. Pellentesque habitant morbi tristique senectus et netus et malesuada fames ac turpis egestas. Vestibulum eget orci. Phasellus risus. Pellentesque lorem. In egestas, pede venenatis sollicitudin ornare, ante diam hendrerit elit, in aliquet magna turpis semper tellus. Mauris odio pede, lobortis at, ornare vitae, pretium sed, libero. Donec auctor. Nulla facilisi. Pellentesque

vitae libero at erat mattis blandit. Ut porta, ipsum volutpat lacinia elementum, risus quam elementum sem, lacinia elementum augue libero at felis.

Lorem ipsum dolor sit amet, consectetuer adipiscing elit. Aenean ac massa at sem euismod mattis. Phasellus nec ligula sit amet tellus convallis accumsan. Pellentesque venenatis velit id nunc. Sed quam tellus, eleifend et, molestie a, accumsan at, tortor. Quisque nibh ipsum, pharetra in, pretium id, tristique a, justo. Vestibulum quis quam. Nulla nec sapien. Cras dolor. Pellentesque habitant morbi tristique senectus et netus et malesuada fames ac turpis egestas. Vestibulum eget orci. Phasellus risus. Pellentesque lorem. In egestas, pede venenatis sollicitudin ornare, ante diam hendrerit elit, in aliquet magna turpis semper tellus. Mauris odio pede, lobortis at, ornare vitae, pretium sed, libero. Donec auctor. Nulla facilisi. Pellentesque vitae libero at erat mattis blandit. Ut porta, ipsum volutpat lacinia elementum, risus quam elementum sem, lacinia elementum augue libero at felis.

Lorem ipsum dolor sit amet, consectetuer adipiscing elit. Aenean ac massa at sem euismod mattis. Phasellus nec ligula sit amet tellus convallis accumsan. Pellentesque venenatis velit id nunc. Sed quam tellus, eleifend et, molestie a, accumsan at, tortor. Quisque nibh ipsum, pharetra in, pretium id, tristique a, justo. Vestibulum quis quam. Nulla nec sapien. Cras dolor. Pellentesque habitant morbi tristique senectus et netus et malesuada fames ac turpis egestas. Vestibulum eget orci. Phasellus risus. Pellentesque lorem. In egestas, pede venenatis sollicitudin ornare, ante diam hendrerit elit, in aliquet magna turpis semper tellus. Mauris odio pede, lobortis at, ornare vitae, pretium sed, libero. Donec auctor. Nulla facilisi. Pellentesque vitae libero at erat mattis blandit. Ut porta, ipsum volutpat lacinia elementum, risus quam elementum sem, lacinia elementum augue libero at felis.

Activity 4 Kerning, Tracking, and Leading

1. Browse to your student data files and open **kerning_tracking_leading**.

2. Click between the "K" and the "e" in Kerning Pairs. Change the kerning to 60. Click between the "P" and "a" in Pairs. Change the kerning to 60.

3. Select the title Tracking in the second article. Change the tracking to 40.

4. Select the text in the first article. Change the leading to 30 pt. Select the text in the second article. Change the leading to 30 pt.

5. Save as **ktl_complete**.

Activity 5 Tabs

1. Create a one-page default document.

2. Create a title at the top left margin spanning to the right margin with a 6p height.

3. Key **Tumblin' Trails** in the title box. Change the font to TwizotHmk or a similar font with a size of 60 pt.

4. Draw a text box in the remaining area. Set a right-justified tab at 44p0. Key in **Gatorade** at the left margin. Press the Tab key; then key **$2.00**. Repeat this for nine other healthy snacks of your choice. Include your best estimate of the price of that item at the right-justified tab.

5. Select all ten snack items and the amounts. Change the font size and font type appropriately.

6. With the ten snacks still selected, adjust the leading to an appropriate amount to space the list of refreshments out so that it is easier to read.

7. Change the tracking for the title to 100.

8. Add an image that will catch the reader's attention in an appropriate place on the flyer.

9. Save as **tumblin_trails**.

EXPLORE (e)

WRITING

1. Using your favorite search engine, search for information on cascading style sheets. Answer the following questions in an article:

   ➡ What are cascading style sheets used for?

   ➡ What are a few of the accessibility issues?

   ➡ What is the history of style sheets?

   ➡ Explain their use in vertical and horizontal centering. Are they effective? Why or why not?

2. Key your article into a word processing document. Include a short title for it. Save as **css_article**.

3. Open **css** from your student data files. Select the Place an article with a title here text in the large text frame. Replace the text with your article.

4. In the text in your article, use leading, kerning, and tracking as appropriate.

5. Key **Cascading Style Sheets** in the top text box. Resize and format appropriately.

6. Click inside the What's Inside text box. Set a tab at 9p0. Key the title of your article in the text box; then press Tab and key **1**.

7. Replace the Place Image Here text box with an appropriate image.

8. Save as **css_final**.

Using Special Characters

Introduction

Typography is not just about the font that you choose. It also includes your attention to other details. In the previous chapter, you studied a special character called a ligature. The careful use of other special characters will give your desktop published document a professionally prepared look.

Quotes

One of the first characters that you need to be aware of are quotation marks. In the days of typewriters the only comparable characters that were available were single or double straight quote marks, similar to those shown in Figure 11.1. As a result the general public began to believe that all quotes were the same. This is not the case. These vertical symbols are actually known as **tick marks**.

Double Curly Quotes

When a person's words are recorded on paper, they are enclosed with quotation marks. Notice that the opening quotation mark curls to the right and the closing ones curl to the left. These are known as **curly quotes**. For a professional-looking document, you should always use curly quotes instead of straight ones. Use of tick marks indicates a novice desktop publisher. Notice the difference in the two marks in Figures 11.1 and 11.2.

Objectives

- *Learn how to use quote marks appropriately.*

- *Understand difference between hyphens and dashes.*

- *Explore symbols and marks you can use to create professional documents.*

- *Learn how to use proofreading symbols when working with printed copy.*

Tick marks are straight quotes found on typewriters.

Curly quotes are marks curved in on either side of a quotation.

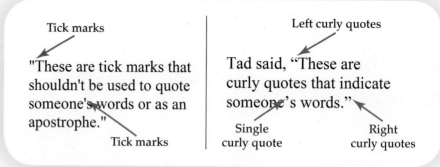

Figure 11.1
Tick marks are often replaced automatically with curly quotes.

Figure 11.2
Curly quotes should always be used as quotation marks to give your document a professional appearance.

Single Curly Quotes

Quotations within quotations are enclosed with single curly quotes. Single curly quotes are also used when an apostrophe is needed, as shown in Figure 11.2.

Primes

Primes look like the quotation marks used with a typewriter except that they are slanted (see Figure 11.3). Double primes are used to indicate feet. Single primes are used as an abbreviation for inches. Many computers automatically apply curly quotes whenever the quote key is selected. You may need to override that choice or insert a specific symbol for primes.

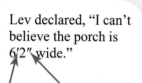

Figure 11.3
Primes appear similar to tick marks except that they are slanted.

Web Symbols

Creating web pages that adhere to professional rules regarding the use of quotes can be quite difficult. The symbols provided as part of standard desktop publishing software are not as easy to access when using web software. Peter K Sheerin, author of "The Trouble With EM 'n EN (and Other Shady Characters)" (http://www.alistapart.com/articles/emen/), provides a clear explanation of ways around this problem.

Primes are slanted marks used to indicate feet and inches.

Hanging punctuation is punctuation such as quotation marks that need to "hang" outside a paragraph rather than line up with the text below.

Hanging Punctuation

Hanging punctuation (usually quotation marks) that appears at the beginning and end of a paragraph can create an awkward design problem. When you key the text, the computer will place the punctuation marks inside the first line so that the margins line up (see top example in Figure 11.4). While this is logical, it is not an attractive design. Instead, the margin should be realigned so that the punctuation falls outside the edges of the text margin, as shown in the second example in Figure 11.4. Notice the difference between the two examples. What happens to the eye in the second example?

> "Send in the second team," begged the crowd.
>
> Hanging punctuation → "Send in the second team," begged the crowd.

Figure 11.4
Hanging punctuation should be visually separate from the line.

Punctuation

Hyphens

In the study of punctuation, there are hyphens and there are dashes. A **hyphen** indicates a compound word such as "merry-go-round" or a break in a word at the end of a line, called **hyphenation**. Figure 11.5 is an example of a hyphenated paragraph. Desktop publishing software provides an option to turn hyphenation on or off. You also have the choice of how closely to hyphenate. Too many hyphens in a row can be a distraction and should be avoided.

> A **hyphen** is a short horizontal line used to separate compound words or to hyphenate a word.
>
> **Hyphenation** is the splitting of a word at a syllable break.

When text is justified, often there are wider gaps in the line than you would like. One of the problems occurs when these gaps fall one above the other. This creates a **river of white**. Notice in Figure 11.6 that your eye is drawn down the river of white space instead of reading the text. Turning on hyphenation can alleviate this design problem, as can be seen in Figure 11.5.

Some hyphenation software is poorly written, breaking parts of a word that should remain together. Often proper names are hyphenated inappropriately. For example, company policy usually states that the name of the business should never be split. If that is the case, then you must manually indicate that the word is to remain unbroken by using a function such as a **nonbreaking space**.

> **Rivers of white** are created when text is justified. As a result, white spaces may appear one above another, creating a distracting "river" of white space.
>
> **Nonbreaking space** is a means of ensuring that a word is not separated during hyphenation.

In the study of punctuation, there are hyphens and there are dashes. A hyphen indicates a compound word such as "merry-go-round" or a break in a word at the end of a line called hyphenation. Desktop publishing software provides an option to turn hyphenation on or off. You also have the choice of how closely to hyphenate. Too many hyphens one after the other in a paragraph is a distraction and is to be avoided.

Hyphenation

Figure 11.5
Hyphens are placed between syllables of a word in order to provide a break at the end of a line.

River of white

In the study of punctuation, there are hyphens and there are dashes. A hyphen indicates a compound word such as "merry-go-round" or a break in a word at the end of a line called hyphenation. Desktop publishing software provides an option to turn hyphenation on or off. You also have the choice of how closely to hyphenate. Too many hyphens one after the other in a paragraph is a distraction and is to be avoided.

Figure 11.6
Consecutive lines in which the openings between words create a distracting river of white space are a possible consequence of justifying text.

One of the questions novice desktop publishers ask is where to place the punctuation following a quotation. Generally, the accepted policy is to place periods and commas inside the quotation mark. Question marks and exclamation marks are placed inside if they apply to the quote itself and outside if they apply to the complete statement. The examples below can help you use this punctuation correctly. Example

"Go with us to the park," pleaded Benjamin.

Why did Ben insist, "Let's go the park"?

Ben asked, "Why won't you go with us to the park?"

An **en dash** is a line the width of the capital letter "N" in whatever font and point size are being used. It is used in ranges of numbers, letters, or dates.

An **em dash** is a line the width of the capital letter "M" in whatever font and point size are being used. It indicates a break in thought.

Drop caps are large, often ornate first letters of a paragraph.

Em and En Dashes

A dash is used to indicate a sudden break in thought or as a "super comma." In the typewriter world, a dash as punctuation was typed as two hyphens. If the typed text was converted to print, the typesetter converted the two hyphens to an actual dash. With the advent of computerized type, that process has changed. It is now possible to set "real" dashes.

Professional typographers actually used two kinds of dashes: an **en dash** (normally used to connect ranges of numbers, letters, or dates), and an **em dash** (as a super comma). The en dash (–) is the width of the capital letter "N" in whatever font and point size are being used; the em dash (—) is the width of the capital letter "M" in whatever font and point size are being used. These dashes are keyed by either inserting them as symbols or by using special keyboard shortcuts, depending on the software being used. If you key two hyphens, often your software will automatically convert those hyphens to an em dash.

Symbols and Marks

Drop Cap

A **drop cap** is the first letter of a paragraph enhanced for emphasis. The letter may be larger or more ornate to create this effect. Use the technique judiciously. Drop caps (see Figure 11.7) create a formal look that might not be appropriate for every document. When you do use drop caps, place them "above the fold," meaning the top half of the page. They should never be used for every paragraph on a page.

Drop caps may be set to drop down any number of lines, but three lines is most common. The regular text can be set to align at the top, middle, or bottom of the cap. Because a drop cap indicates the beginning of a new paragraph, do not indent the paragraph in which it occurs.

Drop cap →

In the study of punctuation, there are hyphens and there are dashes. A hyphen indicates a compound word such as "merry-go-round" or a break in a word at the end of a line called hyphenation. Desktop publishing software provides an option to turn hyphenation on or off. You also have the choice of how closely to hyphenate. Too many hyphens one after the other in a paragraph is a distraction and is to be avoided.

Figure 11.7
A drop cap adds a touch of elegance to text. In this example, the Times New Roman opening letter "I" has been replaced with an Old English one.

Web Drop Caps

Drop caps are actually a graphic masquerading as text. As a result, when you want to include a drop cap in a web page, you must insert it as an image. This is because some of the control that you have in desktop publishing software is not available when using web software.

Dingbat

Dingbats are symbols, such as those shown in Figure 11.8. Dingbats are inserted into text, but they are actually graphics. Dingbats are frequently gathered into a single font family called Wingdings, Dingbats, Symbols, and so on.

Bullets

Bullets are symbols that add emphasis to a list. Most word processing software has options to create bullets automatically, making bulleted lists easy to use. Bullets can be large dots or graphical symbols such as arrows or dingbats. If you use a figure instead of a dot, make sure it does not overwhelm your list. Generally, it is best to indent the second and subsequent lines of text rather than letting them line up beneath the bullet. Figure 11.9 shows an example of a bullet list.

Figure 11.8
Dingbats are graphics that can be keyed into a document just like characters. Each typeface has a different set of images.

Dingbats are graphic symbols or ornaments that appear in a font as characters.

Bullets are symbols used to set off lines of text and draw attention.

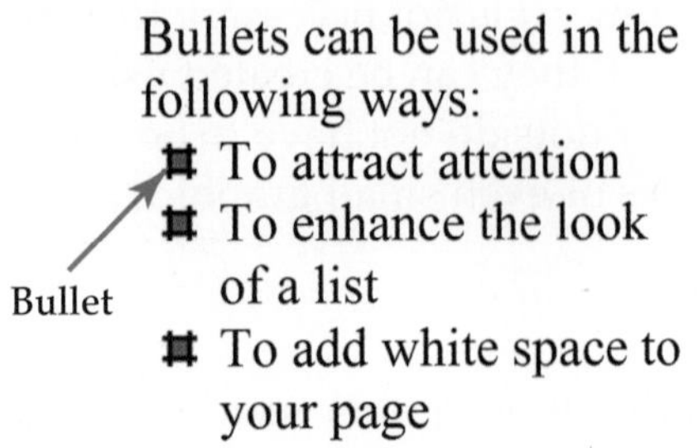

Bullets can be used in the following ways:
- To attract attention
- To enhance the look of a list
- To add white space to your page

Bullet

Figure 11.9
Bullets are an effective means of drawing attention to a list. Usually dots are used as bullets, but they can also be in the form of images.

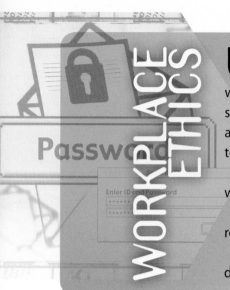

Use of an ellipsis in a quotation requires careful attention to the intent of the quote. Deleting portions (even if indicated with ellipses) of a person's words can be misleading. If the quote is distorted in such a way that the speaker's words are changed, then that is ethically questionable. Make sure that anytime ellipses are used the purpose is to shorten the statement rather than to modify its content.

Compare these two sentences to see how an unethical application of ellipses were used.

The president said that he did not believe that his company should be held responsible for the decision. They were not part of the process.

The president said that … his company should be held responsible for the decision.

Web Dingbats and Bullets

One of the limitations when designing pages for the Web is that the designer is dependent upon the fonts installed on each reader's computer. If a designer chooses to use a specific image that appears in a typeface, and a reader does not have that typeface installed on their computer, a different font will be substituted. As a result, the image may not appear. It's often better to convert dingbat and bullet images to graphics and to use them rather than text to assure they will appear on any computer.

Leader dots are symbols, a series of dots or small images designed to draw the eye across a page.

An **ellipsis** is three dots used to indicate an omitted word or phrase within a quotation.

Locate the information on the pages indicated.
Leader dots

Figure 11.10
Leader dots make it easy for a reader to follow text across a blank page.

Leader Dots

Leader dots are periods or other marks that are keyed in a sequence beginning at the end of one word and ending at the beginning of another (see Figure 11.10). Most programs use leader dots to draw the eye across the page to a name or time. It is not necessary to actually key these dots. Instead, they can be created using the Tab Menu option. Leader dots do not have to be actual dots. They can be dashes or even small graphics.

Ellipsis

Another type of dots is an **ellipsis**. An ellipsis (three dots) indicates an omitted word, phrase, line, or paragraph from within a quoted passage as shown in Figure 11.11. If the ellipsis falls at the end of the sentence, a fourth dot appears as a period. Desktop publishing software provides an ellipsis for you to insert. This is better than merely using periods, which are spaced too closely. Inserting a space between them makes them too far apart unless you kern them closely.

Diacritical Marks

Diacritical marks indicate how parts of a word are pronounced. Used properly, they add clarity to your work. The word "résumé" shows the use of diacritical marks. The letters along with their marks are found in the Symbols font.

Trademark

A **trademark** (™), registered trademark (®), or copyright symbol (©) is a cross between a dingbat and type and is used to indicate specific legal rights. The use of these symbols where indicated will make your work look more professional.

Fractions

You have already read in Chapter 9 that OpenType fonts contain fractions. Fractions that are keyed as separate numbers, as in 1/3, look awkward on the page. Instead, you should use the symbols or the font choices that convert them to a true fraction similar to those shown in Figure 11.12.

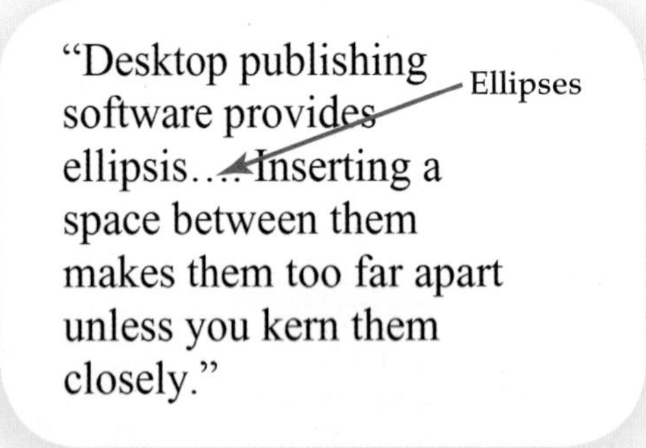

Proofreading (Symbols)

Most proofreading of documents is done directly onto a computer screen. There are times, however, when it is necessary to edit a printed draft of a document. With a series of commonly recognized

"Desktop publishing software provides ellipsis…. Inserting a space between them makes them too far apart unless you kern them closely." — Ellipses

Figure 11.11
An ellipsis makes it easy to quote only the specific text you want to include.

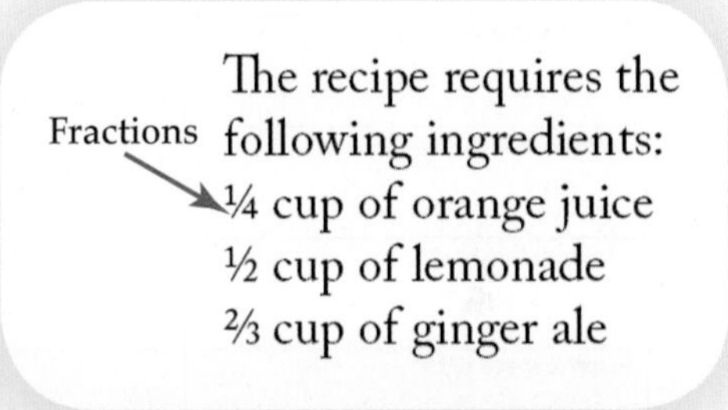

Fractions — The recipe requires the following ingredients:
¼ cup of orange juice
½ cup of lemonade
⅔ cup of ginger ale

Figure 11.12
Using fractions that have been designed as symbols is a design technique that novices don't always use but should.

Diacritical marks are symbols used to indicate the pronunciation of a word.

A **trademark** is a symbol used to indicate legal rights of ownership to a phrase or name.

CHANGING WORKPLACE

Symbols such as fractions, trademarks, copyright, and diacritical marks once required a complicated process to incorporate into a document. Only professional typesetters used them. Early desktop publishing software didn't even offer a means to use them easily. That is no longer the case. Programs such as Adobe InDesign provide special glyphs that make it possible to create your own special symbols as well as to use those that professionals require. There is no longer an excuse to overlook these and other symbols that can give your documents the sharp look you want.

Meaning	Symbol
Insert a comma	
Insert apostrophe or a single quote	
Insert an opening quotation mark	
Insert a closing quotation mark	
Insert something	
Place a period here	
Delete word or words	
Transpose elements	
Close up this space	
Insert a space here	
Begin new paragraph	
No paragraph needed	

Figure 11.13
Proofreading symbols are a commonly accepted means of indicating editing changes.

proofreading symbols, you can mark changes that need to be made to a document.

Figure 11.13 lists proofreading terms and symbols. Figure 11.14 shows a document that has been manually marked using proofreading symbols. Even if you do not edit a document yourself, as a desktop publisher you may encounter these marks on documents others provide.

Hank didnt realize that the guests had al ready arrived but it was too late to do anything about it. Why didn't you tell me? he asked. I replied I thought you knew.

He got only more angrier. He stomped away I threw up my hands in despair.

Figure 11.14
In this example, changes have been indicated using hand-drawn symbols rather than editing on screen.

The difference between a patent, a trademark, and a copyright can be confusing. As a desktop publisher, you need to know the difference so that you can use the correct symbol as needed. The information below is directly quoted from the U.S. Patent and Trademark Office (http://www.uspto.gov/web/offices/pac/doc/general/whatis.htm).

What Is a Patent?

A patent for an invention is the grant of a property right to the inventor, issued by the Patent and Trademark Office. The term of a new patent is 20 years from the date on which the application for the patent was filed in the United States or, in special cases, from the date an earlier related application was filed, subject to the payment of maintenance fees. US patent grants are effective only within the U.S., U.S. territories, and U.S. possessions.

The right conferred by the patent grant is, in the language of the statute and of the grant itself, "the right to exclude others from making, using, offering for sale, or selling" the invention in the United States or "importing" the invention into the United States. What is granted is not the right to make, use, offer for sale, sell or import, but the right to exclude others from making, using, offering for sale, selling or importing the invention.

What Is a Trademark or Servicemark?

A trademark is a word, name, symbol or device which is used in trade with goods to indicate the source of the goods and to distinguish them from the goods of others. A servicemark is the same as a trademark except that it identifies and distinguishes the source of a service rather than a product. The terms "trademark" and "mark" are commonly used to refer to both trademarks and servicemarks.

Trademark rights may be used to prevent others from using a confusingly similar mark, but not to prevent others from making the same goods or from selling the same goods or services under a clearly different mark. Trademarks which are used in interstate or foreign commerce may be registered with the Patent and Trademark Office. The registration procedure for trademarks and general information concerning trademarks is described in a separate pamphlet entitled "Basic Facts about Trademarks."

What Is a Copyright?

Copyright is a form of protection provided to the authors of "original works of authorship" including literary, dramatic, musical, artistic, and certain other intellectual works, both published and unpublished. The 1976 Copyright Act generally gives the owner of copyright the exclusive right to reproduce the copyrighted work, to prepare derivative works, to distribute copies or phonorecords of the copyrighted work, to perform the copyrighted work publicly, or to display the copyrighted work publicly.

The copyright protects the form of expression rather than the subject matter of the writing. For example, a description of a machine could be copyrighted, but this would only prevent others from copying the description; it would not prevent others from writing a description of their own or from making and using the machine. Copyrights are registered by the Copyright Office of the Library of Congress.

SUMMARY

In this chapter you learned how different styles of quotes are used for different purposes. You saw the difference between hyphens and dashes. You explored the various symbols and marks that can be used to create a professional-looking document. You learned to use proofreading symbols when editing a printed copy of document.

KEY TERMS

bullets	em dash	nonbreaking space
curly quotes	en dash	primes
diacritical marks	hanging punctuation	river of white
dingbats	hyphen	tick marks
drop cap	hyphenation	trademark
ellipsis	leader dots	

REVIEW

Answer the following questions on your own computer.

1. What are tick marks?
2. What are marks called that are curved in on either side of a quotation?
3. How are quotations within quotations indicated?
4. What is the difference between tick marks and primes?
5. What is hanging punctuation?
6. When is a hyphen used?
7. What is meant by hyphenation?
8. What can be done to improve design problems caused by a "river of white"?
9. How can you ensure that a word is not separated during hyphenation?
10. What is an em dash?
11. When is an em dash used?
12. What is an en dash?
13. When is an en dash used?

14. What is a drop cap?

15. How can a drop cap be inserted on a web page?

16. What is a dingbat?

17. What are bullets and when are they used?

18. What is the purpose of a leader dot?

19. What is an ellipsis?

20. What is a diacritical marking?

DISCUSS

1. Explain what is meant by "river of white."

2. Identify at least three things to avoid in the use of drop caps.

3. Explain how to create a leader dot.

4. Discuss the use of an ellipsis in desktop publishing software.

5. Explain the use of trademark symbols.

6. Discuss why OpenType fonts should be used when keying fractions.

7. Explain the use of proofreading symbols and why they are not always used.

8. Discuss patents—what they are, how long they last, and what they exclude.

9. Explain the difference between a trademark and a servicemark.

10. Discuss the types of works that are included under copyright law.

APPLY

Activity 1 Special Characters

1. Create a document with 6p left, right, top, and bottom margins.

2. Browse to your student data files and import **special_characters** into your document.

3. Zoom in if necessary. Make the following changes in the sentences:

   ○ Add a double left curly quote in front of the word "Love" and a double right curly quote after the word "friend."

   ○ Add a double left curly quote in front of the word "develop" and a double right curly quote after the word "brightest." Add a left single curly quote in front of "best" and a right single curly quote after "brightest".

to the website at
academic.cengage.com/school/dtp

- Change the dash to an em dash.
- Change the hyphen to an en dash.
- Change all fractions using special symbols so that they are not keyed as three separate strokes.
- Add diacritical marks to the word "resume."
- Add a trademark symbol to Sun Java.
- Add a registered trademark symbol to Silly Putty.
- Add a copyright symbol to Kermit the Muppet.

4. Save as **special_characters_final**.

Toyota Camry Solara

- Convertible
- Certified
- $24,988
- Mileage: 0
- Agile Suspension
- 210-hp VVT-I V6
- Optitron meters
- DVD navigation
- Bluetooth wireless technology
- MP3 compatibility

Sample completed bullets after formatting.

Activity 2 Bullets

1. Create a new document with 6p top, bottom, left, and right margins.

2. Browse to the student data files and import **bullets**. Place it at 6p, vertically spanning to the bottom margin and spanning from the left to right margin.

3. Select the text and then apply bullets to the list.

4. Change the leading in the bulleted list to 45p.

5. Change the bullets to a Webding font with the car image.

6. Add a text box to the top of the document. Key **Toyota Camry Solara** in the text box. Select the text; then change the font size to 40 pt and center the text. Resize the text box and move it as needed to center it in the area.

7. Save as **bullets_final**.

Activity 3 Drop Caps, Leaders and Hyphenation

1. Browse to your student data files and open **drop_caps**.

2. Select all the text in the article titled Conference 2XXX. Change the first-line indent to 1p. Set spacing before the paragraph to 0p6.

3. Repeat this for all other articles in the five-page newsletter. Adjust the font size as needed. Be sure there are no widows or orphans.

4. Set a right-aligned leader tab at 9p5 in What's Inside on the first page. Key the following in the What's Inside text box.

What's Inside	
Conference	1
Scholarship	2
Challenges	3
Making Differences	4
Working Together	5

Conference 1

Scholarship 2

Challenges 3

Making Differences 4

Working Together 5

5. Adjust the leading in the What's Inside text box to 14 pt.

6. Remove the first-line indent in the article on the first page. Add a drop cap that is three lines in height and only applied to one character.

7. Resize the text box. Add an appropriate image in the area below What's Inside.

8. Save as **drop_caps_final**.

Activity 4 Recipe

1. Search the Internet or bring your favorite recipe from home.

2. Create a flyer in landscape orientation with two columns. Determine the best margins for your flyer.

3. Add a title with the name of the recipe. Apply an appropriate font type and size.

4. Key in a list of the ingredients, using bullets. Change leading as appropriate as well as font type and size.

5. Add a numbered list of instructions with an appropriate font type and size. Change leading as needed.

6. Insert an image that adds interest to the flyer.

7. Save as **recipe**.

Activity 5 Famous People

1. In a team of three or four students, each student will write a brief biography of a famous person of their choice. The biography should include at least one quote. It should also include a short paragraph at the end explaining why the student chose to write about that person. Minimum requirement of words is 100. Save as **biography1**, **biography2**, **biography3**, and **biography4**. (The number of students on your team will determine how many files you have saved.)

WRITING

2. Each person will create a newsletter in landscape orientation. Number of pages should be determined by length of articles.

3. Add a text box to the master page that includes the title of the newsletter (Famous People), the date, and the page number.

4. On page 1, key the title **Famous People**. Use your creativity to make the title stand out and catch the interest of readers.

5. Add a text box with the title **What's Inside**. Format the text box for a right-aligned tab with dot leaders. Key the name of each of the famous people that your group wrote about and what page their article appears on. (You may want to leave this text box blank except for the title until you have completed the rest of the newsletter.)

6. Import and place the text appropriately in the newsletter. Turn on hyphenation. Adjust leading and first-line indents as needed. Add one drop cap with appropriate formatting.

7. Add at least two images that increase interest in the newsletter. Size and place appropriately.

8. Check the newsletter for the following and make adjustments as needed:

   ⊃ *Articles fit within their area. Font size changed as needed. Thread as needed with continued on or continued from notices.*

   ⊃ *No widows or orphans.*

   ⊃ *No rivers of white.*

   ⊃ *Quotes correctly formatted.*

   ⊃ *Hanging punctuation adjusted as needed.*

   ⊃ *Hyphens and dashes formatted as en or em dashes.*

   ⊃ *Ellipses, diacritical marks, and fractions formatted appropriately.*

   ⊃ *Nonbreaking hyphens or nonbreaking spaces inserted as needed.*

9. After spell checking your document, print a draft copy and trade with someone on your team. Use proofreader's marks to note any errors that you find.

10. Edit your newsletter from the proofreader's marks.

11. Save as **famous_people**.

EXPLORE ⓔ

WRITING

1. Search the Internet for information on the use of symbols in creating web pages. Read at least two articles pertaining to this topic.

2. Write a summary of your reading that includes the two references in MLA format. Save the summary as **web_symbols**.

3. Create a two-column document with the file **web_symbols** imported into the columns.

4. Use your best judgment and formatting skills to create an eye-appealing document. You may add other elements as needed.

5. Save as **web_symbols_final**.

Independent Project

Podcasting

1. Research podcasting. Using at least three references, write a 500-word review of your research. Save the document as ***podcasting***.

2. Save the resources in MLA format as ***podcasting_resources***.

3. Using your desktop publishing software, design an info sheet on podcasting. Use the following as a checklist:

    - *Create a title that spans from left to right margin and uses reverse type. Apply an appropriate font size and a font type that is used for display.*

    - *Import the text documents. Format them with fonts used for long passages.*

    - *Apply kerning, leading, and tracking where needed. Turn ligatures on.*

    - *Format the paragraphs for a 1p6 first-line indent and p6 spacing after them. The resources should be formatted for a hanging indent.*

    - *Format the first letter of the first paragraph as a drop cap. Apply a font from the blackletter category.*

    - *Reword, if necessary, to add a bulleted list to one of the paragraphs.*

    - *Insert special characters as needed throughout the document.*

    - *Check to be sure there are no widows/orphans.*

    - *Use at least three font effects somewhere in the document.*

    - *Proofread for spelling, grammatical, and formatting errors.*

4. Save as ***podcasting_info_sheet***.

Team Project

projects *projects* *projects*

Designing for Disabilities

1. With your team of students, develop a plan to research several topics, write summaries on the topics, and design a newsletter.

2. Choose topics from the following list:

   - *Fonts for low vision*
   - *Color contrast and partial sight*
   - *Design for the aging population*
   - *Design for partially sighted*
   - *Guidelines for tactile graphics*

3. Write summaries of the topics that were researched. Some of the summaries can be 100 words in length and some should be longer. Within your team, decide on those topics that need more words so not all the summaries are the same length.

4. Save each as: ***topic1***, ***topic2***, ***topic3***, ***topic4***, and ***topic_resources***.

5. Apply appropriate font types, sizes, and effects to demonstrate knowledge of typography.

6. Use special characters as needed, bulleted lists, and tabs.

7. Apply appropriate formatting to paragraphs.

8. Proofread for spelling and grammatical errors.

9. Save as ***designing_for_disabilities***.

Digital Portfolio

Self-Assessment

1. Select five items from Unit 3 that you intend to add to your portfolio. Write an assessment of what you learned from this activity. Include what you learned from creating the content as well as what skills you used in the unit on typography.

   ➲ *What caused you the most difficulty?*

   ➲ *What did you enjoy most about completing the activity?*

   ➲ *What would you do differently if you had the opportunity to repeat it?*

2. Save your self-assessments with the name of the file and **_sa** added to the end of the file name.

Collecting and Organizing Sample Projects

Collect projects and assignments from Unit 3 that you want to include in your portfolio. These assignments do not all need to be your best work. Create the folders for your portfolio. Move the documents to those folders. If available, a copy of the rubric should also be included for each of the projects/assignments that will be included in the portfolio. Back up all files from the portfolio as your plan outlined.

Journalizing Progress

Using a word processing software, tablet PC, handheld device, or blog, add to the journal of this ongoing project. Save the journal as **portfolio_ journal** or give the link to the blog to your instructor. Alternatively, you could keep an audio journal of your work completed by using podcasting or other digital audio methods. Consult your instructor for the journal method to use for this class.

unit4

Communicating with Color

Freelance Production Artist /
Graphic Designer

What I do every day

Typically, clients send jobs that need to be print-production ready. These jobs have had another graphic designer create the art, but the file needs to be set up a particular way in order to print correctly. Other jobs require design work, and in doing the design, I make sure it's also production ready. The types of projects I work on are textbooks, brochures, logos, architectural plans, stationery (business cards, letterhead, and envelopes), web design, packaging, signage, and CD labels.

How I use DTP in my job

Every job described above would be considered DTP, so I use it every day. Three key programs I use are Adobe Illustrator, Adobe Photoshop, and QuarkXpress. More recently, Adobe has introduced InDesign, which could be used in lieu of QuarkXpress.

The best part of my job

I love what I do and try to make clients happy by quickly completing the job and creating a design they are looking for. Freelancing means flexibility! I often work through the night. With no phones ringing and no meetings to run to, I can get a lot done. If I budget my time properly, I can travel and still meet my deadlines.

The worst part of my job

Invoicing. Although this is how I get paid, it has nothing to do with production or design. Therefore, it's hard to stop working and bill for the jobs I've completed.

What I need to know and be able to do

Learning the computer programs is essential, as is a high level of printing knowledge. I try to keep up on design styles, but design doesn't always follow trends; it can be unique. Some of my best jobs are when a client tells me what they want to see, and then I take the time to do something I think would look better. They usually love the new look.

How I prepared to be a production artist/graphic designer

A bachelor's degree is usually necessary (I have a BFA), but also important is a good design sense. In my case, technical ability is a necessity too. During college, I gained experience in jobs at printing companies, newspapers, and studios.

How the Web has impacted this field

The Web has totally changed my field. The only "tool" I still use from 15 years ago is my Pantone Color Book. No more drafting tables, templates, technical pens, or Exacto knives. Delivering or picking up a job from a client is done through the Internet, as are accessing stock photography, buying software/hardware, almost all communication, and delivering a job to the printer. Everything can be done online.

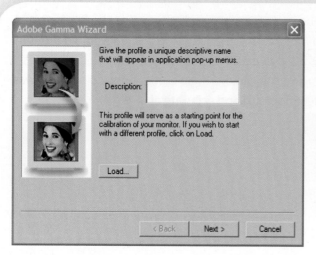

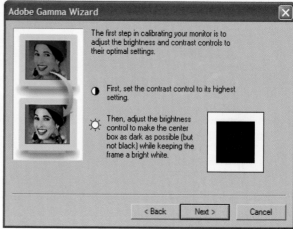

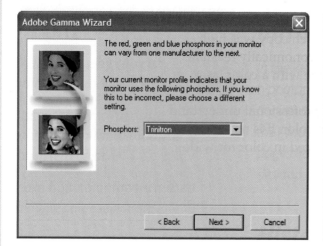

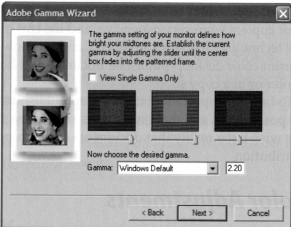

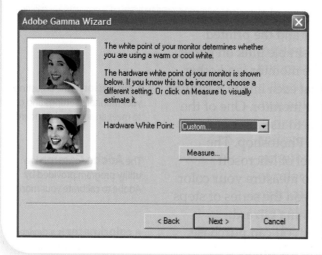

Figure 12.1
The Adobe Gamma software contains a wizard that can lead you through the steps to calibrate a monitor.

of hardware that will allow you to calibrate your monitor. The least expensive and newest is the Huey, which constantly monitors the amount of light falling on your screen and adjusts your system accordingly. Figure 12.2 is a photograph of the Huey.

Calibration is a complex process that requires awareness of the amount of light in a room, the type of monitor, the age of the monitor, and even the color of the walls in the room. Professionals who need to produce absolutely accurate color must go to great lengths to ensure color consistency, beginning with the display on their screen.

White Point

The **white point** is the lightest point on an image displayed on a screen. The appearance of the white point changes with the amount and kind of light that falls on the screen. This light is measured in Kelvins (K) and is called the **color temperature**.

One of the questions that you will have to answer when calibrating a monitor is the type and amount of light in your room, or the color temperature. As this color temperature changes, so will the way your image appears. The industry standard is becoming 6500 K daylight (abbreviated as D65).

Below is a list of color temperatures that are produced by various light sources.

1000–2000 K Candlelight

2500–3500 K Tungsten Bulb (standard household light)

4000–5000 K Fluorescent Bulb

5000–6500 K Daylight

Even if you have a perfectly calibrated monitor and a printer that produces an accurate print, light changes will modify the way your image appears in print. Color seen outside in sunlight may appear quite different from color seen under fluorescent or incandescent light. When you select a color, keep in mind these possible changes.

Gamma Correction

Monitor gamma is a measurement that compares the screen's brightness and contrast. This measurement is set in order to adjust the screen so that the image appears as close to the original as possible. The standard gamma correction is 2.2.

ICC Profiles

Even when a monitor is calibrated, there are additional problems. For one, the **color space** (sometimes called the working space), or the pool of colors that a particular device has available, differs from device to device. This means that a color that is captured by a digital camera might fall outside the working space of a particular printer. When colors cannot be used in a particular working space, they are called **out of gamut**.

Figure 12.2
Pantone markets a device called the Huey that can be used to calibrate your monitor and respond to the light that falls on your display.

© SUSAN LAKE

The **white point** is the lightest pixel on a computer monitor.

Color temperature is the measurement of light that falls on a computer screen.

Monitor gamma is a calibration that measures the brightness and contrast of a computer display.

Color space is the number of colors that a device can display.

Out of gamut is a warning that a particular device is unable to display a color.

The **International Color Consortium** is an organization that works together to ensure that color is consistent regardless of operating systems or software.

ICC Profile is a means of transferring color information from device to device.

In an attempt to ensure that the color of an image is the same regardless of the device used, the **International Color Consortium** (ICC) has developed specifications that are applied to imaging devices such as scanners, digital cameras, monitors, and printers. These color management profiles are accepted as an industry standard. Profiles make it possible for a device such as a printer to convert the information sent to it by a monitor or scanner into an image that approximates the one originally produced.

Printer companies such as Epson provide **ICC profiles** that can be used with programs such as Adobe Photoshop to ensure that colors remain true. The profiles can be downloaded from the website provided by the printer company. ICC printer profiles often include not only the printer but also paper types that may be used, since the paper choice can also affect the way a printed image appears.

Web Color

Viewing colors on the Web using a monitor would seem to be less problematic than printing colors from a monitor. Unfortunately, this is not the case. Just as you must calibrate your monitor to work well with printers, as a web page designer you must take into account the differences that exist from one monitor to another. This just means that you must be aware that the colors you select may not be the colors the reader actually sees. Even differences in light sources will affect the image.

BUSINESS OF PUBLISHING

Businesses spend considerable time and money establishing an identity. One of the means of doing this is through color. Often a company logo will contain a specific color. Any time that logo is used, it is expected that the same color will appear. As a document designer you are required to know what that color is and to ensure that it is used. Almost right isn't good enough.

Color Selection

Types of Color

One of the reasons that accurate color is so difficult to manage is that each device produces color in a different way. A computer monitor creates color by mixing red, green, and blue (**RGB**) spots of color in different concentrations in order to produce an image. This color is projected using light known as an **additive color**. As each color is added to basic black, the image becomes lighter. Notice in Figure 12.3 that when each red, green, and blue is set to its highest number (255), the color produced is white.

Printing presses produce color documents using cyan, magenta, yellow, and black (**CMYK**). CMYK colors are called **subtractive color**. In order to produce white, the percentage of color is set to 0% or subtracted from the color black. Notice the CMYK percentages in Figure 12.3 are zero. In Figure 12.4 all the colors are set to 100% producing black.

RGB is the acronym for red, green, and blue. These are the three colors used to produce an image on a computer monitor or a television.

Additive Color is one that becomes white when all colors have been added.

CMYK is the acronym for cyan (blue), magenta (red), yellow, and black. These are the colors used to produce printed images.

Subtractive color is one that becomes white when all colors have been removed or subtracted.

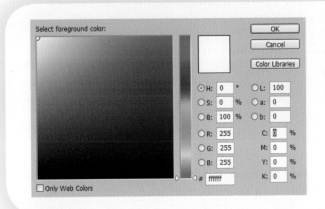

Figure 12.3
Additive color starts with black and adds red, green, and blue to produce white.

Figure 12.4
Subtractive color starts with black and removes cyan, magenta, and yellow to produce white.

Because the image seen on a computer monitor is actually a light and the image seen on paper is a variation of black, it is not surprising that it is quite difficult to produce identical images. A third complication is that personal printers attached to computers use a variety of color techniques to reproduce what is seen on the screen. Some printers use as many as six to eight different color cartridges to produce an image.

Color Theory

Regardless of the way color is produced, **color theory** applies to them all. Color theory consists of an understanding of the relationship of color often used by observing a **color wheel** similar to the one shown

Color theory is the relationship between colors often based on their location on a color wheel.

Color wheel is a visual arrangement of colors in a circle that is similar to the spectrum of light.

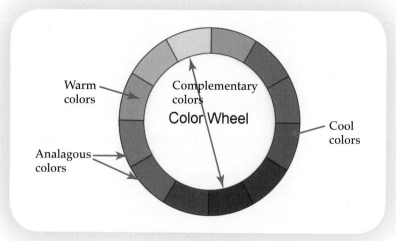

Figure 12.5
A color wheel makes it easy to identify both complementary and analogous colors.

Complementary colors are those that appear directly across from each other on a color wheel.

Analogous colors are those that are near each other on a color wheel.

Cool colors are those near the color blue on the color wheel.

Warm colors are those near the color red or orange on the color wheel.

in Figure 12.5. Colors opposite each other on the wheel are called **complementary colors**. Complementary colors that are combined are seen as attractive or pleasing to the viewer. In addition, **analogous colors**, those next to each color on the wheel, can also be combined successfully.

Another common color concept is the idea of warm and cool colors. Basically, **cool colors** represent the half of the color wheel in which blue appears. **Warm colors** are found in the other half where red/orange appears.

Color Communication

Understanding the use of color to communicate is important. Color itself sends a message that depends on the age, gender, and culture of the person viewing it. Different colors can be expected to send different messages or to create different effects. For example, the following colors are often described with these words:

Black—classic, strong, powerful, mysterious, elegant

Blue—tranquil, peaceful, sad, dependable, cool, constant, quiet

Brown—wholesome, rich, earthy, home-like, stable, rustic, sheltering

Green—soothing, refreshing, healing, natural, fresh

Neutral—classic, quality, natural, timeless, quiet

Orange—sharp, friendly, vital, hot, energizing, inviting

Pink—happy, sweet, romantic, youthful

Purple—sensual, elegant, eccentric, regal, spiritual, mysterious

Red—sexy, exciting, stimulating, provocative, dynamic

White—pure, bright, innocent, clean

Yellow—harmonious, warming, sunny, splendor, anxious (depending upon brightness)

Color Schemes

Colors are often combined to create a particular feel. For example, a combination of warm colors such as those shown in Figure 12.6 create a comforting feel. Cool colors like those shown in Figure 12.7 might be used to replicate the splash from a swimming pool on a hot summer day. Festive colors such as those in Figure 12.8 create a party feeling with all the bright colors. Colors may be combined to create a **color scheme**.

Color scheme is an arrangement of colors designed to create a particular response.

Figure 12.6
Soft browns like these earth tones are soothing.

Figure 12.7
Bright blues and greens create a cool image.

Figure 12.8
Bright colors are used to give readers a sense of festivity or excitement.

Custom Selection

One of the design techniques that desktop publishers have learned to incorporate in their documents is picking up colors from images and using those colors throughout a page. If a graphic has a particularly dominant color such as red, that color (or a version of it) might be reused in a title or a headline or even a frame. Variations of the color can be picked up by enlarging the image so that the pixels are evident. These color variations can then be used elsewhere. Use of these color components gives the document a consistent look.

SUMMARY

In this chapter you learned how to adjust your monitor in order to calibrate it. You explored concepts such as white point and gamma correction. And you learned the importance of ICC profiles. You read about color theory and saw that RGB is an additive color while CMYK is subtractive. You learned ways that color can be used to create feelings and impressions. Now it is time to see how different color modes are used.

KEY TERMS

additive color	color theory	monitor gamma
Adobe Gamma	color wheel	out of gamut
analogous colors	colorimeter	RGB
calibration	complementary colors	subtractive color
CMYK	cool colors	warm colors
color scheme	ICC profile	white point
color space	International Color Consortium	
color temperature		

REVIEW

Answer the following questions on your own computer.

1. Until recently, what was used to add interest when color was not available?

2. What made it possible to print color documents at home? When did that occur?

3. What made reproduction of color possible?

4. What is calibration?

5. What Adobe utility program calibrates your monitor?

6. What is a colorimeter?

7. What is Pantone?

8. What is the name of one of the newest hardwares that is somewhat inexpensive and constantly calibrates your monitor?

9. What is the lightest pixel on a computer monitor called?

10. What is a Kelvin?

11. What is the industry standard for color temperature?

12. What is the calibration called that measures the brightness and contrast of a computer display?

13. What is color space?

14. What is the warning called that a particular device is unable to display a color?

15. What is an ICC profile?

16. What is a color called that becomes white when all colors have been added?

17. What is the relationship called between colors that is based on the location of colors on a color wheel?

18. What is a color wheel?

19. What do you call the arrangement of colors designed to create a particular response?

20. What factors does the message a color sends depend on?

DISCUSS

1. Explain what the International Color Consortium (ICC) has done to solve some of the color problems in monitors.

2. Discuss why accurate color is so difficult to manage.

3. Explain the process used in CMYK to produce white.

4. Analyze the differences in colors on computer monitors and in print and what causes difficulties in producing identical images.

5. Describe the difference in complementary and analogous colors and their relationship to the color wheel.

6. Discuss the concept of warm and cool colors.

7. Explain how dominant colors in images can be used to give a document a consistent look.

8. Identify at least three colors that can be used to create a feeling of festivity and excitement and explain why.

9. Recount why web color is more difficult to produce consistently than one would think.

10. Discuss a few of the most common everyday light sources, the color temperature that they produce, and their relationship to the industry standard.

APPLY

to the website at
academic.cengage.com/school/dtp

Activity 1 Color Communication

1. Using your desktop publishing software, create a default document.

2. Insert a two-column table with five rows.

3. Insert the title Color Communication in the top row. Merge the cells and center the text horizontally and vertically. Change the font size to 24 pt. and the font type to Agency FB or a similar font.

4. On row 2, add column headings Color and Effects. Center the text horizontally and vertically and bold it.

5. Input the list of colors and their effects from the section on Color Communication in the textbook. Resize the columns and rows as needed so there is no word wrap. Add more rows as needed.

6. Change the font size for the column headings and the other rows to 14 pt. with a font type of Arial.

7. Add alternating color fill to the rows with green and yellow shaded at 20%.

8. Change the row height to 3p0 and vertically center the text within the cells.

9. Center the table horizontally and vertically.

10. Save the document as ***color_communication***.

Color Communication	
Color	**Effects**
Black	classic, strong, powerful, mysterious, elegant
Blue	tranquil, peaceful, sad, dependable, cool, constant, quiet
Brown	wholesome, rich, earthy, home-like, stabile, rustic, sheltering
Green	soothing, refreshing, healing, natural, fresh
Neutral	classic, quality, natural, timeless, quiet
Orange	sharp, friendly, vital, hot, energizing, inviting
Pink	happy, sweet, romantic, youthful
Purple	sensual, elegant, eccentric, regal, spiritual, mysterious
Red	sexy, exciting, stimulating, provocative, dynamic
White	pure, bright, innocent, clean
Yellow	harmonious, warming, sunny, splendor, anxious

Activity 2 Color Wheel

1. Using your desktop publishing software, create a default document.

2. Insert a four-column table with nine rows.

3. Insert the title Color Wheel in the top row. Merge the cells and center the text horizontally and vertically. Change the font size to 18 pt.

4. In row 2, column 1, key **Complementary**. Tab to column 2 and key **Yellow/Purple**. (Note that these two colors are directly across from each other on the color wheel. Refer to Figure 12.5.) Tab to column 3. Select the cell and change the fill color to Yellow. Tab to column 4. Select the cell and change the fill color to Purple. Tab to row 3 and continue tabbing until you are in column 2. Key **Green/Red**. Tab, select the cell, and fill with Green. Tab, select the cell, and fill with Red.

Color Wheel			
Complementary	Yellow/Purple		
	Green/Red		

5. Repeat the instructions above for Orange/Blue and Yellow-Green/Violet.

6. In row 6, column 1, key **Analogous**. Tab and key **Yellow/Green**. (These are colors that are found next to each other on the color wheel.) Tab, select the cell, and fill it with Yellow. Tab, select the cell, and fill the cell with Green. Continue these instructions for the following colors: Green/Blue, Blue/Purple, Purple/Orange.

7. Horizontally and vertically center Complementary and Analgous.

8. Vertically center the table. Draw two horizontal guides to use to help in centering the table on the page.

9. Save the document as *color_wheel*.

Activity 3 Color Scheme

1. Using your desktop publishing software, create a flyer advertising a lost dog.

2. Add a title across the top of the flyer. Flyer should contain the *puppy* image from the student data files. Include a text area with a bulleted list of at least six items that describe the dog.

3. Add a text box with the following information keyed: **Last seen on corner of Redmond Blvd. and Richmond Blvd. Contact Javier at (979) 555-0195.**

4. Add a shape at the bottom as an attention-getter. In the shape, key **Reward $50**. This text can be on separate lines if needed.

5. Use at least two different font types. Resize text as needed.

6. Add an earth-tone color scheme to the flyer. Include color changes in text, borders, and at least one fill color. Save the document as **earth_tones**.

7. Change the color scheme of the flyer to cool_blues. Save the document as **cool_blues**.

8. Change the color scheme of the flyer to festive. Save the document as **festive**.

Activity 4 Logos

1. Using your desktop publishing software, create a letter-sized document in landscape orientation.

2. Insert a three-column table with seven rows. In the first row key **Logos**. Center the text and merge the cells.

3. In the second row key **Business Name** [Tab] **Colors** [Tab] **Message**. Center the text horizontally.

4. Choose five businesses' logos. Examine the logo colors and enter the information in the table. What kind of message does this logo send you? Are there any specific emotions the logo evokes in you?

5. Save the document as **logos**.

Activity 5 Movie Review

1. Using your desktop publishing software, create a one-page document.

2. Create a text box and key **Movie Review** in it. Change the font type and font size. Center the text vertically and horizontally. Rotate the text and snap against the left margin. Resize the text box so that it fits from top to bottom.

3. Create three text boxes that are the same size. Write a review of three movies that you have seen recently or that are your favorites. If you can't think of any, go to the Internet and search some of the most recent movies.

4. Key the review in the text boxes with a title for each movie. Check the text for spelling and grammar errors.

5. Add color to each of the movie reviews to enhance the message. For instance, if the movie is a comedy, you may want to create a festive mood with color. Vary the ways in which you add color without overdoing it. Color can be added to text, borders, and as fill color in text boxes or shapes.

6. Save the document as **movie_review**.

1. Use your favorite search engine to search for the following topics: Sir Isaac Newton, Johann Wolfgang Goethe, Johannes Itten, and color meaning.

2. Write an article on each of the above topics that is at least 200 words in length. Save the articles as: **newton**, **goethe**, **itten**, and **meaning**. Keep a resource list in MLA format. Save the resource list as **color_resources**.

3. Read the section in your textbook on Workplace Ethics. Answer the last two questions in that section explaining why you think it is not ethical to use color to manipulate emotions in order to increase sales. Save your written answer as **color_ethics**.

4. Using your desktop publishing software, design a newsletter titled **Color Theory** importing the six documents from instructions 1–3. Use as many pages as necessary.

5. Use the following as a checklist for your final newsletter:

    -   Table of Contents on the first page with use of leader tabs

    -   At least two but no more than three different appropriate fonts

    -   At least one pull quote

    -   At least two images appropriately placed that adds to the message

    -   Use of paragraph formatting for first-line indents, leading, and spaces below paragraph for headings

    -   Footer information on the master page includes page number and date with appropriate tabs

    -   One drop cap following drop cap rules with an appropriate font change

    -   Insertion of special characters as needed

    -   Appropriate use of color in text, borders, and fills

    -   No widows/orphans

    -   No spelling or grammar errors

6. Save the document as **exploring_color**.

Using Color Libraries and Options

Objectives

- *Learn the difference between various color modes available in image software.*

- *Understand the different color options that can be used to change images.*

Introduction

In the previous chapter you learned how to calibrate your monitor and use ICC profiles to ensure that the colors on screen matched those in print. In this chapter you will see what kind of color options are available when using software such as Photoshop or InDesign. When selecting colors, you will be offered a wide variety of choices. This can be quite confusing unless you have an understanding of the differences.

Color Modes

Color mode is the separation of color into channels.

Channels are the division of color modes into separate images.

Colors fall into five basic categories or **color modes**. Each color in a mode is divided into separate **channels** that can be adjusted individually. In Figure 13.1, notice the four CMYK channels that are visible. When the final image is produced, all the channels are combined into a single image. You will learn more about channels in a later chapter.

1. Two colors (black and white)
2. Gray scale (variations of black)
3. RGB (**r**ed-**g**reen-**b**lue)—used on computer screens
4. CMYK (**c**yan-**m**agenta-**y**ellow-**b**lack)—used in print
5. L*A*B (lightness-green/red-blue/yellow)—any device

RGB

RGB colors are based on a scale ranging from 0 to 255, with the higher number representing the purest color. For example, if red and green are set to 0 and blue is set to 255, the result will be a blue as shown in Figure 13.2. Because there are no other colors diluting "blue," this is called a **pure color**. Changing the red and green numbers will alter the blue and create a variation from a pure blue. In the same way, pure red and green are created by assigning 255 to each of the colors and 0 to the other two (as shown in Figure 13.2). As you saw in the previous chapter, this is the method of projecting color that computer monitors use.

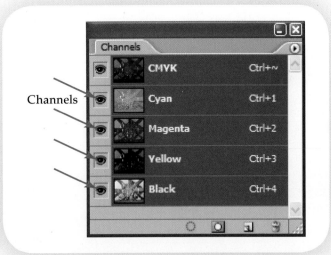

Figure 13.1
Depending upon the color mode in which you are working, an image will be divided into different channels.

Pure colors are those that have a single color component, such as green, without mixing in any other colors.

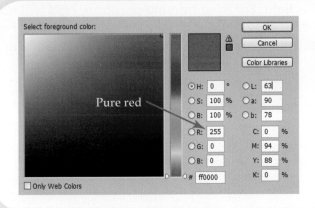 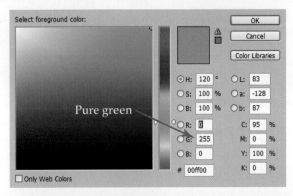

CMYK

CMYK colors are measured as percentages up to 100. If you know that the final product will be in print, selecting the CMYK mode before beginning ensures that the colors you see will match the final output. This step is important because it is possible to create colors in RGB that cannot be matched in CMYK and are out of gamut. In Figure 13.3 the warning icon indicates that the RGB color selected is not printable. Another closely related color will replace it in the printed version.

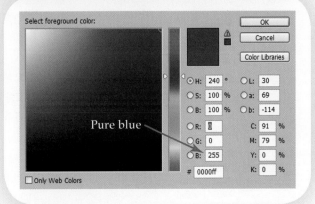

Figure 13.2
Red, green, and blue colors that are set at 255 and zero are called pure colors.

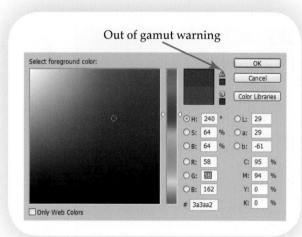

Figure 13.3
The small icon on the color picker is a warning that says "Out of gamut for printing."

CIE-L*A*B

In order to overcome the problem of defining colors, an international company **CIE** (Commission Internationale de l'Eclairage) in 1931 developed a measurement of color based upon the way the human eye perceives color. This is known as CIE-LAB or LAB or **L*A*B**. The color was defined as consisting of lightness or luminosity, and two color ranges. Color "A" was the range of colors from green to red, color "B" was the range of color from blue to yellow. Instead of a color wheel, a triangle is used to describe these color choices.

CIE is an abbreviation for the Commission Internationale de l'Eclairage, a French organization that in 1931 developed measurements for color.

L*A*B is an acronym for the color descriptions developed by the CIE. Often the color is also called CIE-LAB.

HSB is an acronym for hue, saturation, and brightness. Sometimes the "B" is replaced with an "L" for luminescence.

HSB/HSL

Another way to define color is to use hue-saturation-brightness (**HSB**). Hue represents the base color such as blue. Saturation or intensity represents the depth of the base color. Brightness or light determines the amount of white or black added to the base color. In some situations this is also identified as HSL, where "L" is light. For most printing purposes, HSB will not be a concern although it does provide an easy way to change the color. For example, using this mode you can modify the brightness while maintaining the original hue.

Color Picker

The color picker in Photoshop allows you to select any color in a mode and have its corresponding color identified for other modes. This can be helpful if you know the RGB numbers for a particular

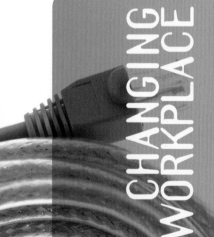

CHANGING WORKPLACE

Understanding how modifications to colors such as hue, saturation, and brilliance affect the image you see is a skill that you carry from your desktop publishing experiences to other situations. For example, modern digital televisions have settings for HSB. Your knowledge of these colors makes it easier for you to adjust a television screen to reflect the actual colors you are seeing. Digital cameras are another area in which an understanding of color settings can make it easier to use the product. You will find that as time goes on, the information and skills that you develop in one area of the workplace will often be useful in other areas. This is particularly true in technology fields such as desktop publishing.

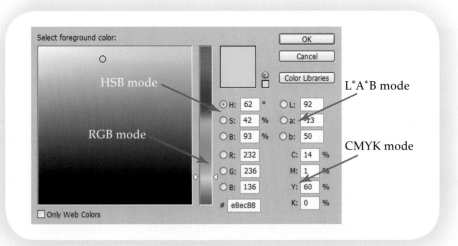

Figure 13.4
The color picker in Adobe Photoshop makes it easy to set colors using any of the modes.

color but want to convert it to CMYK. For example, in Figure 13.4 the RGB color yellow that was selected is (R) 232 (G) 236 (B) 136, but it's 14% cyan, 1% magenta, 60% yellow, and 0% black. L*A*B settings for that color are 92 luminosity, −13 green to red range, and 50 blue to yellow range. The hue is 62, the saturation is 42, and the brightness is 93. Changing any number in the four measurements changes the numbers of the rest.

Color Options

Variations of colors, whether they are viewed on a computer monitor or on a printed page, can be created from any color.

BUSINESS OF PUBLISHING

Screens are a common desktop publishing design tool. Unfortunately, they are also the cause of many printing problems. What looks like a well-designed screen that draws attention to text without obscuring it, in print may become a muddy block of text that is unreadable. The reason this happens is that on screen the gray screen is created using RGB light. In print it is created using CMYK, which is darker. In addition, dot gain, in which ink spreads out on the paper, adds to the dark effect. As a result, it is usually advisable to set screens to a lighter percentage for print than you would only for a monitor.

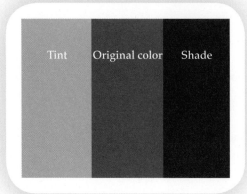

Figure 13.5a
Tints and shades are interesting ways to modify a color without actually changing its basic color.

A **tint** is created when white is added to a color.

A **shade** is created when black is added to a color.

A **screen** is a pale gray background that sets off a body of text from the rest of the page.

PROOFREADING TIPS

It's easy to get carried away with color options that add pizzazz to your page. Unfortunately, not all variations that appear interesting on screen appear as interesting on a printed page. A good proofreading technique is to print a sample of your page using a printer attached to your computer. While the colors and the output may not match exactly, it's a good way to proof a color page. It's helpful if you can compare the output of your personal printer to that of a professional press so you have a good benchmark to use when proofing.

Color Variations

CMYK and RGB colors can be made lighter by adding white. This is called a **tint**. It does not change the color from the original; it merely changes the amount of light.

In the same way, CMYK and RGB colors can be made darker by adding black. This is called a **shade**. It also does not change the color from the original, but merely changes the amount of darkness. In Figure 13.5a the color on the left is a tint of the blue color in the middle. The color on the right is a shade of it.

A **screen** is a light gray background placed behind a body of text to separate it from the rest of the text on the page. This is an excellent design tool that can help draw the eye to a particular passage. Screens are described as percentages of black or tints of black. Figure 13.5b is an example of a 10% screen.

Chapter 1
Getting Started with DTP

INTRODUCTION

You may have noticed that the title of this book, "Digital Desktop Publishing" also includes the phrase "The Business of Technology." These words were chosen carefully to give you a complete idea what you will be studying in this textbook. The word "digital" indicates that you will not be limited to just the study of print. All forms of DTP including that which is used on the Web will be included. The word "business" helps you to understand that the focus will be on business applications rather than the personal use of the technology. Working together, these two phrases give you a clear idea of what you are about to learn.

The term **desktop publishing** describes the process of producing a document using a personal computer. **DTP** software, once called page assembly software, makes it possible to combine both print and graphics on a single page. Once a user creates a desktop publishing document, they can then print a copy using a computer printer, a photocopy machine, or a professional press. DTP also provides the option of creating a digital publication. This allows readers to view a document using a computer monitor rather than a paper copy. DTP requires a wide variety of skills, including an understanding of typography, graphics, layout, and business expectations.

HISTORY

Desktop publishing began even before the introduction of the personal computer. It started with the IBM Selectric™ (1961) and its "golf ball" print head, as shown in Figures 1.1 and 1.2. These allowed users for the first time to change with ease the type style of their text. Before the Selectric™, typewriters were of two types: elite (12 characters per inch) and pica (10 characters per inch). Whatever style your typewriter came with was the style in which you created text. Adding graphics to a document, however, required gluing or waxing the image onto an already typed page.

Macintosh

With the arrival of the Apple Macintosh computer and the ImageWriter printer in 1984, as shown in Figures 1.3 and 1.4, the world of desktop publishing began to change. The Macintosh used a **GUI** (graphical user interface) to simplify the way computers were used. Earlier computers required users to key-in text to access functions. The Mac introduced the use of icons, windows, and menus. Previously only codes built into a document indicated changes in appearance. Now **WYSIWYG** (what you see is what you get) took over in programs such as MacWrite. Suddenly it was possible to choose not only font style but also size and attribute. It was also possible to see those changes on the screen. Graphics could be added digitally to a document in a limited way and

ribbon in the ImageWriter. This made possible the transfer of an image directly to the computer. These early graphics programs were quickly replaced with products such as Corel Draw (1989) and Adobe Photoshop (1990). These newer software programs increased a user's ability to fine-tune artwork and to create renderings that had never been possible in the world of paint and pen.

PageMaker

With the introduction of Aldus **PageMaker** (1985), true digital desktop publishing appeared. With this software, as shown in Figure 1.6, it became easy to move text and graphics around on a page and to create columns with justified text. It did not take long before computers that had originally been used mostly for complex spreadsheet computations became just as important as a means of creating complex digital publications.

OPERATING SYSTEMS

Before moving on to DTP features, it is important to have an understanding of the basic components of your computer. The first place to begin is with the difference between an operating system and the software on your computer. Each provides a different function, but it would be easy to misunderstand these differences. An **operating system** (OS) is the

Figure 13.5b
Screens function somewhat like a callout by drawing attention to a particular body of text.

Patterns

Patterns are created when lines are added to a color to produce variations in colors. Figure 13.6 is an example of colors with patterns.

Gradients

Gradients are created when variations of color are used to create a special effect. Gradients can form a variety of patterns including horizontal, vertical, or radiating from the center. Horizontal or vertical gradients are called **linear**. Those that radiate from the center are called **radial** gradients. Figure 13.7 shows examples of several ways gradient color can be used.

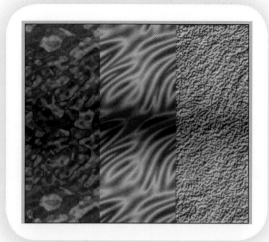

Figure 13.6
Patterns create interesting textures combining color and details as in these three examples. The same color is used for all three, but the patterns are different.

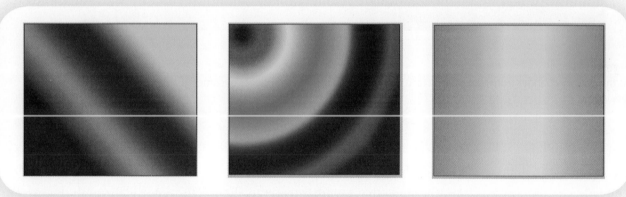

Figure 13.7
Gradients can be created with different colors and designs to produce an interesting color combination.

Opacity

Images and even pages in desktop publishing programs are often created with layers. (You will learn more about layers in later chapters.) Layers are like sheets of paper stacked one on the other. Normally, the top layer covers the bottom layer so that you can only see the part of the bottom layer that is not covered. However, by modifying the opacity, you can change that. **Opacity** is how easy it is to see through an object or color. For example, 100% opacity means that you can only see the image or layer. It is solid in appearance. An opacity setting of 0% makes the image, or layer, invisible. Variations between let you see through to the layer behind with the visible amount determined by the percentage. Figure 13.8 shows examples of an image that is set to four levels of opacity. Notice that the chandelier, which is the bottom layer, becomes less and less visible as the opacity of the yellow top layer increases.

A **pattern** is a series of lines or drawings integrated into color.

A **gradient** is a color technique that spreads variations of color across an image.

A **linear gradient** is a series of colors that are on a vertical or horizontal plane.

A **radial gradient** is a series of colors that spreads out from a central point.

Opacity is the ability to see through one object or layer to another below it.

No opacity

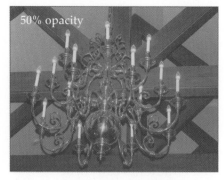
50% opacity

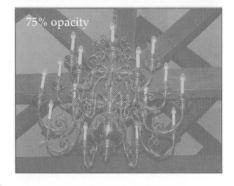
75% opacity

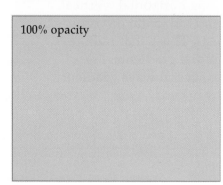
100% opacity

Figure 13.8
As the opacity changes from zero opacity to 100 percent opacity, the chandelier becomes less visible.

Normal
Dissolve

Darken
Multiply
Color Burn
Linear Burn

Lighten
Screen
Color Dodge
Linear Dodge

Overlay
Soft Light
Hard Light
Vivid Light
Linear Light
Pin Light
Hard Mix

Difference
Exclusion

Hue
Saturation
Color
Luminosity

Figure 13.9
Blending options provide you with a series of complex means of combining two layers.

Blending Modes

A **blending mode** is a color technique that combines two layers.

Another way that layers interact to change the color is through the use of **blending modes**. Figure 13.9 shows a list of blending modes available in Adobe Photoshop.

WORKPLACE ETHICS

Be careful when you change an image that has been purchased from a source such as a stock photo shop. Make sure you know what restrictions there are on its use. Some purchase contracts prohibit any changes to the image other than size or resolution. As a result, if you use a special gradient or blend the image with another one, you will be in violation of the contract. It's easy to believe that because you (or your company) paid for it that you can manipulate it in any way that you want. That is not always the case. Just because you have the tools doesn't mean it's legal to use them.

Normal mode is the default in which the top layer obscures the image below it. The other choices use a combination of methods to combine the two layers. For example, Darken compares the top and bottom pixels and displays the darker of the two. Dissolve changes the colors of the bottom layer to match those of the top layer, but only when the opacity is less than 100% (see Figure 13.10). Lower opacity changes more colors. Each blending mode functions in a different way.

When using blending modes, it is important to understand how HSL works. When you select hue, the image is modified so that the hue of the lower layer changes to the hue of the top layer but leaves brightness and saturation alone. Saturation and luminosity blends function in the same way except that the saturation or luminosity of the lower layer changes to the saturation or luminosity of the upper layer. Color blend changes the hue and saturation of the lower layer to the hue and saturation of the upper layer but leaves luminosity alone.

Figure 13.10
In this image the yellow layer dissolves into the chandelier layer, creating an interesting speckled image.

SUMMARY

In this chapter you learned the difference between RGB, CMYK, L*A*B, and HSB. You saw how changing the settings for one mode will affect all the others. You looked at possible variations on color including shades, tints, and patterns. You explored the function of layers with opacity settings and blending modes. Now it is time to learn the different ways that color is handled with print and web pages.

KEY TERMS

blending mode	HSB	pure colors
channels	L*A*B	radial gradient
CIE	linear gradient	screen
color mode	opacity	shade
gradient	pattern	tint

REVIEW

Answer the following questions on your own computer.

1. What is the separation of color into channels called?
2. What are channels?

3. What is the range of the scale that RGB colors are based on?

4. What are pure colors?

5. How are CMYK colors measured?

6. Who developed a measurement of color based upon the way the human eye perceives color?

7. What does HSB stand for?

8. How is a tint created?

9. How is a shade created?

10. What is a screen?

11. How are patterns created?

12. What is the color technique that spreads variations of color across an image called?

13. What is opacity?

14. What does 100% opacity mean?

15. What is a color technique that combines two layers called?

16. What is the default blending mode called?

17. What purpose does the default blending mode serve?

18. How many basic color modes are there?

19. In RGB colors, what does the highest number represent?

20. How is the color of screens described?

DISCUSS

1. Explain why it is important to choose CMYK mode when beginning the project.

2. Discuss the CIE-Lab way of measuring color.

3. Discuss the way of defining color called HSB.

4. Analyze what screens and callouts have in common.

5. Name some of the patterns that gradients can form.

6. Explain how layers work.

7. Identify other choices of blending modes other than the default, and explain how the other blending mode choices work.

8. Explain why it is important to understand how HSL works in blending modes.

9. Explain why the use of screens can cause printing problems.

10. Describe some variations used in patterns that create interesting textures.

APPLY

Activity 1 Screens

1. Research and write a minimum 200-word biography of your favorite actor. Save as **favorite_actor**.

2. Using your desktop publishing software, create a default document. Import the text and place in the middle of the document. Add a title if needed and resize the font to 30 pt., a Modern font, with horizontal centering.

3. Select the text in the article, resize the font to 14 pt. with a font type of Sigvar. Change the first-line indent to 1p6 and the space after the paragraph to 1p0.

4. Add a new layer if possible. On the new layer, add a screen over the text. If needed, change color to CMYK and add a Black screen tinted at 4% over the text.

5. Drag the screen to the bottom layer so that the text is on top.

6. Resize the screen so that there is 0p6 edge around the screen.

7. Save document as **actor_screen**.

Activity 2 Pure Colors

1. Using your desktop publishing software, create a new document.

2. Browse to your student data files and place **color_wheel** in the middle of the document.

3. Draw a text box from left to right margin with a height of 9p. If necessary, change to RGB color mode and apply a pure red fill to the text box. Select the text box, and copy and paste it. Apply a pure green fill to the pasted text box. Drag the green text box down approximately 3p and to the right. Resize the green text box to fit against the right margin.

4. Key **Pure Red and Green** in the green text box. Resize the text to 60 pt. and center horizontally and vertically. Move the red text box to the back if needed.

5. Paste the text box again and apply pure blue to it. Snap the text box to the bottom margin. Copy and paste the green text box from the top to the bottom. Change the text inside to **Pure Blue and Green**.

6. Save document as **pure_colors**.

to the website at
academic.cengage.com/school/dtp

WRITING

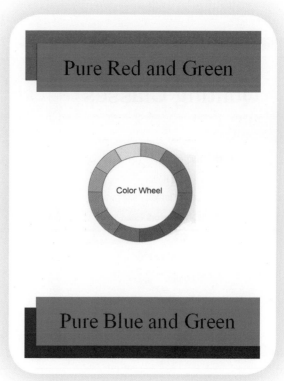

Pure Red and Green

Color Wheel

Pure Blue and Green

Activity 3 Gradients

1. Using your desktop publishing software, create a default document.

2. Draw a text box from left to right margin with a height of 9p. Add a linear gradient with four colors varying from aqua to darker aqua.

3. Key **Buy Now** in the text box. Change the font type to Juice or another font from the Decorative category. Center the text horizontally and vertically and apply a dark blue color to it.

4. Copy and paste the text box. Change the text to **Hot Tub/Spa**. Rotate the text and snap to the left margin, below the first text box. Change the direction of the gradient if possible. Resize the text box to fit the text.

5. Draw a text box below the top text box and even with the side text box. Key **Hot tub/Spa installation** [Enter] **Warranty** [Enter] **Sacrifice at $1,699** [Enter] **Call Ted Smythe** [Enter] **Call (979) 555-0180**. Select the text, change the font size to 36 pt. and center it vertically and horizontally.

6. Place a picture of a spa at the bottom of the ad. Resize the picture appropriately, and center it vertically and horizontally.

7. Save document as **hot_tub_ad**.

Activity 4 Patterns

1. Create a blank default document.

2. Browse to your student data files and import **pattern_1**. Place the image spanning from left to right margin at the top margin to 3p height. Copy and paste the image and snap to the bottom margin.

3. Browse to your student data files and import **pattern_2**. Rotate the image, snap to the left margin and resize as needed. Copy and paste the image, and snap it to the right margin. Adjust as needed to fit within the space.

4. Draw a text box at the top to 9p height. Key **Quilting Classes** in the text box. Select the text, resize to 60 pt., and change the font type to TwizotHmk.

5. Draw a text box that is 3p in height. Fill the text box with a color that picks up a dominant color in the patterns. Drag to place it under the title Quilting Classes.

6. Draw a text box. Key in the text box: **Monday, November 5, 2XXX** [Enter] **6:00 p.m.** [Enter] **Just Quiltin'** [Enter] **2000 Needlework Road** [Enter] **Fabric, TN 30000-0000** [Enter] **(423) 555-0170** [Enter] **$75.00 plus supplies** [Enter] **Just in time for Christmas presents!** Format the text for 24 pt.

7. Save document as **_quilting_patterns_**.

Activity 5 Opacity

1. Using a desktop publishing software, create a blank default document.

2. Draw horizontal and vertical guides dividing the page in thirds, with the zero points set at the top left margin.

3. Browse to your student data files and double click **_flag_** to import the image.

4. Draw a text box. Key **Celebrate Veteran's Day** in the text box. Change the font type to Warnock Pro, the text size to 48 pt., center the text vertically and horizontally. Apply dark blue font color to the font.

5. Copy and paste the text box, and then drag it to the lower third of the document. Replace the text inside the text box with **November 11**.

6. Draw a text box spanning from left to right margin and top to bottom margin. In CMYK mode, fill the text box with pure red. Change the opacity to 40%. Overlay the text box on top of the image and the other text boxes.

7. Save document as **_opacity_celebration_**.

EXPLORE

1. Search the Internet for Adobe Stock Photos. Locate the end user license agreement. Summarize the restrictions in a document saved as **_restrictions_**.

2. Create a new blank desktop publishing document. Create a title with a gradient background titled Adobe Stock Photos. Apply an appropriate color, size, and font type. Center the title vertically and horizontally within the text box.

3. Import the **_restrictions_** document. Use bullets or numbered items to list the restrictions. Adjust the spacing after the paragraphs. Resize the text as needed and place the text box appropriately on the page.

4. On the master page, add a text box at the bottom with Adobe Stock Photos at the left margin and the date at the right margin. Overlay a text box filled with a color that works with the other colors on the page at 30% opacity. This text box should only overlay the footer information. Close the master view.

5. Save document as **_stock_photo_restrictions_**.

14 Distinguishing Print and Web Colors

Objectives

- *Learn what decisions you must make when choosing a print color.*

- *Learn what decisions you need to make when selecting a web color.*

- *Understand the usefulness of a color matching system such as Pantone.*

Adobe RGB 1998 is the working space recommended for use with images that will be printed.

Process color is created by mixing the four basic colors much as an artist would on a palette.

Introduction

Choosing colors is not just about identifying the correct number in a color picker box. Depending upon the purpose of your document, you have other issues to consider. If you are printing a document, the ink that is used to produce CMYK on a professional press requires one set of decisions. If you are going to use the document on the Web, there is another set of concerns.

Print Color

Working Space

Previously, you read about the problems with color space and compatibility between devices. Images that are designed for printing should be assigned a color space of **Adobe RGB 1998**. You should also adjust the color settings in your DTP software to Adobe RGB 1998. This allows you to work in a version of RGB that offers the closest image to the one produced using CMYK inks.

Color Production

Once you have completed a document, there are two ways that color is added to a printed page: process color and spot color. **Process color** uses four colors of ink in different proportions (CMYK) to produce the desired image. The mixing of these four colors approximates the color you want. This is why CMYK colors are labeled as percentages. They tell the press how much of each color to use.

Professional printing is rapidly moving to digital file transfers. This means that a document to be printed is often transmitted using an FTP site or through some other electronic means. Both QuarkXPress and Adobe InDesign are building into their software the means of setting every preference as you design a document. These preferences are then transferred along with the actual file. This speeds up the process for all parties and also helps ensure that fewer mistakes occur. Desktop publishers have to constantly study and read in order to keep up with these changes. Saving your company time and money because you are aware of the latest technology is a true mark of professionalism.

Spot color is a premixed color that is used much like a color you might buy in a paint can.

Color separation is the process of dividing an image into color plates for printing.

Registration is the alignment of printed pages so that a sharp image appears.

Trapping is the slight enlargement of an image on a single plate to allow it to overlap with the image on another plate. This prevents white gaps that might appear as a result of misregistration.

Spot color uses a single ink in the color you choose and applies it to the "spot" you have selected. Spot colors come in a wide variety of premixed colors. If you need a color to look exactly the way you anticipate, spot color is the solution. Use of spot color is a separate printing step that can increase the cost of production, so it is generally only used when black is the only other color present.

Color Separation

To produce a printed color document, a separate printing plate is created for each color (called **color separation**). The process requires each sheet to be printed four times, with a different color applied each time. In the previous chapter, you saw how channels were used to separate each of the colors. Color separation for printing purposes functions in much the same way. In order to produce a sharp image, the page must be carefully aligned each time it is run through the press. This attention to alignment is called **registration**.

Trapping

When a single page is printed with different plates as part of the color separation process, often the images do not register perfectly. The solution to this problem is called **trapping**. Trapping extends the image on a plate so that it is slightly larger than the original. If a gap appears because of an imperfect registration, rather than seeing white, the reader sees a color.

Halftone information

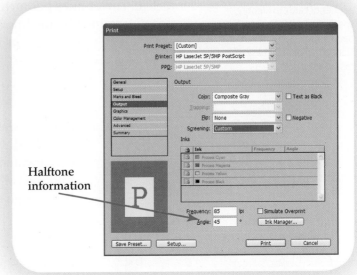

Figure 14.1
The printing option in Adobe InDesign lets the designer set the lines per inch and the angle. This is information provided by your professional printer.

Misregistration, or the failure to print each plate exactly in the same spot on a page, is a problem that has plagued printers since color separation began. Where most people see this problem is in the Sunday comics in the newspapers. Images overlap in such a way that it is sometimes difficult to even see the picture. The overlaps create nearly a 3-D effect. In the days when typesetters and designers did all their work by hand, it was considered a fine art to be able to trap an image to avoid these problems. Today trapping options in software make it much easier. Good trapping techniques, however, are still as much art as they are technology.

Halftone is the process of converting an image to dots for printing.

Line screen is the measurement of the number of lines used to create a printed image. The measurement is given as LPI or lines per inch.

Halftone screen is a means of changing a printed image into dots suitable for printing.

A **swatch** is a color selection that is given a name.

The **Pantone Color Matching System** uses a series of cards to identify specific colors. Each color has been established as a Pantone standard, making it easy to reproduce a color.

Desktop publishing software can be set to trap, but today most printers prefer to use their own trapping software.

Halftones

In order to print an image, **halftone** images are created using a series of dots that are arranged in rows called **line screens**. Line screens are identified as LPI or lines per inch. Different angles are used to fool the eye into believing that the image is a solid mass of color. Depending upon the type of paper and the printer used, different line screens and number of dots per inch are recommended by your professional printer. A line-screen ruling of 150 LPI with small dots creates a high-quality image. A line-screen ruling of 60 LPI to 85 LPI with large dots creates an image that is less crisp and clear. Fewer lines per inch create a coarser image. The size of the dots is also determined by the line screen. Before images were created digitally on screen using pixels or dots to display an image, **halftone screens** were used to break up images into dots.

Swatches

A color **swatch** in Photoshop is a color that has been identified with a particular name. You can create your own swatches and name them, so it is always easy to find the color you want. Learning to use swatches effectively is an essential desktop publishing skill.

Pantone

Pantone is a company that has worked with the printing industry for many years. Their **Pantone Color Matching System** consists of a series of color samples on cards (see Figure 14.2). With these cards, it is easy to select a particular color by name or number. Because

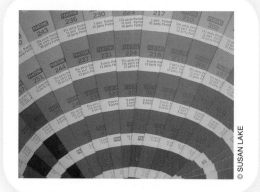

Figure 14.2
Pantone charts or sample cards allow you to select an exact color for use by a printer.

© SUSAN LAKE

different paper produces different results, there are cards for various kinds of papers such as coated and uncoated.

Image editing software such as Adobe Photoshop includes these same colors in its **swatches library**. In swatch libraries specific colors are gathered together as a group and labeled, as shown in Figure 14.3. This group of swatches can then be loaded into your document to ensure that you are using colors that meet your needs. Hovering over a particular color reveals the color's Pantone number, if the view is set to thumbnail, or its name, similar to those shown in Figure 14.4.

A **swatches library** is a collection of swatches gathered into a single library of colors.

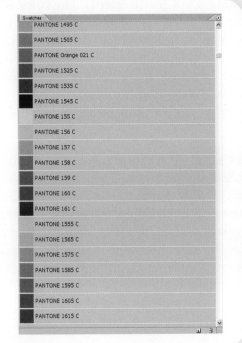

Figure 14.3
The Adobe Photoshop swatches library lists a number of different options from which to choose a spot or process color.

Figure 14.4
Using the Adobe Photoshop swatches library list, you can load specialized Pantone colors arranged by name and number.

When you designate a specific color based upon a Pantone color chart, the printer knows the proportion of C-M-Y-K that will produce that process color or the single ink that matches that spot color. This means that if your company logo uses a specific Pantone blue, it will always appear the same.

Other Color Systems

Pantone is not the only company that produces spot color. As you can see in Adobe Photoshop, there are a variety of swatches preloaded into the library (see Figure 14.3).

PROOFREADING TIPS

One of the most important proofreading issues when using color in a document is ensuring that you have not indicated a spot color when you intended to use a process color. This mistake can cost companies huge expense and sometimes results in the desktop publisher losing a job as well. Spot color is an expensive process because it requires another plate and another run through the press. Several of these mistakes could mean that a print job that should only have required four plates might need a far greater number than that. Fortunately, most professional printers check for this problem before beginning a run. Real desktop publishers, however, check for themselves before sending the file to be printed.

sRGB is the working space recommended for use with images that will be viewed on the Web.

Web-safe colors are the 216 colors that all users can see regardless of their computer displays.

Some of the companies that are included in the Photoshop library are Toyo (Japanese), ANPA (American Newspaper Publishers Association), Trumatch, and HKS (European). Visibone is for web pages. Each color system creates its own colors from scratch, so it is sometimes difficult to match colors from one system to another.

Web Colors

While print documents are produced using CMYK, web documents have a different set of requirements. The color space for web pages is slightly different from the standard RGB. The color space (or range of colors that can be seen) that is used for web pages is **sRGB** because it is the closest color that can be seen on the majority of computer displays. If you are working in a program such as Photoshop, you will want to select that color space instead of Adobe RGB 1998, which is used with print.

Web-Safe Colors

Images are projected using RGB colors, but some computer monitors are not able to display a full range of RGB colors. The most limited computer screen can only display 216 colors. In order to address this problem, a palette of colors designated **web-safe colors** has been developed. Image editing software usually has a feature that automatically limits the color choices to web-safe colors. Figure 14.5 shows a selection of web-safe colors.

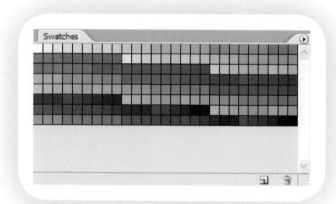

Figure 14.5
Web-safe colors provide a limited palette of colors.

As computer video cards become more powerful and as displays using 24 bit-high color (thousands of colors) and 32 bit-true color (millions of color) become common, the use of safe colors is less of a concern. Unless you know that your audience will be using out-of-date technology, you do not have to limit your colors to those declared web safe.

Named

While RGB colors are identified with numbers from 0–255, web pages are unable to determine colors from that information. One way to identify colors on a web page is to indicate a color name such as "red." Unfortunately, HTML is only able to use 16 color names: aqua, black, blue, fuchsia, gray, green, lime, maroon, navy, olive, purple, red, silver, teal, white, and yellow (and sometimes orange).

Mistakes happen. Even the most diligent desktop publisher is going to publish a document that has an error. If the error is one that could have occurred as the result of a printing problem, it's tempting to blame the printer. Your employer may not know that it was your fault, and you can avoid loss of prestige by placing the blame elsewhere. While this does happen, don't let it happen to you. If you were the one who made the mistake, take responsibility for it. Making ethical decisions is not always easy, but admitting your own mistakes is a place to start.

Hex Colors

Since you do not want to be limited to only 16 colors on a web page, you need to learn how **hex** (hexadecimal) **numbers** are used to provide other color choices. In order to define a web color, each RGB number is converted to a hex number, a numeric system created using base 16 that is written using the symbols 0–9 and A–F. The hex number for a color is created as a triplet in the RGB order. For example, if you have a color that is R-45 G-83 B-205, then R = 2D, G = 53, and B = CD. Combined, the hex number for that color would be #2D53CD. Hex numbers for an RGB combination are supplied by image editing software for any color that you select. Figure 14.6 shows the color this produces.

Hex numbers are hexadecimal numbers derived from base 16 that are used to describe web colors.

Generally, hex numbers are used for colors rather than named colors even if one is available. If you want to see what color a hex number is, you can enter that number in your image editing software to produce that color.

Download Time

Images with many colors in them take longer to display on a web page than those with fewer colors. If you are concerned that your readers might not have a fast connection or might not be patient enough for your page to load, you should consider the number of colors used in your images. Some image editing software such as Corel Paint Shop Pro will count the number

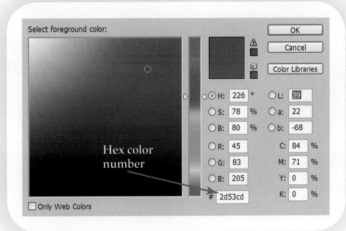

Figure 14.6
Image management programs convert color selections to a hex number for you.

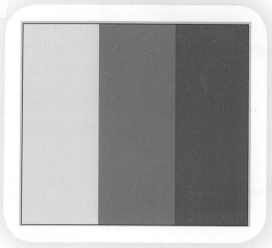

Figure 14.7
These stripes are limited to three colors, which makes them an ideal candidate to be converted to an index color.

Index colors, usually used with GIF files, are colors assigned a number for each pixel.

of colors for you and provide an option to reduce the number of colors. This can be very useful unless you need to reproduce a full-color photograph.

One way to reduce download time is to use GIFs instead of JPGs as images. GIFs use **index colors**, which identify each pixel in an image as one of 256 colors. If there are only a few colors used, the file sizes are much smaller and the time to open on a web page is reduced. Index colors are not appropriate for images with many colors because the file sizes become too large, increasing download time.

Figure 14.7 shows examples of ways to use index colors. The stripes saved as a JPG produce a file that is 68 K. The same image saved as a GIF is only 3 K. This works well in this example because there are only a limited number of colors in the image.

SUMMARY

In this chapter you learned how to set a working space for both print and the Web. You discovered the technique used to create a four-color image in print. You saw how swatches can help you find colors and how a color matching system makes it easier to select the correct color. You read about web-safe colors and when they are appropriate choices. You learned how to name a color for use on a web page using a hex number or a name. And you discovered an option for reducing the size of an image using a GIF file.

KEY TERMS

Adobe RGB 1998

color separation

halftone

halftone screen

hex numbers

index colors

line screen

Pantone Color Matching System

process color

registration

spot color

sRGB

swatch

swatches library

trapping

web-safe colors

Answer the following questions on your own computer.

1. What is the name of the working space recommended for use with images that will be printed?

2. What are the two ways that color is added to a printed page?

3. What is color separation?

4. What is the alignment of pages of print called so that a sharp image appears?

5. What is the process called of converting an image to dots in order to print the image?

6. What is a line screen?

7. Line screens are measured in LPIs. What does LPI stand for?

8. What is an example of an LPI number that would give a high-quality image?

9. Where does a designer get the information to set the lines per inch and the angle for printing?

10. What is a swatch?

11. What is a swatches library?

12. What type of color does Pantone produce?

13. What is the color matching system by Visibone used for?

14. Why is it sometimes difficult to match colors from one system to another?

15. What is the color space that should be chosen when creating web pages?

16. How many web-safe colors are there?

17. How many colors with names (and no numbers) can HTML recognize?

18. What is a hexadecimal number?

19. What are index colors?

20. What is one way to reduce download time for a web page?

DISCUSS

1. Explain the process used in process color.

2. Explain the process used in spot color.

3. Sometimes images do not register properly. Identify the solution to this problem.

4. Analyze the differences in line screens and the result in the printing of an image.

5. Explain the Pantone Color Matching System.

6. It is anticipated that in the future, web-safe colors will become less of a concern. Explain what factors are expected to cause this.

7. Explain the hexadecimal numbering system.

8. Analyze the importance of download time for images on the Web.

9. Discuss the cost difference between using spot and process colors.

10. Describe the change in how documents are transferred for professional printing.

APPLY

to the website at
academic.cengage.com/school/dtp

Activity 1 Swatches

1. Using your desktop publishing software, create a new document that is 24p0 × 24p0 in size.

2. Draw a text box from left to right margin 8p in height.

3. Change the Color Mode to Pantone Pastel Uncoated. Add Pantone 9460 U, Pantone 9441 U, Pantone 9443 U, and Pantone Red 0331 U to the Swatches.

4. Apply Pantone 9443 U to the fill in the text box and a 3 pt. stroke of Pantone Red 0331 U. Draw a smaller text box filled with Pantone 9460 U with a stroke of the same color. Drag the smaller text box in the larger one. Resize as needed. Use shear or skew to change the perspective on the second text box. Key **Free Health Screening** in it.

5. Add a new layer and name it **date**. Draw a text box. In it, key **Trinity Medical, Inc.** [Enter] **9000 Hospital Road** [Enter] **Dothan, AL 36302-0001** [Enter] **(334) 555-0119.** [Enter twice] **November 20, 2XXX** [Enter] **9:00 a.m. – 5 p.m.**

6. Add a new layer and name it **date**. Draw an ellipse filled with Pantone 9460 U with a 3 pt. stroke of Pantone 9460 U. Drag the ellipse over the date and time in the other text box. Resize as needed to fit the text.

7. Change the font size in Free Health Screening to 18 pt. Apply navy blue (C = 100, M = 90, Y = 10, and K = 0) to all text.

8. Save document as **health_screening**.

Activity 2 Hex Colors

1. Using your desktop publishing software, create a blank default document.

2. Import the text file **hex_colors** and place it approximately 2 inches from the bottom margin.

3. Create a new layer named **screens**. Add a black tint at 15% screen over the code in which the color words identify the colors. Add a text box over the hex color numbers with a yellow tint at 27%.

4. Add a text box spanning from left to right margin at 9p height. Fill it with a brown swatch (C = 0, M = 68, Y = 100, K = 44).

5. Key **Color Identification** [Enter] **for Web Pages** in the text box. Change the text size to 48 pt., white, with a Vrinda font type. Center the text horizontally and vertically.

6. Add a 10 pt. White Diamond stroke or other similar stroke in white to the text box.

7. Save document as **web_colors**.

Activity 3 Matching Colors

1. Using your desktop publishing software, create a new blank document.

2. Draw a text box beginning at 8p horizontally and ending at 9p horizontally from left to right margin.

3. Import the image **sun_valley**. Resize the image so that it fits in the space above the text box and spans across horizontally to 9p. This image has three colors in it. Normally, to find these colors so you could match them, you could open it in an image editing software and use the eyedropper tool. This has been done for you, so you will add these colors as swatches: Logo Purple (C = 44, M = 69, Y = 14, K = 0), Logo Yellow (C = 0, M = 19, Y = 89, K = 0), and Logo Green (C = 85, M = 14, Y = 100, K = 2).

4. Create a linear gradient using the three logo colors. In the gradient, add the yellow at the left, green in the middle, and purple at the right.

5. Draw another text box in the space left above the gradient text box. Key **Sun Valley Estates** [Enter] **"Here for Life."** Apply Logo Green to the top line and change the font size to 36 pt., Trebuchet MT font type. Apply Logo Purple to the second line and change

---

Color Identification For Web Pages

```
<!DOCTYPE html PUBLIC "-//W3C//DTD XHTML 1.0 Transitional//EN" "http://www.w3.org/TR/
xhtml1/DTD/xhtml1-transitional.dtd">
<html xmlns="http://www.w3.org/1999/xhtml">
<head>
<meta http-equiv="Content-Type" content="text/html; charset=iso-8859-1" />
<title>Designating Web Page Colors</title>
</head>

<body>
<p>One way to identify colors on a Web page is to indicate a color name such as &quot;red.&quot;
Unfortunately HTML is only able to use sixteen color names: <font color="aqua">aqua</font>, <font
color="black">black</font>, <font color="blue">blue</font>, <font color="fuchsia">fuchsia</font>,
<font color="gray">gray</font>, <font color="green">green</font>, <font color="lime">lime</font>,
<font color="maroon">maroon</font>, <font color="navy">navy</font>, <font color="olive">olive</font>, <font color="purple">purple</font>, <font color="red">red</font>, <font color="silver">silver</font>, <font color="teal">teal</font>, <font color="white">white</font>, and <font
color="yellow">yellow</font>(sometimes <font color="orange">orange</font>). </p>
<p>Since you don't want to be limited to only sixteen colors on a Web page, you need to learn how
hex numbers are used to provide other color choices. In order to define a Web color, each RGB
number is converted to a hex number. This is a numeric system created using base 16. It is written
using the symbols 0-9 and A-F. The hex number for color is created as a triplet in the RGB order.</p>
<p>Examples:</p>
<p><font color="#CC0000">Dark Red </font></p>
<p><font color="#003399">Dark Blue </font></p>
<p><font color="#006600">Dark Green </font></p>
</body>
</html>
```

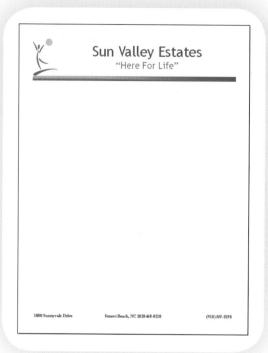

the font size to 24 pt. Bold both lines. Center the lines horizontally and vertically.

6. Draw a 1p text box across the bottom from left to right margin. Set a center tab and right-justified tab at appropriate places. Key **1000 Sunnyvale Drive** [Tab] **Sunset Beach, NC 28468-0120** [Tab] **(910) 555-0198** at the left margin. Apply Logo Green to the text and bold the text. Center the text vertically within the text box. Move the text box as needed to snap to the bottom margin.

7. Lock the position of each of the objects in order for them not to be moved accidentally.

8. Save document as *sunny_letterhead*.

Activity 4 Goldfish

1. Using your desktop publishing software, create a 24p × 24p document.

2. Browse to your student data files and import **goldfish**, placing it from left to right margin and top to bottom margin. If your software has a layers palette, name the layer **goldfish**.

3. Add a new layer named **green overlay**. Draw a text box from left to right margin and top to bottom margin, filling it with green (C = 75, M = 5, Y = 100, and K = 0). Set the opacity at 40%.

4. Add a new layer named **text**. Draw a polygon and key **Goldfish** [Enter] **Available** [Enter] **(902) 555-0140** in it. Change the text to Toledo 18 pt. Apply a yellow color from the small yellow leaf in the corner (C = 2, M = 7, Y = 80, K = 0). Bold the text.

5. Fill the polygon with an orange color from the goldfish (C = 4; M = 60, Y = 66, K = 0). Add a stroke with a green from the leaves (C = 75, M = 5, Y = 100, K = 0). Change the stroke weight to 4 pt.

6. Save document as *goldfish_available*.

Activity 5 Golf Tournament

1. Using your desktop publishing software, create a document.

2. Browse to your student data files and import **golf**. Resize the image from left to right margin at a 9p height.

3. Draw a text box from left to right margin underneath the image. (It will be moved and resized later, so don't worry about its size or placement.) Key **Tournament** in the text box. Fill the text box with black and apply white to the text. Rotate the text box and snap it to the left margin below the golf image. Resize as needed.

4. Draw a text box in the bottom half of the space left. Change the font size to 24 pt. Set a right-aligned dot leader tab at the right margin. Key **Monday** [Tab] **Practice Round** [Enter] **Wednesday** [Tab] **Practice Round** [Enter] [Tab] **Par 3 Contest** [Enter] **Thursday** [Tab] **Competition Round** [Enter] **Friday** [Tab] **Competition Round** [Enter] **Saturday** [Tab] **Competition Round** [Enter] **Sunday** [Tab] **Final Competition Round**. Resize and move the text box to the bottom of the margin.

5. Draw a polygon in the blank area at the top. If possible, adjust the Star Inset of the polygon. Key **December 1–7, 2XXX** [Enter] **8:30 a.m.– 6:30 p.m.** [Enter] **Par 3 Contest at 1:00 p.m.** [Enter] **REGISTER** [Enter] **Call (300) 555-0120** in the polygon:. Fill the polygon with red. Resize Register to 60 pt., Goudy Old Style. Adjust the paragraph spacing after Register to 1p5.

6. Change the stroke to 8 pt. black. Resize the polygon as needed and adjust the placement so it is balanced on the page.

7. Save document as **golf_tournament**.

EXPLORE

1. Using your favorite search engine, read some articles on color. Write three articles of at least 150 words, summarizing your reading. Search for information on some of the following topics. The information should add to what you have already learned in the textbook.

   ➥ What is color?

   ➥ What are color characteristics?

   ➥ What are color attributes?

   ➥ What are the color classifications?

   ➥ What is color harmony?

   ➥ What is color psychology?

2. Save the written articles as **color1**, **color2**, and **color3**. Save the resources as **color_resources**. Be sure the resources are in MLA format.

3. Using your desktop publishing software, design a newsletter using your articles and the resources. Include the following in the newsletter:

   ➥ Addition of Pantone color selections or other swatches added to the file.

   ➥ Designation of process color.

- ⊃ Color theme evident in design.
- ⊃ Table of Contents included on page 1.
- ⊃ Footer with page number and any other relevant information added to the master page.
- ⊃ Heading for newsletter with appropriate font type and size, color, sizing, and placement.
- ⊃ Titles for each of the articles with appropriate font type, size, and color.
- ⊃ Addition of other elements that adds to the message of the newsletter.
- ⊃ Appropriate paragraph formatting in all articles: first-line indent, drop cap, spacing after paragraphs, and no widows/orphans.
- ⊃ Creativity demonstrated in using skills learned in textbook.
- ⊃ No errors in spelling or grammar.

4. Save document as **color_research**.

Independent Project

Banner Color

1. Do research on the Internet to find information about five well-known local, national, or international businesses. Decide what type of newsletter they would use and what type of color communication should be used. Will any of the businesses have a need for serious newsletters and brochures or will they be more entertaining? What colors are normally used in the business logos?

2. Using your desktop publishing software or image editing software, create two banners for each of the five businesses. One of the banners for each business should use CMYK for print and the other should use RGB for the Web using web-safe colors.

3. Use a variety of color techniques such as gradients, patterns, and opacity.

4. Insert both banners into a document using your desktop publishing software.

5. Write a brief article explaining how you determined the colors that would be used.

6. Save as **banner_cmyk1, banner_rgb1, banner_cmyk2, banner_rgb2, banner_cmyk3, banner_rgb3, banner_cmyk4, banner_rgb4, banner_cmyk5, and banner_rgb5**.

Team Project

Newsletter Color

1. In a team of three or four students, plan a cookbook or a newsletter of some of your writings from a class in another discipline such as English, science, or history. The finished document should include:

   ➲ *Title page*

   ➲ *Three sections*

   ➲ *A minimum of six other pages*

2. As a team, create a sketch of the newsletter, including plans to add color to the communication that will create a personality for the document. It should be designed to use as a print document as well as a PDF document to post on the Internet.

3. Once decisions have been made about what articles or recipes to include, each member of the team should create the newsletter. The newsletters do not have to be exactly the same; however, colors used should be similar. Use as many of the color concepts as possible that were learned in Unit 4.

4. Save as ***newsletter_color***.

Digital Portfolio

Self Assessment

1. Select five items from Unit 4 that you intend to add to your portfolio. Write an assessment of what you learned, focusing on color. Include what you learned from creating the content as well as what skills you used in the unit on color.

   ➲ *What caused you the most difficulty?*

   ➲ *What did you enjoy most about completing the activity?*

   ➲ *What would you do differently if you had the opportunity to repeat this activity?*

2. Save your self assessments with the name of the file and **_sa** added to the end of the file name.

Collecting and Organizing Sample Projects

Collect projects and assignments from Unit 4 that you want to include in your portfolio. These assignments do not all need to be your best work. Move the documents to those folders. If available, a copy of the rubric should also be included for each of the projects/assignments that will be included in the portfolio. Back up all files from the portfolio as your plan outlined.

Journalizing Progress

Using word processing software, tablet PC, handheld device, or blog, add to the journal of this ongoing project. Save the journal as **portfolio_journal** or give the link to the blog to your instructor. Alternatively, you could keep an audio journal of your work completed by using podcasting or other digital audio methods. Consult your instructor for the journal method to use for this class.

unit 5

Designing with Images

Career Profile | Graphic Designer—Corporate

What I do every day

I work in the corporate environment as the primary creative services liaison for one of my company's distribution channels. I provide the channel marketing team with strategic design solutions and contribute to the creative brainstorming process as it relates to our corporate goals. I also communicate marketing initiatives to the creative services team and provide design and creative direction to them.

How I use DTP in my job

Using a Macintosh computer with Adobe CS software, I design and produce marketing materials for print, the Web, and CD formats.

The best part of my job

Working with a creative, high-performance team that has a clear direction and an open mind toward new ideas is a rewarding aspect of my position.

The worst part of my job

Not having enough time in the day. There is always plenty to do, so I really need to manage my time effectively and efficiently and communicate regularly with my team regarding priorities in order to accomplish all our objectives.

What I need to be able to do

Learn and be comfortable with the necessary software programs and communicate effectively with all team members. Approach each project with the business objective in mind; it adds value to what I bring to the table as a designer. Produce design solutions instead of focusing on the tangible product that will be created in the end.

How I prepared to be a graphic designer

My path to becoming a graphic designer was very indirect. My major was in business administration with a minor in fine art, and my goal was to work in marketing. After an internship with an ad agency, I decided I wanted to be on the design end of the marketing process. I took a course in Adobe PageMaker and accepted an entry-level graphic design position. My advice is to get as much on-the-job experience as possible while in school through internships, part-time work, or volunteering.

How the Web has impacted this field

The Web has significantly altered the way design is approached. The criteria for creating a web-based promotion is quite different than print, from both a technical and creative standpoint. Print jobs are much more linear from concept to production, while the Web is much more interactive and alive, with the ability to link multiple concepts through a user-guided presentation. Since usability is a huge issue with the Web, the ability to seamlessly integrate design with function is what creates a high-performance site.

15 Modifying Bitmap Graphics

Objectives

- *Understand how to convert an image from one format to another.*

- *Learn to transform an image by cropping, resizing, flipping, and rotating it.*

- *Develop an awareness of the tools available in image editing software.*

- *Learn how layers can be used to modify an image.*

- *Discover how channels can be used for more than color separation.*

- *Practice special techniques with images*

Introduction

One of the desktop publishing tasks you will need to become proficient at is modifying bitmap or raster graphics. Depending upon the complexity of the changes you need to make, you can modify images in your actual desktop publishing software or you may need to use specific image editing software such as Photoshop. In previous chapters you have seen how you can make minor changes using your DTP software. In this chapter you will see how you can make more extensive ones using image editing software.

Paint Programs

Remember that bitmap graphics are made up of a series of pixels that are so small that your eye sees them as a single object. Changing these pixels creates a modified image. Pixels are edited using paint programs.

The paint programs most often used by desktop publishers are Adobe Photoshop, Corel Paint Shop Pro, or Macromedia Fireworks. In addition, Microsoft is developing a series of graphic programs under the name of Expression. Microsoft Expression Graphic Designer can be used to edit bitmaps or raster graphics.

Format Conversion

You may want to convert a bitmap image from one file format to another. This is easily done within a paint program. Merely opening a raster file and then saving it to a new file format will automatically convert it for you. Figure 15.1

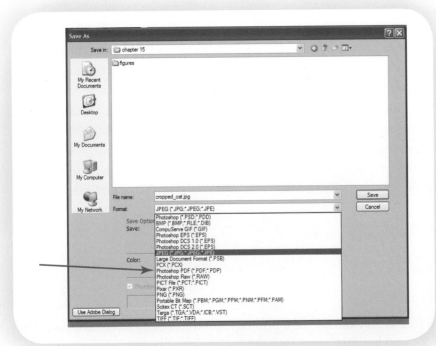

Figure 15.1
Using the drop-down menu under Save As allows you to convert an image from one format to another.

shows you the Save As screen with the drop-down menu for a different format. The most common conversion will be from a JPG to a TIF since TIF files are often used in print.

In an earlier chapter you studied optimization. One type of compression uses a lossless process in which no pixels are deleted. Graphics in a TIF format are saved as a lossless image. Others, such as JPG, use a lossy compression that removes or changes pixels to create a smaller file size. When you convert an image from one format to another, optimization occurs automatically.

Transformations

Images can be modified or **transformed** easily using a variety of actions. You have already seen how you can transform an image in a desktop publishing program. In this chapter you will see that there is more transformation control in an image editing program.

Transformation is the modification of an image using actions such as cropping or flipping.

Cropping

Cropping is the process of removing part of an image. Cropping is one of the most valuable tools a desktop publisher has. Cropping is not just about removing edges that might have a distracting element. Cropping is also about pulling out a single element that can be used in a way not possible if the entire image is selected.

Becoming an expert in image editing software is challenging. While many desktop publishers use the software on a limited basis to make minor changes, often they are not considered professionals. Spending time acquiring the skills to use a program such as Photoshop is one way to be considered a highly desirable desktop publisher. There are courses available at many community colleges, online, and at special seminars. It is well worth your time to begin taking these courses in order to build your skills. Image editing software is not learned quickly. Be patient with yourself and plan on putting in the time it requires to become knowledgeable. You won't regret the decision.

Figure 15.2 is an example of a photograph that needs to be cropped. The socked foot and leg intruding into the picture are distracting. Figure 15.3 demonstrates how cropping was used to eliminate the problem.

Figure 15.2
This image has several problems that can be fixed by cropping.

Figure 15.3
Removing the leg is the first step in making this a useful image.

This image is better, but some problems still exist. The chairs are not attractively arranged. There is a newspaper on the table. In addition, there is no focus point in the room. The poster wants to draw your eye, but the white chairs intrude.

This image is not a total loss, however. There are a number of elements that can be cropped from this image and used in a desktop published brochure advertising this facility in New Orleans. The most

Figure 15.4
The poster on the wall could be used as an ad for this hotel.

Figure 15.5
The white chairs beneath the poster draw attention to the poster.

Figure 15.6
The cabinet cropped from the original photograph contains interesting elements.

obvious is to crop out the poster on the wall, as shown in Figure 15.4. An option that results in an interesting combination is leaving the chairs with the poster (see Figure 15.5). The glassed display case, shown in Figure 15.6, can also be used. The table, lamp, and plant arrangement in Figure 15.7 makes another nice image.

With nothing but the cropping tool, you have created three or four useful images from one that might have been discarded. One of the added benefits of using this technique is that all the images have the same lighting, resolution, and "feel" since they came from the same source.

Resizing

Resizing is easy to do. You can resize within a desktop publishing program, but it is better to resize in an image editing program such as Photoshop. By saving within an image management program, you will reduce the file size of your image and, therefore, of the final document. You may need to make minor size adjustments once the image is placed in a document. Resizing is also called scaling since you scale the size up or down.

Keep in mind that while resizing, you want to maintain the proportions of your image. Images that are resized without maintaining the ratio of height to width take on a distracting and unnatural look. This distortion is one of the surest signs of a novice designer.

Figure 15.7
The plant and table cropped from the photograph provide a sense of warmth missing from the original image.

It is tempting to want to squeeze an image slightly to make it fit into an open spot on a page. Compare Figure 15.8 to Figure 15.9. In the second image, the distortion caused by improper resizing is immediately apparent. In Figure 15.10, however, the resizing is not as noticeable to the untutored eye. As a matter of fact, the woman in the picture probably would be delighted at the thinner image. While you may think you can get away with this much change, it is still a distorted image and should be avoided.

Figure 15.8
The original image of the young woman may not fit where you want it placed and may require resizing.

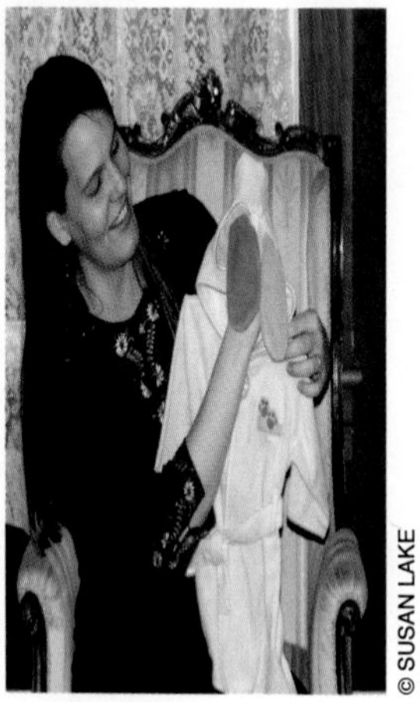

Figure 15.9
This image has been resized without maintaining the ratio of height to width. The result is jarring to the reader.

Figure 15.10
This image is also nonproportional, which is noticeable when observing the image carefully.

CHANGING WORKPLACE

Originally all photographs included in a print document were converted to halftones using a series of dots to produce image using ink. Generally the original photographs were printed from 35 mm film. In just the last few years this has changed dramatically. The megapixel cameras now on the market have made it possible to work with digital images that can be imported directly into a document. Even magazines that once would not have considered anything but an actual print are beginning to move to digital. As digital cameras continue to improve, the last holdouts will convert from film to digital images. Soon film cameras will go away just as typewriters have been replaced by computers. Striking changes such as this may not seem significant, but the lesson to be learned is important. As technology continues to evolve, there will be other changes that are just as dramatic. Desktop publishing is a field that requires you to be constantly aware of new equipment and new techniques.

Flipping

Flipping an image vertically or horizontally is an option. Flipping is particularly useful when working with images of people. Generally it is best if a person's eyes are focused into a page rather than away from it. Notice in Figure 15.11 that the baby's eyes pull you away from the information in the ad. In Figure 15.12, the baby's eyes are facing into the page and the focus is now inward as well. One concern to be aware of is that the

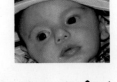

Figure 15.11
This ad has a problem. The baby's eyes draw the reader outward instead of into the page.

Figure 15.12
Flipping the image of the baby horizontally makes for a much more effective ad.

human face is not exactly the same on both sides. If you flip a face so that it is reversed as in a mirror, the face may appear slightly different.

Rotating

Photographs that have been shot horizontally rather than vertically need to be rotated before they can be used, which is easy to do and easy to see. This is more important, but less easy to see, when an image has been photographed slightly tilted. Figure 15.13 is an image that needs to be rotated 90 degrees clockwise to produce a vertical image. Figure 15.14 shows the result, but notice

Figure 15.13
Images are often photographed in such a way that they must be rotated before they can be used.

Figure 15.14
Rotating this image still leaves the designer with a problem; it is not straight.

Figure 15.15
Fine rotation adjustments can be made to an image, resulting in vertical or horizontal lines that are non-jarring to the reader.

that the vertical lines behind the bed are slanted, creating an awkward effect. This image needs to be rotated incrementally. Notice the difference in Figure 15.15 where a 7 degree rotation was used to straighten the image. The distracting white blanket was also cropped out of the photo.

Tools

Desktop publishing software has several painting tools that allow you to create your own images from within the software. These are limited in nature, but they can be used quite effectively.

Eyedropper

The Eyedropper tool makes picking up a specific color to reuse in another way quite simple. The eyedropper changes the foreground color to the one selected. Once the foreground color is modified, you can then use the color information to determine the RGB or CMYK settings for that color.

Lines

A **rule** is a term used by desktop publishers to describe horizontal or vertical lines used as dividers.

Lines are an essential tool in desktop publishing. Straight lines are generally called **rules** and are used to separate features within a page. Rules can be various sizes, usually measured in points. They can be different colors. Rules can consist of more than one line, similar to the one shown in

Figure 15.16. A **hairline** is the thinnest rule available in both your desktop publishing and image management software. Holding down the Shift key as you draw a rule will **constrain** it to a straight angle.

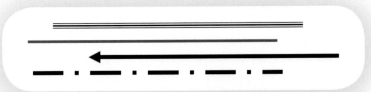

A **hairline** is a very fine rule.

Constraining is the process of using the Shift key to draw lines so that they are straight or to draw shapes so they are squares or perfect circles.

A **stroke** is the border of a shape or a letter.

A **fill** is the interior of a shape or a letter.

Figure 15.16
Rules can be added in desktop publishing software, or they can be created in image editing software. No matter how they are created, they can be an important design feature.

Shapes

Rectangles, ellipses, and polygons can be created using the DTP software. Squares can be created holding down the Shift key as you draw a rectangle. Perfect circles are produced by holding down the Shift key as you create an ellipse. The lines used to create the borders of these shapes are usually called **strokes**. The area inside the shape is called a **fill**. Figure 15.17 contains a rectangle with a wide stroke and a pattern fill.

Image editing programs generally have a feature that allows you to select simple predesigned figures such as arrows, hearts, or musical notes. Corel Paint Shop Pro has a series of images grouped together called picture tubes that can also add interest.

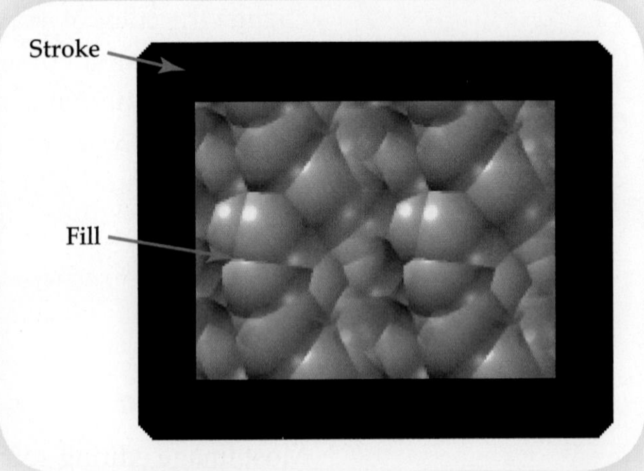

Brushes

There are a wide variety of brushes, shapes, and dynamics available in image editing software. These can be used to create images, but they can also be used to enhance the look of an image that has already been created. An example of the way a brush can be used to modify an image is shown in Figure 15.18. Compare the two figures. A small white brush with a minimum opacity level was painted over the teeth of the person in the second image, brightening them. Countless techniques such as this are used every day by image editing experts.

Stroke

Fill

Figure 15.17
Strokes are the borders around a shape, and fill is the color within the shape.

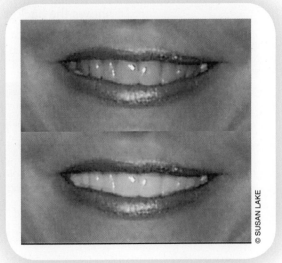

Figure 15.18
Brushes can be used to draw objects, but they can also be used for other purposes. A slightly opaque brush was used to whiten the teeth in this image.

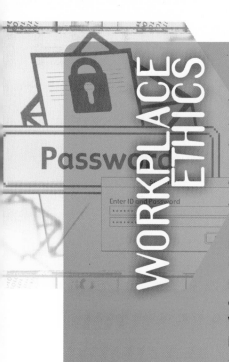

WORKPLACE ETHICS

With the growth of digital image usage have come frequent scandals about news photographs that have been "doctored" or changed. Sometimes these changes are designed to fool the public. Other times the photographs are changed to improve the image of the person in the photo. For example, an actress might have wrinkles removed or her body slimmed in places. Changing photographs to intentionally mislead an audience is completely unethical. No desktop publisher or photographer should be willing to participate in such an action.

The predicament you face comes when images are changed for other purposes. Few people would object to red eye being removed from an image. Even removing a slight blemish from a face is excusable. From that point on, you will have to make your own judgments. Is it acceptable to change the color of a car in order to make it more attractive for an ad? What are the ethics of removing a person from a group image because they haven't given permission to use the image while the others have? What about extracting a person's image from one location and placing them in another background? Designers face all these questions and many more every day.

Magic Wand

Most image editing software has a tool similar to a magic wand. With this tool you can select an area that has similar colors. Once the area is selected, you can delete or modify it with ease. This provides one way of deleting a background, thus helping an image to stand out. Notice in Figure 15.19 that the background can be selected with a few simple clicks. Figure 15.20 shows the background erased.

Figure 15.19
Tools such as Photoshop's magic wand make it easy to select areas of similar colors.

Figure 15.20
Once the background of this image was selected, it was deleted, allowing the image to float in its own background.

Healing Brush Tool

One brush that is particularly useful is the Healing Brush tool. With this tool, small imperfections that might be unwelcome in an image you want to use can be erased. Notice in Figure 15.21 the small blemish on the girl's forehead. Using the Healing Brush tool, it was quickly removed.

Red Eye Removal

Another commonly used tool removes the red eye caused by a camera's flash. It focuses specifically on the red in an eye and replaces it with a more natural color. Figures 15.22 and 15.23 demonstrate how red eye problems are not limited to humans.

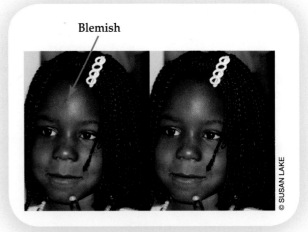

Blemish

Figure 15.21
The Healing Brush tool makes it possible to remove blemishes without disturbing the rest of the image.

Figure 15.22
Red eye is a frequent problem when a camera with a flash is used.

Figure 15.23
Image editing software includes tools that make red eye removal easy.

PROOFREADING TIPS

Proofreading images requires you to carefully scrutinize the images you plan to use. Look for images that are slightly tilted. Pay attention to distracting elements that might be at the side or edge. Watch for red eye. Make sure that the eyes of people in a photo are facing inward. Make sure that if you flip an image, it doesn't change the way the actual image looks. Check images that have been resized to make sure that they have been scaled proportionally. These and other details require you to pay close attention to any photographs or other images you use.

Layers

The use of layers is one of the techniques that provide you with considerable control of your images. Using layers on top of an image allows you to make changes without modifying the original figure. You learned in an earlier chapter that modifying an image without actually changing it is called nondestructive editing. This allows you to experiment as much as you need without worrying about losing your original.

An **adjustment layer** is a special layer that allows you to modify image adjustments such as levels and contrast.

A **fill layer** provides you with a nondestructive layer that can be filled with any color you want.

Flatten is the process of merging all the layers into one.

There are several different kinds of layers in image editing software. The most obvious is an empty layer onto which you can add elements. In addition, you can create a layer that duplicates another layer. An **adjustment layer** allows you to make a wide variety of changes in that layer such as curves, levels, and color balance. A **fill layer** places a color or gradient over the image below. Changes to any of these layers creates changes in the visible image, but in a nondestructive manner.

As a final step you will generally want to **flatten** all your layers to reduce the file size.

Opacity

Opacity is a feature often used in image editing programs to fine-tune changes. A layer can be assigned its own opacity, allowing you to make fine changes. In Figure 15.24 a pink layer to match the pink of the dress was overlaid on the original image. Since the pink layer was placed on top of the image, initially you would see a solid pink image. The opacity of the pink layer was changed to 20 percent and therefore only placed a slight pink enhancement to the image.

Figure 15.24
A layer set to a low opacity level allows a color or an image to merge to the layer below it.

Dropped Shadows

Dropped shadows are one of the most common techniques used to enhance images and can be created in image editing or desktop publishing software. The shadows that are formed create a three-dimensional effect, giving depth to an image. The angle of the light and the amount of shadow can be adjusted as needed. With a DTP program, you can only shadow an entire image. An image editing program allows you to select specific elements within an image to add shadows to.

In Photoshop, dropped shadows are attached to the layer in which the image is placed. In Figure 15.25 a text layer with a drop shadow was added to the image.

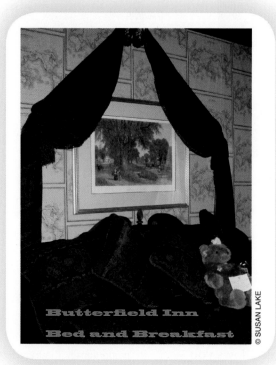

Figure 15.25
Using a drop shadow makes the text on this image appear to be floating over the image.

Combining Images

One important use for layers is the ability to combine several images to create a collage. Each image is placed on a separate layer, allowing you to move them around until they are placed exactly as you want. Figure 15.26 duplicates two images to create an interesting single image.

Channels

You have already seen how channels are used to divide an image into the RGB or CMYK colors that make up the image. Channels are also used to create **masks**. A mask is a means of selecting an area within an image that you do not want affected by any changes you make. Creating a mask requires placing a layer over the original image and then covering or masking parts of the image.

To understand a mask, imagine an image such as that seen in Figure 15.27. Place over that image a piece of film that has a section cut away similar to

Figure 15.26
Combining one or more images is an excellent way to create the exact picture you need.

Mask

Figure 15.27
This image is waiting for an area to be selected.

Figure 15.28
A mask has been created around the cat so that just the cat will be selected.

Figure 15.28. The area outside the cutaway is the mask. The area that is visible through the cutout is the selection.

A mask is created using a special **alpha channel**. This channel is nondestructive and can be used as a means of selecting specific parts of an image in order to work with just that part. This process, however, provides you with far more control of your image. Using an alpha

A **mask** is a means of covering an area within a graphic to prevent it from being selected.

An **alpha channel** is a special channel used to store masks. Other channels separate the RGB or CMYK colors that make up an image.

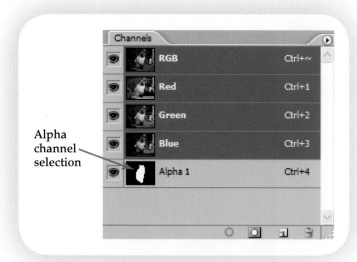

Figure 15.29
Photoshop provides a thumbnail of the mask so that you can see what area has been selected.

Alpha channel selection

A **quick mask** serves the same purpose as a standard mask except it does not save the alpha channel for future work.

A **vignette** is a fuzzy border around an image.

channel allows you to select an area and then go back and add to or subtract from that selection area.

When you are working in the alpha channel, a red tint indicates the area that is not selected or is masked. The original color indicates the selected area. To remove the red tint, paint with a white paintbrush to unmask the area. To add the tint, paint with a black paintbrush to mask or deselect an area.

The completed mask is then loaded onto the original channels. You can then make changes by applying a single action to the selected area. For example, a mask could be used to blur a selected area or change its contrast.

Masks fall into two categories: quick and alpha. A **quick mask** gives you the same control that an alpha channel does, but it does not save the channel information for future use.

The black and white image in Figure 15.29 is the cutout that can be seen in the alpha channel. Notice that if you superimposed the black and white image over the ruby-tinted cat, it is the only part of the image with color visible.

Techniques

There are many other techniques that you can use to enhance or change an image.

Fuzzy edge

© SUSAN LAKE

Figure 15.30
A vignette makes for an interesting image with the fuzzy outline.

Feathering

In an earlier chapter you saw how feathering slightly blurred the edges of an image. Feathering can be used to create a **vignette** (pronounced vĭn-yĕt), which is a photograph similar to the one shown in Figure 15.30. The edges fade out slowly. This technique is one frequently favored by desktop publishers.

Filters

Filters are useful for enhancing the look of an image. Sometimes you may want to slightly blur your image using a Gaussian blur filter. You may want to sharpen the details using the unsharp mask filter. You may want to create an image of a painting using a brush stroke filter. Images can be **sheared** or angled to give an interesting effect. The term **skewing** is sometimes used instead of shearing. The possibilities are endless.

Shearing/skewing is the process of twisting an image.

Figure 15.31 uses shearing to add the impression of movement in the pond. Figure 15.32 converts the pixels to a watercolor effect. A sponge filter is used for Figure 15.33. Figure 15.34 converts the colored image to a

Figure 15.31
Shearing requires careful consideration since it distorts the image. In this case, the shearing adds motion to the image.

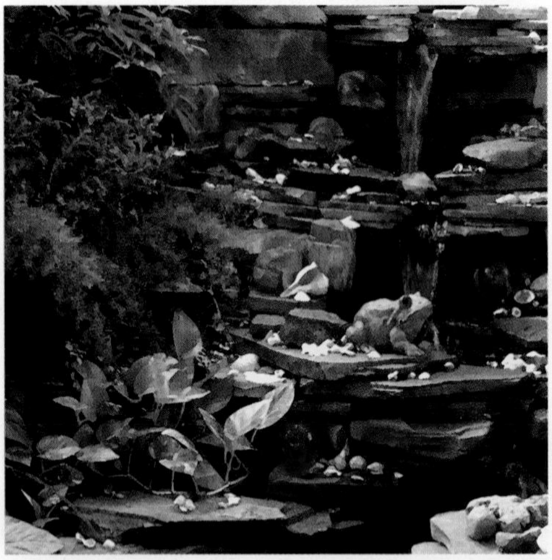

Figure 15.32
Special filters such as this watercolor modify an image to produce a photograph that you could not create yourself.

Figure 15.33
The sponge filter softens the lines of this image, making the rocks less harsh.

Figure 15.34
The graphic pen filter removes the color from image and converts it to a pen and ink drawing.

pen and ink drawing. The liquefy technique is used to change the water to a more liquid state in Figure 15.35.

Lining Up

The moving of images on a document page is a common practice. You have already done that in a number of exercises. An important technique to remember when lining up the faces of people is to always arrange the figures so that the eyes are on a horizontal line.

In Figure 15.36, four family photos have been moved into a line. Two of the photos are similar in size. One is much smaller, while one is much longer. More importantly, the eyes are all at different levels. Figure 15.37 shows the images lined up with a horizontal blue line used as a means of measuring eye height. In addition, the figures have been rearranged so that all the

Figure 15.35
Liquefying the water falling from the stones creates a special feeling without distorting the original image.

Figure 15.36
Desktop publishers often are given mug shots or face shots to place together on a page.

Figure 15.37
Lining up a series of mug shots requires making sure that the eyes are on the same level.

images face inward. The smaller image has been enlarged proportionally to match more closely the size of the other three family members. Figure 15.38 shows the final image. The last step was to crop the images so that they were all of the same height. Notice that cropping can often be done more closely than you expect without distorting the image's effectiveness.

© SUSAN LAKE

Figure 15.38
Cropping and rearranging the images creates a series of faces that appear cohesive.

Drawing Tablets

Drawing tablets are exquisite tools to use whenever you must work with images. The ability to do fine work is greatly enhanced. The specialized tools that are incorporated in a tablet's software can speed up the production of any project. Drawing tablets come in different sizes and with different features. The one that works best for you will depend upon your work environment. A tablet usually consists of a specialized mouse, a stylus, and a responsive pad on which you can use the stylus or the mouse (see Figure 15.39). The stylus is designed to be pressure sensitive so that you can increase or decrease the size of some tools as you use them.

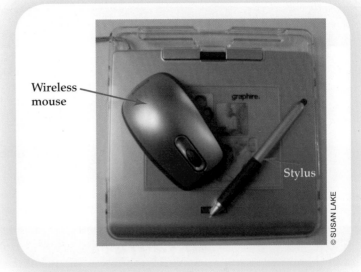

Wireless mouse

Stylus

© SUSAN LAKE

Figure 15.39
A tablet such as this Wacom Graphire4 is a tool that lets you modify images with ease.

Web Images

Learning to modify a bitmap or a raster graphic is just as important when designing web documents as print ones. The same skills are used, but you must be far more aware of the file sizes of your images. Other than that, the transformation techniques, image editing tools, layering, and channel knowledge that you have learned here will transfer completely to a computer screen. One tool that is available specifically for web usage allows you to slice an image into a series of parts. This slicing allows you to upload an image quickly onto a web page because each part is sent separately.

SUMMARY

In this chapter you learned how paint programs can be used to create images for your desktop publishing documents. You learned how to convert from one file format to another. You saw how transformations can be used to crop, rotate, resize, and flip an image. You saw how tools such as the eyedropper, healing brush, and red eye remover can be used to enhance an image. You read about using layers, including ways to add a drop shadow to a specific part of an image. You learned techniques such as feathering, filters, and mug shots. In addition, you saw that a drawing tablet can be a useful addition to a desktop publishing program.

KEY TERMS

adjustment layer	flatten	shearing
alpha channel	hairline	skewing
constraining	mask	stroke
fill	quick mask	transformation
fill layer	rule	vignette

REVIEW

Answer the following questions on your own computer.

1. What programs are used to edit pixels?
2. What type of image files are often used to print?
3. In image editing, what is transformation?
4. What is the process of removing part of an image called?
5. What is another term used for resizing?
6. What is meant by resizing an image proportionately?
7. What is the Eyedropper tool used for?
8. What is a rule?
9. What is the name of the thinnest rule available in your desktop publishing or image editing software?
10. What is constraining?
11. What is the border of a shape or letter called?
12. What is the interior of a shape or letter called?

13. What is the purpose of the healing brush?

14. What is the process of merging all the layers into one called?

15. What is a mask?

16. What is an alpha channel?

17. What is a quick mask?

18. What is a vignette?

19. What is the process of twisting an image called?

20. When working with images, what device can greatly enhance and speed up your work?

DISCUSS

1. Explain the process of converting a bitmap image from one file format to another.

2. Discuss the difference between a TIF file format and a JPG format.

3. Describe some ways that cropping can be used to improve an image.

4. Explain why it is better to resize an image in an image editing software rather than in desktop publishing software.

5. Discuss flipping an image of a person. Include why and how to flip images.

6. Explain how to create a perfect circle or square.

7. Describe the use of the Magic Wand tool.

8. Discuss the different type of layers used in images and their uses.

9. Explain ways in which the use of drop shadows can enhance an image as well as the value of creating drop shadows in an image editing program.

10. Describe the use of channels and masks and how one relates to the other.

APPLY

Activity 1 Cropping

1. From your student data files, open *lighthouse* in your image editing software.

2. Use the Crop tool to create three different images from the one image. Save as *image1*, *image2*, and *image3*. The images can be varying sizes.

3. Open *lighthouse* again and save as *lighthouse* with the file type JPG.

go to the website at
academic.cengage.com/school/dtp

Activity 2 Rotating

1. From your student data files, open **squirrel** in your image editing software.

2. Rotate the squirrel image 90 degrees clockwise.

3. Resize the image to half the width, keeping the proportion.

4. Save the document as **rotated_squirrel**.

5. Rotate the squirrel again at 45 degrees clockwise. Save as **arbitrary_squirrel**.

Activity 3 Tools and Layers

1. From your student data files, open **aggie_bonnets** in your image editing software.

2. Crop the image so that most of the green does not show and the image focuses on the flowers.

3. Use the Eyedropper tool to pick up three colors from the flower. Write the CMYK numbers down for the three colors. Pick up colors that are light, medium, and dark from the colors in the flowers.

4. Add new layers for each of the elements you add to the image. Draw a perfect circle and place it on the image. Draw two more perfect circles that are each getting smaller in size. Color each one of them a different color from the colors you picked up with the Eyedropper tool. Draw a rectangle. Use the Text tool and key **Aggie Bonnets** in the rectangle. Change the font type and size appropriately. Center the text horizontally in the rectangle. Apply the light and dark color to the text and rectangle.

© KAREN BEAN

5. Use the magic wand to remove the fence from the image.

6. Use the Clone Stamp tool or other available tools to add greenery and flowers to the removed fence area.

7. Save the document as **aggie_bonnets_edited**.

Activity 4 Mask Mode

1. From your student data files, open **bluebonnets** in your image editing software.

2. Draw an Elliptical selection around the house. In a Mask mode, apply a Gaussian Blur with a radius of 25 or use another similar filter if that one is not available. Exit the Mask mode or return to Standard mode.

3. Invert your selection and fill with white. Press the Delete key.

4. Crop the image so that the house is centered.

5. Save the document as **masked_house**.

Activity 5 Creative Story

1. Using your desktop publishing software, write a creative story using the images created in Activities 1–4.

2. Place all the images in your scratch area so that you can see them. Write the story either using story editor, a word processing software, or directly into a text box. The story should contain a minimum of 200 words.

3. Decide on a title for your story and create a text box with a title. Apply appropriate colors and font type, size, and style.

4. Place the images in appropriate places with appropriate sizes in the story.

5. Proofread and spell check the story.

6. Save the document as **creative_story**.

EXPLORE

1. Using your favorite search engine, search for information on bitmap or raster graphics or images.

2. Write a 200-word report from your research. Save the report as **bitmap_graphics**. Include the resources in MLA format in a file saved as **resources_bitmap_graphics**.

3. Using your desktop publishing software, import the files into a two-column document. Add a title and at least two images that have been modified using techniques learned in this chapter. Include the images before they were modified as well as after modifying for a total of four images in the document. Do not include resizing as part of modifying. Resize any image before placing it in the document.

4. Add a short article to the document explaining what you did to the two images and why you chose to modify them in that way.

5. Keep in mind and use any desktop publishing techniques such as design priniciples, typography, and color that you have learned prior to this chapter.

6. Proofread and spell check the document.

7. Save the document as **rg_research**.

16 Incorporating Vector Graphics

Objectives

- *Develop an understanding of how vector images are created.*

- *Learn about tool options available in vector editing software.*

- *Learn about functions such as tracing found in vector software.*

- *Discover how clip art can be used creatively.*

Introduction

You learned in the previous chapter how to use bitmap or raster graphics to edit images for your desktop publishing projects. In this chapter you will see how vector graphics can be just as important as part of the design process.

Draw Program

Remember that vector graphics are made up of a series of lines or arcs that are defined mathematically. Changing the size of the lines or arcs modifies the image. It is important to be aware that if you need to make a complete image smaller or larger, all the lines and arcs must be selected before the transformation takes place. For those who are used to working in bitmaps, this requires a change in mindset.

Vectors are edited using drawing programs such as Adobe Illustrator. Other programs such as Adobe Photoshop and Corel Paint Shop Pro incorporate some vectors into images, but they are primarily bitmap software. Microsoft Expression Graphic Designer allows you to work in either a bitmap or a vector layer with all the features available to each.

Illustrations

Before we learn to use the tools and techniques that are possible with a vector drawing program, we will look at an example to see how vectors differ from bitmaps.

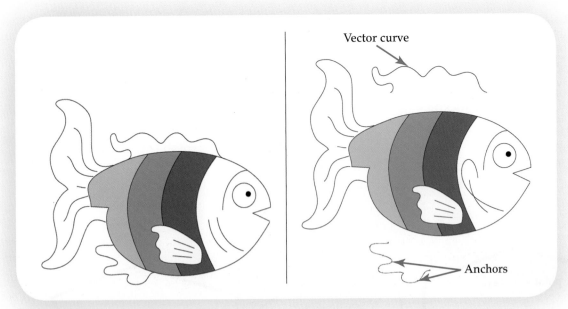

Figure 16.1
Vector images may appear similar to bitmap ones, but they are actually created with lines and curves rather than pixels.

Figure 16.2
Vector images allow you to modify separate parts without disturbing the sections adjacent to the parts.

Figure 16.1 appears to be a graphic much like the ones you worked with in the previous chapter. In Figure 16.2, notice that the fins have been moved away from the body of the fish. These "fins" are actually a series of curves that can be moved independently of the rest of the image.

Paths

Vector lines or curves are called **paths**. A path consists of one or more lines or arcs. Notice the bottom fins show a series of dots. These are points or **anchors** that can be adjusted to change the shape of the path. The beginning and end of each path has an anchor point called an **end point**.

A **path** is the term used for the lines or curves created in vector graphics.

An **anchor** is a point along a line or a curve that can be used to change the shape of a vector.

An **end point** is an anchor that appears at the start and end of a path.

BUSINESS OF PUBLISHING

One of the most common uses of a program such as Adobe Illustrator is in the creation of ads. In the publishing world, most camera-ready ads are Illustrator files that incorporate both vectors and bitmaps. Camera ready means that the desktop publisher has no work that must be done on the ad. It can be placed in a document just as it is. The ability to develop camera-ready artwork is important for many businesses. It provides the business with more control over the image and can greatly reduce the cost of an ad. Time is also saved because it's not necessary to have the ad created and then submitted for approval. Often one of the tasks assigned to an in-house desktop publisher is the creation of camera-ready ads for use in professional publications.

A **corner point** is an anchor at a point that changes direction along a path.

A **smooth point** is an anchor along a curve.

A **direction line** is a line that appears when a smooth point is selected. The line is used to adjust the shape or angle of a curved vector.

At places along the path where the angle changes, a **corner point** appears (see Figure 16.3). **Smooth points** are anchors along the curve of a path.

A path can be open, as in a straight line, or closed as in a circle. Paths that are curved can be changed using **direction lines** as shown in Figure 16.4. Paths that are lines are changed by moving the end points as shown in Figure 16.5.

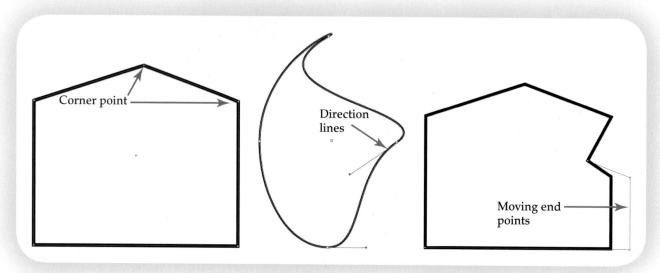

Figure 16.3
Corners are points that change directions along a vector path.

Figure 16.4
Direction lines allow you to change the shape of vector curves.

Figure 16.5
Changing the shape of a path can be done easily using anchors and end points.

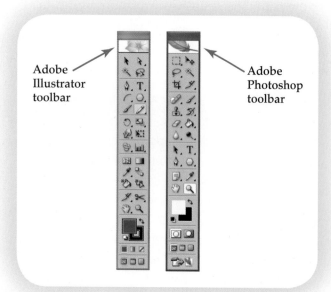

Figure 16.6
Adobe Illustrator (vector software) and Adobe Photoshop (bitmap software) have toolbars that appear similar.

Tools

There are a wide variety of tools available to use with vector drawings. Many of these are similar to those you have seen in painting programs such as the selection tool, paintbrush, and eyedropper. Figure 16.6 lets you compare the toolbars available in Illustrator and Photoshop.

Shapes

Even though the Shapes tool seems identical to the one you have seen in painting programs, it does not produce the same result. One shape creates a vector and the other creates a bitmap shape. For example, Figure 16.7 shows two polygons. The one on the left is a vector version. The one on the right was created as a bitmap. Other than the anchors at each point, both of them appear the same. If you look at a close-up in Figure 16.8, you will see that the bitmap polygon has a series of jagged edges. In Figure 16.9 the bitmap one is smooth. If you are printing from the vector image, you will get a sharper edge and a smoother image. No matter how much you enlarge the vector image, no jagged edges will ever appear.

Figure 16.7
Both polygons appear on screen to be identical, but they are not.

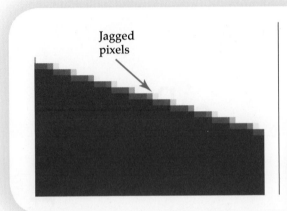

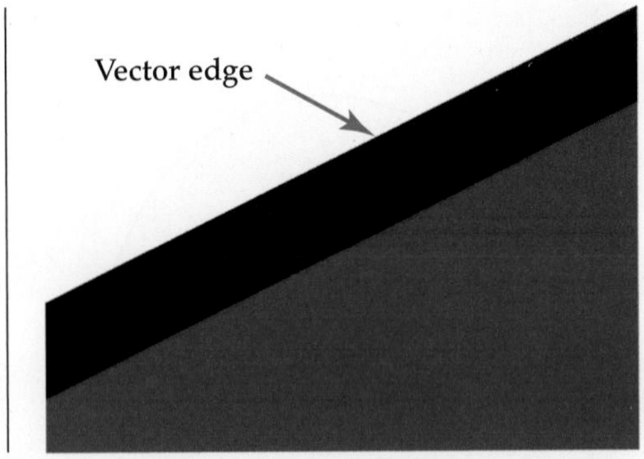

Figure 16.8
Enlarged bitmap images reveal a series of jagged edges.

Figure 16.9
No matter how much a vector image is enlarged, the edge remains smooth.

Pen Tool

While the Shapes tool provides you with basic figures such as rectangles and ellipses, often you will want to use additional shapes. The Pen tool allows you to draw any shape that you want. Novice users are tempted to click and draw as if they had an actual pen. The result is a series of direction points and curves. Instead it is easier to produce what you want if you begin by clicking on a point and then clicking on the next point, creating a series of anchors.

Live Paint Bucket

The paint bucket in Adobe Illustrator does not function as you might expect. Instead of being able to pour a color into an area as you would in a painting program, you must first convert a vector drawing to Live Paint. If there are any gaps in your drawing, they must be closed before you will be able to pour paint into the image.

Symbols

The Symbol Sprayer tool in Adobe Illustrator provides you with a series of images that have already been created. Figure 16.10 is an example of several

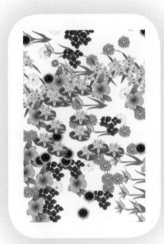

Figure 16.10
The Symbol Sprayer in Adobe Illustrator makes it easy to add images to a page.

flower symbols that have been sprayed onto a page. The use of symbols in Illustrator is much like the use of picture tubes in Paint Shop Pro.

The use of symbols that are high-quality vector images can speed up production. You can also add your own symbols to the group to reuse as you want. Company logos are often included as a symbol because of the frequency with which they are used.

Cutting Tools

The Scissors and Knife tools allow you to cut out a part of a path. Notice in Figure 16.11 that the ellipse has had a slice removed. The scissors are used with straight paths, and the knife is used with curved ones.

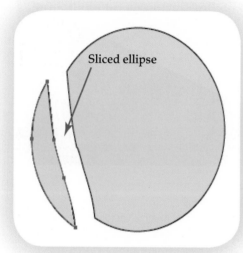

Figure 16.11
Slicing a circle with the knife allows you to easily modify the image. Once the slice is made, Illustrator replaces the path, closing the circle.

Figure 16.12
Typing on a path is an interesting way to add pizzazz to your image.

Text

Text keyed into a vector program is vector based. As a result, you have a number of options as to the placement. Text is not restricted to horizontal or vertical placement. Text can be keyed into a path as shown in Figure 16.12, or it can even be included within a shape.

Selections

Because of the different selection needs, there are more options available for vector graphics. In a bitmap image, selection consists of a Marquee tool or a lasso to select an area and the Move tool to place the area in a new location. In a vector drawing, you have a series of lines that can be moved as well as resized. As a result there are three selection tools: a Standard selection tool, a Direct selection tool, and a Group selection tool. The lasso and magic wand can be used to make selections just as they can in a bitmap image.

The Standard selection tool places a bounding box around the image. This bounding box can be resized or rotated. A Direct selection tool allows you to click on an anchor and resize the line in which the anchor appears. Figure 16.13 shows how an anchor has been pulled to reshape a part of the fish's fin. The Group selection tool works much like the standard one except that it only allows you to move the selection.

Figure 16.13
The Direct selection tool makes it simple to change the shape of any path.

Functions

Two functions that you may have used elsewhere are grouping and order. These functions are also used when working with vector images.

Grouping

Grouping is the ability to tie together two or more sections that are then treated as a single object. These parts are then included in the bounding box that is visible with the selection tool. The action applied to one part applies to all the parts grouped together.

Arrangement

The second function that is important to understand is arrangement. This is the placement of one object above or below another. Arrangements are ordered within a single layer. Figure 16.14 demonstrates the arrangement of two smaller fish on top of a larger one.

Ordering and layering are quite similar. In arranging, all the action occurs in a single layer. However, it is also possible to order layers so that images on one layer are moved above or below another layer. If you wanted to be able to adjust each fish separately, you might want to place each one on its own layer instead of merely arranging them in a single layer.

Figure 16.14
Creating an image often requires placing one part of the design on top of or below another part.

Cropping

Cropping an image in a drawing program is more difficult than cropping in a painting program. There are no cropping tools similar to those you saw in the previous chapter. Instead you must select an area (called a **clipping path**) using the Shapes tools or the Pen tool to create an area that will be visible. Once the area is done, you will create a **clipping mask** that covers up rather than removing the part of the image that is masked. You can move this mask to any point in the image, revealing what is beneath

A **clipping path** is a drawing or shape that will be used to crop an image.

A **clipping mask** is the area outside the clipping path.

 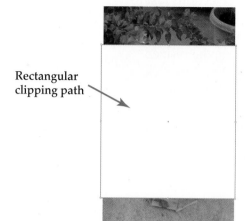 

© SUSAN LAKE

Rectangular clipping path

© SUSAN LAKE

Figure 16.15
This image imported into Adobe Illustrator needs to be cropped, but there are no cropping tools.

Figure 16.16
Cropping requires a clipping path, which in this case is in a rectangular shape.

Figure 16.17
Once a clipping path is created, the selection of a clipping mask cuts away the masked area.

it. Figure 16.15 shows an image that needs to be cropped. In Figure 16.16 a rectangle has been created to cover part of the image. Figure 16.17 shows the result once a clipping mask has been created.

Tracing

Bitmaps can be added to vector drawings, but they can only be slightly modified. Even though they are part of a vector image, they cannot be edited like a vector. One solution is to convert the drawing to a vector using the **tracing** function. Tracing is an action that converts bitmap images into lines and curves. This is quite memory intensive, so it is advisable to

Tracing is the process of converting a bitmap image to a vector one.

WORKPLACE ETHICS

Password

B eing able to convert a photograph or image to a vector image is a wonderful tool. One problem you need to be aware of is that this would be considered a derivative work. This means that you have changed the art that someone else created in order to make a new work. If you are using someone else's image, there may be a copyright restriction on creating derivative work that prevents you from using your new image without the artist's permission. Some stock photo companies specifically indicate that no change can be made to images. As a professional desktop publisher, you need to be conscious of such laws.

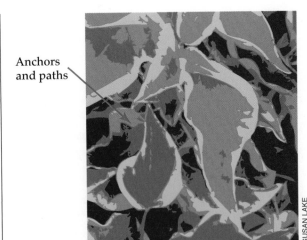

Anchors and paths

© SUSAN LAKE

© SUSAN LAKE

Figure 16.18
Live tracing is a technique that lets you convert a bitmap image to a vector image. It's often necessary to reduce the number of colors used to keep the file size manageable.

Figure 16.19
A close-up of a live trace image shows that the leaves now have paths and anchors.

convert only images that have a few colors. Figure 16.18 is an example of a bitmap image that has been converted to a vector. Figure 16.19 is an enlargement of part of the flower image. Notice that you can see the anchor points in the image.

Clip Art

Clip art is frequently used by desktop publishers as a shortcut. The wide variety of clip art collections makes this easy to do. Often clip art is created as a vector graphic, which can then be modified.

CHANGING WORKPLACE

Vector images were once restricted to simple line drawings that could not create the interest that bitmap images generated. This is no longer true. With techniques such as live tracing available and computers powerful enough to generate even complex images, converting bitmaps to vectors is becoming more common. Since the print quality of such images is often higher than bitmap ones, they can be more widely used. Learning to manage the complexities of such transformations is an important skill.

It's easy to make mistakes when adding text to an image. Since this text becomes part of the image, rather than part of the regular copy, errors are often overlooked. Part of the problem is that when a spelling check is run on a document, this material is not included since it's viewed as an image rather than text. Make a point of proofing all images that contain text, looking for the same type of spelling and punctuation mistakes that you would find in a document.

Figure 16.20
Clip art can be a useful addition to a desktop published document, and many clip art images are vectors.

Figure 16.21
Clip art can be modified in creative ways to produce an image unlike the original.

Figure 16.20 is an example of a Microsoft clip art image. Figure 16.21 shows how that same image has been modified in several ways to create a new and unique image. One of the window frames is now green, and the entire image has been clipped.

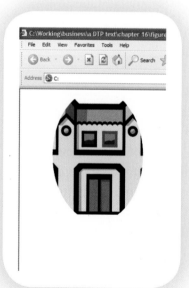

Figure 16.22
SVG images are special web vector images that are coded into the page.

Web Vectors

Vector images generally have to be converted to bitmap images before they can be used on a web page. This is easy to do using the Save for the web option. You can then choose a GIF or a JPG with the appropriate compression options selected.

SVG (scalable vector graphics) is another option for web use that allows you to maintain the sharpness and small file size that vector drawings provide. One drawback is that currently an Adobe plug-in is required to view an SVG. Figure 16.22 shows an SVG image loaded onto a web page.

SVG files are different from most images in that they are coded into the web page with statements similar to the ones below.

```
<polygon fill-rule = "evenodd" clip-rule = "evenodd" fill =
"#FFB5B5" points = "85.545,29.521 84.713,70.986 103.723,57.442
103.248,10.393 85.545,29.521 85.545,29.521 " /> <polygon fill-
rule = "evenodd" clip-rule = "evenodd" fill = "#FFB5B5"
points = "234.416,29.521 234.416,74.194 254.495,56.491
253.545,10.393 234.416,29.521 234.416,29.521" />
```

SUMMARY

In this chapter you learned what a vector path is and how anchors function. You learned about shapes, Pen tools, the Live Paint Bucket, and scissor functions. You saw how grouping and ordering parts can be used to create an image. You learned how to crop and trace a vector image. You saw how vector clip art can be used creatively.

KEY TERMS

anchor	corner point	path
clipping mask	direction line	smooth point
clipping path	end point	tracing

REVIEW

Answer the following questions on your own computer.

1. What is a vector graphic?
2. What is used to edit vector graphics?
3. What are anchors?
4. What is a path?
5. What is an end point?
6. What is a corner point?
7. What is a smooth point?
8. Where do direction lines appear?
9. What are direction lines used for?
10. What is used to change the shape of a path?
11. What vector tool allows you to draw any shape you want?
12. What kind of path is the scissors tool used on?
13. What kind of path is the knife tool used on?
14. In order to crop an image in a vector graphic program, what must be done?
15. What function would be used to convert a bitmap to a vector graphic so that it can be modified within the program?

16. What must be done to vector graphics before they can be used on a web page?

17. What does SVG stand for and what does it mean?

18. What is required in order for an SVG image to be viewed?

19. What is meant by camera ready?

20. What is meant by derivative work?

DISCUSS

1. Explain the difference between a vector and bitmap graphic and how this affects editing the image.

2. Describe the visual differences in a shape drawn with a vector tool and a shape drawn with a bitmap tool.

3. Explain the best process for using the Pen tool in bitmap graphic programs.

4. Explain the process of using the Live Paint Bucket tool.

5. Describe and explain the three selection tools found in a vector graphic program.

6. Discuss why it is easy to miss mistakes when text is added to an image.

7. Explain the use and advantages of a Symbol Sprayer tool.

8. Describe some advantages of the use of vector-based text.

9. Discuss why it is easier to crop an image in a drawing program rather than a painting program.

10. Explain the use of tracing in converting bitmap images to use with vector drawings.

APPLY

to the website at
academic.cengage.com/school/dtp

Activity 1 Vector Tools

1. Create a new document 200 pt. × 200 pt.

2. Using the Shapes tool, draw a square that is the size of the document. Fill with Black.

3. Draw a stop sign using the Polygon (or Octagon if there is no Polygon) tool. Fill the Octagon with Red. Change the Line color to White.

4. Using the Text tool, key **STOP**. Change the font type to Arial, font size to 18 pt. or appropriate size for the shape that you drew, and font color to White.

5. Order the rectangle, octagon, and text as needed.

6. Group the Octagon shape and text.

7. Create a symbol using your new shape.

8. Save the document as **stop**.

Activity 2 Bitmaps Converted

1. Open **stop** from your student data files.

2. Using the tracing function, convert the bitmap to a vector image.

3. Using the Scissors or Knife tool, edit the vector image to a different shape.

4. Save the document as **stop_edited**.

Activity 3 Text Paths

1. Using the Pen tool, create a shape that looks similar to a teepee. You may want to show guides so that each side of the teepee is the same.

2. Use the Text tool, key **Driving** on one side of the teepee and **School** on the other. You may need to use the space bar to adjust spacing between the words so that each appears on one side of the teepee.

3. Change the stroke of the line you drew with the Pen tool to 2 pt. Change the color of the stroke to Blue. Change the color of the font to Red. Adjust the font size as needed.

4. Crop the image.

5. Save the document as **driving_school**.

Activity 4 Standard Sign Colors

1. Create a document that is 333 pt. × 333 pt.

2. Draw nine equal size squares covering the entire document.

3. Fill each square with one of the nine standard traffic sign colors: red, pink, orange, yellow, yellow green, green, blue, purple, and brown.

4. Save the document as **standard_sign_colors**.

Activity 5 Driver's School Flyer

1. Using your desktop publishing software, create a flyer for a driver's school.

2. Include a list of at least five purposes of traffic signs. The purposes can be found on the Internet by searching for a manual of traffic signs. Use appropriate bullets for the list of purposes.

3. Import the images created in the four activities above.

4. Add any other elements to create a balanced, well-designed flyer.

5. Save the document as ***driving_school_flyer***.

EXPLORE

1. Search the Internet for information on standard sign typefaces.

2. Write a summary of what you learned about the typefaces used in traffic signs. The summary should be a minimum of 200 words. Save the summary as ***sign_typefaces***.

3. Using a vector-based software, create at least three images to use in your summary. These images should use as many tools as you can that were learned in this chapter and add to the message of your summary.

4. Save the document as ***summary_sign_typefaces***.

Using Digital Photography

Introduction

Although many large corporations and businesses have professional photographers who provide photographs for ads and other uses, desktop publishers must often rely on their own skills to produce photographs for use in their documents. With the increasing affordability of digital cameras, it is becoming accepted that page designers can capture images that meet their needs. While you may not be expected to be a photographer capable of producing award-winning images, you may be expected to take pictures of people and places.

Objectives

- *Understand how digital cameras are an important part of desktop publishing.*

- *Learn features available in a digital camera.*

- *Discover decisions necessary in creating a good composition.*

- *Learn why an image release form is important.*

Digital Cameras

An important consideration when selecting a digital camera is the number of pixels the camera can record. Camera makers define these recordable pixels using the term **megapixels**. Megapixels are calculated by multiplying the horizontal pixels of an image by the vertical ones. For example, a 5 megapixel camera produces images that are $2560 \times 1920 = 4{,}915{,}200$ pixels (rounded up to 5 million).

The greater the number of pixels, the better the quality of a photograph. The use of more pixels, however, creates larger file sizes. Depending on the purpose of the photograph, the maximum number of pixels may not be required.

Megapixels describes the size of images captured by a camera.

Resolution

In order to determine if an image is acceptable for print, you must consider its **resolution**. Image resolution is measured using the number of horizontal pixels and the number of vertical pixels. An image produced using a 5 megapixel camera has a resolution of 2560 × 1920.

For print purposes an image should be printed using at least 150 to 300 **pixels per inch** (PPI). Dividing the number of horizontal and vertical pixels by the required number of PPI gives a maximum effective print size. For example, an image approximately 3300 × 2100 to be used in a document that requires 300 PPI can be printed at a maximum size of 11" × 7" (3300/300 = 11 and 2100/300 = 7). The image can be printed at a smaller size than that with no difficulty.

Web Principles

On the Web, high-resolution photographs only slow down the speed at which a page is viewed. It's best to use images with a resolution of 640 × 480. Because of their relatively small file size, they are able to load more quickly when viewed.

Digital Advantages and Disadvantages

Digital cameras have advantages over traditional film cameras that make them perfect for desktop publishing. Digital cameras require no film but instead often use internal memory cards. By eliminating the need to develop film and then print a copy, the savings in both time and money can be significant.

One often overlooked benefit of using digital media is that a greater number of shots can be taken, thus increasing the chances of capturing the perfect picture. Special effects such as different angles or lighting can be tried without additional expense. Digital cameras can take close-ups with ease, and the camera itself can impose special effects such as sepia tones to give a feeling of antiquity to a modern scene.

One drawback to digital photographs is that they can be lost easily if the camera or computer on which they are stored malfunctions. As a result, it is a good idea to back up all digital images to a CD or other storage.

Care of the Camera

Digital cameras are sturdy, but they should be treated with care, just as you would traditional cameras. Follow these rules to keep your camera in good working order:

- ➦ Keep the lens area clean by using a soft cloth designed especially for camera lenses.
- ➦ Keep the lens cap on when the camera is not in use.

- Beware of dropping the camera even from a short distance such as onto a counter.
- Never force a memory card in or out of a camera if there is resistance.
- Never force an uncooperative switch; instead find out why the latch or door is unable to function properly.
- Protect your camera from unfriendly elements such as extreme heat or cold, wetness, dirt, and sand.

Features

Digital cameras are available with a wide variety of features. Some features are common to all. These include a power switch, an option to view pictures already taken, flash choices, optical or digital zoom options, battery location, and a means of saving photographs and sending them to a computer. If you have a camera, determine which features your digital camera includes by reading your owner's manual or find information about your camera on the Web. Check to see if your camera has any special features, such as the ability to modify a picture using the camera's built-in software. One popular camera allows the user to choose whether the photograph is a fast-moving action shot or a long shot such as that of a mountain. Figures 17.1, 17.2, and 17.3 show features available on one particular camera. Your digital camera may have similar features that may appear in different locations.

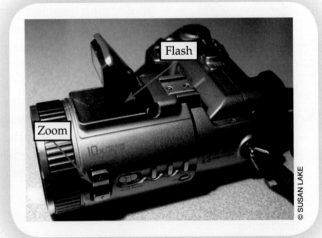

Figure 17.1
The zoom feature is one of the most popular features on digital cameras. Flashes are also built in.

Figure 17.2
The LCD monitor of a digital camera allows you to see what your image will look like. More expensive digital cameras also have traditional eyepieces to view the image.

Figure 17.3
A jog dial similar to this one is often found on a digital camera. It is used to change the camera functions. The switch to turn the camera on and off is often located near this dial.

Macro

A **macro** is a camera function that allows close-ups.

Optical zoom on a camera uses a lens to actually magnify the image.

Digital zoom is the enlargement of an image in a camera lens. This is done electronically by merely enlarging the pixels rather than actually capturing more of the image.

PROOFREADING TIPS

There is nothing more frustrating that submitting a well-designed publication that includes the perfect image only to receive a printed version in which the image is pixelated. Pixelated images are photos that have been enlarged so much that the individual pixels are visible. To avoid this, be sure to proofread images and files to verify that the resolution of an image is large enough for the purpose you intend.

Occasionally the reason this happens is that a low-resolution image is placed FPO (for position only). Using a low-resolution image keeps the file sizes small until it is time to print. Sometimes the low-quality image is not replaced with the better image, resulting in a disappointing product. Include a check for the correct image as part of your proofreading process.

A **macro** feature on a camera allows you to photograph images at very close range. This feature is one of the advantages of using a digital camera. In the past, only film cameras with special lenses had this capability. Inexpensive film cameras had to be at least three feet from an image in order for the photograph to be sharp. Today, even moderately priced digital cameras have macro functions allowing you to photograph within inches of a subject. Good photographers have learned that closer is generally better.

Zoom

Just as a macro feature lets you get close, a zoom feature allows you to photograph a subject from a great distance. The zoom enlarges the image so that it appears to have been taken at close range. Zoom features make it possible to capture images you are unable to get close enough to. It is also useful when photographing subjects that might be camera shy because they are unaware that their picture is being taken.

Cameras generally have two zoom functions: **optical** and **digital**. The digital zoom is merely a software function of the camera designed to make your eye believe that the image is enlarged. It does not actually zoom. An optical zoom uses a lens to enlarge the image. Cameras with only digital zoom are less desirable than those with an optical zoom.

Flash

Flashes that create additional light when the natural light is insufficient are built into most cameras. Additional flash equipment can usually be added as a separate component to the camera. Flashes can be tricky, though, because too much light will cause a glare to appear on your subject.

Cameras generally allow you to override the automatic flash function preventing the camera from flashing. If you are taking pictures in a large room or one with high ceilings such as an auditorium, it is often better to turn off the flash and allow the camera to compensate. Modern digital cameras have built-in software that reads the amount of light and opens the lens wider to allow more light to enter when necessary.

File Formats

Digital cameras save images in a number of formats. The most common file is a JPG, but cameras can often save as TIF or RAW as well. Each format has advantages and disadvantages.

JPG is the format of choice for most images. The file size is small because of compression, and the save time is short. JPGs can be used on the Web as well as in print. The JPG file format is the one with which most people are familiar.

TIF images produce larger file sizes because they are not compressed. The time required to save this image format is also often

The RAW file format is becoming increasingly popular. More cameras come with RAW capability, and photographers are beginning to appreciate the control that RAW provides. Using this digital negative requires a more extensive knowledge of areas such as white balance, exposure, shadows, and temperature. The difference between 8-bit and 16-bit images is another consideration. This is just one more example of the need to keep current in the changing field of technology.

longer than for a JPG. As you have read, print publications generally use TIF images. As a result, saving images as TIFs may be a good choice if the amount of time to save and the amount of memory card space required are not a problem.

The **RAW** file format is used primarily by professional photographers. The file size produced by this format is quite large, and the save time is often long. The advantage to RAW is that with specialized image conversion software, the photographer can make significant changes to the original image. Figure 17.4 is an example of the Adobe RAW converter. Often RAW is defined as the equivalent of a negative from which you can produce an image that is modified as you want.

Figure 17.4
The RAW converter software allows you to make changes to the basic image and then to save in the file format of your choice.

Memory

Digital cameras once saved images to floppy disks, CDs, or internal memory. Today most digital cameras use some type of **memory card**. These cards range in memory sizes from as small as 32 megabytes to over 2 gigabytes. Generally cards fall into three categories: memory sticks, compact flash cards, and SD (secure digital) cards. Memory cards are not limited to these three. Each year a new kind of card or a variation of an old one appears on the market.

RAW is a camera file format that acts like a negative, allowing you to make significant changes to the original image.

A **memory card** is a flash storage device in which digital photographs are captured.

Figure 17.5
Memory cards for cameras come in a variety of sizes and types. Different cameras require different types of memory cards.

Figure 17.6
A card reader allows you to transfer your images from a memory card to your computer.

Flash memory is a type of electronic storage that retains information even with power turned off. The information in this type of memory can be erased and new information recorded.

Photographic composition describes the selection and arrangement of subjects within a photograph.

Regardless of the type of card, each one uses **flash memory** and the major difference is size and cost. Memory sticks are about the size of a piece of chewing gum. Compact flash cards are larger (about 1.5" × 2") and the least expensive. SD memory cards are tiny, being less than an inch long and about 3/4" wide. Figure 17.5 allows you to compare the size of each memory card type.

Transfer

Transferring images from a digital camera to a computer can be accomplished in many ways. Some cameras have cables that connect directly to the computer or a dock. Some computers have built-in slots for the various memory cards. You can also use an external memory card reader similar to the one shown in Figure 17.6.

Some cameras include software that automatically reads the images they capture and then copies them to your computer. Generally, these are stored in folders identified by dates. You can also transfer the images yourself just as you would move a file from one folder to another or from a CD to your computer.

Steps to Good Composition

Knowing how to use a digital camera to take satisfactory photographs requires an understanding of the design principles of **photographic composition**. Composition is the selection and arrangement of subjects within the picture area. Your choices of what to include and where to locate your subject in the photograph can make the difference between a picture that conveys a message and one that merely captures a random moment.

Focus

When beginning to consider your shot, ask yourself what you are taking a picture of. This is not as obvious as it sounds. There will be many items in the typical snapshot. Capturing all of them does not provide a focus.

Moving the camera just a few inches can make the difference between effective and ineffective composition. Take the time to walk around a subject, looking for the most appropriate angle.

Centering the Subject

The most frequent mistake amateur photographers make is placing the object of attention in the center of the photograph.

Publishing isn't just about putting down words on paper and then making them appear attractive on a page. Publishing is also about attention to detail. It requires you to keep track of sources of images and releases. It requires you to learn new skills and to develop others. This may mean knowing which kind of memory card your camera uses and what the best price is for it. It requires you to understand how to transfer images from a camera to a computer and how to make backups in case of a computer failure. Desktop publishing is a field that requires you to have a broad range of skills and to add to them continuously. Photographic skills are a good example of the need to stay current.

Psychologically, the human brain prefers to "wander" around a photograph, deciding for itself what is important. Centering removes this satisfying movement. Place the focus point in such a way that the eye can move about the picture.

Rule of Thirds

Just as in page design, the Rule of Thirds is an important consideration when choosing composition. Dividing the photograph horizontally or vertically into thirds provides a satisfying balance, allowing for many composition options. Compare Figures 17.7 and 17.8. The second figure has a set

Figure 17.7
The cake is the focus of the image, but other components such as the light fixture and the plates add interest.

Figure 17.8
The grid on the image makes it easy to see how the Rule of Thirds applies to this photograph.

of grid lines drawn over the image. In this second example, the grid makes it apparent that the arrangement of the cake is intentional. The cake appears in the left side rather than in the center of the photograph. The stack of plates on the right side of the picture counters the cake. These design choices make for a better balance.

Background

Pay close attention to the background information your photograph includes. You may see it as nonessential "clutter," but your viewer will give it more attention. Make sure it adds to your photographic story rather than detracts from it.

The horizon is an important background to consider in outdoor shots. It should be straight, and its prominence in a photograph should be gauged. Horizons that are low in the photograph give importance to the sky, as shown in Figure 17.9.

Figure 17.9
Notice how the prominent sky is dwarfing the boat on the water.

Figure 17.10
The framing of the window and the curtains draws the eye out to the mountain beyond the window.

You may want to look for a background that will frame your picture in some way. Framing is effective in giving the viewer a sense of location and distance. In Figure 17.10, notice how the window frame in the image encourages your eye to move out to the image beyond it.

Unifying Elements

One way to help the eye "wander" around a photograph is to use lines within an image, as shown in Figure 17.11. These lines could be vertical, horizontal, diagonal, S shaped, or curved. Lines help pull the eye along in the direction you intend. Lines can also tie together objects within a photograph, thus reducing the jumble of objects in a photograph.

Figure 17.11
The lines of the vertical poles draw your eye into the image and give the eye a series of interesting points to observe.

Special Effects

The choice of distance from which you photograph an object can make an ordinary picture distinctive. In Figure 17.12, the combination of the fall trees with the ship beyond creates an unusual effect. Close-ups or different angles give viewers a perspective they might not otherwise have considered. Shooting up or down rather than straight on is an effective means of getting your viewer's attention by giving the eye something unusual to see. The light you choose and the angle from which it comes are another effect to consider. Notice in Figure 17.13 how the reflection of the water adds to the effectiveness of the image.

Figure 17.12
The combination of close-up trees and the distant ship creates an image that attracts the reader's attention.

Figure 17.13
Angles and reflections create a special image of the glacier. The weaving together of ice, water, and mountains makes for a striking image.

Action

With a digital camera it is now much easier to capture action shots, such as the movement of a sports figure or even a child in a swing, than it was with a traditional camera. In the past, special film speeds were used to produce effects that are common in today's digital cameras. Figure 17.14 is an example of an action image. If you look closely, you can even see the dirt clods flying up from the horses' hooves.

Because movement was difficult to capture in the past, amateur photographers tended to capture only posed pictures with people facing into the lens. That is no longer necessary or desirable. Just as viewers want to move their eyes through the elements of a photograph, those same viewers prefer to feel they are seeing a moment captured as it happened, not as it was posed. Learning to capture and include motion in your photographs will communicate the message that the photograph recorded the event as it happened. Try to avoid staged photographs with people standing in a row.

Figure 17.14
Action shots are easier to photograph with a digital camera than with film cameras.

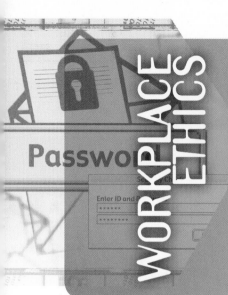

Sometimes you may not have the perfect photograph to use in your project, but someone else does. Most people would be thrilled to have one of their photographs used in a publication. You have already read about how important it is to verify that you have permission to use an image, but another consideration is giving credit. Too often images are published without identifying the photographer. Just because someone is pleased to see his or her work used is no excuse for not giving proper credit. Always assign a credit line to a photograph—particularly one you didn't take yourself.

An **image release form** gives you permission to use a photograph in a document or on a website.

Image Release Form

If you are going to photograph images of people to be used in your desktop publishing documents, you should get in the habit of having **image release forms**, or releases, signed. These documents give you permission to use someone's photograph in a publication. Depending upon the type of publication, some organizations require use of specific releases.

Regardless of what release you have to acquire later, having your own releases with pertinent information simplifies the process. Figure 17.15 is an example of a typical image release form. This form generally includes the following:

- A release statement that may or may not include the purpose for which the photograph will be used
- Information about the person photographed
  - Name
  - Address (including city, state, and ZIP Code)
  - Telephone
  - E-mail
- Signature of the person photographed
- Date the form was signed

If you are taking pictures of a company activity for use in the business' newsletter, releases are not usually needed. However, you might find at a later time that you

Figure 17.15
A release form like this should be used whenever you anticipate using a photograph in a publication.

would like to use these same images in another publication. Having releases already on file makes the process much simpler. Keep in mind that photographing children and using their images requires approval of the parent or guardian.

SUMMARY

In this chapter, you looked at the differences between digital and film cameras and read about how to care for your digital camera. You learned about the features that are available in digital cameras. You learned how to create good digital photographs by using the rules of composition. This included learning about focus, the Rule of Thirds, backgrounds, and special effects. You also read about why you should get release forms signed.

KEY TERMS

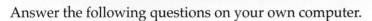

digital zoom	memory card	pixels per inch (PPI)
flash memory	optical zoom	RAW
image release form	photographic composition	resolution
macro		
megapixels		

REVIEW

Answer the following questions on your own computer.

1. What are megapixels?
2. How are megapixels determined?
3. What is resolution?
4. What should be considered in determining if an image is acceptable for print?
5. What is PPI?
6. What is one of the most popular features on digital cameras?
7. On a digital camera, what allows you to see what your picture will look like?
8. What is the name of the dial on most digital cameras that is used to change the camera functions?

9. On a digital camera, what allows you to photograph images at a very close range?

10. On a digital camera, what feature allows you to photograph an image that is at a great distance?

11. What are the two zoom functions on a digital camera?

12. What is digital zoom?

13. What is optical zoom?

14. What is the most common file format that digital cameras use to save images?

15. What is RAW?

16. What is a memory card?

17. What is flash memory?

18. What is photographic composition?

19. What is an image release form?

20. What is a pixelated image?

DISCUSS

1. Explain pixels as it pertains to file size and quality of image.

2. Review how to determine the maximum size that an image can be printed effectively.

3. Discuss why high-resolution photographs should usually be avoided for use on the Web.

4. Discuss the advantages of digital cameras over traditional film cameras.

5. Explain the use of flash on a digital camera, giving some specific tips for best use of flash.

6. Describe the RAW file format. Include advantages and disadvantages of using this format.

7. Review the three types of media generally used to save files on a digital camera.

8. Discuss the different methods used in transferring files from a camera to a computer.

9. Explain the importance of the background of a photograph. Give specific details.

10. Discuss the purpose and importance of keeping an image release form on file.

to the website at
academic.cengage.com/school/dtp

Activity 1 Maximum Print Sizes

1. Using your desktop publishing software, insert a table to use for the following. Calculate the answers for the blank column. Round to the nearest whole number to get the maximum print size.

MATH

Camera Megapixels	Required PPI	Horizontal Pixels	Vertical Pixels	Maximum Print Size
1	300	1280	960	
3	150	2048	1536	
5	200	2560	1920	
5	300	2560	1920	
4	300	2304	1792	
4	150	2304	1792	
8	300	3328	2304	
10	300	3840	2560	

2. Save the document as **maximum_size**.

Activity 2 Features Comparison

1. Using your own digital camera or one available in the classroom, explore its features including optical and digital zoom, macro, and flash.

WRITING

2. Using an object, person, or animal, take as many images as you want using the various features.

3. Pick what you consider the best and the worst of your images that demonstrate zoom, macro, and flash. Save as **zoom_good**, **zoom_bad**, **macro_good**, **macro_bad**, and **flash_good**, **flash_bad**.

4. Using your desktop publishing software, import the images into a document. Create a title for the document called Features Comparison. Write a short summary of what makes each image good or bad and what you did to take a good image. Place the images on the document using appropriate design principles. Format text using good typography principles and add some color.

5. Save the document as **features_comparison**.

Activity 3 Good Composition

1. Most communities have something they are known for. It could be a lake, a park, a historical monument or building, or a building with special architecture. Practice using the steps to good composition as

WRITING

outlined below by taking images from that area of your community. If you cannot travel to that area of your community with a digital camera, use your school as the subject of this activity. Take at least three images, focusing on each area of good composition:

- *Focus—What are you taking a picture of? Take three different pictures, moving the camera just a few inches each time.*

- *Centering the Subject—What is your main subject of the picture? Take a picture with the object in the center. Take two more pictures with the object not centered.*

- *Rule of Thirds—Take three pictures, with the subjects on the left or right third of the picture, countered by other objects that are not quite as important but provide balance to the image.*

- *Background—Take three pictures, focusing on the background and how it adds to the picture.*

- *Unifying Elements—Take three pictures, focusing on providing lines such as diagonal, S shaped, or curved in the pictures.*

- *Special Effects—Take three pictures at different distances and angles to provide interest or to gain the reader's attention.*

2. Choose six pictures from your photographs that best exemplify the six areas of good composition. Write a report of the area you photographed. You may need to do some research about the area from the Internet or brochures obtained from the Chamber of Commerce. Save the report as **good_composition**.

3. Using your desktop publishing software, create a brochure of this area of interest. Insert a minimum of six images with information from your report added in various places on the brochure. Use previously learned desktop publishing skills to set up and enhance the brochure.

4. Save the document as **community_brochure**.

Activity 4 Action

1. Attend an event either in school or in the community. Take a number of action shots where people or animals are actively involved in a sport or activity.

2. Write an article on the event that could be included in a newsletter or newspaper. Include images that will add interest to your article.

3. Save the document as **reporting_action**.

Activity 5 Digital Science

1. Choose three different plants to take images of. You may want to visit a nursery to take the pictures so that you know the exact name of the plant. Take a number of different pictures of each of the three plants.

2. Research the plants to find their scientific name and other scientific information about them. Write a summary with a minimum of 100 words of each plant. Save the summaries as *plant1*, *plant2*, and *plant3*. Keep a log (in MLA style) of any resources you used and save the document as *plant_resources*.

3. Using your desktop publishing software, create a newsletter for the Science Gardening Co., Inc. Include the three articles, and several of your best images of each plant. Use colors from the plant images in the newsletter. Use other desktop publishing skills learned in previous chapters to enhance the newsletter.

4. Save document as *plant_newsletter*.

EXPLORE

1. New digital camera technology is constantly on the market. A desktop publisher should always keep up with the latest that is available. In a team of three or four students, research the current market for digital cameras. After reviewing features, decide on two cameras that you would consider purchasing, given a budget of $400.

2. Each member of the team should create a flyer for each camera, pointing out its best features. In the footer of the flyer, give credit to any websites from which you obtained information or images that were used in the flyer.

3. Save document as *camera1* and *camera2*.

Objectives

- *Understand how tables are added to desktop published documents.*

- *Learn differences between various chart types.*

- *Develop design techniques for charts and graphs.*

- *Learn ways to design effective maps.*

Introduction

Images are not the only objects you may want to add to a document. Tables, charts, graphs, and maps can also make worthwhile additions to a page. Objects such as these allow you to publish data in a visual manner.

Tables

Tables allow information to be displayed in an organized format, making it easier for your reader to understand facts and figures. Tables can be created in a spreadsheet program such as Microsoft Excel and then imported directly into programs such as QuarkXPress and Adobe InDesign. Tables can also be created within desktop publishing programs themselves.

Design

When designing your table, keep in mind that the first row is usually a header used to identify the information listed in each column.

Table borders add visual interest. The borders can be different widths, colors, or styles. Figure 18.1 is an example of a table with special borders and colors. Tables that have no visible borders still function as tables, but cell outlines do not show on printed copy. This allows you to create borderless columns, as demonstrated in Figure 18.2. Notice that the data appears to have been entered in columns.

Tables are considered text boxes in desktop publishing software. They can be resized and assigned the same

	megapixels	length	width
1228800	1	1280	960
2076672	2	1664	1248
3145728	3	2048	1536
3981312	4	2304	1728
4915200	5	2560	1920
5614272	6	2736	2052
7151808	7	3088	2316
7990272	8	3264	2448

Figure 18.1
Notice the blue outline border and the dotted border between the first and second column.

megapixels		length	width
1228800	1	1280	960
2076672	2	1664	1248
3145728	3	2048	1536
3981312	4	2304	1728
4915200	5	2560	1920
5614272	6	2736	2052
7151808	7	3088	2316
7990272	8	3264	2448

Figure 18.2
Tables without borders can be used to create column designs within a page.

formatting you use with text including drop shadows and text wrapping.

Modifications

Once a table is created, it is easy to add additional rows or columns. If you need extra rows, press the Tab key at the end of the last column and a new row will be inserted. To add additional columns, you generally must use a menu option. You can delete tables, rows, columns, and cells in the same way that you add them by using the menu option.

You are not limited to uniform columns and rows. Two cells can be merged or split to overlap between two (or more) columns or rows. In Figure 18.3 the subheading "resolutions" is in two cells that have been merged.

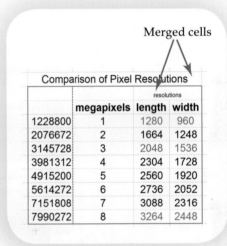

Merged cells

Comparison of Pixel Resolutions

		resolutions	
	megapixels	length	width
1228800	1	1280	960
2076672	2	1664	1248
3145728	3	2048	1536
3981312	4	2304	1728
4915200	5	2560	1920
5614272	6	2736	2052
7151808	7	3088	2316
7990272	8	3264	2448

Figure 18.3
Table cells can be merged or split to provide more design options.

Charts and Graphs

Statistics are converted from numbers into graphics using charts and graphs. The easiest way to create these graphics is to use the charting/graphing tools available in spreadsheet software such as Microsoft Excel. Charting tools make it possible to record data and then to experiment with the resulting chart or graph until your visual information needs are met. The best way to convey your information may not be apparent to you until you have tried several different approaches. Do not choose too quickly. Give yourself the opportunity to look at several different ways of presenting your information.

A chart with too much information can be confusing. A chart type that does not fit the type of information being displayed is inaccurate. And a chart that does not include significant figures is misleading. At each point, decisions must be made by the chart designer—decisions that require significant thought. There are no automatic answers. You must know what message you are trying to convey and the best means of doing that.

ables and charts are a staple of business publications. Learning how to produce readable and interesting charts is an excellent desktop publishing skill to acquire. Knowing how to discuss charting terms such as series and data points is a true mark of a professional. It's not a skill that comes easily. You need to build many charts and spend some time looking at the techniques others have used in order to become proficient at it. It will be worth the effort in the long run. Desktop publishing of business documents requires you to know all the tricks of producing quality charts and graphs. Something as simple as understanding how to convert a basic chart into one that contains pictographs can give you the edge you need.

Types

When making a decision about what type chart to use, there are a wide variety of chart types from which to choose. Figure 18.4 shows some of the choices and describes their purposes.

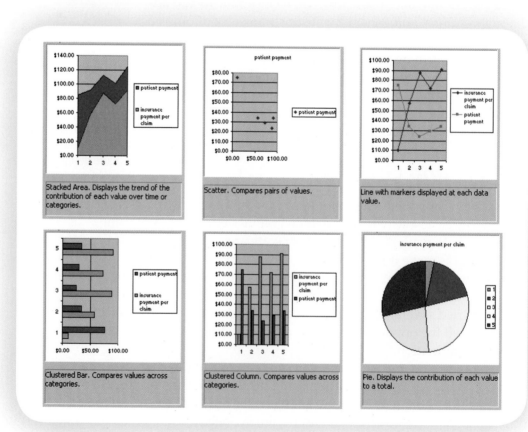

Figure 18.4
Microsoft charting provides you with a description of each chart type's purpose.

Charts and graphs need to be honest. That means that the numbers and data being represented should not be manipulated just to make a point. The reader relies on you to provide data that can be trusted. Setting up a chart just to satisfy your own agenda is unethical. Much like the statement "everybody is doing it," when you only know of two other people who fit the description, pulling out figures that distort the reality is unfair to your reader. There is a fine line between simplifying data to make it easy for the reader to understand and distorting data. Make sure you do not fall into that trap when designing tables and charts.

When you select the option to insert a chart in Microsoft Excel, as shown in Figure 18.5, a long list of chart types becomes available. This list, as shown in Figure 18.6, includes column, line, pie, bar, area, scatter, stock, surface, doughnut, bubble, and radar. Within each of these types, there are a number of design options.

Figure 18.5
Choosing to insert a chart in Microsoft Excel opens a window filled with possibilities.

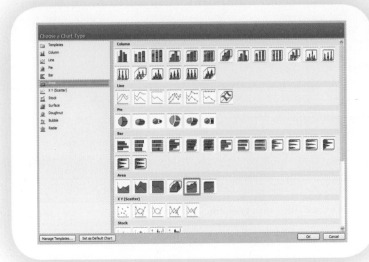

Figure 18.6
The chart window lists both chart types and variations within each type.

Most charts fall into four basic types: bar, pie, line, and area. For example, a column chart is merely a vertical bar chart. The difference between one type of chart and another is the use for which it is designed. Vertical column charts generally are used to compare categories, while horizontal bar charts show value.

In addition, within each chart type there are multiple subtypes designed to let you choose the most effective way to display information. One of the options available involves the decision about dimensions. Most charts can be either two- or three-dimensional, so a column chart can be a series of flat rectangles or a series of boxes that appear to stand out from the background. Figure 18.6 showed that there are 19 different ways to display columns. Some are two-dimensional choices, and others are three-dimensional.

Design

Once you have made a choice as to the type of chart to use, you must now add the significant details. Charts contain three types of information. Two are defined on the chart axes, and the third is indicated visually as the series name. Chart design uses a series of standard identification features that include axis labels, gridlines, legends, and titles. Figure 18.7 is an example of a chart with all the expected features.

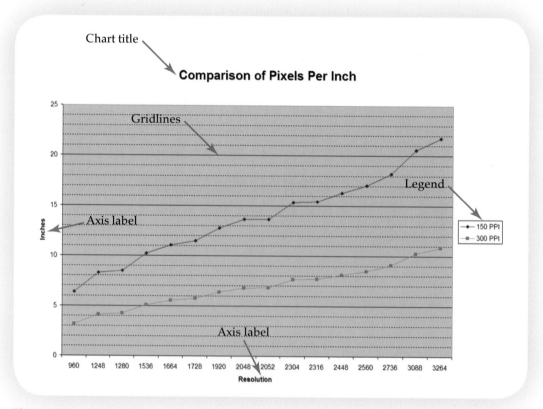

Figure 18.7
Notice that this chart contains all the basic chart components: legend, title, X-axis designation, Y-axis designation, and gridlines.

When designing a chart, one of the first issues you must be aware of is the purpose of the horizontal and vertical **axes**. This is where your data will be plotted. Generally, the horizontal axis (X) shows categories while the vertical axis (Y) shows values. Reversing this standard can be confusing for your audience, so keep these conventions in mind.

Axis labels identify the data type. A data type in the form of a date and dollar amount is easily identified. Some axis labels, however, such as sales figures by type, may not be so easily identified. Do not assume that your audience will be able to tell what each axis is measuring.

Data range is the highest and lowest number assigned to each category value. A chart limits the upper and lower numbers shown based upon this range. In the example in Figure 18.7, the data range was from 0 to 25.

A **series** on a chart is a list of categories to which numerical information (data) is assigned. The series data is demonstrated using bars, lines, or circles. In the example, the pink and blue lines indicate the data series.

A **legend** identifies the series categories. Legends can be boxed with color or shade keys to identify the category, or the categories can be identified directly on the chart. As the designer, you must choose the best way to visually communicate the information supplied by the chart.

The lines that separate points on a chart are called **gridlines**. Gridlines can be set at narrow or wide increments depending upon your design. If the reader needs to be able to determine a number closely, then you will need to use narrow gridlines. If only an approximate number is needed, lines can be set at wider intervals. Gridlines fall into two categories: major and minor. Major gridlines are usually in increments of 10 (if the data range is broad enough) and minor ones fall between. Gridlines can be shown on both the X- and the Y-axes if necessary. Often gridlines are only shown on the Y-axis. In Figure 18.7 the major gridlines were in bold and the minor ones were dotted. Since the data range only ran from 0–25, the major gridlines were in increments of 5 with the minor gridlines at 1.

A title provides the reader with information about a chart's overall content. The title should be concise yet clear. A title is not a "throwaway" feature. Often it conveys as much information as the chart itself. For example, a chart titled "Income" is not as helpful as one titled "Income Comparison." Sometimes chart titles can reduce the need for additional information such as axis labels.

Pictographs

Pictographs are small images used in graphs to represent quantity. For example, if you are creating a chart that measures the number of books found in homes, you might replace the standard colored bar with a series of small books. The books are pictographs. Microsoft Excel has a function that makes it easy to add pictographs to your chart.

Axes is the vertical (Y) or horizontal (X) value or category defining information on a chart.

The **data range** is the upper and lower numerical limit of the Y-axis.

The **series** is the area of the chart in which data is recorded visually using elements such as columns or lines.

Legend is a key, generally found in a box, used to identify the series on a chart or a map.

Gridlines are horizontal or vertical lines designed to make it easy to track information (usually numerical) on a chart.

A **pictograph** is a chart that uses images to represent the numbers in a chart's columns or bars.

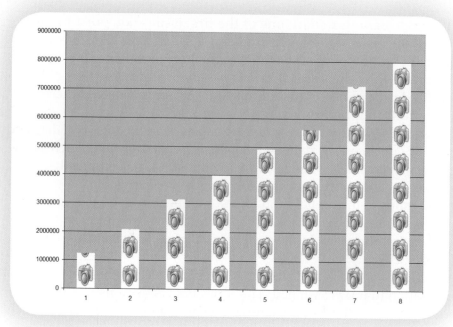

Figure 18.8

Images of cameras are used as pictographs for this chart. Partial camera images indicate that the upper range falls between gridlines.

Figure 18.8 is an example of a pictograph. Notice that a partial image is used in the first column to indicate the upper range of the data series.

Guidelines

Even though the nature of a chart is its simplicity, do not leave out significant details such as the date the information was gathered and the conditions under which it was compiled. Footnotes or addendums providing this information can give credibility to your statistical image. These features are important tools because they help make your chart readable and informative.

As a chart designer, remember that what seems obvious to you when you are creating a chart may not be obvious to your audience. Including features such as a legend helps make your chart more readable and informative. Do not leave these features out unless you are sure that the information is completely clear. It is better to include unnecessary information than to risk confusing your reader.

The most important feature to remember when designing a chart is to keep it simple and easy to read. Try to avoid too many technical details that might be confusing. Desktop publishing skills require you to be able to understand your audience and to know what level of knowledge they bring to your chart. If a chart contains information that your audience cannot understand or that they misunderstand, then no matter how accurate or complete it may be, you have failed to communicate. Effective communication is the absolute test of your chart.

To design effective informational charts or graphs, keep in mind the following guidelines:

- ○ Avoid being overly technical or overly simple.
- ○ Have a specific goal in mind rather than just providing a compilation of information.
- ○ Make sure the information is current.
- ○ Use column charts to compare categories such as changes over time.
- ○ Use bar graphs to display values rather than trends.
- ○ Use pie charts to compare parts to the whole.
- ○ Use line graphs to show trends.
- ○ Use area charts to show both trends and contributions to the whole.
- ○ In a pie chart, limit the pieces to no more than five.
- ○ In a line graph, use no more than three lines.
- ○ Indicate any special conditions under which information was gathered.
- ○ Include a title, axis labels, and legend as appropriate.

Maps

Sometimes as part of a document design, you may be called upon to place a map in a publication. These maps may include directions to your business or the location of a specific room within a building. You may be sending a letter notifying someone of a meeting, publicizing an event, or even placing an ad in the phone book.

Mapping functions can be found on the Web using Google or Yahoo. Microsoft has a full-featured mapping program called MapPoint as well as a less complex one called Streets and Trips. Most map software has a function that allows you to make a copy of a map as a JPG or GIF file. Once you have completed your map design, you can then add it as an image to your document.

CHANGING WORKPLACE

Maps once were limited to those on huge wall hangings in a classroom or those folded into a car's glove compartment. That is no longer the case. GPSs (global positioning systems) that use satellites to track locations, cell phones that know your location, and web-based mapping services have changed the way the world thinks about maps. Those living in large towns often print out directions to a new business before leaving the house. Car manufacturers advertise the advantages of their mapping systems built into the car. It seems like maps are now everywhere. As a result, your readers have become sophisticated map users. Keep this in mind when you design maps for your documents.

Design

Pushpins are map images used to locate a specific place. Generally the images look like pins, but they are not limited to that design.

One of the rules of map designing is "simple is better." When designing a map, eliminate as many details as possible. Leave only essential information, keeping it simple and easy to read. For example, if only one major highway is generally used to access the road on which your business is located, include only the portion of the map that is needed once the highway exit has been reached. Include a text statement indicating the major highway used to reach the exit.

If there are several ways to reach your location, use the highlighting tool provided in most mapping programs to indicate the best choice. It is usually considered a standard convention to indicate north on maps. Be sure to also include other helpful information such as distances between major points.

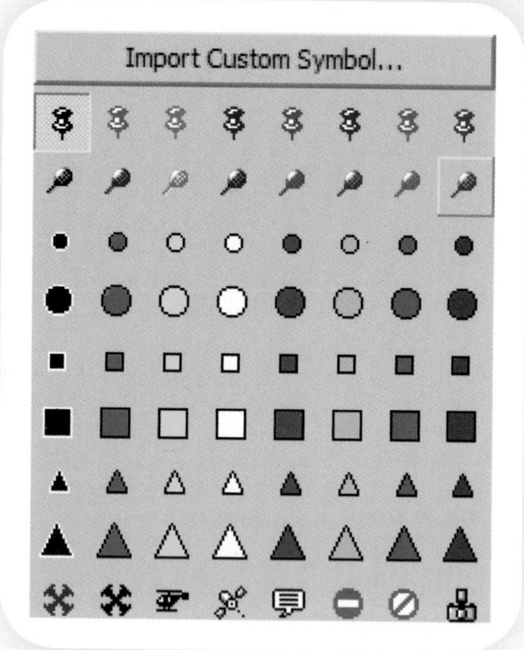

Pushpins

Pushpins are used to locate specific sites on a map. They can appear in a variety of forms as shown in Figure 18.9. These pin selections are available in Microsoft MapPoint, but other mapping software programs also provide multiple choices. Pushpins are useful for indicating points of interest or destinations. Using different style pins makes it easy to identify quickly what information the reader is seeing. Figure 18.10 uses pushpins to indicate a starting and ending point of the route from Lubbock to New Orleans.

Figure 18.9
Pushpins can be designed using a wide variety of figures, not just the standard image of a tack.

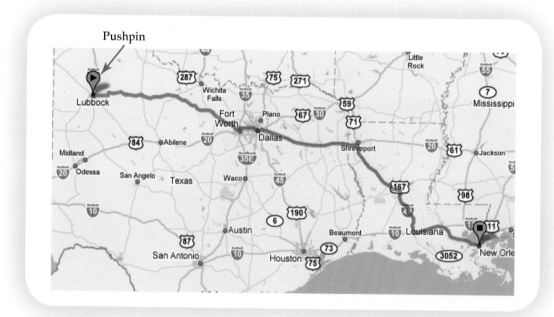

Figure 18.10
Pushpins are important components of a map because they draw the reader's attention to a specific location. Small balloons are used as pushpins on this map.

Zooming

The ability to zoom in or out of a particular site or area on a map is one of the functions included in mapping software. Zooming in enlarges and zooming out reduces the area visible on the screen. Details that are not visible on a map at one size often appear when you zoom in. This is one of the advantages of using computerized maps. Details can be omitted at different resolutions to reduce the visual clutter. A selection tool is also usually included, allowing you to select the specific area that you want to zoom into and then precisely perform the function in one step. Figure 18.11 shows a close-up of a highway intersection in Atlanta, Georgia, making it easy for the reader to see the necessary exits.

PROOFREADING TIPS

Once a map is created, step back and look at it from your reader's perspective. Imagine that you are seeing the image for the first time. Ask yourself if someone unfamiliar with the area shown by the map will understand what you are capturing. It's amazing how the simplest things can interfere with your readers' understanding. Sometimes a map actually needs to be two maps—the first zoomed out showing the location of a second, close-up map. Sometimes even having north designated might make a difference. Even though you may have pushpins marking a particular location, sometimes it's helpful to have an additional arrow pointing to the starting point. Always put yourself in the reader's place in order to see potentially confusing items. It doesn't sound like proofreading, but it is.

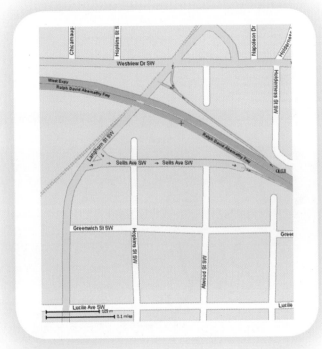

Figure 18.11
Using the zoom feature of a map allows the reader to see details up close.

Once you have zoomed into an area you want to see, you may need to move small distances to adjust what is visible. **Panning** moves across an area by means of a "hand" to guide the user. A panning hand allows you to easily direct your motion with more control that you would get using only standard vertical or horizontal scroll bars.

Panning is the use of a "hand" to move small distances on a map.

Legend

The legend identifies parts of a map and color codes. Colors help differentiate between areas of information. Just as in the creation of charts, legends provide helpful information for those using a map. Legends are particularly important because they help your audience understand details that might otherwise be missed. Legends sometimes are merely a scale showing the number of inches to a mile, as in Figure 18.11. This legend informs the reader that an inch represents just .1 of a mile on the map.

Directions

Many map programs provide written directions to guide the user from one destination to another. These directions often include points of interest along the way, road conditions such as construction delays, distances, time to complete the trip, and even the cost of the trip. They can be an excellent addition to a document that includes a map. Figure 18.12 shows ways that you can incorporate a map and directions guiding the reader from the airport to a location in Raleigh, North Carolina.

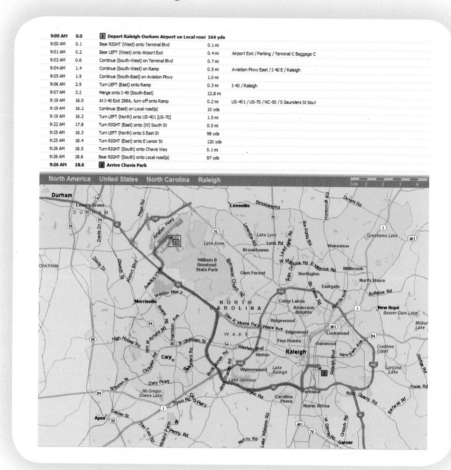

Figure 18.12
Maps can be an important addition to a document. They can be used to visualize data, provide directions, and simplify instructions.

Web Principles

Maps on the Web are readily available. As a result, rather than reproducing a map in a web document, it's more productive to merely link to a Yahoo or Google map that points to a location. The only difficulty is that occasionally mapping software changes location, making the link no longer effective. Keep this option in mind when designing documents that are to be used on the Internet.

SUMMARY

In this chapter you learned how to include tables in a desktop published document and then how to modify them. You read about the difference between types of charts and graphs and how to design them effectively. You saw how pictographs can add interest to a chart. You learned how to create a map for a document and how to incorporate maps with directions, making them a useful part of a page.

KEY TERMS

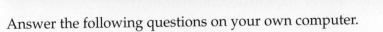

axes

data range

gridlines

legend

panning

pictograph

pushpins

series

REVIEW

Answer the following questions on your own computer.

1. What is the purpose of using a table to display information?

2. What can be used to create tables?

3. What is the first row of a table usually called, and what is it used for?

4. What adds visual interest to your tables?

5. Once a table has been created, how do you add a new row to it?

6. What feature in a table allows you to create rows and cells that are not uniform?

7. How can statistics be converted from numbers into graphics?

8. What are the four basic types of charts?

9. What is the difference between one type of chart and another?

10. What dimensions are most charts displayed in?

11. What elements are included in a chart's standard identification features?

12. What is the axis on a chart?

13. What is the purpose of the horizontal and vertical axis?

14. What is data range?

15. What is a series?

16. What is a legend?

17. What separates points on a chart?

18. What two categories do gridlines fall in?

19. Which axis are gridlines most often shown on?

20. What is a pictograph?

21. What are two of the most important things to remember when designing a chart?

22. What is the test of a well-designed, effective chart?

23. When designing a map, what should be eliminated?

24. What mapping tool can be used to indicate the best way to reach your location if there are several possibilities?

25. What are pushpins?

26. What is the difference between zooming in and zooming out?

27. What is panning?

28. Rather than reproducing a map that you want on a web document, what is more productive and why?

29. How do data ranges work?

30. What are some uses of maps in document design?

DISCUSS

1. Explain how a table with no visible borders functions.

2. Discuss why tables are considered text boxes.

3. Discuss designing of charts that can cause errors in how readers interpret the information and their ability to understand the information accurately.

4. Describe the difference in the use of vertical column charts and horizontal bar charts.

5. Explain the differences between two- and three-dimensional charts.

6. Discuss the use and purpose of different settings on gridlines.

7. Explain the importance of a title on a chart.

8. Explain what gives credibility to the information in your statistical image.

9. Describe at least five guidelines for designing effective informational charts.

10. Give some examples of pictographs and their uses.

APPLY

Activity 1 Imported Tables

go to the website at academic.cengage.com/school/dtp

1. Using your desktop publishing software, import **cell_phone_usage** from your student data files to a default document.

2. Select any blank columns or rows and delete them.

3. Select the title and change it to 18 pt. font size. Select the header row information and center the text.

4. Adjust column width so that the source appears on one row without wrapping text.

5. Align center all the text vertically.

6. Resize the text box to fit the table. Add vertical guides so that you can move the table to center it. Move the table so the top starts at 9p0.

7. Draw a horizontal 2 pt. line from the margin to 18p0 on the horizontal ruler above the source line.

8. Save the document as **cell_phones**.

Activity 2 Pasted Charts

1. Open **cell_phone_charts** from your student data files. Click on a white area of the chart. From the menu bar choose File > Copy.

2. Open **cell_phones** that was created in Activity 1. Paste the copy of the chart into the document.

3. Using the horizontal guides, center the chart below the table.

4. Save the **cell_phones** document again.

Activity 3 Pictographs

1. Open **pictographs** from your student data files. Click on the Cell Phones tab to be sure the chart is showing. Select the chart.

2. From the menu bar choose File > Copy.

3. Create a new desktop publishing document with landscape orientation. From the menu bar, choose File > Paste.

4. Center the chart in the document.

5. From the Sheet1 tab, copy the source information. Return to the desktop publishing document. Paste the source information below the chart.

6. Save the document as **cell_phone_pictographs**.

Activity 4 Maps

1. Go to http://www.fbla-pbl.org. Find information on the current year's National Conference. Make a note of where it is located and the date.

2. Go to http://www.mapblast.com. Create a driving direction map using the city you live in as the Starting Point and the location of the National FBLA Conference as the Ending Point.

3. Use Print Screen or another available program to capture the map. Save the file as **fbla**.

4. Create a default desktop publishing document. Insert **fbla** from your student data files. Resize the image of the map as needed.

5. Create a title for the document. Key in the title **FBLA National Conference** [Enter] **Location of Conference** [Enter] **Date of Conference**. Format the font with appropriate font type, size, and color.

6. Save the document as **fbla_map**.

Activity 5 Desktop Publishing Competition

1. Using your desktop publishing software, import the file **desktop_publishing_skills** from your student data files.

2. Insert two columns to the right of the one column. Adjust column width to fit within the margins, with the last two columns 10p0 in column width. All row heights of the table should be 4p0, centered vertically.

3. Insert three rows above the first row of the table. Merge all columns in the first row; then merge all columns in the second row.

4. Key **Business Professionals of America** in the top row. In the second row, key **Desktop Publishing (24)**. Center the text in both rows. Change font size to 24 pt. and font color to Navy (R = 44, G = 46, B = 115).

5. In the third row, leave the first cell blank. In the second column, key **Points by Grader 1**, and in the second column, key **Points by Grader 2**. Bold and horizontally center the text in both cells.

6. Insert a row below the last row of the table. Merge the row and then key **Source: Business Professionals of America, http://www.bpa.org, 2004**.

7. Move the table so that the top row begins at 6p0 horizontally.

8. Add a table with three rows at the bottom of the document page. Key **Student** in the first row, **School** in the second row, and **Grader's Signature** in the third row. Change the font type to Tahoma and the font size to 14 pt. Add a Thick-Thin border of 4 pt. to the table.

9. Save the document as **bpa_desktop_publishing**.

10. Choose a school to invite to this competition. Add another page to the document in front of the current page. Design a flyer that includes all important information for when and where this event will take place. Include some ideas that will make students want to enter and attend this event. Be creative! Include a map to your school somewhere on the flyer.

11. Save the document as **desktop_publishing_competition**.

1. Search the Internet for more information on how to choose the most appropriate chart type. Write a report with a minimum of 500 words on the four most common chart types used in business: column, row, line, and pie. Include a title and four side headings. Save the document as **chart_types**.

2. Create a desktop publishing document designed as a newsletter with two columns. Import **chart_types**, placing the text as appropriate.

3. Add images, font changes, color, and other design elements to your newsletter as appropriate. Include the sources of your information either as footnote information or in an article within the newsletter.

4. Save the document as **chart_types_research**.

Independent Project

Relay for Life Designs

1. You have been asked to assist the Committee Chair for the Sponsorship Committee for this year's Relay for Life. Your job is to design banners and flyers for the event.

2. Go to your local Chamber of Commerce and read about the Economic Development of your community if it is available. Create banners to display at the Relay for Life event of the top three businesses in your community. You should find information about the businesses on the Chamber of Commerce website or the businesses' websites.

   ⊃ *Take images of the business or use the businesses' logo or both.*

   ⊃ *Use other image tools such as cropping, masks, layers, Eyedropper tool, Text tool, and others to create your banner.*

   ⊃ *Banners should be created in a size of 800 × 400 pixels.*

   ⊃ *Use colors, typography and design that best represent the business.*

3. Save the document as ***01banner***, ***02banner***, and ***03banner***.

4. Use vector tools to create a logo for Relay for Life for the current year. Go to the current website to see the current logo to get ideas. Use as many vector tools, including text paths, as possible to demonstrate skills learned in this unit. Save the document as ***relay_logo***.

5. The event will take place at a local football field. Determine the exact location appropriate for your situation. Create a flyer with the date, time, and place of the event including a map to the exact location. Save the document as ***event_flyer***.

6. Create two flyers that include cancer facts. Research the Internet or interview a survivor to gather facts to use on the flyer. Include at least one table or chart on each of the facts flyers. Use the logo created with vector tools. Save the documents as ***01_cancer_facts*** and ***02_cancer_facts***.

Team Project

Volunteer Event

1. In a team of three or four students, volunteer to create a newsletter reporting on an event at a school in your area.

2. Take action pictures at the event, using the skills learned in this unit.

3. Use image editing tools to edit the images for use.

4. As a team, decide on what will be included in the newsletter and the design.

5. Create at least one vector image to use in the two-page newsletter.

6. As a team, discuss the skills learned in the unit that can be used in creating the newsletter.

7. Each member should create his or her own newsletter, using the design ideas from the meeting.

8. Save the document as ***volunteer_event***.

Digital Portfolio

Self-Assessment

1. Select five items from Unit 5 that you intend to add to your portfolio. Write an assessment of what you learned from this activity. Include what you learned from creating the content as well as what skills you used that you had learned in the unit. What caused you the most difficulty? What did you enjoy most about completing the activity? What would you do differently if you had the opportunity to repeat it?

2. Save your self-assessments with the name of the file and **_*sa*** added to the end of the file name.

Collecting and Organizing Sample Projects

Collect projects and assignments from Unit 5 that you want to include in your portfolio. These assignments do not all need to be your best work. Move the documents to those folders. If available, a copy of the rubric should also be included for each of the projects/assignments that will be included in the portfolio. Back up all files from the portfolio as your plan outlined.

Journalizing Progress

Using a word processing software, tablet PC, handheld device, or blog, add to the journal of this ongoing project. Save the journal as ***portfolio_journal*** or give the link to the blog to your instructor. Alternatively, you could keep an audio journal of your work completed by using podcasting or other digital audio methods. Consult your instructor for the journal method to use for this class.

unit 6

Business Publications

Freelance Writer & Graphic Designer

What I do every day

I help my clients communicate with their customers by advising on marketing strategies, then executing marketing plans. This involves creating materials that speak to specific target audiences about their needs and the solutions that my clients offer.

How I use DTP in my job

I use DTP as a tool for creating visual materials that communicate my clients' messages effectively to their customers. I design logos and corporate identity, and printed materials such as mailers, brochures, advertising, and websites.

The best part of my job

What I enjoy most is the moment when a concept comes together in my head, matching the client's objective to specific pieces of language and visual elements. I strive for creating designs in which the words and images work hand in hand.

The worst part of my job

Being a freelancer, I am only paid when I work, and I only work when I go out and find it. The downside of this is when, after a lengthy period of being extremely busy, I complete my projects and find myself without work. That's because when I'm busy with projects I have no time to be chasing down new work. That "uh-oh" moment is the worst part of my job.

What I need to know and be able to do

First and foremost, I need to know my clients and what matters to their customers. The world's best creator of pretty layouts is worthless without this knowledge, because graphic design is art with a purpose. The purpose is communication. Secondly, I need to know how to use the tools available to acquire visual materials and create designs. This means software and the Internet.

How I prepared to be a freelance writer and graphic designer

I have a BA in Journalism and years of experience in the marketing and advertising industry. I began freelancing in the post-9/11 economic slowdown and have not been disappointed.

How the Web has impacted this field

Immeasurably! The Web enables near-instantaneous research into products, services, concepts, and my clients' competition—all of which assist me in the creative work I prepare. Gone are the days of poring over stock photography source books or images on CD. All photo research can be done online using the robust search engines developed just for this task. The Web has radically transformed the approval process as well. Instead of driving across town to meet with clients or mailing hard copies of design mockups to distant clients, I use the Web to transmit detailed high-resolution files that are viewable on any computer.

19 Maximizing Production Time

Objectives

- *Develop understanding of using templates to speed up design.*

- *Learn to use style sheets to manage text and paragraphs quickly.*

- *Understand how Find and Change functions can reduce the time it takes to make changes.*

- *Discover how joining a database or spreadsheet to a desktop-published design can personalize a document.*

Templates are predesigned documents intended to be used as a base design, with text and images replacing greeking and placeholder images.

Introduction

One of the issues that every businessperson faces is time management. Desktop publishers continually struggle with the need to produce more in less time. Making typography decisions can be time-consuming. So can finding the right image. Design choices can consume a desktop publisher's day. While it is often not possible to speed up those parts of the process, there are tools and techniques that can help you maximize your desktop publishing time. This chapter is designed to teach you how to use these tools to produce a quality product in a shorter time.

Templates

One of the best ways to produce more in less time is to use a template. A **template** is a predesigned page, or pages, created for use in a number of different ways. The designers of templates are often professionals who have spent the time necessary to make good typography and layout choices. Your task is to fill the space provided with text and to replace the template images with your own. InDesign and QuarkXPress offer some templates as part of their software purchase. Other templates can be purchased from professional design businesses.

Uses

Templates often include greeked text that can be replaced with the text you want to include. Placeholder images can be replaced with your own images. Figure 19.1 is an example of a brochure template supplied by Adobe InDesign.

Figure 19.1
This brochure is laid out in three columns with places for your own images and text.

PROOFREADING TIPS

If you are using a template, watch out for greeked text that you failed to delete. It's easy for a line or even a word to remain behind when you overwrite text. If you are importing text from another source into a document, it's easy to overlook these stray pieces. Always do a final read when you are finished and ready to print a document.

Notice the text and figures that can be replaced while still maintaining a professional design. Even a return postcard is provided as part of this layout. Figure 19.2 shows the inside design of this double-sided brochure. While the document is designed to be used to advertise a hotel, it could easily be adjusted to work for other uses.

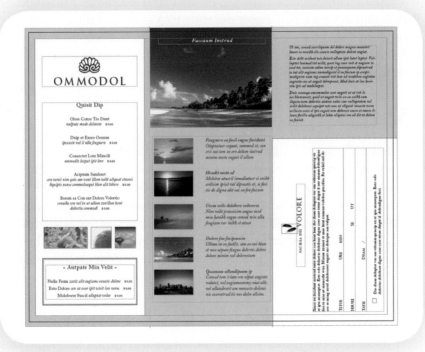

Figure 19.2
The template of the inside of this brochure includes a placeholder for a menu.

Templates are designed to be copied. Often we get so used to avoiding any hint of unethical use of other's work that we forget some work is supposed to be borrowed. Templates are a good example. However, just because they are designed to be used, you are not free to share them with others. If you have purchased a template from a design source, there are limitations to the way you can use them. Sharing them with others is not allowed unless the license specifically indicates that you have such a right.

Templates are designs that you can turn into exactly what you need. Do not feel restricted by the original use for which they were designed. For example, if you needed a flyer to advertise an event that included a meal that requires a reservation, the brochure in the previous figure would be an excellent choice. The attached postcard could then be used to indicate the number of people planning to attend the dinner.

Saving

Templates are saved with slightly different extensions. For example, InDesign templates are saved as .indt. QuarkXPress templates are saved as .qpt. When you save a template, it defaults to a standard file format. This helps ensure that you are not overwriting your template. To save changes to a template, you must specifically indicate that you want it saved as a template.

Style Sheets

Style sheets are a set of formatting choices that can be applied to text or a paragraph.

A **style sheet** is a design shortcut that is not used nearly enough. Desktop publishers who use style sheets find that their workload is much less demanding. Style sheets allow you to set a style for a paragraph or a character that you can apply to any paragraph or word in a document. If you design a style with a specific font or size or paragraph spacing and then apply it to text, the font or paragraph is changed instantly to the style. In addition, if you change the style, all text with that style is also changed.

Character

Character styles are choices applied only to text.

In desktop publishing programs such as InDesign and QuarkXPress, styles fall into two categories: character and paragraph. A **character style** includes a wide variety of decisions: font family, font style, font size, leading,

The use of style sheets is an industry standard. It's expected that documents will be developed with style sheets. Not using them is a sign of a novice desktop publisher. Even if you are often making a one-page flyer, get in the habit of establishing styles. Once the document is complete, consider saving it as a template so that you can reuse the design in another way. If a style has been set for text such as headings, you can change the font size or style quickly by just modifying the style. Learning to work quickly is an essential skill, and templates and style sheets help you do it.

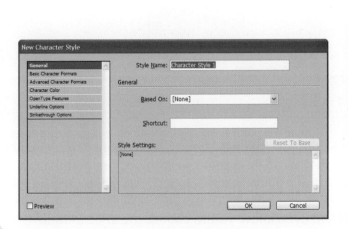

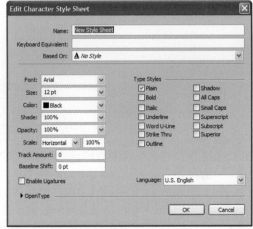

Figure 19.3a
InDesign character styles are changed using the list on the left of the dialog box.

Figure 19.3b
QuarkXPress character styles are changed using checkboxes and drop-down menus.

kerning, tracking, case, and position. In addition, you can select character color, underlining, strikethroughs, and even languages. Character styles only apply to text. Figures 19.3a and 19.3b show examples of character style choices.

Paragraph

A **paragraph style** defines the way a paragraph is formatted, including all the options listed above for characters as well as others. You can choose indents, spacing, tabs, hyphenation, justification, drop caps, bullets, numbering, and rules. Basically anything that you can select when creating

Paragraph styles are choices applied to both text and paragraph formatting.

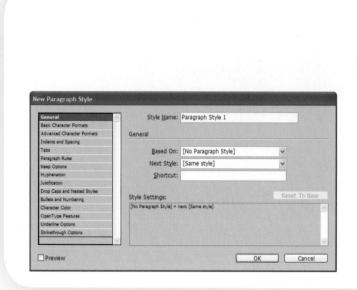

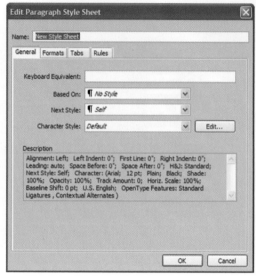

Figure 19.4a
InDesign paragraph styles include all the choices for characters as well as paragraph choices.

Figure 19.4b
QuarkXPress paragraph styles use a series of tabs to move among choices.

a paragraph can be set with a style. Figures 19.4a and 19.4b show examples of paragraph style choices.

Creating

Styles can be created from text that has already been defined or by making custom style choices. Styles can be based upon other styles and then modified. You can also assign shortcuts to styles to reduce the time required to assign a style.

Paragraph styles will even allow you to choose the style to follow the paragraph in which you have assigned a style. For example, if you always want a text paragraph to follow a heading paragraph, you can indicate that in the style. This means that you will not have to assign a style to the next paragraph. Simply styling the initial paragraph as a text paragraph will do this for you. Figures 19.4a and 19.4b included drop-down boxes from which you could choose a "based-on" style, as well as the next style.

Naming

Assigning a unique name to a style will make it easier to select the one you need in the future. When naming a style, keep in mind that you may be using this style months later when you have forgotten exactly what its purpose was. Naming a style carefully gives you valuable information. For example, a style named "style 1" is not much help. A style named "figure caption" tells you instantly that you want to use this style for text that describes an image.

Desktop publishing rules do not remain the same from year to year. Changes occur on a regular basis. For example, for years the words "Internet" and "Web" were always capitalized. Today some publishers still use that rule. Others, such as the publisher of *Wired* magazine, have decided that it is not necessary. Tools such as Find and Replace are useful when you must make global modifications because of rule changes such as these.

Find and Change

The Find and Change function in desktop publishing software can allow you to make changes instantly. For example, if you realize after you have completed a document that you used two spaces after each sentence instead of one, you can use the Find function to locate each time you spaced twice. The Change function can then change the two spaces to one. InDesign provides an option that allows you to search for specific formats (see Figure 19.5). This means that if you want to change every instance of bold to italic, you can do so easily. Find and Change is a time-saving tool that all desktop publishers should use.

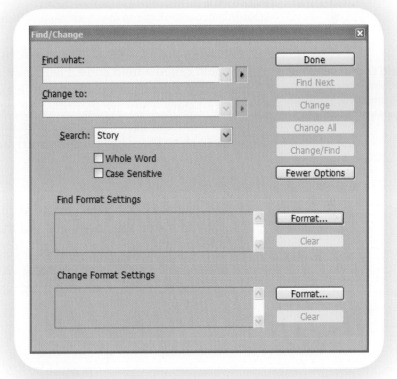

Figure 19.5
The InDesign Find/Change dialog box allows you to choose the area in which you will search. You can limit it to a single story or the entire document.

Mail Merge

One of the best uses of technology to maximize time is the Mail Merge feature available in desktop publishing software. **Mail merge** is the process of creating personalized documents using a database or a spreadsheet. A single document such as a business letter can be created that is then mail merged to create multiple documents, each of which contains a single record.

Mail merge joins a spreadsheet or database to a document in order to individualize the document using the data.

Field Codes

Databases and spreadsheets are created using headers that define the information in each column or field. For example, in Figure 19.6, the headers consist of first, last, address, city, state, and zip. Each of these lists

	A	B	C	D	E	F	G
1	first	last	address	city	state	zip	
2	Marvin	Taylor	3567 103rd	Mason	OH	45050	
3	Corinne	Allen	215 Briarwood Lane	San Angelo	TX	76904	
4	Victoria	Bailey	3311 Sandalwood	Russellville	AK	72801	
5	Sara	Rauch	2566 Samuel Blvd.	Tallahassee	FL	32309	
6							
7							
8							
9							

Figure 19.6
Spreadsheets gather data into rows and columns. Each column of information is a field.

A **field code** is a means of identifying information that is to be entered from an attached spreadsheet or database.

represents a field. To mail merge a document, you must insert the name of a field called a **field code**. Field codes identify the data that must be inserted in the document. Notice in Figure 19.7 the field codes for name, city, and state. They are identified by two arrows on each side of the field name. InDesign uses the Data Merge palette to attach the data to the document. QuarkXPress uses add-on software.

Merging

Once a document has been created with the appropriate field names, then it is time to merge the document and the data. This creates a new document for each line of data or record. Notice in Figure 19.8 that the field

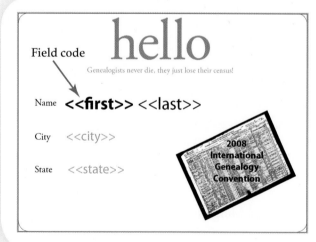

Figure 19.7
Field codes "read" the data from a spreadsheet or a database.

Figure 19.8
Merging a document creates a new document for each record.

codes in the nametag have now been replaced with a person's name and address.

Labels

One of the most common uses of mail merge is to create labels or envelopes. Label design is different from other mail merge documents in that each page will have more than a single record. Notice in Figure 19.9 that the same set of field codes are duplicated four times so that four records appear on a single page. Often the manufacturers of labels will provide a template for use with different size labels, making the process easier.

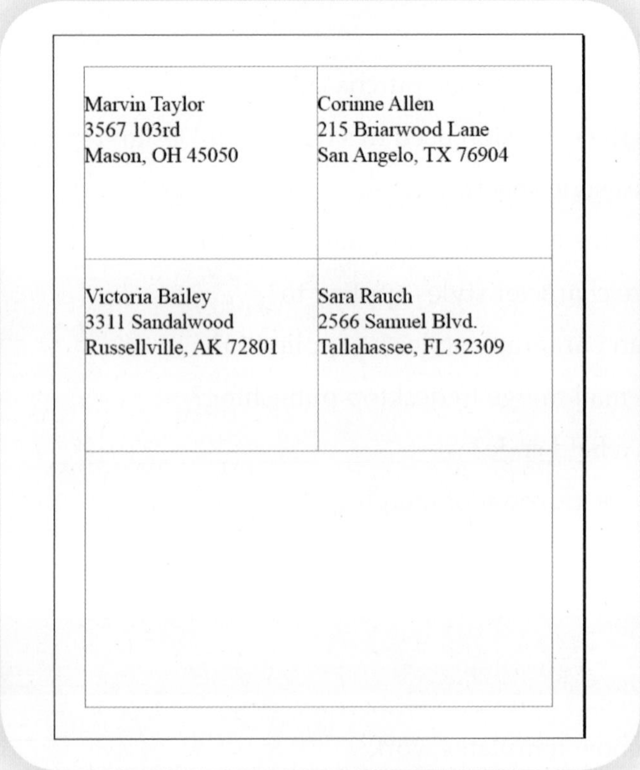

Marvin Taylor 3567 103rd Mason, OH 45050	Corinne Allen 215 Briarwood Lane San Angelo, TX 76904
Victoria Bailey 3311 Sandalwood Russellville, AK 72801	Sara Rauch 2566 Samuel Blvd. Tallahassee, FL 32309

Figure 19.9
Labels incorporate multiple records into a single page.

SUMMARY

In this chapter you learned how templates can be used to maximize production time. You saw that style sheets allow you to change a character or paragraph style just once, which will then change all occurrences of that style. You learned how Find and Change can make it easy to find errors and change them without having to manually look for them. You discovered that mail merge makes it possible to create multiple documents from a single design using data from a spreadsheet or database.

KEY TERMS

character styles	mail merge	style sheets
field code	paragraph styles	templates

REVIEW

Answer the following questions on your own computer.

1. What is a template?
2. Where can templates be purchased?
3. What is the extension used in saving an InDesign template?
4. What is a style sheet?
5. What are the two categories that styles fall into?
6. What are character styles applied to?
7. What can paragraph styles be applied to?
8. What is mail merge in desktop publishing?
9. What is a field code?
10. What is the purpose of merging?

DISCUSS

1. Explain how templates work.
2. Discuss how the process of saving templates helps you to avoid overwriting the template.
3. Review some of the formatting that can be used in character styles.
4. Review some of the formatting that can be used in paragraph styles.
5. Explain how styles are created.
6. Explain why the name you choose for a style is important.
7. List some uses of mail merge in desktop publishing.
8. Explain the ethical use of templates.
9. Explain the use of find and change.
10. Give an example of something you should always look for in proofreading when using templates.

to the website at
academic.cengage.com/school/dtp

Activity 1 Templates

1. Create a new document that is 8-1/4" × 13" with no facing pages. If possible, save the preset as **cereal box**.

2. Change the preferences to inches if needed.

3. Draw a text box on the entire background filled with light yellow. Extend the text box to the edges rather than only the margins.

4. Draw a text box at 1" vertically that is about 1/4" in height. Extend the text box to the edges rather than only the margins. Fill the text box with white with a black drop shadow.

5. Draw a text box that is 4" × 3". Move it so that it is on top of the white filled text box with the left edge of the box starting at 1/4". Fill the text box with red with no border. Add feathering to the text box that has a width of 1" with Diffused Corners and no Noise.

6. Key **Brand Name** in the text box. Change the font to Vivaldi font type, 48 pt. Center the text horizontally and vertically in the text box. Apply blue to the text with an outline of red.

7. Draw a 2" × 2" picture box. Move the picture box to 2" on the horizontal ruler and 2" on the vertical ruler.

8. Draw a 4" × 2" text box. Rotate the text box 10 degrees. Move the text box with the top left corner aligned at 2-1/2" on the horizontal ruler and 3" on the vertical ruler.

9. Key **Name of Cereal** in the text box. Change the font type to Toxica, 40 pt. Center the text horizontally and vertically. Apply a red stroke to the name of the cereal.

10. Draw a picture box from left to right margin, beginning at 2" on the vertical ruler and ending at 8-1/2".

11. Draw a text box, beginning at 11" on the vertical ruler and ending at the bottom margin. Fill the text box with blue. Key **Net Wt. 00.0 oz.** [Enter] **(0 lb. 0.0 oz.) (000 g).** Apply small caps and white to the text. Resize the text box to fit the text; then move the text box to the bottom left corner.

12. Draw a text box that is 4" × 3". Drag to the bottom right corner. Key **Advertisement for inside of box** in the text box. Apply a 10 degree shear to the text box.

13. Save the document as **cereal_box_template**. Change the file type to save as a template.

Activity 2 Creating Styles

1. Create a letter-sized document with two columns and no facing pages.

2. Draw a text box from left to right margin, down to 6p0 on the vertical ruler. Key **Style Sheets** in the text box. Change the font type to

Volkswagen, 60 pt. Fill the text box with orange feathered at .5 Feather Width and Noise at 10% if available. Center the text vertically and horizontally.

3. Import the following files into the columns, threading text as needed: **style_sheets, character_styles,** and **paragraph_styles**.

4. Create a new paragraph style sheet that includes Cambria font type, 18 pt. font size, and 10 pt. leading. Alignment should be set at center with an orange color applied to the heading. If available, add rules below the heading. Name the paragraph style **heading**.

5. Apply the heading style that was created in Instruction 4 above to the three headings in the document.

6. Create a new paragraph style named **paragraph**. Change size to 14 pt., first-line indent to .5, and Space Before and After to .2.

7. Apply the paragraph heading style to all three paragraphs.

8. Create a new paragraph style named **subheading**. Set the alignment to left, Space Before and After to .2, and font size to 14 pt.

9. Apply the subheading paragraph style to the two subheadings.

10. Click on the headline text box across the top. If available, create a new object Style. Name it **headline**.

11. Save document as **styles**.

Activity 3 Find and Change

1. Create a new blank document using the defaults.

2. Place the **find_and_change** file from your student data files at the top left margin of the document.

3. Select all the text in the document and change the font size to 18 pt.

4. Use the Find/Change feature on your desktop publishing software to find Cameron and change to Albuquerque. Do not change the first instance. You should have two total changes for the document.

5. Use the Find/Change feature on your desktop publishing software to find Albuquerque and change the text to Bauhaus font style with red font color.

6. Save document as **albuquerque**.

Activity 4 Data Merge

1. Create a blank document using the defaults.

2. Import **primary_document** from your student data files into the page. Reformat the information to create a flyer. Add eye-catching elements

to the flyer to gain attention. Leave a space for the name of the homeowner that the flyer will go to.

3. Use **data_source** from your student data files to merge with the primary document. Only include the field code for the person's name on the flyer. Perform the merge.

4. Save document as **homeowners_flyer**.

5. Use **data_source** from your student data files and your desktop publishing software to create labels to mail the flyer.

6. Save document as **homeowners_labels**.

Activity 5 DTP Book

1. Import and save the following files into your desktop publishing software. Create the appropriate number of pages needed to import all text in the file. Save each one as a separate file with the same file name as the imported file. You should have four solution files when you are finished.

   1_getting_started_with_dtp

   2_planning_your_document

   3_creating_your_document

   4_importing_graphics

2. Create a new book. Save it as **dtp_book**.

3. Add the four documents in step 1 to the book. Create the following paragraph styles:

   heading – Font type Arial Bold, Font size 18 pt., centered, navy blue color

   subheading – Font type Arial, Font size 14 pt., centered, navy blue color

   paragraphs – First-line indent .5", .2" before and after paragraphs, keep lines of paragraph together with two lines on one page and at least two lines on the next page

4. Apply the three paragraph styles to all documents in the book. Add pages as needed and place or thread text as needed in each chapter of the book.

5. If available, use automatic pagination with the page numbering continuing from previous document.

6. Save the book again.

7. Save **1_getting_started_with_dtp** as **book_template** with a template file type.

1. Using your favorite search engine, search for desktop publishing shortcuts or use your specific desktop publishing software with the word "shortcuts." For example, search for InDesign CS2 Shortcuts or QuarkXPress 7 Shortcuts.

2. Bookmark at least five sites that include tips, tutorials, or free downloads on templates or creating styles. When bookmarking the sites, organize the bookmarks in a folder with your name and shortcuts.

3. Download one of the templates to use, or follow one of the tutorials on creating a style. Use the template or the new knowledge you have acquired to create a reflection journal. Reflect back for at least a week or 10 days on what you have accomplished in school as far as completion of assignments, tests, quizzes, etc. Reflect on the use of your time at home for completion of these projects. Include in your reflection all of your classes and activities. In the reflection also include a plan to improve what you may have accomplished if needed. This plan for improvement can be a separate article, paragraph, or list, or it can be a part of your reflection. Be honest with yourself! The content in this project is for your own self-improvement.

4. Save document as ***exploring_shortcuts***.

Using Logos

Introduction

Now that you have learned a variety of desktop publishing skills such as typography and layout, it is time to put these skills to use in business documents. Nearly every document that is distributed by a business uses desktop publishing in some way. This includes letters and the envelopes in which they are mailed, handouts available at presentations, business cards given to potential customers, and ads. Most of these will include the company logo.

Objectives

- *Understand design features of a logo.*

- *Learn to integrate logos into standard business publications.*

Logo

One of the most important components of any business publication is the company logo. A **logo** is an image that instantly identifies a business, containing a graphic element and a logotype. A **logotype** is text that is set using a specific typeface and may be arranged in a particular way. Special fonts may be designed just for this purpose. The logotype could consist of the company's name, initials, and sometimes a **slogan**. A slogan is a phrase that identifies the company's mission or purpose. Slogans may also be short statements designed to encourage purchase of a product, such as Coca Cola's "The Real Thing." Figure 20.1 is an example with an image, logotype, and a slogan.

Usually logos are designed by professionals and then used by desktop publishers. However, it is important to understand how logos are designed so that you can use them effectively.

A **logo** is an image and text combined to identify a business or organization.

A **logotype** is the text included in a logo. It may be a distinctive typeface.

A **slogan** is a statement or phrase that identifies a company's mission or image.

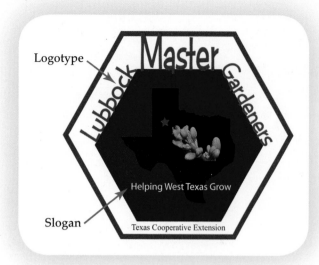

Figure 20.1
This logo uses a brown background and a simple colored flower to project the gardening image it represents.

Images

Images are often incorporated into business logos. These images can become so firmly attached to the name of the company that even without the company name, the business is recognized. For example, a picture of a Quaker man instantly calls up the name Quaker Oats. Images are usually simple line drawings rather than complicated photographs. Often the best logo images are connected in some way to the corporate name. A good example is the shell used by Shell Oil Company. Other companies use images of the products they sell, such as the Mercedes steering wheel.

Color

You have already studied the impact of color on emotions and the senses. The use of color in logos is important for these same reasons. Companies often select colors that reflect their identity such as the use of green for a tractor company or the use of pink for a business that sells makeup. Notice in Figure 20.1 the use of green and browns to reflect the gardening theme.

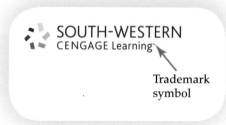

Figure 20.2
The South-Western logo is simple yet distinctive.

Logotype

Often logos are created using the actual letters of the name of the company rendered in a distinctive typeface. The Cengage logo (the publisher of your text) is an example of this (see Figure 20.2). South-Western is a part of Cengage Learning. The logo consists of the parent company with the subsidiary's name above. Notice the TM (trademark) symbol has been integrated into the logo.

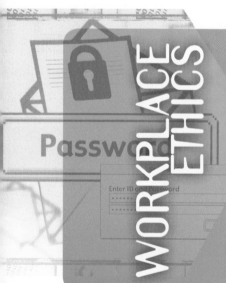

WORKPLACE ETHICS

As you have read, businesses spend time and money developing a logo. The distinctive logotype is part of their brand. Others who borrow their logo are stealing something of more value than may appear at first glance. If someone publishes the logo in such a way that it detracts from the good image of the company, the business can suffer. As a result, companies are diligent in protecting their logos and branding.

There are a number of ways that words are used as a logo. Often letters are joined together, sharing common vertical strokes as shown in Figure 20.3. Sometimes they are joined using the horizontal strokes or crossbars. Occasionally part of a stroke is removed to use the white space between the letters as a visual connection. Some designers reverse the second letter of the name to use white space to make the letter visible. Another technique is to crop away part of the letters. Interlocking letters is a frequently used technique. Letters can be layered over one another using transparency. Finally, letters can be contained in a box. When text is used in this way, the letters are handled more like graphics than type.

In order to use these techniques, you need to experiment with different typefaces and styles. Thick and thin strokes can be used creatively. Use of serifs is an interesting way to join letters. Notice in Figure 20.4 how changing from a sans serif to a serif font creates a different look to the logotype.

Slogans

Slogans can be an important part of a logo when they are distinctive enough that the statement alone identifies the company. "Just Do It" does not require the Nike name for the audience to recognize the connection.

Uses

With a logo in place, it often falls upon desktop publishers to design standard business documents for use by the organization. Once these designs are created using desktop publishing software, either templates or mass printings are created for use by others. For example, letterhead may be designed and then printed in bulk. Others use the preprinted pages for their letters instead of blank paper.

Figure 20.3
This logotype joins the initials of the organization in such a way that they appear to be a single unit.

Figure 20.4
Looping letters within each other makes for an interesting image.

Challenges

Logos are used in many ways. The three most common placements are in letterheads, business cards, and envelopes. Often the three are designed as a package to provide a sense of continuity. The challenge of using the same logo for each of these is that the sizes differ so widely. The ratio of length to width gives an idea of the difference between each one. A letter has a 1:1.3 ratio, a business card is 1.75:1, and a #10 business envelope is 2.3:1. Merely placing a logo in the same place on each piece makes for an awkward design. Using components of the logo such as color, slogans, and images to create a slightly different arrangement while still maintaining the overall image is one way to use a logo for design.

Letterhead

When designing letterheads, keep in mind the information that needs to be included. Letterheads require the name of the company, the address, the phone number, and usually the business logo. Often the web address of the company is also included. Sometimes a footer is used at the bottom of the page as a location for information such as an address or phone number. Obviously, you must also anticipate the space needed for the text of the letter. Standard business letters use 1" margins; however, the logo may extend beyond that. Figure 20.5 is an example of one way that a letterhead can be designed with a logo.

Figure 20.5
A letterhead such as this one eliminates the need for the sender to include the business information within the letter.

Occasionally, a business will create a **watermark** that is imprinted into paper intended for use as letterhead. This watermark can be a pale version of the company logo.

A **watermark** is a pale image or text imprinted into paper.

Business Card

A business card contains information similar to that found in a letterhead. Keep in mind that most business cards are 2" × 3.5" but that you do not have that full space to work with. You must build into your design at least a .125" margin within that size. In addition, there must be a place for the name of the person for whom the card is designed, the person's job title, phone numbers (work and mobile), and that person's email address. Figure 20.6 uses the same information found on the letterhead but with a slightly different design. Notice how much more prominent the logo is.

Figure 20.6
This business card is preprinted, requiring only the addition of the card holder's name.

Envelope

Envelopes require much less information than a business card or letter. The envelope generally uses the logo as well as the company name and address. When designing a business envelope, pay close attention to mailing regulations. There are restrictions that limit the placement of information on the envelope so that it does not interfere with the machines that read the recipient's address. Figure 20.7 uses a small version of the logo and the address to create an envelope design.

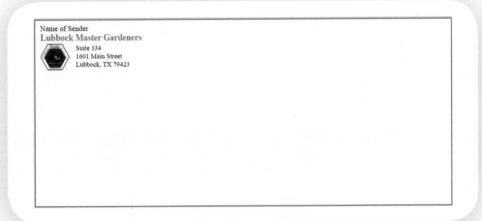

Figure 20.7
Business envelopes are typically long and thin with limited space. The logo is reduced in size to make it fit into the allowable space.

Email

Occasionally businesses design email templates that include a logo, but generally the senders merely use a signature that includes company information.

PROOFREADING TIPS

When designing a logo or using one in a document, think carefully about the colors and fonts you select. Proofread for color and font appropriateness. It's easy to make a decision today that won't seem so appealing tomorrow. Always allow yourself time to separate from your design and then go back to consider it with fresh eyes. Have others give you their impression of your color and font choices. The exotic font that appeals to you may send a different message to others. Proofreading isn't just about finding mistakes. It's also about reviewing work you have already completed.

Memos

Memos are similar to letters except they are much briefer. The logo and company information is generally limited to the upper portion of the memo with designations for the person receiving the memo (TO), the person sending it (FROM), the date, and the subject. The margins for a memo are similar to those for a business letter.

Other Documents

Other documents such as handouts, proposals, and reports may also need to be desktop designed. The logo and other details that you include in a business card or letterhead will usually be included as identifying information. Since these documents will generally be printed on standard letter-size paper, placement and size may be similar to those you used on the letterhead.

Keep in mind that proposals and reports are usually bound on the left side, which means that instead of a 1" side margin you will need one that is 1.25". This may require an adjustment to your design if you are using the same one created for your letterhead.

Standard Design

As you have seen, there are a number of different uses for the same logo. Businesses often establish a series of designs for each situation and then provide these to anyone who might need them.

SUMMARY

In this chapter you learned that logos consist of images, color, logotypes, and slogans. You saw that it is a challenge to use a logo in the design of standard business documents such as a letterhead, a business card, and an envelope because of the difference in proportions. You learned that logos are often included in the design of most documents produced by a business.

KEY TERMS

logo   slogan   watermark

logotype

REVIEW

Answer the following questions on your own computer.

1. What is a logo?
2. What is a logotype?

3. What is a slogan?

4. What is the purpose of a slogan?

5. When designing a letterhead, what information should be included?

6. What is a watermark?

7. What is the standard size of a business card?

8. What should the margin be on a business card?

9. When designing a business envelope, what should you pay close attention to?

10. What is the difference between memos and letters?

DISCUSS

1. Explain some ways in which words can be used as a logo.

2. Discuss the three most common uses of logos in business documents and how the logos vary in each of them.

3. Explain logotype, how it relates to the logo, and what can be included in a logotype.

4. Discuss the importance of a slogan in the identity of a company.

5. Explain the design of email templates.

6. Review the differences that should be considered in designing proposals and reports.

7. Discuss how changing a logo that has been in place for a long period of time could affect a business.

8. List some tips that help in designing logos.

9. Explain why companies are diligent in protecting their logos and branding.

10. Discuss some design choices that need to be considered if you are designing for an international market.

APPLY

Activity 1 Examining Logos

1. From the Internet, locate three logos that you have noticed recently. Save a copy of each image. Alternatively, if you cannot find these on the Internet, use printed copies and scan each image. Crop the images you save so that each only contains the logo.

to the website at
academic.cengage.com/school/dtp

2. Create a new desktop publishing document and insert a two-column table. In the first column, place a copy of the image. In the second column, write a description of the design of the image, including the following:

    ⊃ Brief description of the entire logo

    ⊃ Brief description of the logotype

    ⊃ Brief description of the colors used

    ⊃ Any other element used in the logo that captured your attention with an explanation of why

    ⊃ Your overall impression of the logo including any thoughts on why this design was used

3. Save the document as ***logo_ideas***.

Activity 2 Logo and Slogan Design

1. Design a logo of your initials using your image editing software. Use colors, fonts, and other elements as desired to create an identity symbol of yourself.

2. Save document as ***logo_design***. This logo will be used in some of the remaining activities.

3. Using your image editing software, design a slogan for yourself that includes two or three words only.

4. Save the document as ***slogan_design***.

Activity 3 Business Set

1. Design a letterhead, business card, and envelope using your logo and slogan created in Activity 2. Be sure to read the information in the textbook and follow the guidelines provided for information required on each document, sizes, and margins required.

2. Save the document as ***letterhead_design***, ***business_card_design***, and ***envelope_design*** with the file type of template.

Activity 4 Memo Design

1. Design a memo using your logo, slogan, and headings TO, FROM, DATE, and SUBJECT.

2. Save document as ***memo_template*** with the file type template.

3. Write a three-paragraph memo to your instructor on what you have learned in this chapter. Limit the memo to one page.

4. Save the document as ***instructor_memo***. Get specific instructions from your instructor on printing the memo on your memo template.

Activity 5 Team Logo

1. In a team of three or four students, decide on a business to begin. Name the business and create a slogan for the business with two or three words only.

2. Elect a member to keep a logo of the team's design ideas. Using desktop publishing software, the elected member should insert a two-column table. In the left column, key **logo**. Key some design ideas in the second column for the team logo. In the next row, key **slogan** and **design ideas** in the second column. In the third row, key **letterhead** and design ideas in the second column. In the fourth row, key **business card** and **design ideas** in the second column. Each member should give input for the design ideas. Save document as ***team_ideas***.

3. Each member should use the design ideas to create a logo, slogan, letterhead, and business card for the company that their team has created. Save documents as ***team_logo***, ***team_slogan***, ***team_letterhead***, and ***team_business_card***.

EXPLORE

1. Using your favorite search engine, search for the history of watermarks.

2. If available, use the story editor to write an article that includes an explanation of the purpose of watermarks, where they originated, what type of documents they were normally used on, and the differences in paper and digital watermarks. The article should be no less than 150 words. Include at least two resources. Save document as ***watermark_history***.

3. Format the desktop publishing document in proper academic report format with a title and the resources included.

4. Save document as ***watermark_history***.

Objectives

- *Learn which components make up a newsletter.*

- *Discover design techniques that make newsletters easier to read.*

Introduction

One of the most common desktop publishing tasks is creating a newsletter. Newsletters are similar to newspapers in that they contain many of the same components. The difference is that a newspaper is designed to record current information and distribute it to readers immediately. Newsletters are printed less frequently and are not as current. They are used for a number of purposes. Newsletters can be used as a sales tool, a means of distributing information about a particular topic, or a publicity medium.

Components

A newsletter is designed using standard components, many of which you have already studied in this text. You can create a newsletter of your own design, or you can choose to use a template. Newsletter template designs contain various standard components, but you may need to add other components yourself.

Nameplate

A **nameplate** contains the name of the newsletter along with other information such as the date, issue, and volume number.

The **nameplate** is made up of information found at the top of the opening page. It contains the name of the newsletter as well as other information such as the volume number, the date of publication, the company logo or motto, and other identifying details. Generally, the nameplate appears in the top 1/4 or 1/3 of the page, although some designs place it along the left column or even in the middle of the page. Figure 21.1 shows an example of a newsletter with the nameplate at the top of the page.

Nameplate

Figure 21.1
This nameplate combines the motto, the table of contents, issue number, volume number, date, and name of the publication into a splashy nameplate.

PROOFREADING TIPS

If you are including a table of contents on the front page of your newsletter, be sure to verify the page numbers as a final stage before sending the document to be printed. It's easy to move an article at the last minute and forget to change the matching page number. Make the same check for jump lines. It's a sign that you aren't paying attention to details when a jump line directs the reader to the wrong page.

Table of Contents

While newsletters are generally only a few pages long, a table of contents serves an important purpose. While it may not be essential to locating information, it is frequently used as a means of encouraging readers to read past the first page. Often a table of contents uses cryptic words to describe articles in an effort to tease readers into searching for an article. Notice in Figure 21.2 that the table of contents is brief, yet designed to attract attention.

Header

A **header** is similar to a nameplate in that it repeats the name of the newsletter and the page number and often includes the date. However, the header appears on pages other than the first one. Often a complete header is used on every page, or it may only appear on one side of a two-page spread. Figure 21.3 shows a header that spreads across two pages.

A **header** restates the newsletter name and usually provides the page number and sometimes the date.

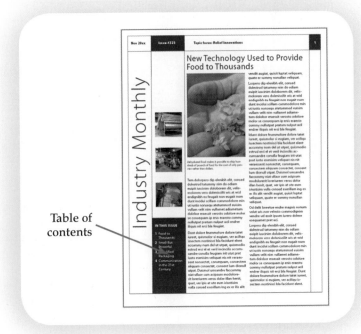

Table of contents

Figure 21.2
A table of contents draws the reader's interest into the remainder of the newsletter.

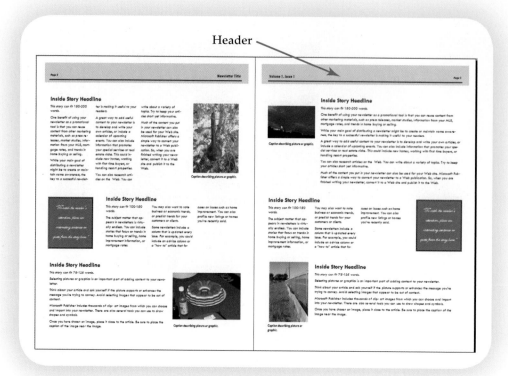

Figure 21.3
The blue border at the top of the pages identifies this newsletter's header.

A **masthead** contains contact information that identifies who publishes the newsletter.

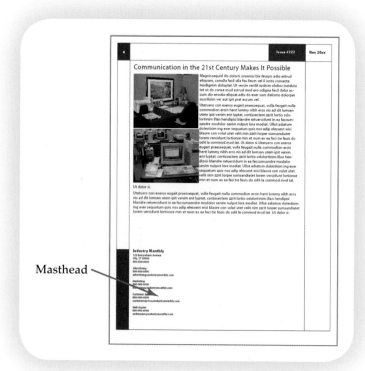

Figure 21.4
The masthead in this newsletter is brief but contains enough information to make it possible to contact the publisher.

Masthead

The **masthead** is often placed on the first inside page (page 2). It contains publication information such as the names of those who contributed articles; the address, phone numbers, and web address of the business; and subscription policies. Contact information including an email address is also usually included. The masthead in Figure 21.4 provides ample information about the publisher of the newsletter.

It is sometimes easy to forget to include a masthead since they are often left out of template designs. A masthead is particularly important for those reading the newsletter who might not be part of your expected audience. For example, the complete address might be of interest to someone unfamiliar with the organization that produced the newsletter, and that person might not know in what town the business is located.

Newsletters are big business. Often we think of them as just in-house documents used to notify employees about insurance policy changes or new babies. That is not the case. Newsletters are also sold on a subscription basis to a specialized audience. For example, some financial newsletters charge several hundred dollars to update readers on the latest stock purchases and changes in the financial industry. Genealogy newsletters appeal to those searching for information on their ancestors. Even car enthusiasts subscribe to newsletters to learn about the latest changes in the automobile industry. Having the skills to produce a readable and interesting newsletter is valuable to those looking for information that is not always available to the general public.

Headlines

Headlines are not titles. A title is a line of text that contains no verb or implied action. **Headlines** are miniature sentences that have action. Newsletters that use headlines rather than titles are more readable. Because headlines need to be shorter than a standard sentence, there are several shortcuts to use. The headlines in Figure 21.5 provide a sense of activity that would be missing if only titles were used.

Headlines are brief sentences that summarize the content of an article.

Figure 21.5
The opening page of this newsletter contains standard headlines as well as a kicker and a deck.

Headline Guidelines

1. Eliminate words such as "a," "an," and "the."

2. Use a comma instead of the word "and."

3. Remove as many adjectives and adverbs as possible.

4. Do not use end punctuation.

A sentence might read, "The new factory will be opened by March 1, and at that time there will be a guided tour of the facilities." A headline would read "Factory to open March 1 with guided tour." Notice how compressed the ideas are while still conveying the information.

Headlines can be **upstyle**, meaning that every word is capitalized, or **downstyle**, meaning that only the first word and proper nouns are capitalized. The example above used downstyle.

Variations of headlines include a **kicker** that is a short phrase over the headline. It is often used to make the article more intriguing by including information of particular interest. A **deck** is text that is placed between the headline and the actual article. Decks can be longer than headlines and may expand on the primary headline.

Subheads are small headlines or titles that are placed at intervals within an article to draw the reader from one part of an article to another. It is a way of making long text appear less dense.

Upstyle capitalizes all words in a headline.

Downstyle capitalizes only the first word and proper nouns in a headline.

A **kicker** is a brief headline or title that appears above the main headline. It is designed to draw attention to the main head.

A **deck** is a longer headline that appears below the main head. It provides additional information about the article.

A **subhead** is a brief title that separates paragraphs within an article. It is designed to make it easier to read long blocks of text.

A **byline** identifies the author of an article.

Figure 21.6
The byline on this page identifies the author of this particular article and gives author information at the end.

Byline

A **byline** is the name of the author of each article within a newsletter. Often newsletters are written by a single person with only a few pieces provided by others. If the newsletter editor is the primary author, often no bylines are given for those articles. Bylines can be placed at the beginning of an article or at the end. If a byline is placed at the end, often a short biographical description is included as well as contact information. You can see in Figure 21.6 that the byline gives credit to the author.

Articles

Newsletter articles are generally written for an audience with a common interest. Subjects are those that will appeal to this specific audience. Jargon and terms used by this audience do not have to be explained in the same way that a writer would need to do for a broader audience.

Because audiences are often looking for a "quick read," the writing is generally more compact. Sentences and paragraphs are shorter. Information is delivered as succinctly as possible.

Humor is an important component of newsletters. Jokes, cartoons, and bits of fun add interest and readability to newsletters. Dates and reminders are also frequently included in the content, often in the form of a calendar. Newsletters are designed to inform. All content is written with that in mind.

Illustrations

Illustrations add interest to a newsletter either in the form of a photograph or a drawing. Newsletters may be printed in black and white or they may have color. As color printing becomes more affordable, more newsletters are using color to create interest. Regardless of the type of illustration, captions are an important addition. Captions are widely read and add interest and information to the page.

Design

When designing a newsletter, there are special conventions that are used to make it easier to read. Other features are used to create interest.

Jump Lines

You have already studied jump lines in a previous chapter. These are used to guide a reader from one page to another on which an article is continued. It is tempting to place an entire article on a single page, but one of the conventions of newsletters is that articles are broken so that more articles can appear on the front page or earlier pages. These articles are then continued on later pages to encourage readers to view every page.

CHANGING WORKPLACE

Newsletters are not always distributed as print documents. Often they are published as PDF files or as web pages. This means that not only is a newsletter designer required to understand the demands of print, but the designer must also be able to work in a Web environment. It's important to understand the limitations as well as the possibilities that this change in method of distribution creates. On the Web, colors are available that might not be used in print. Links to other sites of interest are more easily accessible. Jump lines are seldom used and the table of contents becomes a navigation guide instead. Creative newsletter designers will begin to see more ways to use the Web to enhance their pages and make them more readable. Today's newsletter will not be the same as the one you will read next year.

Continuation Heads

A **continuation head** restates the original headline to simplify the process of finding an article that has been continued from a previous page.

Continuation heads are used in conjunction with jump lines so that the reader can find the continued article. Sometimes continuation heads are identical to the headline used when the article is first introduced. Other times they are modified slightly to draw interest. Figure 21.7 shows how continuation heads and jump lines make it easy for the reader to follow the article from page to page.

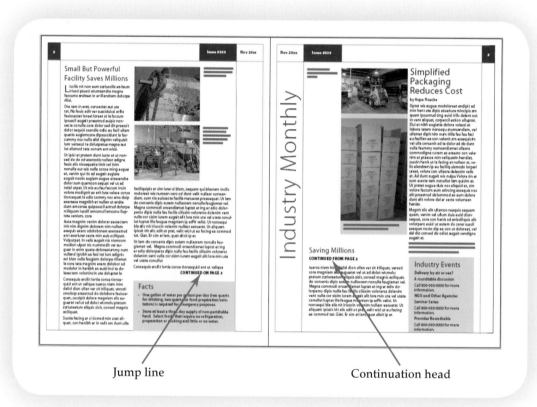

Jump line

Continuation head

Figure 21.7
Jump lines and continuation heads simplify the reading process.

End Signs

End signs are dingbats or symbols used to indicate that an article is complete. End signs are used less frequently today, but they can be a useful design feature. Often the sign is one that is similar to the company logo to give continuity to the page. Figure 21.8 uses end signs that add a touch of whimsy.

Tombstoning

Tombstoning is a design flaw. It occurs when two headlines are placed directly across from each other. This practice makes the two headlines appear connected when they are actually separate. Placing an image or figure above a headline is the most common means of avoiding this problem. Figure 21.9 is an example of a set of headlines that are tombstoned.

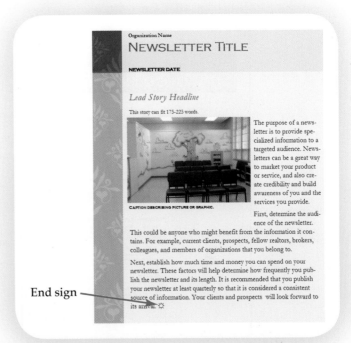

Figure 21.8
The sunshine symbol at the end makes it clear to the reader that the article is completed on this page.

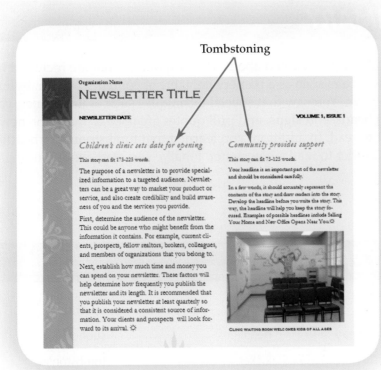

Figure 21.9
Even with the small space between the two columns, it would be easy for a reader to think that the two headlines are connected.

End signs are symbols or images that are used to indicate that an article is complete.

Tombstoning is the placement of two headlines across from each other, creating possible confusion when readers move their eyes across the page.

Pull Quotes

You have already seen pull quotes in a previous chapter. They are frequently used in newsletters as a means of attracting interest by quoting a particular passage from an article. Pull quotes are most often found on the front page, but they can appear wherever needed. The pull quote in Figure 21.10 adds to the content of the newsletter.

Binding

Most newsletters are printed on ledger-size paper (11" × 14"). They are usually bound using staples in a saddle stitch. If only two sheets are folded together (forming an eight-page document), occasionally no binding is used. Newsletters that are printed on letter-size paper (8.5" × 11") may be merely stapled in the upper corner.

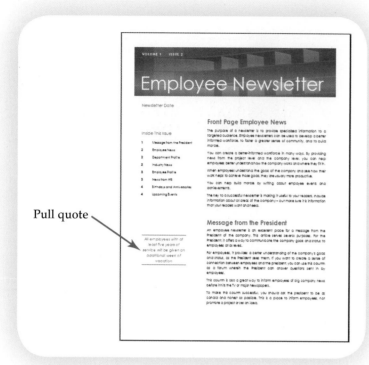

Pull quote

Figure 21.10
Pull quotes such as this one provide the reader with an idea of the significant content in the article.

SUMMARY

In this chapter you learned about the components that are included in most newsletters such as a nameplate, table of contents, header, byline, and masthead. You saw that special techniques such as jump lines, continuation heads, end signs, and pull quotes are used to make the newsletter easier to read. In addition, you learned that tombstoning of headlines makes it harder to read a newsletter. Finally, you read about binding options.

KEY TERMS

byline	header	upstyle
continuation head	headlines	subhead
deck	kicker	tombstoning
downstyle	masthead	
end signs	nameplate	

REVIEW

Answer the following questions on your own computer.

1. How are newsletters similar to newspapers?
2. What contains the information at the top of the page?
3. What is the primary purpose of a table of contents in a newsletter?
4. How is the header similar to a nameplate?
5. What information is contained in a masthead?
6. Why is it sometimes easy to forget to include a masthead in the newsletter?
7. What does upstyle mean?
8. What does downstyle mean?
9. What is a kicker?
10. What is a deck?
11. What are subheads?
12. What is a byline?
13. When are no bylines given for an article in a newsletter?
14. What is an important addition to illustrations in a newsletter?
15. What is the purpose of a jump line?
16. What is an end sign?
17. What is tombstoning?
18. Where are pull quotes most often placed in a newsletter?
19. Discuss the size of paper used to print newsletters and the binding most often used.
20. Other than print, what other ways are newsletters distributed?

DISCUSS

1. Review the information that is included on a nameplate.
2. Explain why a masthead is important for those reading the newsletter who might not be part of your expected audience.
3. Explain the difference between a headline and a title.
4. Discuss the placement of bylines and other information that may be included in a byline.
5. Review some of the characteristics of an article in a newsletter.

6. Explain why more newsletters are being printed in color.

7. Explain the purpose of placing as many articles as possible on the first page of a newsletter.

8. What is a continuation head?

9. Discuss some important last-minute proofreading tips of newsletters.

10. Discuss precautions that should be used when quoting others in a newsletter.

APPLY

to the website at
academic.cengage.com/school/dtp

WRITING

Activity 1 Identifying Components

1. Obtain a copy of a newsletter either by searching the Web or receiving one personally through membership in a specific organization.

2. Locate and label as many examples of the following as you can find in the newsletter: byline, continuation heads, deck, downstyle, end signs, headlines, kicker, masthead, nameplate, upstyle, subhead, and tombstoning.

3. Write an article listing at least six items that you found. In the article include the following information: explanation of where the item was located, description of the formatting of the item, and an explanation of how it was or was not used effectively.

4. Import your article into your desktop publishing software. Add the activity title to the document.

5. Save the document as **component_id**.

Activity 2 Nameplates

1. Using your desktop publishing software, create three different nameplates for newsletters using different placements for each. Review the figure in the chapter and the information in the chapter for design ideas. Each nameplate should be for a different newsletter.

2. Save the documents as **nameplate1**, **nameplate2**, and **nameplate3**.

Activity 3 Newsletter Design

1. Obtain a copy of a newsletter either by searching the Web or receiving one personally through membership in a specific organization. (You can use the same newsletter you used in Activity 1 as long as it is at least four pages in length.)

2. Key the articles that you intend to use in a word processing software so that they can be imported into the newsletter.

3. Using your desktop publishing software, redesign the newsletter using the information you learned from this chapter. If your example

is longer than four pages, make some decisions on what should be omitted to create a four-page newsletter. Add any components that you can that were not included in the original newsletter.

4. Save the document as ***newsletter_design***.

Activity 4 Team Newsletter

1. Divide into a team of four students. Within that team divide into partners. One partnership should write two articles on components and the other partnership should write two articles on design of a newsletter. Each person in the team should write at least one article.

2. The articles should contain at least half the content from information other than the textbook. Research the Internet for information to include in your article. Keep a journal in MLA style of the resources used so that the team can compile a resource list.

3. Key your article into a word processing document. Have the team members proofread the articles. Prepare a document compiling all resources.

4. Each member of the team should create a newsletter using the four articles and resource list. Use as many components as needed in the newsletter.

5. Save the document as ***team_newsletter***.

6. As a team, critique the four newsletters for design and component usage. Be sure when critiquing to always include positive things first. When critiquing those things that can be improved on, include suggestions for improvement.

7. Each team member should write a summary of the critique of the four newsletters.

8. Import the summary into your desktop publishing software and add a title.

9. Save the document as ***team_critique***.

Activity 5 Newsletter Creation

1. Use a topic of your choice for this two-page newsletter. It could be for an organization that you belong to such as a school club or church, or you could choose a topic that you are interested in and want to research.

2. Use various sources to gather information for your articles. At least one of the sources should be through an interview. Write all articles. Keep a resource list, including the person interviewed in the resource list.

3. Gather illustrations to use in your newsletter and plan for components that you intend to use in the design of your newsletter.

4. Using your desktop publishing software, create the newsletter.

5. Save the document as ***newsletter_creation***.

EXPLORE e

WRITING

1. Search the Internet for the history of newsletters. Include a resource list in MLA style, using a minimum of two resources.

2. Write an article about the history of the Internet.

3. Design an illustration for your article using your image editing software. Save document as ***history_illustration***.

4. Import your article and illustration into your desktop publishing software.

5. Save the document as ***newsletter_history***.

Publishing to a Professional Printing Service

22

Introduction

In the earliest days, printers set type letter by letter (see Figure 22.1) and created documents from information provided by a customer using presses such as the one shown in Figure 22.2. In time the printing technology improved, streamlining the process so it was no longer necessary to set type by hand. Page design, however, was still done manually.

An even bigger change occurred when it became possible to use computers to create desktop published documents. As a result, many people now produce their own materials using a laser or ink jet printer and a photocopy machine.

Sometimes, however, it's easier, quicker, or more cost-effective to take desktop publishing files to a printer to have documents produced on professional presses. Upon your first experience with a professional print shop, you may run into some unfamiliar terminology and expectations that are often quite different from your own printing experience.

Before beginning, it's important to clarify the words **printer** and **press**. At home or work, a printer is the device that produces a paper document you created on your computer. At a professional print business, the device that produces that paper document is called

Figure 22.1
In order to create a printed document, it was once necessary to set type by hand, placing each letter separately.

© SUSAN LAKE

Objectives

- *Learn how professional printing produces a document.*

- *Understand why incorrect use of fonts can cause problems in a print project.*

- *Discover steps you must take before submitting a document to be printed.*

- *Learn what you must do when giving final print approval.*

- *Learn questions to ask when seeking the services of a printer.*

A **printer** is a person who uses a press or a device that produces a document using a computer.

A **press** is a piece of equipment used by professional printers to create a document.

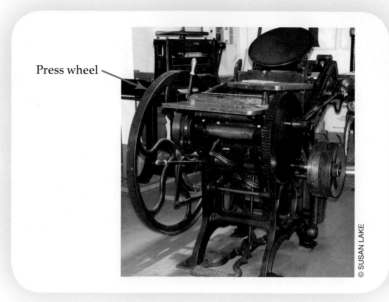

Press wheel

Figure 22.2
Presses such as this one made in the late 1800s required no electricity since they were run by hand turning the large wheel.

a press and the person who runs it is referred to as the printer. To add confusion, the term "printer" also refers to the business itself. The press is a high-level printing device that functions like your printer at home or work.

Printing

A professional printer can produce a document in two ways. The first process allows the printer to make copies from an original, or **master**, that you have already printed. The result is very much like making your own copies on a copier except that a press is used and the final copies are of higher quality than those from a copy machine. Quick-print shops often provide this service. With the other process, the printer creates the master using specialized equipment.

A **master** is a printed page or plate used to print a document.

Service Bureau

A **prepress service bureau** is a business that converts documents to files that can be used by a printer.

RIPping is the process of converting a file to an electronic form that can be used to create film.

Most printers have an in-house **prepress service bureau** whose job is to convert your desktop publishing files to a form that can be used by the printing equipment. These electronic files are then used to create an image of the page that is recorded on film in a process called **RIPping** (raster image processing or processor). In simple terms, RIPping is similar to sending your files to your home or office printer. However, RIP is able to produce a much higher resolution image than the printer in your home or office. The high-resolution master means a crisper, better-looking final product coming off the press. During the RIP process, the software can often perform other functions as well, such as checking for missing fonts and images, color trapping, and more.

Printers usually use an **imagesetter** such as a **Linotronic** to RIP files. Print shops have different types of Linotronic imagesetters that require specific software to convey information between your computer and the printing equipment. This software is called a **print driver**. Your print shop personnel can tell you which print drivers work best with their equipment.

Just as the printing process was streamlined when it was no longer necessary to manually set type by hand, improvements continue to speed up the printing process. Many print shops today no longer create the film that is used to produce a plate. Instead, computers send electronic files directly to a plate maker, bypassing the intermediate step.

Camera Ready

One of the first terms you will encounter when working with a print shop or service bureau is **camera-ready**. For a camera-ready document, no work is required of the print shop other than the actual printing.

If a document is not camera-ready, printers are required to create **mechanicals**, which are boards onto which all the text and graphics are placed using glue or wax (see Figure 22.3). Even if a mechanical is provided by the person needing the service, sometimes photographs have to be specially prepared and then placed, or **stripped**, into an open area on the board. Placeholders, often noted as **FPO** (for position only), are created for images in the document.

An **imagesetter** is the hardware used to RIP files.

Linotronic is a common brand of imagesetter.

A **print driver** provides information to desktop publishing software about the printing equipment to be used.

Camera-ready is when a file is ready to go to the press without intervention on the part of the printer.

A **mechanical** is a layout created by hand using paper, glue, and often a gridded board.

Stripping is the process of converting images to film.

FPO is an acronym for "for position only," indicating a placeholder image being used in place of the one intended for actual printing.

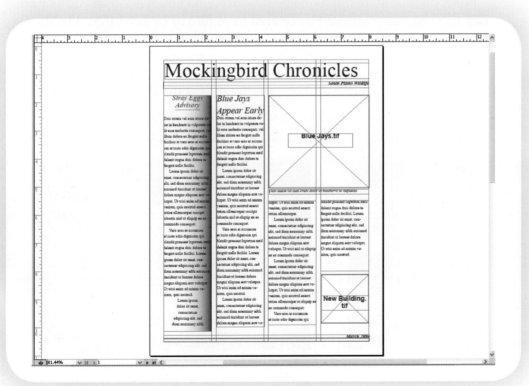

Figure 22.3
Pasteups such as this one use placeholders and boards to lay out the design of a page.

Printing is a competitive business with more companies seeking the same business. The Internet has changed how print shops do business. No longer are they limited to clients within a few miles of their business. Printers can now search for customers all over the world. Files can be emailed or transferred to the print shop's server from wherever the customer's computer is located. Prompt shipping options make it possible to package and send print products to the next state or country. Because of the stiff competition, it's important for printers to keep costs low and to use all the resources available to them. Creative marketing and efficient personnel are some of the tools that are required of printers in today's world.

Because mechanical work is already completed, a desktop publishing document is considered camera-ready. Few customers of print shops today require mechanicals to be constructed.

Offset is a printing process that transfers an image from a plate to a blanket that is offset to paper.

Lithography is the process used to print documents on an offset press.

A **plate** is a paper or metal sheet on which an image is cut or etched to be used on an offset press.

Presses

Offset presses (using **lithography**) are the type most frequently found in print shops. Figure 22.4 is an example of an offset press. In order to use an offset press, a plate must first be produced. As you read in an earlier part of this chapter, plates can be created from film or be produced directly from a computer. A **plate** similar to the one shown in Figure 22.5 can be metal, paper, or any substance that will retain an image.

The plate is then attached to a roller on the press. During the printing process, ink is rolled over the plate. Because of the chemical nature of

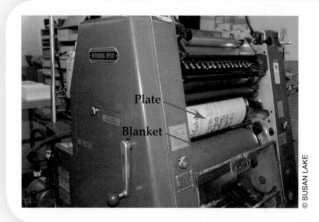

© SUSAN LAKE

© SUSAN LAKE

Figure 22.4
This offset press is produced by Heidelberg, a company renowned for manufacturing fine presses.

Figure 22.5
This plate appears to be paper, but it is actually a thick sheet of metal.

It takes time to create a quality print product. The time you took to create your desktop published document is only one factor. Once your file is complete, the printer must finish a number of steps that you do not see. Your file must be RIPped, plates created, press time scheduled, setup completed, and proofs approved. All these steps must be finished before your document can be completed. Trying to hurry these steps may result in a product that is not as good as it could be. Treating your printer with respect means understanding the time he or she needs to do a good job. Find out how much lead-time is necessary and then meet those deadlines. Asking a printer to produce a print job in less time than is needed is unfair.

the plate, only the image attracts ink. The plate with the ink passes through water, which washes off the unneeded ink. Next, the press transfers the page's image on the plate to a surface or blanket roller. The blanket is then pressed or rolled upon the sheet of paper (see Figure 22.6).

While this sounds like a complicated process, you have probably experienced it yourself. If you press your hand on a page of wet ink, the words from the page will transfer to your hand. If you then quickly blot it on another page, you will have created an offset print.

A **web press** is a specialized offset press that uses large rolls of paper to produce continuous pages of print. Newspapers are generally produced using a web press.

Offset is called **indirect printing** because the plate is not directly printed on the page. Other press types such as flexography, gravure, intaglio, and letterpress are considered **direct printing**. Some of these processes engrave the image into the plate, while others raise the image above the surface of the plate. In both cases, ink is applied to the plate, which then rolls onto the sheet of paper.

Digital printing, a process similar to printing with a laser printer, is becoming more common, although offset is still generally less expensive. Digital printing, however, provides more flexibility and will continue to grow in importance.

Preparation

While it is possible to create a printout of a document using software such as Microsoft Publisher or Word, professional printers usually discourage

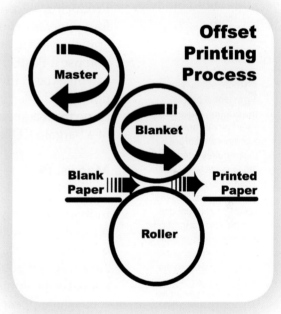

Figure 22.6
While one brand of offset press may appear somewhat different from another, they all use the same printing process.

A **web press** is an offset press that prints on long rolls of paper such as newsprint.

Indirect printing is the process of offsetting an image to create a printed document.

Direct printing is the process of printing a document directly from a plate.

Digital printing transfers an electronic file directly from a computer to a press.

Proofreading is an essential part of the printing process. Four-color printing is a complicated process that requires attention to detail, particularly when it comes to registration. A minor slippage as the paper moves from one color press to another can create a page that is blurry. Pages that are carefully registered are sharp and clear. A printer is expected to proof for that before starting to run a print job, but as the consumer you should also check. Another problem that occurs when printing color is the accuracy of the color output. The amount of ink that a printer uses can change the way a color looks. The difference between pink and red is merely one degree. Check the accuracy of the colors being printed during your final press proof. You have the right to expect colors to meet your expectations.

use of low-end software. In order to use your files, the printer must employ the same software used to create the files, and the software must be a type and version compatible with the printer's printing system. The software packages most frequently accepted are QuarkXPress, Adobe PageMaker, Adobe InDesign, and Corel Ventura.

Adobe Acrobat files and PostScript files do not require a printer to have your specific software, and these are quickly becoming acceptable options. However, some printers do not yet use a process that accepts these types of files.

Problems

A document that looks fine on your own laser printer may not necessarily appear the same way when it is printed professionally. There are a number of reasons for this.

Fonts

Producing a document on your own printer allows you to use whatever font appeals to you. Some fonts, such as those used by the computer's operating system, are not designed for print. Generally, printers request that you use a PostScript or OpenType font to ensure that your fonts will print as you expect. (System fonts are not designed for print; therefore, they are not a valid selection when designing your document.) Fonts should always come from a quality source, such as Adobe, since fonts purchased as part of a bargain CD may not print well.

Mac vs. PC

The Macintosh computer is the most common platform in the printing industry. In many cases, businesses use PCs. This creates a platform issue particularly when it comes to fonts. Mac fonts and PC fonts cannot be exchanged easily, although each platform has fonts that are quite similar. As a result, if you create your document on a PC and send it to a Mac-only shop, the PC fonts will be replaced by Mac ones. Since all typefaces (even those that appear to be alike) have slight differences in spacing and height, the length of a document and its spacing on a page can differ depending upon the font selected.

Faux Fonts

In some software, when you apply an attribute instead of selecting the actual font, the computer creates a faux font (see Chapter 2 for more information). A faux font may not print correctly on an imagesetter.

Fonts are designed and organized into font families. A font family includes the plain (or roman) style as well as all the different styles for that particular font, such as bold or italic. Each style is stored in a separate file. For example, the Times New Roman font family includes Times New Roman, Times New Roman Bold, Times New Roman Italic, Times New Roman Bold Italic, and others. You are probably accustomed to adding a style (or attribute) such as bold or italic to a font by selecting a section of text and clicking a button on your software's toolbar. Figure 22.7 is an example of a toolbar that allows you to select attributes. When you do this in programs such as Adobe PageMaker or QuarkXPress, the software links the attribute to the font, and the selected text appears correct on the screen. It probably even looks right when you print it on your laser printer.

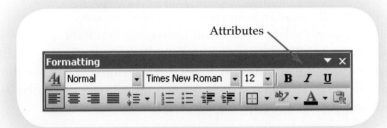

Figure 22.7
This Microsoft Word formatting toolbar allows you to select attributes such as bold and italic.

During RIPping, the imagesetter may see the font name but not recognize that an attribute is linked to it. The linked information is lost and the font or text style you expect does not make it onto the master. For example, what you intended to be bold may come off the press as plain text. This is especially a problem if the font you want to use does not exist on your system. In that case, when you apply an attribute instead of selecting the actual font, the computer creates a faux font that looks like the actual font. Since the actual font does not exist, the imagesetter cannot find the font file with the information it needs to create the master. In this case, the imagesetter will often substitute a default font. To avoid this problem, be sure to use the correct font in your documents—do not just add an attribute to a selection of text. If you intend a selection of Times New Roman to be bold, select Times New Roman Bold from your font list. You can review the fonts on your system by returning to the font folder or by looking at the list from within your application. Linking of fonts and attributes is not a problem in programs such as Photoshop, Illustrator, and InDesign because they use a different system to identify fonts.

Images

Graphics in the form of photographs or drawings are an essential component of desktop publishing documents. They can also prove the most troublesome element. Once again, the image that prints well on your printer at home or work may not work as well when it is converted by a print shop. If you intend to use graphics in your document and are unsure about how they will look in your final printed product, talk to your printer. He or she can provide specific settings and feedback about how to get the best-quality images. In the meantime, here are some basic guidelines for using graphics in your files:

- The **hairline** setting for rules or borders and for fill patterns for frames often does not turn out as you expect. Ask your printer about using these elements in your file.

A **hairline** is the narrowest line that can be produced by a printer.

- Web graphics in a JPG or GIF format are not print friendly. Instead, use TIFF or EPS graphic files in your publications.
- Color images should be converted from RGB (web colors) to CMYK (print colors). If you are given the option, select UCR (undercolor removal) rather than GCR (gray component replacement).
- Resize and rotate all images in the graphics program in which you created them instead of in your desktop publishing software.
- Digital photographs and scanned images should have a resolution of at least 300 dpi. The size of the image will affect its final appearance. To determine the optimum size that can be printed, divide the dimensions (in pixels) by 300. If your image is originally 640 × 480 pixels, it will print best at a size no larger than 2.1 × 1.6".

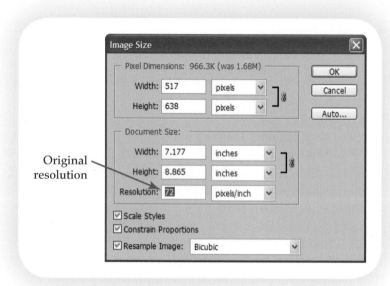

Original resolution

Figure 22.8
This image is originally set to 72 dpi, which is often the default size.

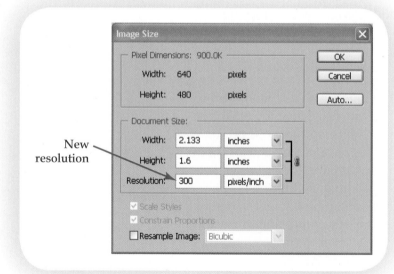

New resolution

Figure 22.9
This image has been changed to 300 dpi and had resampling turned off.

One way to modify your image resolution is to use image editing software such as Adobe Photoshop. In Photoshop, choose Image > Image Size. As a default setting, the width and height are shown in pixels (see Figure 22.8). The document size is shown in inches. The original resolution may be only 72 pixels per inch. This is fine for a computer screen, but does not work for print.

If you change the resolution to 300 pixels per inch (turning off the Resample Image option), the new size is 2.1 × 1.6", which is the size at which your image should be printed (see Figure 22.9). Enlarging the image in your desktop publishing software will not improve its resolution.

Preflight

When you send your files to a printer, it is essential that you provide all the information needed to complete the project. A crucial detail that is often overlooked is information on the fonts used in a document. As explained previously, if the RIP does not recognize a font, it will substitute a different one. To avoid this problem, you may need to provide copies of the fonts you have used if the printer does not have them in its system. In addition, you will need to provide copies of all images and files that you have used to create your document. It is easy to forget a small file such as an unusual rule that you placed on a page. One of the ways to avoid this is to use the **preflight** feature provided in most high-end desktop publishing software (see Figure 22.10). This feature ensures that all the parts are gathered into the folder you will send to the printer. (See the specific application's user manual for more information on how to preflight your files.) Alternatively, you may decide to send a test file to the printer for preflight. Many printers will process up to 16 pages for a small fee or even without charge. The test file you send should include an example of every element and type of art you expect to use in your document.

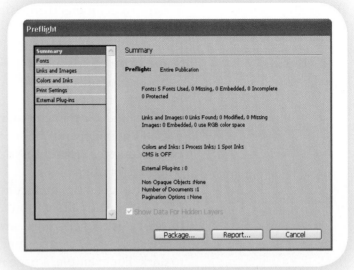

Figure 22.10
Adobe InDesign makes it easy to preflight a document before submitting it to a printer.

Color

Color documents are printed using two processes: process color and spot color.

Process color, or four-color printing, uses cyan (process blue), magenta (process red), yellow, and black (CMYK) to produce color images. Different combinations and concentrations of these four colors can produce a wide variety of colors. In process printing, each color is printed separately, requiring the printing paper (sheet) to be run through a press four times. As the layers of ink are applied to the paper, they combine to form all the colors in your document. Modern presses are actually a series of presses joined as one with each component able to print a different color. Figure 22.11 is an example of a five-color press with the fifth color reserved for special page treatment.

Because the same page must be printed multiple times in four-color printing, there is a good chance the sheet of paper may shift a little each time. The term **registration** refers to how well the sheet lines up each time it goes through the press. If the registration is off, the sheet has shifted during one of its trips through the press and one or more colors have been printed in a slightly different spot instead of directly on top of one another. The result of bad registration can be a blurry image or color that is not quite what you intended. To account for the possible shift in registration, it may be necessary to use the trapping option provided by most desktop publishing software.

Single color press

© SUSAN LAKE

Figure 22.11
This machine is actually five presses combined into a single press, meaning that it is not necessary to change colors in the press or reposition the paper as it moves from color to color.

Preflight is software that checks a desktop published file for any problems the printer might encounter.

Registration is the alignment of pages when a page is printed more than once. It is essential that pages printed in multiple colors be registered. Registration marks provide guides.

Trapping is an electronic process that overlaps the colors of an image in such a way that a slight difference in the placement of a page through the press will not distort the color or clarity of the image. Some print shops apply trapping during the RIP process.

Spot color (also called PMS color) is an alternative way to add color to a page. In spot color printing, only two colors are used: black and another ink color. Each page is printed twice. One run places the black ink on the page, and the second run prints a "spot" of color. (Technically, you could create an entire document with one spot color and not use black ink at all.)

You can get more impact and variety with spot color than you might think. Spot color allows you to choose from a wide range of options, such as those included as Pantone selections. The use of different quantities of ink makes it possible for the same color to appear on a page in ranges from light to dark. For example, a page might contain a logo in a light red that appears pink. On the same page, a headline might appear in a bold red. In each case only a single color is actually used, but the logo is printed at a 30 percent concentration of the red ink and the headline is printed at 100 percent.

It is very important that you do not designate any spot color if you are planning on a four-color print. It is just as important not to accidentally designate a photograph as CMYK if you are only planning on spot color. During the RIP stage, the software looks for color designations. If both process color and spot color are used in a document, this will cause confusion and additional cost for you. Many times, the printer will catch such a mistake at the RIP stage and give you a chance to correct your files, but you are better off finding it yourself.

Whenever color is going to be used, a separate page must be produced for each color. High-end desktop publishing software has an option for **color separation** that prints onto each page only the information that appears in that color (see Figure 22.12). It is helpful to check color separation before sending your document to the print shop.

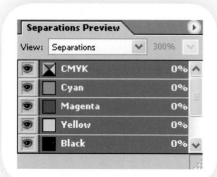

Figure 22.12
Adobe InDesign allows you to print each page as a separate color.

Transmittal

Since desktop publishing files are often quite large, you will need to work with the printer personnel to determine the best way to transfer the information they need from you. You may burn a CD or place the files on a Zip disk or a flash drive. Some printers provide server space so that you can place the files on their computer using **FTP** (a way to transfer data using the Internet). It is important to know how the printer wants to receive the files. You should clarify this when you first discuss your job with the printer.

Paper

Once you have decided to have your work professionally printed, you will find that there is a large selection of paper to choose from. The printer will ask your preference of paper properties such as size, weight, and type. Paper can be cut in all sizes, but the most common sizes fall into two

categories: American and metric. Print shops are not limited to standard sizes, although the product will be chosen from a standard size. Once a document is printed, it can be cut or trimmed. Review Chapter 2 for more paper options. It is important to realize that selecting an unusual paper size can be expensive. Even though the paper from the trimmed page is discarded, you are still paying for it. Unless there is a good reason to use an unusual paper size, it is best to select standard sizes.

Another consideration when selecting paper is to know how porous it is. Porous paper absorbs more ink so the dot gain is greater (see Chapter 2). The higher the dot gain, the fuzzier your print will appear on the page. For crisp, clear print, the dot gain needs to be as small as possible.

Figure 22.13
The printer's control station is a combination easel and computerized panel that allows changes to be made to the press with the touch of a button.

Folding

Documents can be folded in a variety of ways. Each variation comes with its own name (see Chapter 2), but the process is designed to use a single sheet of paper to create multiple pages that are each viewed separately.

A sheet of paper folded in half is a **folio**. Each half of the folio is one page; therefore a single folio would have four pages (two on each side). Several folios placed one inside the other create a **signature**. Multiple signatures make a book.

A **folio** is a printing term used to describe a folded page.

A **signature** is a collection of folios.

Binding

Documents can be bound in a variety of ways. Saddle stitch places staples in the middle of folded pages, creating a booklet. Spiral binding can use metal coils or plastic combs that loop around the outside, allowing the pages to lie flat. Perfect binding glues the edges, forming a book (such as found in a paperback).

Cost

Printing is expensive in terms of both time and money. Printers understand this and can often provide a less expensive solution to a problem than one you may have thought of. For example, sometimes a printer might know that a color print job with one customer can be combined with yours to reduce the cost to both. Occasionally, a printer might have purchased special paper in bulk that will allow you a better-looking product at a cheaper price. Some printers charge a premium for work that must be completed quickly. Planning ahead or being willing to wait a little longer for your print job may save you money.

Proofing

A **proof** is the process of checking a printed page for errors before final publication.

A **dummy** is an early proof used in page design planning.

A **comp** is an image of a layout.

A **page proof** is a final copy of a page used to do a last check for errors before printing occurs.

A **galley** is another term for a page proof.

Once a document is ready to be printed, you are generally expected to **proof** the final product before production begins. There are actually a number of proofing stages. A **dummy** proof is used in planning and is often merely an approximation of the design. A **comp** (composite) proof is used in the early stage of the design and is intended for internal use only. A press or **page proof** is used to verify that the images and colors are correct. A **galley** is another name for a page proof. It is important that you proof final pages carefully, since once you have given your approval, any mistakes that appear are your responsibility. Take the time you need to read carefully.

Communication

The key to a successful professionally printed job is communication. It is essential to talk with your printer before even beginning to work on a desktop publishing document that you want printed. Problems with fonts and image resolution can be solved before they become major issues. Each service bureau and printer has its own requirements. Learning what yours are will make for a successful project that is less expensive and less time-consuming for everyone involved.

Understanding the process and the terms as explained in this chapter will make it easier for you to know what questions to ask and to understand the answers you receive.

1. What type of press do you use?
2. Which software do you have that I also have?
3. Are you a Mac or PC shop? Or do you offer both?
4. How do you want me to send you my files?
5. Should I use a special print driver?
6. Do you have my fonts?
7. Should I do my own trapping?
8. What will be my dot gain?

9. What paper should I use?

10. What are my folding options?

11. What are my binding options?

12. How much time will it take to complete the print job?

13. Whom should I call if I have questions?

14. How much will this cost?

15. Is there any way to reduce the cost without sacrificing quality?

SUMMARY

In this chapter you learned what to expect when seeking the services of a professional printer. You saw how a press works and what issues you need to take into consideration such as font choices. You learned the importance of preflight and proofing. You considered decisions such as paper, binding, folding, and cost. You learned that it is essential to know what questions to ask and why those questions are important.

KEY TERMS

camera-ready	imagesetter	press
color separation	indirect printing	print driver
comp	Linotronic	printer
digital printing	lithography	proof
direct printing	master	registration
dummy	mechanical	RIPping
folio	offset	signature
FPO	page proof	stripping
FTP	plate	trapping
galley	preflight	web press
hairline	prepress service bureau	

REVIEW

Answer the following questions on your own computer.

1. What is a printer?

2. What is a press?

3. What are the two ways a professional printer can produce a document?

4. What is the name of the service that converts desktop publishing files to a form that can be used by printing equipment?

5. What does RIPping stand for?

6. What other functions can software perform during the RIPping process?

7. What is an imagesetter?

8. What does camera-ready mean?

9. What is a mechanical?

10. What is the name of the process used to convert images to film?

11. What does the acronymn FPO stand for?

12. What is offset?

13. What is the "plate" that is used in offset printing?

14. What is the process used in offset presses found in print shops?

15. What is digital printing?

16. Why would someone choose to use digital printing over offset printing?

17. What are the names of the software packages that most professional printers accept?

18. What type of files do not require a printer to have the specific software?

19. To prepare for printing, what should the resolution be for digital photographs and scanned images?

20. What graphics formats are best for printing?

21. What is preflight?

22. What is registration?

23. What is trapping?

24. What is another name for spot color?

25. What is color separation?

26. What does FTP stand for and what does it mean?

27. What attributes make up paper properties?

28. What are the most common categories of sizes to use for paper?

29. What is a folio?

30. What is it called when several folios are placed one inside another?

1. Explain the process of how type was set in the early days.

2. Discuss what has to be done if a document is not camera-ready.

3. Explain how plates are produced and used in offset printing.

4. Discuss the similarities and differences between indirect and direct printing.

5. Identify the fonts that are designed for print and those that are not.

6. Explain what types of problems can occur if you send your PC-designed document to a Mac shop for printing.

7. Explain why it is better to use the font Times New Roman Bold rather than Times New Roman and then applying the Bold style to the text.

8. Give details of printing using process color and review how it works.

9. Explain the process of printing using spot color.

10. Identify the different ways to transfer files needed for printing to the professional printer.

APPLY

Activity 1 Checklist

1. Create a checklist from the preparation section in the textbook on things that you should remember when preparing a document that will be sent to a professional printer.

go to the website at
academic.cengage.com/school/dtp

2. Create a tabloid-size poster that is 11 × 17 to place in the office as a reminder of what should be remembered when preparing a document that will be sent to a printer. As you are creating the poster, remember that this poster will be sent to a printer and should be planned for accordingly.

WRITING

3. Format the poster information and add elements that will attract attention and yet look businesslike.

4. Save the document as **checklist**.

Activity 2 Printer Questions

1. Visit someone who sends desktop published documents frequently to a professional printer, or visit a professional printer.

WRITING

2. Obtain a copy of a project that they have had printed, or take one of your own projects to ask questions about.

3. Interview the person, obtaining the answers to as many of the 15 questions in the textbook under the Communications section as possible.

4. Write a summary of the answers and then import the summary into a desktop publishing document. Include information about your resource in the summary.

5. Save the document as *printer_questions*.

Activity 3 Printing Newsletter

1. In a team of three or four students, decide on three topics other than the history of printing to do some research on.

2. Each student should write a separate article, with all students also working together on an article on the history of printing. Save the articles: *topic1*, *topic2*, *topic3*, and *printing_history*. Keep a document with your resources listed in MLA format. Save as *print_resources*.

3. Each student in the team should create a two-page newsletter using the articles and the resources. Demonstrate skills that you have learned in this desktop publishing course, including addition of other attributes to make the newsletter interesting.

4. Save the document as *printing_newsletter*.

Activity 4 Postcard

1. Using your desktop publishing software, create a postcard to send to prospective buyers of offset printers. The postcard should advertise a specific brand and model number of offset printer that you locate on the Internet or through a brochure by visiting a store. Invite the prospective buyers for a demonstration of the product at your office. Use a date two weeks from the current date. Be creative with your design of the postcard.

2. Using a phone book or the Internet, locate at least five businesses to send the postcard to. If you have the Merge Documents feature on your desktop publishing software, use it to merge the names of the printing businesses you looked up with your postcard to personalize it.

3. Save document as *post_card*.

4. Use the Merge Documents feature to create labels for the businesses.

5. Save the document as *post_card_labels*.

Activity 5 Greeting Card

1. Using your desktop publishing software, create a 5 × 7 (folded) greeting card with an image on the front, copyright information on the back, and a short poem or quote on the inside. Design the greeting card with the knowledge that you will send it to a professional printer for printing.

2. Using an online source or local print shop, determine what type of paper you will have the greeting cards printed on. Include any information for the printer on the pasteboard in your file. Calculate the cost of printing 100 greeting cards. Include the details on the pasteboard.

3. Save the document as **greeting_card**.

EXPLORE

1. Using your favorite search engine, search the Internet using keywords such as "printing press cost." Do a cost and features comparison of three presses by different manufacturers with a comparison of at least three of their attributes.

2. Using your desktop publishing software, place your information from your research in a table. Add a title and demonstrate as many skills as you can that you have learned about creating tables including formatting the tables and data within them.

3. Save the document as **press_comparison**.

4. Pick one of the presses that you included in your table. Create a flyer advertising the press. You should add at least one image of the press if at all possible.

5. Save the document as **press_flyer**.

23 Creating Yearbooks

Objectives

- *Understand steps to follow before beginning a yearbook.*

- *Learn how producing a yearbook requires knowledge of design, photography, and writing.*

- *Discover why it is difficult to sell a yearbook.*

- *Understand final steps to production.*

Introduction

For students, one of the most challenging desktop publishing experiences comes from creating a school's yearbook. Yearbooks are unusual in that they are larger documents than those created in a standard desktop publishing class. Its size and durable nature sets the yearbook apart from other desktop publishing projects. All of the skills you have developed up to this point in this book can be used to create a school yearbook. Most publishers allow schools to use standard desktop publishing software such as QuarkXPress, Adobe InDesign, *or* Adobe PageMaker *when creating a yearbook. Some yearbook companies even provide special toolbars that can be added to this software. Other companies may choose to provide their own software for students. This software is frequently limited and does not provide as many options as* Quark *and* InDesign.

Planning

Yearbooks do not just happen. They are the result of careful planning and attention to detail. Planning often begins even before school starts during special workshops. Frequently, these workshops are held by yearbook publishers, or they might be a "camp" held at school during the summer. During this planning time, decisions must be made that will guide the staff the rest of the year.

Yearbooks are permanent. For many people, yearbooks are the only record they have of their years in school, or their parents' or grandparents', for that matter. Yearbooks are dug out and read decades after the person has left school. Because of this longevity, the choices a yearbook staff makes today will continue to have an impact far into the future. This puts a particularly challenging burden on everyone involved. What might seem like a funny joke today could appear cruel and heartless in the future. Photographs that place a person in an unflattering position are humorous today but hurtful or damaging tomorrow. As a result, it is essential that everyone understands the importance of good judgment and mature decisions.

Leaders

Yearbooks are guided by two people: the adviser and the editor. Unlike most classrooms, the instructor is an adviser for the project, rather than a teacher. The adviser's task is to provide an environment for the staff to work and to learn. The final "test" is the yearbook, and the final grade is given by the students, faculty, staff, and community members who read it. The student editor carries the burden of ensuring all deadlines are met and assignments are completed.

A yearbook **theme** is a concept that is used throughout the book to act as a unifying agent. The theme may be revealed through images or color.

Theme

Generally, yearbooks have a unifying **theme** that is carried from page to page. A theme may include color and images. For example, a circus theme might be selected that would include figures of clowns and bright colors. It is important to make overall decisions, such as the theme, before beginning work on the actual yearbook. Since the cover usually introduces the reader to the book's theme, it must also be carefully considered during this early stage. Figure 23.1 is an example of a cover that introduces the theme of a puzzle. Notice in Figures 23.2 and 23.3 that this idea of "pieces" is carried throughout the book.

Figure 23.1
The puzzle cutout on the yearbook's cover draws the reader into the book.

Figure 23.2
The page designer has extended the theme of pieces by using cutout letters.

Organization Division/Megan Rhodes 69

Figure 23.3
The divider continues the puzzle theme. Pieces are even used to indicate page numbers.

Layout	Pg	Pg	Layout	
XXXXXXXXXXXXXXXXXXXXXXXXX		1	Title Page/TOC	
Opening	2	3	Opening	Color
Opening	4	5	Opening	
STUDENT LIFE DIVIDERS	6	7	STUDENT LIFE DIVIDERS	Color
	8	9		
	10	11		Color
	12	13		
	14	15		Color
	16	17		
	18	19		Color
	20	21		
	22	23		Color
ORGANIZATIONS DIVIDERS	24	25	ORGANIZATIONS DIVIDERS	
	26	27		Color
	28	29		
	30	31		Color
	32	33		
	106	107		
	108	109		
	110	111		
ACADEMIC DIVIDERS	112	113	ACADEMIC DIVIDERS	
	114	115		
	116	117		
	118	119		
	120	121		
	122	123		
	124	125		
	126	127		
	128	129		
	130	131		
	132	133		
	134	135		
FACULTY/ADMIN DIVIDERS	136	137	FACULTY/ADMIN DIVIDERS	
Faculty/Staff	138	139	Faculty/Staff	
Faculty/Staff	140	141	Faculty/Staff	
Faculty/Staff	142	143	Faculty/Staff	
Faculty/Staff	144	145	Faculty/Staff	
Faculty/Staff	146	147	Faculty/Staff	
FRESHMEN DIVIDERS	148	149	FRESHMEN DIVIDERS	
Freshmen pictures	150	151	Freshmen pictures	
Freshmen pictures	152	153	Freshmen pictures	
Freshmen pictures	154	155	Freshmen pictures	
Freshmen pictures	156	157	Freshmen pictures	
Freshmen pictures	158	159	Freshmen pictures	
Freshmen pictures	160	161	Freshmen pictures	
Freshmen pictures	162	163	Freshmen pictures	
SOPHOMORE DIVIDERS	164	165	SOPHOMORE DIVIDERS	
Sophomore pictures	166	167	Sophomore pictures	
Sophomore pictures	168	169	Sophomore pictures	
Sophomore pictures	170	171	Sophomore pictures	
Sophomore pictures	172	173	Sophomore pictured	
Sophomore pictures	174	175	Sophomore pictures	
Sophomore pictures	176	177	Sophomore pictures	
Sophomore pictures	178	179	Sophomore pictures	
JUNIOR DIVIDERS	180	181	JUNIOR DIVIDERS	
Junior pictures	182	183	Junior pictures	
Junior pictures	184	185	Junior pictures	
Junior pictures	186	187	Junior pictures	
Junior pictures	188	189	Junior pictures	
Junior pictures	190	191	Junior pictures	
Junior pictures	192	193	Junior pictures	
	194	195	Junior pictures	
SENIOR DIVIDERS	196	197	SENIOR DIVIDERS	Color
Senior pictures	198	199	Senior pictures	Color
Senior pictures	200	201	Senior pictures	Color
Senior pictures	202	203	Senior pictures	Color
Senior pictures	204	205	Senior pictures	Color
Senior pictures	206	207	Senior pictures	Color
Senior pictures	208	209	Senior pictures	Color
Senior pictures	210	211	Senior pictures	Color
Commencement	212	213	Commencement	
Commencement	214	215	Commencement	
Commencement	216	217	Commencement	
Commencement	218	219	Commencement	
Commencement	220	221	Commencement	
ADVERTISING DIVIDERS	222	223	ADVERTISING DIVIDERS	
Local Ads	224	225	Local Ads	
Local Ads	226	227	Local Ads	
Local Ads	228	229	Local Ads	
Local Ads	230	231	Local Ads	
Local Ads	232	233	Local Ads	
Ads	234	235	Ads	
Ads	236	237	Ads	
Ads	238	239	Ads	
Ads	240	241	Ads	
Ads	242	243	Ads	
Ads	244	245	Ads	
Ads	246	247	Ads	
Ads	248	249	Ads	
Ads	250	251	Ads	
Ads	252	253	Ads	
Ads	254	255	Ads	
Ads	256	257	Ads	
Ads	258	259	Ads	
Ads	260	261	Ads	
Index	262	263	Index	
Index	264	265	Index	
Index	266	267	Index	

Figure 23.4
A ladder is a means of tracking each page of a yearbook.

Ladder

A **ladder** is a list of pages in a yearbook that includes the content for the page and the person responsible. Deadlines may also be marked on a ladder.

Once a theme is selected, a page-by-page plan, called a **ladder**, is completed. The ladder shows the areas that will be included in the book and the order in which they will be produced. Using the ladder, tasks are assigned to each member of the yearbook staff. For example, copy must be written and photographs must be taken. Figure 23.4 is an example of a ladder that is ready to be filled in. Sometimes, to reduce cost, color may be limited to only a few pages within the book. If that is the case, then these special pages need to be considered in the planning process. In Figure 23.4, notice that the color pages are listed in the far right column.

Because of the size of a yearbook, the entire book is not sent to the publisher at once. Instead, sections in the form of signatures must be completed at regular intervals during the year. Each section has its own deadline. It is vital that these interval deadlines be met. If they are not, yearbook staffs often find that their expenses increase with each missed deadline as contracts with publishers typically include late penalties.

Ads

The size of the yearbook, or number of pages, is usually determined based on the expected cost and the amount of revenue available. One source of revenue that can help offset some of the costs associated with producing a yearbook is ads. Often, ads are sold even before the yearbook is begun.

Ads can be sold in a variety of sizes. Yearbook ads are typically set up as a percentage of the page, such as 1/8–1/4–1/2–1 as shown in Figure 23.5. Some business owners may provide a business card to use as the content for their ad, since this fits well within the smaller ad size. Others provide camera-ready ads created by professionals that might be a full page or part of a page.

Yearbook staffers are sometimes asked to create ads themselves, using logos and other information provided by the business. If the staff is asked to create an ad, it is important that the final design be provided to the business so that the ad can be proofed for accuracy.

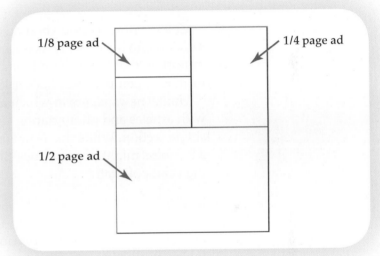

1/8 page ad
1/4 page ad
1/2 page ad

Figure 23.5
Ad sizes can be mixed on a page to provide a variety of size options. This full page ad has been broken down into a page with a variety of ad sizes.

Yearbook publishing is big business. Schools all over the country produce yearbooks each year, and publishers understand the importance of providing a quality product. Contracts are carefully negotiated with schools because each customer is valuable to the publisher. Yearbook advisers learn that they have negotiating power and often use it to receive special benefits for their schools and classes. In addition, publishers often have connections to photographers that provide school pictures. This can be an additional revenue source for the publisher since they make money off the student photographs as well as the yearbook. Student editors can learn much from being involved in this process.

Color is moving into yearbooks at the same rapid speed that it is moving into businesses. As a result, if color is to be used in an ad, it is important that the staff understand the proper use of color in advertising formats. Refer back to Chapter 15 to review the use of color.

Unlike newspapers in which ads are placed on each page interspersed with articles and photographs, most yearbooks gather all their ads into a single section. While this is not as effective an advertising placement as a business might hope, it does simplify the layout and design process for the yearbook staff.

Sales

Because of the high cost of producing a yearbook, it is usually necessary to presell each copy before production begins. The yearbook publisher is then supplied with an exact number to print that represents the number sold. Students must pay for a yearbook before they even see it. As a result, a marketing plan must be developed and put into place that encourages buyers to purchase an expensive product sight unseen. Yearbook staff members who are able to succeed at this possess sales skills that will be admired in the business world.

Production

Coverage

Yearbooks are designed to record and recognize events and activities that occur during a single school year. Most of these events will be school related. Some events outside the school, such as a natural disaster, may be important enough to include. The areas most frequently included in a yearbook are student life, academics, sports, organizations, and people. The yearbook will include photographs of every student organized by grade level as well as of faculty and administration.

A yearbook is not just a gathering of pictures. It is also a written account of the year. Unfortunately, the body copy is often written as last-minute fill rather than carefully prepared text. Just as it is important to capture the shot of the winning touchdown, it is vital to record the emotion of the event in the written word.

Photography

Digital photography has dramatically changed the way yearbooks are produced. In the past, in order to produce quality photographs, schools were required to have full-featured darkrooms. Today, with the use of digital cameras, students can focus on learning to be good photographers rather than on learning to develop film. And, since it is no longer necessary to develop every image taken, yearbook photographers are free to shoot pictures of every facet of school life. Even the simplest school moment can now be captured. Photographers should learn to look for the ordinary that can be turned into an extraordinary photograph.

Because there is often a large number of images to choose from, a good yearbook staff must learn to judge images for their impact. More is not always better. Instead, it is important to identify images that will best express the message you are trying to convey. Part of this process involves learning to cull out everything but the best.

Page Design

Unlike other documents that are sent to professional printers, yearbooks often have limitations on type and color. Yearbook publishers have a selection of fonts from which the staff is expected to choose. Inadvertently using a font that is not on the list of accepted choices can create problems during printing. With professional printers, you can overcome this problem by packaging the font along with your document. That is not the case with most yearbook publishers. Color selections have similar limitations, and a choice of colors is provided. Choosing a color outside the selection can add cost to the yearbook production since spot colors have to be used instead of process ones.

Generally, good yearbook design requires consistency. A template may be created that includes the fonts chosen, the alignment of text, the column choices, and the margins. If no template is used, each staff member must be aware of the overall design decisions and maintain them throughout the book. Within these limitations, creativity separates good yearbooks from the ordinary. Looking at sample yearbooks from previous years is a good way to find ideas that you can rework to make your own.

Placement of photographs works best if you use one dominant photograph on a page or a spread. Then add three to seven smaller images related to the dominant one. Allow at least one pica as a margin separating the photographs. Each page should have a headline, body copy, and captions for the photos. White space should go toward the outside edges rather than being trapped.

PROOFREADING TIPS

Page proofs are part of the challenging process of producing a quality yearbook. The proofs often arrive while the staff is engaged in the next set of pages, and it's easy to view this part of the process as unimportant. Nothing could be further from the truth. The page proof portion of the process is the last chance the yearbook staff has to find those mistakes that will be seen as soon as the first reader opens the book. Time should be set aside for careful reading and notation of any problems. Some advisers and editors offer incentives for any mistakes that proofreaders find as a way of encouraging attention to detail.

Submission

Yearbook pages are submitted as one or more signatures. They can be sent to the publisher in several ways. Some yearbook publishers allow electronic transmittal using an FTP process. Others require the staff to mail a CD onto which the electronic files have been burned. It is important to follow carefully the steps supplied by the publisher to prevent problems.

Because the yearbook is printed in stages, the staff will receive page proofs to double-check at intervals. These are pages printed exactly as they will appear in the book, although not at the same resolution. It is essential that they be read carefully and returned quickly so that the production process can continue. Major changes to these pages can be quite costly. Only changes that correct significant errors should be considered. Changes that are the result of errors by the publishing company are not charged to the yearbook staff.

SUMMARY

In this chapter, you learned who provides leadership in a yearbook production. You discovered how themes and ladders play a part. You saw the importance of ads. You saw the importance of a yearbook sales campaign. You learned the steps needed to produce a yearbook including writing, photography, and page design. And finally you learned how to use page proofs.

KEY TERMS

ladder   theme

REVIEW

Answer the following questions on your own computer.

1. What is one of the most challenging desktop publishing experiences for a student?

2. What is the difference between yearbooks and documents created in a standard classroom?

3. Who guides the yearbook?

4. What is the final test in a yearbook class?

5. What is a yearbook theme?

6. What is a ladder?

7. What function does the ladder serve?

8. In what form are sections of a yearbook sent to the publisher?

9. What is the usual result of missed deadlines?

10. What factors determine a yearbook's total number of pages?

11. What is one source of revenue available to offset the cost of producing a yearbook?

12. If the yearbook staff is asked to produce the ad for a business, what is an important step in this process?

13. What is the purpose of a yearbook?

14. What is one example of a non-school-related event that may be included in a yearbook?

15. What does good yearbook design require?

16. What separates good yearbooks from extraordinary yearbooks?

17. What is a good way to find ideas for a yearbook?

18. What text should be placed on each page of a yearbook?

19. Why is it necessary to presell copies of yearbooks before production begins?

20. What is the plan called that encourages buyers to purchase an expensive product sight unseen?

DISCUSS

1. Discuss the software options that may be provided by yearbook publishers.

2. Review some examples of the uses of themes.

3. Explain what type of ads are often used in yearbooks.

4. Identify the differences in the placement of ads in a newspaper and a yearbook.

5. Discuss the impact of digital photography on yearbook production.

6. Explain limitations in page design that yearbook staffers must respect. Identify the consequences of not following these limitations.

7. Review how templates can help in designing yearbooks.

8. Discuss effective placement of photographs.

9. Explain the different methods of submitting completed pages of a yearbook.

10. Explain the page proof process and results of not checking page proofs.

go to the website at academic.cengage.com/school/dtp

Activity 1

1. Review five yearbooks from the school library or family or friends' personal copies. Look for the central theme in each one and identify three to five ways the theme was used in the yearbook. Keep notes on your review.

2. Using the notes you kept on reviewing the yearbooks, write and create a newsletter explaining the uses of the themes.

3. Save the document as **yearbook_themes**.

Activity 2

1. Choose a page from one of the yearbooks that you reviewed in Activity 1 to recreate. Use similar photographs with the exact copy and create the page with your desktop publishing software.

2. Save the document as **practice_page**.

Activity 3

1. Plan a theme for the current year to use in the yearbook. Write a summary of why this theme was chosen. In your summary, explain a minimum of three to five ways the theme will be used. Save your summary as **theme_summary**.

2. Using the theme discussed in your summary, use your desktop publishing software to create the cover page for this year's yearbook.

3. Save the document as **cover_page**.

Activity 4

WRITING

1. Attend an event at your school. This could be an athletic, academic, or social event. Write an article for the event and take pictures of it. Save the document as **event**. Save one image to use as the central image **(central_image)**. Save at least three other images as **image1**, **image2**, and **image3**.

2. Using your desktop publishing software, create a page for the yearbook covering your chosen event. Save the document as **event_page**.

Activity 5

1. Using your desktop publishing software, create a projected cost of production, sales, and revenue figures for a yearbook. Include the over-all projected cost for producing a yearbook. You may want to visit a yearbook sponsor or publisher to get this cost. Project how many sales will be needed for the yearbook as well as how many ads will need to be sold. Save the document as **cost_projection**.

MATH

2. Write a marketing plan to sell your yourbook. Answer the following question in your plan: *What will be in the yearbook that will make someone want to purchase it?* Save the document as **marketing_plan**.

WRITING

3. Create a plan to sell ads. List the businesses in your area, with their phone numbers and addresses, that should be contacted to sell ads. List at least two ways to sell ads other than through businesses. Save the document as **ad_plan**.

EXPLORE

1. Through research on the Internet or other contacts, locate at least two yearbook publishers. Review their methods of publishing such as submission methods, page design, and cost of production, including penalties for missed deadlines.

2. Write a summary of your findings, including which publisher you would choose and why.

3. Save the document as **publisher_choice**.

24 Using the Business of Technology

Objectives

- *Understand stages of team development.*

- *Determine activities that team performs.*

- *Follow publication process.*

Introduction

Desktop published documents are not often created by a single person. In the preceding chapters, you learned that a diverse set of skills is needed, often requiring the work of a team. Teamwork is not simply a matter of gathering a group of people and asking them to complete a task. Functioning as a team requires specialized skills on the part of both the team leader and the team members. Just as it is important to learn how to manage images, create layouts, and make typography decisions, it is also vital that you know how to add your expertise to that of others in order to produce a product.

Stages of Team Development

Teams generally go through the four stages shown in Figure 24.1. These include forming, storming, norming, and performing. Each stage is fairly predictable, and the issues that arise must be addressed in order for your team to be successful. **Forming** represents the creation stage when a team is formed. **Storming** represents the stage in which personalities begin to mesh, sometimes with initial conflict. **Norming** represents the stage during which conflicts are resolved and plans are begun. The **performing** or last stage is the moment when the team becomes a functioning, productive group. Learning to recognize and work through each stage will give you a stronger team.

Forming is the first stage of team development when the team is formed.

Storming is an early stage of team development during which conflicts develop.

Norming is a later stage of team development during which conflicts are resolved.

Performing is the final stage of team development during which the team is fully functional and productive.

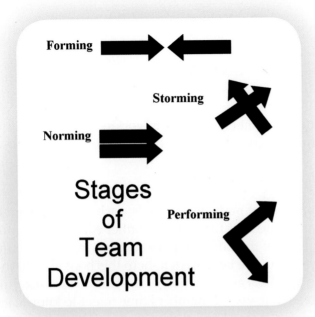

Figure 24.1
Teams go through four expected stages of development.

Team Charter

Beginnings are important times for teams. As a general rule, groups should be created quickly and begin to work on their project as soon as possible after they are formed. If extended periods of time are allowed to lapse between creation and work, the energy of the team can become lost.

Once a team starts to work, it must understand its purpose. A team with a fuzzy focus cannot be expected to accomplish much of importance. Part of a team's responsibility is to understand why it was formed. When it knows its reason for existence, it must establish a **team charter** to specifically identify its goals, values, and approach. While this may seem pointless, in the long run a team will achieve much more if it spends time clearly identifying the path it plans to follow before beginning work on a

A **team charter** specifically identifies the team's goals, values, and approach to handling the task at hand.

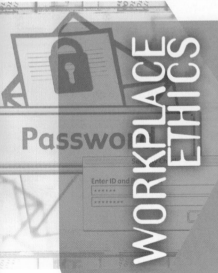

Teams require honesty. Too often, team members think that they must be polite and avoid all conflict. The nature of good teamwork is that a variety of opinions are joined to produce a single product. If a team member keeps those opinions to him or herself, the team cannot function. This does not mean that you should be verbally hostile as you reveal your point of view. Instead, you must be willing to share and then to listen. It's a difficult task to learn since we tend to think our ideas are best. A good team member learns to overcome this tendency and to work in unison.

project. The following questions are areas that should be addressed in the team charter:

- Why was the team created?
- What is the team to accomplish?
- How will the team track its progress?
- What will the members gain from working on this team?
- What happens when team members need help?

Team Building

Teams are comprised of many individuals, each with different ideas, experiences, and concerns. Teams must gather each person into the group, meshing all of the different personalities, in order to function as a single entity. One of the best ways to help this happen is to include team-building activities as a function of the team. These activities are generally recreational, giving members time to get to know each other and develop trust. Food, games, and recognition activities are frequently used to build team spirit and help reduce conflict.

Team Leader

Every member of a team is important and should contribute in a significant way. The team leader is merely one member of the group—not someone special. The team leader's significant function is to facilitate communication. A good team leader is one who can encourage communication, enhance team productivity, and provide essential structure and organization. Selection of a team leader should be based on these skills and not on how well the person is liked.

In some organizations the team leader is selected by an immediate superior or the task is assigned as part of the job responsibility. If this is the case, the team leader needs to be aware of the essential skills of a good leader and work on improving any skills in which he or she may be weak.

BUSINESS OF PUBLISHING

Too often, the costs of producing documents within a business using a copy machine or printer are not taken into consideration. Supply costs such as binders, plastic coils, paper, and toner are not factored into the decision-making process. The personnel costs are often ignored as well. The business of publishing requires desktop publishers to keep in mind all costs so that effective decisions can be made about the usefulness of a print document. A good desktop publisher knows how much it costs to use the photocopier as well as to mail a document. The ability to perform a cost analysis and compare different production methods is an essential skill. With this knowledge, you can produce documents that perform the task intended while keeping expenses low.

Team Communication

Communication within a team is essential to the success of the organization. Too often, fear of ridicule prevents team members from voicing essential information. Some fear entering into conflict with other members. Some so strongly want to see their point accepted that they refuse to allow others to add ideas. These and other communication problems can destroy the effectiveness of a team. Ways must be found to encourage members to listen to each other, be open in their opinions, and be willing to accept diverse opinions. The team leader is an important component in this process.

Team Activities

Team Meetings

One of the activities that a team engages in is to meet and report on the progress and concerns of its members. These meetings should have beginning and ending times and clearly stated purposes. As a good team member, do not keep the others waiting. In addition, do not prolong the meeting past the time it should end.

An agenda is the guiding hand at team meetings. With a well-thought-out agenda, members know the subjects to be discussed and the material to be presented. Agendas should be delivered before the meeting so that everyone is prepared.

These meetings are not chat sessions or recreation. Members should keep discussion centered on the meeting's purpose and not deviate to other issues unless appropriate. While meetings are designed to allow members to give their opinions, they should not go into long, rambling speeches. Limit your discussion to the essential points. Often individual discussions that take up the team's time can be better held outside the meeting.

Good team members adhere to rules that make meetings productive. They include the following:

- Be on time.
- Start on time and end promptly.
- Use agendas that include the purpose, time for discussion, and desired outcome of the meeting.
- Come prepared with the information needed by others.
- Stay on task.

Team Decisions

As part of any meeting, decisions must be made by the team. It is during this decision-making process that conflict can arise. Learning to make decisions as a team is a skill that can reduce long-term conflict and increase the team's effectiveness. As part of the decision-making process, everyone in

PROOFREADING TIPS

One of the advantages of working as a publication team is that there are others to proofread the portions of a document that you produced. This helps find those mistakes that are so easily overlooked. No one likes to make mistakes. And no one wants others to point them out. Learn to accept editing comments without feeling defensive. Instead, accept any recommended changes as a gift that can help improve your work. If you can learn to do this, you and your team will produce far better publications.

the team should understand issues related to each decision, including the following questions:

- ➲ What are the specific details of the decision to be made?
- ➲ What is the deadline for the decision?
- ➲ What impact will the decision have on the team?
- ➲ Who will be involved in the outcome of the decision?
- ➲ How will the decision be made?

There are a number of ways to make decisions. The two most frequently used means of reaching agreement are to gain a consensus or to allow the majority to rule. **Consensus building** requires that everyone or nearly everyone agrees with the final decision. Majority rule requires most, but not all, of the members to agree. Some decisions are made by a small subgroup of team members or by a single member once the team as a whole contributes their ideas. Each means of making a decision can be appropriate at various times. Your team should consider each option and its consequences whenever making a decision.

As a member of the team, it is important that you listen carefully to all points. When giving your opinion, you should not seek conflict but neither should you avoid it just to keep peace. Everyone should participate, even those whose opinions go against the feelings of the majority. The leader and others in the team should check often for understanding by restating the points being made to ensure that everyone is aware of all the issues. Continually search for alternative solutions that meet the goals of every member. The purpose of a team decision is to use all the ideas that can be generated rather than only those of a single person.

Consensus building is the process used to reach agreement by a team of people.

Collaborative Tools

Collaborative computing is growing in importance as software is developed to encourage its use as part of a team activity. Brainstorming software, such as *Inspiration*, is sometimes used to gather and sort ideas. *Microsoft PowerPoint* is also used to brainstorm. Its Notes features can be used to add ideas as they occur to members of a group using this software.

CHANGING WORKPLACE

Members of a publication team no longer must be in the same city or the same country. Collaborative publication tools make it easy to share work easily between groups using online technology. It's important to understand that even though a member of a team is not physically present, all the same steps in building a team are still useful. Good team members take time to get to know those who are physically removed. This includes asking the same social questions by email or phone that you would in person. Sending holiday greetings is an example of these social exchanges that add to effective teams. Team members who ignore these social conventions find that the performing stage is not arrived at as easily as they might wish.

Any software that facilitates the gathering of ideas and the tracking of information can be an important collaborative tool.

Technology has provided teams with ways to collaborate even when the team is not able to meet in person. Video conferencing provides members with a means of meeting using a video camera. Teleconferencing, using phone lines, is another way. Calendars and databases that can be accessed by everyone in a team provide collaborative tools that are useful.

Software such as *Adobe Acrobat* and *Microsoft Word* allows you to create a document, send it on to others for their comments, and then use the Reviewing toolbar to accept or reject any suggestions. Figure 24.2 demonstrates the use of this process during the creation of a textbook using *Word*. Notice the revisions as well as comments on the right side of the document. With collaborative tools such as these, teams can be far more productive than in the past. It is just one way technology has had an impact on business.

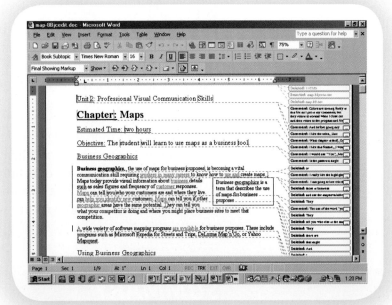

Figure 24.2
Collaborative software makes it easier for a team to provide input.

A **flow chart** helps a team see each stage of work required to complete the task.

A **mock layout** is a drawing demonstrating the document being produced.

Publication Process

When planning a desktop publishing project, there are a number of considerations that must be addressed. You have already learned to consider the audience and purpose. Other concerns include the time available to complete the project, the cost of the project, and the life of the publication. A **flow chart** may be established to indicate what is required for each stage of the project (see Figure 24.3). Often, information must be gathered first. Each person on the team may be assigned a particular part of that step. Once the content is available, a **mock layout** may be created allocating space for text and graphics.

Once the size of a document has been decided, then costs can be determined. If a document is going to

Tasks	Personnel	Deadlines
Planning Meeting (assignments)		
Audience		
Purpose		
Content Acquisition (outline)		
Writing		
Photography		
Design		
Layout		
Cost Determination		
Proofing		
Final Document Preparation		
Printing		
Distribution		

Figure 24.3
A flow chart does not have to be a complicated document. In this example a simple spreadsheet makes it possible to track deadlines and personnel.

be printed professionally, several bids may be solicited in order to compare prices. If the document is going to be printed in-house using your own equipment, it may still be necessary to determine supply costs. One often overlooked consideration is the life of a publication. A pamphlet that will be read once and thrown away does not have to be as durable as a handbook that must be maintained and used as a frequent reference.

The next steps require the team members to produce the required pages, proof them, and then gather the document into its final format. Once the document is complete and in a printed form, it must be distributed. Desktop published documents may be mailed, handed out, or distributed by means of the Web. Usually a final step is evaluating the process and the product to determine how future work can be improved.

SUMMARY

In this chapter you learned that there were specific stages of team building. You saw how a team charter, team building, a team leader, and team communications can improve the function of a team in business. You learned about activities that teams engage in, such as meeting, decision making, and collaboration. You saw how all of these come together in the publication process.

KEY TERMS

consensus building	mock layout	storming
flow chart	norming	team charter
forming	performing	

REVIEW

Answer the following questions on your own computer.

1. What are the four stages of team development?

2. What is the name of the stage in team development that represents creation?

3. What occurs during the storming stage of team development?

4. What is the name of the stage in team development in which conflicts are resolved?

5. What occurs during the performing stage of team development?

6. What is a team charter?

7. What is the significant function of the team leader?

8. What should the selection of a team leader be based on?

9. What is the guiding hand at team meetings?

10. When should an agenda be delivered and why?

11. What are the two most frequently used methods of reaching agreement?

12. What is the meaning of consensus building?

13. What is the meaning of majority rule?

14. How can a leader and team members check for understanding to be sure all participants are aware of the issues?

15. What is the purpose of a team decision?

16. Name a software program that is considered a collaborative tool.

17. What is a flow chart?

18. What is a mock layout?

19. In considering cost, what is often overlooked?

20. What is a final step in the publication process?

DISCUSS

1. Discuss what should occur at the beginning for teams to work and why.

2. Review the purpose of a team charter and what it should include.

3. Explain what is meant by team-building activities.

4. Discuss the selection process of a team leader.

5. Discuss communication problems in a team that can destroy its effectiveness.

6. List some characteristics of a good team meeting.

7. Discuss the rules that should be adhered to in order to make a team meeting productive.

8. Review the issues related to decisions that should be understood by all team members.

9. Describe some ways that a team can collaborate even if they cannot meet in person.

10. Explain the process and considerations of cost analysis of a job.

go
to the website at
academic.cengage.com/school/dtp

Activity 1 Class Team

WRITING

1. A class can be considered a team. Think about the class that you are in and answer the following questions:

   ● Why was the team created?
   ● What does the team need to accomplish?
   ● How will the team track its progress?
   ● What will the team members gain from working on this team?
   ● What happens when team members need help?

2. Using your desktop publishing software, create a flyer about your class with the answers to these questions. Be creative.

3. Save document as **class_team**.

Activity 2 Team Development

WRITING

1. In a team of three or four students, use the four stages of team development to create an emergency plan for your classroom. There should be an emergency plan posted on the wall; however, write a plan for what should occur in order to get everyone from the classroom effectively and in an organized way. The plan on the wall may only cover what occurs outside of the classroom.

2. Using desktop publishing software, each team member should create a journal explaining what occurred or what decisions were made during each of the stages of team development while your team created the emergency plan. Include at least one image of your team in the journal. Also include discussion of any conflict during the stages. How was it handled? How could it have been handled better?

3. Save the document as **team_journal**.

Activity 3 Emergency Plan

WRITING

1. Using your desktop publishing software, create a poster of your emergency plan from Activity 2 that can be posted on the wall of the classroom.

2. Save the document as **emergency_plan**.

3. Print your **emergency_plan**. Meet back in your original team of three or four students to evaluate the finished product. Approve one of the plans using consensus. Submit this plan to your instructor with a written explanation as to why the team chose this plan. The written explanation should be added to the original poster document as a second page.

4. Save the written explanation document as **best_emergency_plan**.

Activity 4 Student Organization

1. Members of a student organization can be considered a team. Attend a meeting of a student organization on your campus. Using the information learned in this chapter, write a summary of the team's meeting. Use the following list as a guideline.

   - Be on time.
   - Start on time and end promptly.
   - Use agendas that include the purpose, time for discussion, and desired outcome of the meeting.
   - Come prepared with the information needed by others.
   - Stay on task.

2. Using your desktop publishing software, create a document with your summary.

3. Save the document as *student_organization_summary*.

Activity 5 Class Trip

1. In a team of three or four students, plan a class trip. Begin by creating a team charter.

2. Use your desktop publishing software to publish the charter for your team. Save the document as *trip_charter*.

3. Plan and participate in at least one team-building activity. Using your desktop publishing software, create a document explaining this activity with discussion on its effectiveness in building trust in team members. Save the document as *trip_team_building*.

4. Each member of the team should create a flyer with details of the class trip. Save the document as *trip_flyer*.

EXPLORE

1. Search the Internet for books or articles on effective team building, participation, and/or meetings.

2. Using MLA style, create a list of at least six articles or books that can be used to extend your learning from the textbook. Include an annotation below each resource that states what you believe would be gained from using the book or article as a resource.

3. Save the document as *more_team_resources*.

Independent Project

Yearbooks Plus!

1. A yearbook is usually a recording or commemoration of school activities; however, it does not have to be restricted to this. It can also be a report or summary of statistics or facts of other events.

2. Create a mini yearbook commemorating an event from one of the following:

   ➲ *Historical event*

   ➲ *Family gathering*

   ➲ *School activity*

   ➲ *Report of a business*

3. The mini yearbook should include the following:

   ➲ *Theme that is used on all pages*

   ➲ *Cover page that includes the theme with appropriate titles and images*

   ➲ *At least one page template*

   ➲ *At least one style sheet containing a minimum of two styles*

   ➲ *Minimum of four pages*

   ➲ *Minimum of five images*

   ➲ *Effective use of font type, size, color*

   ➲ *Appropriate balance of images, headlines, and other text, including captions and articles*

   ➲ *Effective use of desktop publishing skills*

4. Save as ***mini_yearbook***.

Team Project

Marketing Samples

1. Create a folder of marketing samples for an auto insurance company. Decide on a name for the auto insurance company.

2. Include at least three examples of each of the following items:

    - *Logo*
    - *Slogan*
    - *Letterhead saved as a template*
    - *Newsletter templates (two pages) with a style sheet and two different styles.*

3. Templates should include a minimum of the following:

    - *Nameplate*
    - *Table of Contents*
    - *Header*
    - *Masthead*
    - *Headline*
    - *Tombstoning*
    - *Pull Quote*

4. Design three other documents to use in marketing the company. Choose from the following:

    - *Sign for the front of the building*
    - *Flyer*
    - *Ad for newspaper*
    - *Cover page for folders*
    - *Billboard*
    - *Brochure*
    - *Poster*
    - *Bulletin Board display*

Digital Portfolio

Self-Assessment

1. Select five items from Unit 6 that you intend to add to your portfolio. Write an assessment of what you learned from this activity. Include what you learned from creating the content as well as what skills you used that you had learned in the unit. What caused you the most difficulty? What did you enjoy most about completing the activity? What would you do differently if you had the opportunity to repeat this activity?

2. Save your self-assessments with the filename with **_sa** added to the end of it.

Collecting and Organizing Sample Projects

Collect projects and assignments from Unit 6 that you want to include in your portfolio. These assignments do not all need to be your best work. Move the documents to those folders. If available, a copy of the rubric should also be included for each of the projects/assignments that will be included in the portfolio. Back up all files from the portfolio as your plan outlined.

Journalizing Progress

Using word processing software, a tablet PC, handheld device, or blog, add to the journal of this ongoing project. Save the journal as **portfolio_journal** or give the link to the blog to your instructor. Alternatively, you could keep an audio journal of your work using podcasting or other digital audio methods. Consult your instructor for the journal method to use for this class.

projects projects projects

Source: http://www.fbla-pbl.org/docs/FBLA_CMH_2006/FBLA_Tab5.pdf

Future Business Leaders of America Phi Beta Lambda

FBLA Chapter Management Handbook (2006–2007)

"FBLA-PBL is the premier student business association. Our mission is to bring business and education together in a positive working relationship through innovative leadership and career development programs."

FBLA Desktop Publishing Competition

School-Site Testing

Two (2) hours will be allowed for the skill test at the school-testing site. Additional time will be allowed for general directions. Participants will complete problem(s) that may include application of the following:

- Graphics
- Text creation
- Layout creativity
- Selection of appropriate fonts and type sizes

Production Test Rating Categories

Usability

Document effectively meets goals of the project

Document addresses appropriate audience and shows good grasp of the concept

Information effectively synthesized

Technical Features

Appropriate font selection (i.e., size, font type, mix, leading)

Effective text treatment (i.e., paragraph indents, bullets, hanging indents, alignment, text wrapping)

Effective application of a special effect(s), which may include but is not limited to drop cap, shadowing, reverse type, screens, and mirror images

Layout

Creative, original

Appealing

Selection and effective use of graphic(s)

Overall Effort

- Comprehensive approach to the project
- Effective use of technology for the task
- Final product indicates a clear thought process and an intended, planned direction with formulation and execution of a firm idea

Computer Competency Classes

(written by Diana Crites, Sherando HS, Virginia)

Introductory Computer Class

Objectives

- Students will produce the written report from the student descriptions and information presented for the Community Service Project. They will follow the technical requirements regarding report content, report cover, table of contents, and general requirements as outlined in the Chapter Management Handbook.
- Students will focus on graphic design throughout the report and for the report cover.

Competencies/Standards (Align with Your State Competencies/Standards)

- Proofread and edit documents
- Compose a variety of documents
- Enhance layout of documents by using formatting features

- Import graphics using a variety of peripherals
- Analyze writing tool suggestions (e.g., speller, thesaurus, grammar check)
- Incorporate intermediate word processing operations
- Identify the purposes and goals of the student organization
- Participate in course activities sponsored by the student organization

Procedures

- Students will gather the information and develop the written report as outlined in the FBLA Chapter Management Handbook. Students will incorporate graphics, tables, and formatting features to enhance the report. Students will proofread and edit the report. Students will receive a project grade based upon the rubric, which can be downloaded by going to http://www.fbla-pbl.org/docs/rubrics/IntroComputerReportRubric.doc. The instructor will use the rubric to determine the winning project. All instructors of this course will then determine the final winning project from all classes (if more than one class is participating.) Recognition should be given to the final winner and the winners from each class. The winning project will be distributed to the advanced classes.

Advanced Computer Class

Objectives

- Students will review the winning written report chosen from the introductory computer class. They will ensure that the developer followed the technical requirements (regarding report content, report cover, and table of contents) and general requirements as outlined in the Chapter Management Handbook.
- Students will enhance the report using more advanced word processing skills (styles, etc.).
- Students will enhance the report using more advanced graphic enhancements.
- Students will develop at least a 20-slide presentation of the Community Project as described in the report (possibly imported from the styles in the report) and add any additional features needed.
- Students will print the presentation in handout format.

Competencies

➩ Produce multipage documents incorporating tables, templates, macros, style sheets, and other advanced word processing functions

➩ Create a professional document (e.g., brochure, annual report, newsletter) demonstrating established principles of layout design in desktop publishing

➩ Import text, graphics from other sources

➩ Research and organize information for an original multimedia presentation

➩ Plan and build a multimedia presentation using advanced features

➩ Enhance the multimedia presentation layout according to principles of effective design

➩ Enhance a multimedia presentation with features (e.g., color, transitions, timing, backgrounds, graphics, charts, graphs)

➩ Enhance the multimedia presentation using customized options (e.g., original artwork organizational charts, tables)

➩ Incorporate visual elements using scanned images, digital photography, video images, and downloadable images from the Internet

➩ Incorporate audio elements, such as music and voice sounds, digital audio (.wav) files, and MIDI interface files

➩ Proofread and edit a multimedia presentation

➩ Create handouts and other visuals

➩ Identify the purposes and goals of the student organization

➩ Participate in course activities sponsored by the student organization

Procedures

➩ Students will take the winning report created by the introductory students and enhance the written report using advanced word processing features. Students will review and choose enhanced graphics to incorporate as submitted by the Desktop/Multimedia students. Students will proofread and edit the report and will develop a 20-slide multimedia presentation. The winning presentation will be printed and added to the appendix. A project grade will be given based upon the rubric. The rubric can be downloaded by going to http://www.fbla-pbl.org/docs/rubrics/Advanced ComputerPowerPointRubric.doc and http://www.fbla-pbl.org/docs/rubrics/AdvancedComputerReportRubric.doc. The instructor will use the rubric to determine the winning report and project. The instructors will determine the final winning report and presentation from all classes (if more than one class is participating). Recognition should be given to the final winner and the winners from each class. The winning report will be submitted to the Content Committee for final review before submitting to FBLA state competition. The winning presentation will be submitted to the Publicity/Presentation Committee for final review.

Desktop and/or Multimedia Class

Objectives

- Students will enhance photos of the Community Service Project using appropriate software. They will use techniques such as cropping, feathering, layering, shaping, etc.
- Students will find appropriate graphic clip art related to the Community Service Project. They will use clip-art programs and the World Wide Web as resources. They will enhance the clip art to gain reader interest or understanding of the project.
- Students will merge graphics with photos and add text for enhancement.
- Students will ensure that images are compressed for *PowerPoint* usage.
- Students will plan, compose, and produce a trifold teaser brochure.
- Students will incorporate enhanced graphics in the brochure to create an excellent appearance.
- Students will prepare and print the brochure for distribution.

Competencies

- Gather/compose (in exportable format) documents and graphics for use in designing various desktop publishing applications
- Apply principles of design, layout
- Incorporate original and/or imported text and graphics from a variety of software applications
- Incorporate visual elements using scanned images, digital photographs, or images imported from the World Wide Web
- Draw and edit objects incorporating features such as fills, borders, and lines
- Identify the purposes and goals of the student organization
- Participate in course activities sponsored by the student organization
- Describe ways that desktop publishing and multimedia presentations can be used in business and industry
- Compose headlines and captions
- Proofread and edit text for format, mechanics, and clarity using standard proofreader's symbols
- Incorporate journalistic principles in layout
- Gather/compose (in exportable format) documents and graphics for use in designing various desktop publishing applications such as flyers, brochures, or newsletters
- Apply principles of design, layout, and typography
- Design a layout for ease of readability and attractiveness (e.g., white space, column position and spacing, page margins, graphic text placements)

- Enhance appearance of document using desktop features (e.g., graphic boxes, lines, illustrations, images)
- Create multipage and multicolumn documents
- Incorporate original and/or imported text, graphics, tables, and charts from a variety of software applications
- Incorporate audio and/or visual elements using scanned images, digital photographs, or images imported from the World Wide Web
- Identify the purposes and goals of the student organization
- Participate in course activities sponsored by the student organization

Procedures

- Students will enhance photos for the Community Service Project, using appropriate software. Techniques such as cropping, feathering, layering, shaping, etc. should be used. The completed graphics will then be used in the written report, the *PowerPoint* presentation, and the brochure.
- Students will plan, compose, and produce a trifold (1/3 text, 2/3 graphics) brochure which will correlate with the written report. The winning brochure will be printed and added to the appendix to the winning report. A project grade will be given based upon the rubric, Which can be downloaded by going to http://www.fbla-pbl.org/docs/rubrics/Desktop-MMBrochureRubric.doc and http://www.fbla-pbl.org/docs/rubrics/Desktop-MMPowerPointRubric.doc. All instructors of this course will then determine the final winning brochure from all classes (if more than one class is participating). Recognition should be given to the final winner and the winners from each class. The winning brochure will be submitted to the Publicity/Presentation Committee for final review before distribution to the public or submission for FBLA state competition.

File Formats

Raster or Bitmap Graphics	Extension
Windows or OS/2 Bitmap	bmp
Windows Clipboard	clp
Windows or OS/2 DIB	dib
FlashPix	fpx
CompuServe Graphics Interchange	gif
Amiga	iff
GEM Paint	img
JPEG 2000	jp2
Joint Photographic Expert Group	jpg or jpeg
Deluxe Paint	lbm
MacPaint	mac
Portable Bitmap	pbm
Kodak PhotoCD	pcd
Macintosh Paint	pct or pict
Zsoft Paintbrush	pcx
PC Paint	pic
Portable Network Graphics	png
Photoshop	psd
Paint Shop Pro Image	psp
Pixar	pxr
Sun Raster Image	ras
Raw File Format	raw
SciTex Continuous Tone	sct
Silicon Graphics Image File	sgi

Truevision Targa	tga
Tagged Image File Format	tiff
WordPerfect Bitmap	wpg

Vector Graphics	**Extension**
Adobe Illustrator	ai
Corel Draw	cdr
Computer Graphics Metafile	cgm
Micrografx Designer/Draw	drw
AutoCAD Interchange File	dxf
Windows Enhanced Metafile	emf
Encapsulated PostScript	eps
Macromedia FreeHand	fh
Ventura	gem
Macintosh Draw	mpnt
Lotus Development	pic
Encapsulated PostScript	ps
Word Pro Draw	sdw
Scalable Vector Graphics	svg
Windows Meta File	wmf
WordPerfect	wpg

Glossary

A

Accordion fold An accordion fold divides a page into fourths.

Acrobat Reader Acrobat Reader is software that can be downloaded without cost. It is used to read Adobe Acrobat, or PDF, files.

Additive color Additive color is one that becomes white when all colors have been added.

Adjustment layer An adjustment layer is a special layer that allows you to modify image adjustments such as levels and contrast.

Adobe Gamma The Adobe Gamma is a utility program provided by Adobe to calibrate your monitor.

Adobe RGB 1998 Adobe RGB 1998 is the working space recommended for use with images that will be printed.

Alignment Alignment is the placement of text or graphics on a line. The placement can be to the right, to the left, or centered.

Alley Alley is the space between columns.

Alpha channel An alpha channel is a special channel used to store masks. Other channels separate the RGB or CMYK colors that make up an image.

Analogous colors Analogous colors are those that are near each other on a color wheel.

Anchor An anchor is a point along a line or a curve that can be used to change the shape of a vector.

Anchors Anchors are design tools that tie parts of a page together or elements to the page.

Arranging Arranging is the term that Adobe InDesign uses to describe the process of moving a layer up or down.

Ascender An ascender is the part of a lowercase letter that extends above the x-height, as in the letter "t."

Ascender line The ascender line marks the upper limit of the ascender, which is usually the tallest letter. If the capital is taller, the term "cap line" is sometimes used.

Asymmetry Asymmetry is when one or more elements on a page are not balanced.

Axes Axes is the vertical (Y) or horizontal (X) value or category defining information on a chart.

B

Background Background is the bottom layer of a design.

Balance Balance is the use of elements so they counter each other, for example in opposite corners of a page.

Bandwidth Bandwidth is the speed at which a computer can transmit information along a network.

Baseline A baseline is the line on which type "sits."

Bitmap Bitmap is a type of image created using pixels.

Bitmap fonts Bitmap fonts are those used to display text on a computer screen.

Blackletter fonts Blackletter fonts imitate an antique European font.

Bleed Bleed is a design that places a graphic or color so that it extends to the edge of the page leaving no visible margin.

Blending mode A blending mode is a color technique that combines two layers.

Bond paper Bond paper is usually used in a photocopier or a personal printer.

Book paper Book paper is a better quality than bond.

Booklet   A booklet is a desktop published document that consists of two pages printed front and back on a single sheet of paper.

Bounding box   Bounding box is the area surrounding a frame.

Bracketed serif   Bracketed serif is a curved serif that fills in the area between the serif and the stroke.

Bullets   Bullets are symbols used to set off lines of text and draw attention.

Business letter fold   A business letter fold folds a page into thirds to fit in a standard business envelope.

Byline   A byline identifies the author of an article.

C

Calibration   Calibration is the adjusting of your monitor's settings and color to meet an accepted standard.

Callout   Callout is a word or words that explain a point in a graphic.

Camera-ready   Camera-ready is when a file is ready to go to the press without intervention on the part of the printer.

Caption   Caption is a phrase or sentence describing a graphic.

Channels   Channels are the division of color modes into separate images.

Character styles   Character styles are choices applied only to text.

CIE   CIE is an abbreviation for the Commission Internationale de l'Eclairage, a French organization that in 1931 developed measurements for color.

Clip art   Clip art is usually a line drawing that is created as a vector graphic. Clip art is often supplied with word processing programs.

Clipping mask   A clipping mask is the area outside the clipping path.

Clipping path   A clipping path is a drawing or shape that will be used to crop an image.

Closure   Closure is the desire by the human brain to complete a drawing or design.

CMYK   CMYK is the acronym for cyan (blue), magenta (red), yellow, and black. These are the colors used to produce printed images.

Coated paper   Coated paper is one to which a finish has been added, producing a better-quality print.

Color mode   Color mode is the separation of color into channels.

Color scheme   Color scheme is an arrangement of colors designed to create a particular response.

Color separation   Color separation is the process of dividing an image into color plates for printing.

Color space   Color space is the number of colors that a device can display.

Color temperature   Color temperature is the measurement of light that falls on a computer screen.

Color theory   Color theory is the relationship between colors often based on their location on a color wheel.

Color wheel   Color wheel is a visual arrangement of colors in a circle that is similar to the spectrum of light.

Colorimeter   A colorimeter is a device used to calibrate a computer monitor by recording the image that appears on the display.

Comp   A comp is an image of a layout.

Complementary colors   Complementary colors are those that appear directly across from each other on a color wheel.

Compression   Compression in graphic files is the process of reducing the size of the image.

Consensus building   Consensus building is the process used to reach agreement by a team of people.

Consistency   Consistency of design is when the same choice is made for similar parts of a page such as a typeface or spacing.

Constraining   Constraining is the process of using the Shift key to draw lines so that they are straight or to draw shapes so they are squares or perfect circles.

Continuation head   A continuation head restates the original headline to simplify the process of finding an article that has been continued from a previous page.

Cool colors   Cool colors are those near the color blue on the color wheel.

Copyright   Copyright is the legal protection any artist has for the work he or she creates.

Corner point   A corner point is an anchor at a point that changes direction along a path.

Counter   Counter is the open area inside a letter such as that which appears in the letter "D."

Cover stock paper   Cover stock paper is a heavy stock.

Cross-platform   Cross-platform is a term that indicates that a file can be read on both Macs and PCs.

Cross-platform compatibility   Cross-platform compatibility is the ability or inability of software or fonts to function on both Windows and Macintosh computers or any other operating system such as Linux.

Curly quotes   Curly quotes are marks curved in on either side of a quotation.

D

Data range   The data range is the upper and lower numerical limit of the Y-axis.

Deck   A deck is a longer headline that appears below the main head. It provides additional information about the article.

Decorative fonts   Decorative fonts are those used for display purposes.

Default   Default, as it is used with software, is a setting that is already established when the software is first opened.

Descender   A descender is the part of a lowercase letter that extends below the baseline, as in the letter "g."

Desktop publishing   Desktop publishing is the use of word processing software or specialized desktop publishing software on a personal computer to create a document in which graphics and text enhance the message.

Diacritical marks   Diacritical marks are symbols used to indicate the pronunciation of a word.

Digital printing   Digital printing transfers an electronic file directly from a computer to a press.

Digital zoom   Digital zoom is the enlargement of an image in a camera lens. This is done electronically by merely enlarging the pixels rather than actually capturing more of the image.

Digitally signed   Digitally signed indicates that the font has been tested to meet specifications.

Dingbats   Dingbats are graphic symbols or ornaments that appear in a font as characters.

Direct printing   Direct printing is the process of printing a document directly from a plate.

Direction line   A direction line is a line that appears when a smooth point is selected. The line is used to adjust the shape or angle of a curved vector.

Display type   Display type is specifically designed to be used in a large size.

Dot gain   Dot gain describes the spreading of ink once it is applied to paper. Dot gain is a concern particularly when using a low-quality paper such as newsprint.

Dot matrix   Dot matrix is a means of printing by placing a series of dots closely together so that they give the appearance of printed letters.

Downrules   Downrules are vertical lines between columns.

Downstyle   Downstyle capitalizes only the first word and proper nouns in a headline.

Drop caps   Drop caps are large, often ornate first letters of a paragraph.

Drop shadow   Drop shadow is a dark blurred edge around an image to give it a feeling of depth.

DTP   DTP is an acronym for desktop publishing.

Dummy   A dummy is an early proof used in page design planning.

E

Ellipsis   An ellipsis is three dots used to indicate an omitted word or phrase within a quotation.

Em dash   An em dash is a line the width of the capital letter "M" in whatever font and point size are being used. It indicates a break in thought.

Em space   An em space is a space the width of a capital letter "M" in the font and point size being used.

En dash   An en dash is a line the width of the capital letter "N" in whatever font and point size are being used. It is used in ranges of numbers, letters, or dates.

En space   An en space, half the size of an em space, is the width of a capital letter "N" in the font and point size being used.

End point   An end point is an anchor that appears at the start and end of a path.

End signs   End signs are symbols or images that are used to indicate that an article is complete.

F

Facing pages   Facing pages is a DTP term indicating that there are right and left sides.

Faux font   Faux font is a regular font that has been modified by software to appear as if it has an attribute such as bold.

Feathering   Feathering is a graphic enhancement that blurs the edges of the image.

Fibonacci sequence   The Fibonacci sequence is a series of numbers beginning with 1. Each number in the series is added to the next in order to create a third number.

Field code   A field code is a means of identifying information that is to be entered from an attached spreadsheet or database.

File format   File format is the type of program that created an image. The extension (two to four letters after the period) at the end of the file name indicates its format.

Fill   A fill is the interior of a shape or a letter.

Fill layer   A fill layer provides you with a nondestructive layer that can be filled with any color you want.

Firewall   A firewall is a means of preventing access to a network

Flash memory   Flash memory is a type of electronic storage that retains information even with power turned off. The information in this type of memory can be erased and new information recorded.

Flatten   Flatten is the process of merging all the layers into one.

Float   Float is a description of a figure that indicates it can be placed anywhere on a page.

Flow   Flow is the visual path created by arrangements of elements within a page design.

Flow chart   A flow chart helps a team see each stage of work required to complete the task.

Flush   Flush is an alignment term indicating that the line begins at the left or ends at the right margin.

Focal point   Focal point is the visual element in a page design that the viewer notices first.

Folio   A folio is a printing term used to describe a folded page.

Font   Font originally included typeface, style, and size, but the term now is interchangeable with typeface.

Footer   A footer is recurring information that appears at the bottom of the page.

Foreground   Foreground is the top layer of a design.

Forming   Forming is the first stage of team development when a team is formed.

FPO   FPO is an acronym for "for position only," indicating a placeholder image being used in place of the one intended for actual printing.

Frame   A frame is a DTP enclosure for text or images that allows you to move the information as a unit.

FTP   FTP is an acronym for file transfer protocol. It is a way of transferring files from a computer to a server using the Internet.

G

Galley A galley is another term for a page proof.

Gatefold A gatefold folds the sides into the middle of a page.

Golden ratio The golden ratio is a number (pi). The approximate result is derived by dividing 5 by 3, arrangements often found in nature.

Gradient A gradient is a color technique that spreads variations of color across an image.

Graphics Graphics is a broad term that describes anything on a page that is not text.

Greeking Greeking is a series of nonsense words, often derived from Latin, used as a placeholder in a desktop publishing document.

Grid A grid is the division of a page into a design on which text, figures, or white space are placed in order to design a page.

Gridlines Gridlines are horizontal or vertical lines designed to make it easy to track information (usually numerical) on a chart.

Grunge type Grunge type is a decorative font that appears to be beat up.

GUI GUI, an acronym for graphical user interface; indicates that pictures rather than text allow the user to work with the computer.

Guides Guides are nonprinting lines that provide visual points of reference, making it easy to align text, images, or frames.

Gutter Gutter is the inside margin of a document with facing pages. It is slightly wider than the outside margin to allow for binding space. The term "gutter" is also used to mean the space between columns.

H

Hairline A hairline is the narrowest line that can be produced by a printer.

Half fold A half fold divides the page in half. It is often a booklet fold.

Halftone Halftone is the process of converting an image to dots for printing.

Halftone screen Halftone screen is a means of changing a printed image into dots suitable for printing.

Hanging indents With hanging indents, a paragraph's first line is flush left but the remaining lines are indented.

Hanging punctuation Hanging punctuation is punctuation such as quotation marks that need to "hang" outside a paragraph rather than line up with the text below.

Harmony of design Harmony of design is when all the elements on a page are arranged in an effective way.

Header A header is recurring information that appears at the top of the page. A newsletter header restates the newsletter name and usually provides the page number and sometimes the date.

Headlines Headlines are brief sentences that summarize the content of an article.

Hex numbers Hex numbers are hexadecimal numbers derived from base 16 that are used to describe web colors.

High-end program A high-end program is software that has many features and is often used by professionals.

Hot spots Hot spots are locations that transmit a wireless signal for use by those in the vicinity.

HSB HSB is an acronym for hue, saturation, and brightness. Sometimes the "B" is replaced with an "L" for luminescence.

Hyphen A hyphen is a short horizontal line used to separate compound words or to hyphenate a word.

Hyphenation Hyphenation is the splitting of a word at a syllable break.

I

ICC profile ICC profile is a means of transferring color information from device to device.

Image release form An image release form gives you permission to use a photograph in a document or on a website.

Imagesetter An imagesetter is the hardware used to RIP files.

Index colors   Index colors, usually used with GIF files, are colors assigned a number for each pixel.

Indirect printing   Indirect printing is the process of offsetting an image to create a printed document.

Inkjet   Inkjet is a printing method that sprays a series of ink dots onto a page, allowing it to reproduce both text and images with fine detail.

Inline   Inline describes frames that are placed within text and must stay with that text.

Input device   An input device allows users to enter information into a computer.

International Color Consortium   The International Color Consortium is an organization that works together to ensure that color is consistent regardless of operating systems or software.

J

Jump line   A jump line is the statement at the end of text on one page indicating the page on which the text continues (or was continued from).

Justified   Justified alignment places text so that it fills the entire line from the left to the right margin.

K

Kerning   Kerning is spacing of letters generally to make them move closer together.

Kerning pairs   Kerning pairs are sets of letters designed to be spaced closely together.

Kicker   A kicker is a brief headline or title that appears above the main headline. It is designed to draw attention to the main head.

L

L*A*B   L*A*B is an acronym for the color descriptions developed by the CIE. Often the color is also called CIE-LAB.

Ladder   A ladder is a list of pages in a yearbook that includes the content for the page and the person responsible. Deadlines may also be marked on a ladder.

LAN   LAN is a local area network that connects computers located in proximity to one another. Since cables are required to connect each to a single connection point, the physical distance limits the size of a LAN.

Landscape orientation   Landscape orientation is a page design in which the longest side is the top of the page.

Layering   Layering is the practice of placing text and images on top of each other in a design.

Leader dots   Leader dots are symbols, a series of dots or small images designed to draw the eye across a page.

Leading   Leading is the spacing between lines of a paragraph.

Ledger   Ledger is a standard American paper size that is 11 × 17 inches. It is also known as tabloid size.

Legal   Legal is a standard American paper size that is 8.5 × 14 inches.

Legend   Legend is a key, generally found in a box, used to identify the series on a chart or a map.

Legibility   Legibility is the measurement of text that determines how easily the eye can decipher the words. Legibility is used for display text or short passages.

Letter   Letter is a standard American paper size that is 8.5 × 11 inches.

License   License is the permission granted to use a work of art without transferring ownership.

Ligatures   Ligatures are letters that have historically been attached, creating a single character.

Line screen   Line screen is the measurement of the number of lines used to create a printed image. The measurement is given as LPI or lines per inch.

Linear gradient   A linear gradient is a series of colors that are on a vertical or horizontal plane.

Linotronic   Linotronic is a common brand of imagesetter.

Linux   Linux is an open source operating system that generally runs on PCs.

Lithography   Lithography is the process used to print documents on an offset press.

Logo   A logo is an image and text combined to identify a business or organization.

Logotype   A logotype is the text included in a logo. It may be a distinctive typeface.

Lorem ipsum   Lorem ipsum is the first two words of the original greeking text. It is sometimes used instead of the word "greeking."

Lossless   Lossless compression does not change any pixel data.

Lossy   Lossy compression reduces the size of an image file by removing information that is not essential.

M

Mac   A Mac (Macintosh) is a computer marketed by Apple Computers that uses the Macintosh operating system.

Macro   A macro is a camera function that allows close-ups.

Mail merge   Mail merge joins a spreadsheet or database to a document in order to individualize the document using the data.

Malware   Malware is a broad term that describes software designed to be destructive to a computer. It can include viruses, worms, Trojans, adware, or spyware.

Margins   Margins are the white space surrounding a page.

Mask   A mask is a means of covering an area within a graphic to prevent it from being selected.

Master   A master is a printed page or plate used to print a document.

Master pages   Master pages contain recurring items such as page numbers as well as other design elements.

Masthead   A masthead contains contact information that identifies who publishes the newsletter.

Mechanical   A mechanical is a layout created by hand using paper, glue, and often a gridded board.

Megapixels   Megapixels describe the size of images captured by a camera.

Memory card   A memory card is a flash storage device in which digital photographs are captured.

Mock layout   A mock layout is a drawing demonstrating the document being produced.

Modern fonts   Modern fonts have unbracketed serifs, vertical stress, and uneven strokes.

Monitor gamma   Monitor gamma is a calibration that measures the brightness and contrast of a computer display.

Monospace fonts   Monospace fonts mimic the spacing produced by a typewriter. All the letters are the same width.

N

Nameplate   A nameplate contains the name of the newsletter along with other information such as the date, issue, and volume number.

Native   Native formats are those that can only be read by a single program.

Negative space   Negative space is another term for white space or areas on the page where no text or graphics are located.

Newsprint paper   Newsprint paper is low quality and inexpensive.

Nonbreaking space   Nonbreaking space is a means of ensuring that a word is not separated during hyphenation.

Nondestructive editing   Nondestructive editing makes changes to an image without actually affecting the original image.

Norming   Norming is a later stage of team development during which conflicts are resolved.

O

OCR   OCR (optical character recognition) is a process that converts a scanned representation of text into editable "live" text on a computer.

Offset   Offset is a printing process that transfers an image from a plate to a blanket that is offset to paper. Offset is another term for standoff.

Oldstyle fonts   Oldstyle fonts have bracketed serifs, angled stress, and strokes that move gently from thick to thin.

Opacity   Opacity is the ability to see through one object or layer to another below it.

Open source   Open source software is developed by individuals and offered free to the public. "Open" means that its code can be modified in any way that a user needs.

OpenType   OpenType combines both PostScript and TrueType in a font with advanced features.

Operating system   An operating system (OS) is the software that allows a computer to function. It includes features such as how a monitor displays an image and how files are accessed.

Optical zoom   Optical zoom on a camera uses a lens to actually magnify the image.

Orientation   Orientation is the vertical or horizontal position in which a page is printed.

Orphans   Orphans are single lines of text that appear at the top of the column or page, with the rest of the paragraph appearing in the previous column or page

Out of gamut   Out of gamut is a warning that a particular device is unable to display a color.

Outline fonts   Outline fonts are typefaces that can be scaled up or down in size without losing sharpness.

Output device   An output device allows users to transfer information in a computer to print or display.

P

Page description language   Page description language is software that allows a printer to produce a printed page that includes text and graphics.

Page proof   A page proof is a final copy of a page used to do a last check for errors before printing occurs.

PageMaker   PageMaker was the first true desktop publishing software developed for use on a computer.

Pagination   Pagination is the setup of a document including margins, columns, headers, footers, and orientation.

Palette   A palette is a bar or area on the screen that provides additional features for tools.

Pangram   Pangram is a sentence used as an example because it contains all the letters of the alphabet.

Panning   Panning is the use of a "hand" to move small distances on a digital map.

Pantone Color Matching System   The Pantone Color Matching System uses a series of cards to identify specific colors. Each color has been established as a Pantone standard, making it easy to reproduce a color.

Paragraph styles   Paragraph styles are choices applied to both text and paragraph formatting.

Pasteboard   Pasteboard is the area outside the document page itself.

Path   A path is the term used for the lines or curves created in vector graphics.

Pattern   A pattern is a series of lines or drawings integrated into color.

PC   PC is an acronym for a personal computer. Generally, PCs are computers that use the Microsoft Windows operating system.

PDF   PDF is an acronym for portable document format. It is an extension for Adobe Acrobat and Acrobat Reader files.

Perfect binding   Perfect binding uses glue along the edge of pages to create a book.

Performing   Performing is the final stage of team development during which the team is fully functional and productive.

Photographic composition   Photographic composition describes the selection and arrangement of subjects within a photograph.

Pica   Pica is a printer's measurement equal to 1/6 of an inch.

Pictograph   A pictograph is a chart that uses images to represent the numbers in a chart's columns or bars.

Pixel   A pixel (picture element) is a data representation of a specific color at a specific location in a matrix or grid. A rectangular collection of pixels can produce a representation of an image on a computer screen or on a printed page.

Pixels per inch (PPI)   Pixels per inch (PPI) describes the number of pixels in each inch of print.

Placeholder   A placeholder is a means of assigning space for a text or graphic without having to place the actual copy.

Plate   A plate is a paper or metal sheet on which an image is cut or etched to be used on an offset press.

Platform   Platform is another term for an operating system.

Point   Point is a printer measurement equal to 1/72 of an inch.

Portrait orientation   Portrait orientation is a page design in which the shortest side is the top of the page.

Positive space   Positive space is the area on a page where text or graphics are located.

PostScript   PostScript is a programming language that describes the appearance of images (which includes text) on the printed page.

PPD   PPD is a file sent to a printer that provides it with all the information it needs to create a postscript document.

Preflight   Preflight is software that checks a desktop published file for any problems the printer might encounter.

Prepress service bureau   A prepress service bureau is a business that converts documents to files that can be used by a printer.

Press   A press is a piece of equipment used by professional printers to create a document.

Primes   Primes are slanted marks used to indicate feet and inches.

Print driver   A print driver provides information to desktop publishing software about the printing equipment to be used.

Printer   A printer is a person who uses a press or a device that produces a document using a computer.

Printer driver   A printer driver is software installed on a computer that allows a printer and computer to communicate.

Printer font   Printer font is a typeface designed to be printed.

Process color   Process color is created by mixing the four basic colors much as an artist would on a palette.

Proof   A proof is the process of checking a printed page for errors before final publication.

Proportion   Proportion is the arrangement of elements on a page making more important ones larger than less important ones.

Proportional fonts   Proportional fonts are spaced according to the size of the letter.

Pull quote   A pull quote is a statement or phrase pulled from an article. Generally, the most interesting quote is used to attract a reader's attention.

Pure colors   Pure colors are those that have a single color component, such as green, without mixing in any other colors.

Pushpins   Pushpins are map images used to locate a specific place. Generally the images look like pins, but they are not limited to that design.

Q

Quick mask   A quick mask serves the same purpose as a standard mask except it does not save the alpha channel for future work.

R

Radial gradient   A radial gradient is a series of colors that spreads out from a central point.

Ragged right   Ragged right describes left alignment that leaves white space at the end of each line.

Rasterizing   Rasterizing converts a vector graphic to a bitmap.

RAW   RAW is a camera file format that acts like a negative, allowing you to make significant changes to the original image.

Readability   Readability is the measurement of text that determines how quickly the eye can process information. Readability is used for small text and long passages.

Recto pages   Recto pages are the odd-numbered pages in a document with facing pages.

Registration   Registration is the alignment of pages when a page is printed more than once. It is essential that pages printed in multiple colors be registered. Registration marks provide guides.

Repetition   Repetition is the duplication of elements or details on one or more pages.

Resolution   Resolution describes the number of vertical and horizontal pixels in an image.

Reverse type   Reverse type is white type on a dark background and is designed to make the type stand out.

RGB   RGB is the acronym for red, green, and blue. These are the three colors used to produce an image on a computer monitor or a television.

Rhythm   Rhythm is the flow and movement of a page.

RIPping   RIPping is the process of converting a file to an electronic form that can be used to create film.

Rivers of white   Rivers of white are created when text is justified. As a result, white spaces may appear one above another, creating a distracting "river" of white space.

Roman   Roman describes a font without additional attributes such as italics.

Rotation   Rotation is the movement of an image along a center axis.

Router   A router is one type of hardware that connects computers in a network. Hubs and switches are also used to connect networks.

Royalty free   Royalty free is a term that describes a work of art that can be used without having to pay a fee or royalty each time you use it.

Rule   A rule is a term used by desktop publishers to describe horizontal or vertical lines used as dividers.

Rule of Thirds   The Rule of Thirds states that a page (or image) that is designed in thirds is more appealing to the eye than other designs.

S

Saddle stitch   A saddle stitch places staples in the middle of folded pages.

Sans serif   Sans serif is a typeface without serifs.

Scaled   A scaled image is one that has been enlarged or reduced.

Scaling   Scaling is the enlarging or reducing of a font or an image.

Scratch area   Scratch area is the area outside the document page itself.

Screen   A screen is a pale gray background that sets off a body of text from the rest of the page.

Screen font   Screen font is a typeface designed to be viewed on a computer monitor.

Script fonts   Script fonts are designed to imitate handwriting.

Series   The series is the area of the chart in which data is recorded visually using elements such as columns or lines.

Serif   Serif is a typeface with extensions at the ends of the main strokes that define each letter. These extensions are called serifs.

Shade   A shade is created when black is added to a color.

Shearing/skewing   Shearing/skewing is the process of twisting an image.

Signature   A signature is a collection of folios.

Slab serif fonts   Slab serif fonts have heavy serifs, vertical stress, and even strokes.

Slogan   A slogan is a statement or phrase that identifies a company's mission or image.

Slug   Slug is a nonprinting area in which details about the document are stored for other uses.

Small caps   Small caps are smaller uppercase letters that are about the same height as lowercase letters. They are used for emphasis.

Smooth point A smooth point is an anchor along a curve.

Spiral binding Spiral binding uses plastic or metal combs.

Spot color Spot color is a premixed color that is used much like a color you might buy in a paint can.

Spread A spread is made up of two facing pages of a document.

sRGB sRGB is the working space recommended for use with images that will be viewed on the Web.

Standoff Standoff is the space between an image and text.

Stickiness Stickiness is a design that encourages the reader to keep reading or to stay on a page.

Stock photos Stock photos are professional photographs gathered into a library of images and marketed for use in documents or on the Web. They are often cataloged with keywords to help you find the one you want.

Storming Storming is an early stage of team development during which conflicts develop.

Stress Stress is the angle determined by the narrow strokes of a letter.

Stripping Stripping is the process of converting images to film.

Stroke A stroke is the line that defines a letter or the border around an object or text.

Style sheets Style sheets are a set of formatting choices that can be applied to text or a paragraph.

Subhead A subhead is a brief title that separates paragraphs within an article. It is designed to make it easier to read long blocks of text.

Subtractive color Subtractive color is one that becomes white when all colors have been removed or subtracted.

Swash Swash is an exaggerated serif.

Swatch A swatch is a color selection that is given a name.

Swatches library A swatches library is a collection of swatches gathered into a single library of colors.

Symmetry Symmetry is when elements on a page are evenly balanced.

T

Tabs Tabs are places on a ruler used to line up text.

Team charter A team charter specifically identifies the team's goals, values, and approach to handling the task at hand.

Templates Templates are predesigned documents intended to be used as a base design, with text and images replacing greeking and placeholder images.

Tension Tension is the opposite of harmony. It can add interest to a page or cause it to feel incomplete.

Text paper Text paper is very high quality.

Theme A yearbook theme is a concept that is used throughout the book to act as a unifying agent. The theme may be revealed through images or color.

Threaded text Threaded text is copy that moves from one column to another or from one page to another.

Tick marks Tick marks are straight quotes found on typewriters.

Tint A tint is created when white is added to a color.

Tombstoning Tombstoning is the placement of two headlines across from each other, creating possible confusion when readers move their eyes across the page.

Tracing Tracing is the process of converting a bitmap image to a vector one.

Tracking Tracking is the spacing between letters in a word.

Trademark A trademark is a symbol used to indicate legal rights of ownership to a phrase or name.

Transformation Transformation is the modification of an image using actions such as cropping or flipping.

Transitional fonts Transitional fonts have bracketed serifs, vertical stress, and uneven strokes that move quickly from thick to thin.

Transparency Transparency is a graphic enhancement that lightens the image so that you can see the image or text behind it.

Trapping Trapping is a process used by printers to adjust images so that gaps in colors are not visible when registration is slightly off.

Trifold Trifold is much like a Z fold but with both sides containing print.

Trim size Trim size is a paper size that is reduced or cut from a standard size.

TrueType TrueType was developed by Apple Computer in conjunction with Microsoft in order to replace PostScript.

Two-page spread Two-page spread is a design that incorporates both sides of a layout.

Typeface Typeface is the design for the letters, numbers, and symbols that make up a font.

Typography Typography is the study of all elements of type including the shape, size, and spacing of the characters.

U

Upstyle Upstyle capitalizes all words in a headline.

V

Vector A vector is an image created by using a series of lines and curves rather than pixels. The beginning and ending points of the objects are defined mathematically, making the image easier to resize or scale.

Verso pages Verso pages are the even-numbered pages in a document with facing pages.

Vignette A vignette is a fuzzy border around an image.

VPN VPN is a virtual private network that provides a WAN to members of a widespread organization.

W

WAN WAN is a wide area network that uses devices such as telephone lines, satellite dishes, and radio waves to connect computers to a network.

Warm colors Warm colors are those near the color red or orange on the color wheel.

Watermark A watermark is a pale image or text imprinted into paper.

Web press A web press is an offset press that prints on long rolls of paper such as newsprint.

Web-safe colors Web-safe colors are the 216 colors that all users can see regardless of their computer displays.

White point The white point is the lightest pixel on a computer monitor.

White space White space is the blank area on a page designed to provide a visual break and to give other elements greater impact.

Widows Widows are single sentences or phrases at the bottom of a column or page. The rest of the paragraph appears on the next page or column.

Wi-Fi Wi-Fi is a term used to describe a wireless network.

Windows Windows is an operating system marketed by Microsoft that is used on computers generally identified as PCs.

Wired Wired networks are those that are connected using Ethernet cables such as CAT5.

Wireless access points Wireless access points are locations from which network signals are transmitted using an antenna.

WYSIWYG WYSIWYG, an acronym for what you see is what you get, means that the image that appears on a computer display is the same as the printed version.

X

X-height line The x-height line is the line under which type "sits." Fonts designed with high x-heights are harder to read than those placed at the standard height.

Z

Z fold Z fold divides a page into thirds, with print on one side.

Z pattern Z pattern is a visual path that draws the eye from top left to top right down to bottom left and then to bottom right.

Zero point Zero point is the point on the vertical and horizontal page where the ruler is set to zero.

Index

greeking, 109–110
greeting cards, printing, 354–355
gridlines, 289
grids, 91, 94
grouping graphics, 261
grunge type, 154
guidelines
    charts, 290–291
    headers, 330
guides, 39, 50
GUI (graphical user interface), 5
gutters, 23

H

hairlines, 243
half folds, 25
halftones, 220
hanging indents, 166
hanging punctuation, 174
harmony of design, 96–103, 107
headers, 327
    guidelines, 330
    proofreading, 46
headlines, 329
headphones, 11
Healing Brush tool, 245
help, 9
Help menus, 17
hex colors, 223, 227
history
    of DTP, 5–6
    of fonts, 149–151, 161
HSB (hue-saturation-
    brightness), 208
HSL (hue-saturation-light), 208
hyperlinks, 46
hyphens, 175, 184

I

ICC (International Color
    Consortium) profiles, 195
identifying fonts, 156
illustrations, 256–258, 331.
    See also graphics; vector
    graphics
images
    backgrounds, 276
    combining, 246–247
    digital photography. *See*
        digital photography
    feathering, 120, 248
    fills, 41
    filters, 248–250
    focal points, 78–81
    formats, 52–54
    lining up, 250–251
    logos, 318
    managing, 6
    modifying, 212
    moving, 59
    options, 62–64
    permissions, 64–65, 68

printing, 281, 345–346
proofreading, 55
release forms, 278–279
transferring, 274
types of, 56–57
web pages, 251
imagesetters, 341
importing
    files, 315
    graphics, 57–59
    tables, 297
    text, 45
indents
    hanging, 166
    spacing, 170–171
indexes, 224
indirect printing, 343
inkjet printers, 13
input devices, 10–12
interfaces, 5
International Color
    Consortium. *See* ICC
Internet
    document distribution, 28
    web documents. *See* web
        documents

J

journalizing progress, 189
JPG files, 55
jump lines, 42, 331
justified, alignment, 114

K

kerning, 163, 164, 171
keyboards, 10
Knife tool, 260

L

labels, 311
ladders, 358–359
landscape orientation, 22
LANs (local area networks), 14
laser printers, 12, 19
layers, 119–120, 129
    bitmaps, 245–247, 254
    blending modes, 212
layouts
    components, 91–94, 106
    documents, 21–23
    measurements, 35–37
LCD monitors, 271
leader dots, 178
leaders, 184
    teams, 368
    yearbooks, 357
leading, 164, 170, 171
ledger size paper, 24
legends, 289, 293
legibility, 142
letterheads, logos, 320

letter size paper, 24
letter width, 162–163
licenses
    images, 65
    software, 11
ligatures, 164
linear gradients, 211
lines, 138–139, 242–243
    ascender, 139
    design, 124
    jump, 331
    screens, 220
lining up images, 250–251
links, 114
Linotronic, 341
Linux, 6–7
lithography, 342
Live Paint bucket, 259
local area networks. *See* LANs
logos, 196, 205, 317–319
    business cards, 321, 324
    design, 322, 324
    email, 321–322
    envelopes, 321
    letterheads, 320
    memos, 322, 324
    uses of, 318–322
    viewing, 323–324
logotype, 317, 318
long text passages, 142
Lorem ipsum, 110, 127–128

M

MacDraw, 6
Macintosh
    history of DTP, 5–6
    operating systems, 6–7
    printing, 344
MacPaint, 6
Macromedia FlashPaper, 8–9
macros, 272, 282–283
Magic Wand, 244
Mail Merge, 309–311
maintenance, cameras, 270–271
malware, 15
managing
    deadlines, 22
    images, 6
    projects, 189
maps, 291–294
    design, 292
    directions, 294
    legends, 293
    pushpins, 292
    zooming, 293
margins, 40, 119
marks. *See also* symbols
    diacritical, 179
    proofreading, 179–181
    special characters, 176–179
Mask mode, 254–255
master pages, 46, 50–51,
    120–121, 340